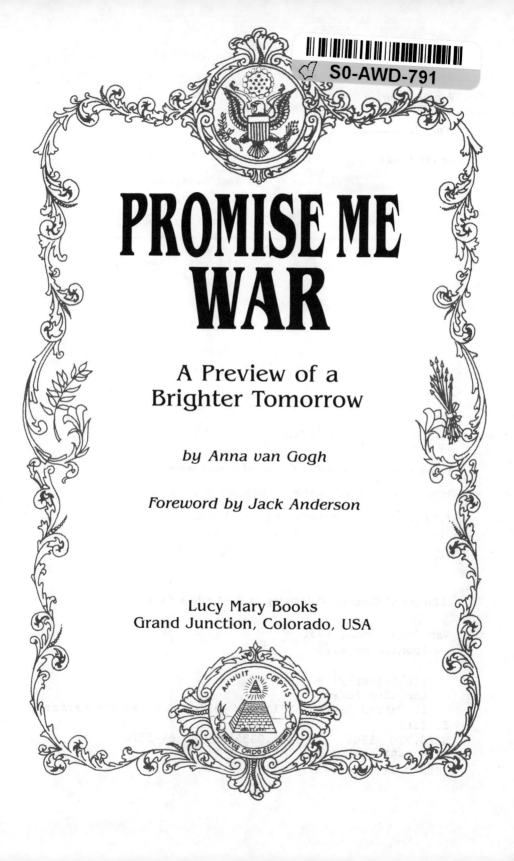

PROMISE ME WAR

A Preview of a Brighter Tomorrow

by Anna van Gogh

Foreword by Jack Anderson

Lucy Mary Books
Grand Junction, Colorado, USA

Limited Edition

No. ———————

of 150 books

Published by Lucy Mary Books, P.O. Box 2381, Grand Junction, Colorado 81502

Indexed by GeorgAnna Buckel Goe

Printed and bound by BookCrafters in Chelsea, Michigan

Library of Congress Cataloging in Publication Data

Van Gogh, Anna, 1931–
   Promise me war.

   Bibliography: p.
   Includes index.
   1. United States--Military policy. 2. Atomic warfare.
I. Title.
UA23.V26 1984   335'.0335'73   84-3876
ISBN 0-913829-03-X
ISBN 0-913829-00-5 (pbk.)

To The Children

That great wealth
of human compassion
that surrounds us

Is the only truly
renewable resource
found on this planet Earth.

It is available
for the purpose
of nourishing
the human soul.

Anna van Gogh

Preface

This book is about war. It is not about violence and it is not about killing. This book is about the eternal war of competing ideas; it is about war as a decision making process. This book is also about wealth. It is not about money and it is not about material goods. This book is about that wealth of information that surrounds us; it is about that wealth of knowledge that freedom of information exchange could provide to everyone. Thus, this book is about the dynamic dualism of war and wealth.

The armed peace of the industrial elite has threatened nuclear war for so long that citizen participation has been effectively eliminated from the decision making process we once called democracy. The false measure of material wealth has enforced underutilization of human resource for so long that freedom of choice has been effectively eliminated from the economic prosperity we once called capitalism. Thus, this book has been written for those who have grown weary of being held hostage by obsolete behavior patterns associated with an old style democratic capitalism.

Now there is a new wealth of information replacing an old capitalism of material goods. And there is a new war of ideas replacing an old democracy of political consensus. Along with that replacement comes also an unprecedented opportunity for democracy and capitalism to interchange their classical roles.

Political consensus was once cooperative; now the war of ideas can bring competition. Access to material goods was once competitive; now the wealth of information can bring cooperation. Stimulating competitive ideas of democracy can come from the many special interest groups; cohesive cooperative actions of capitalism from protective environmental action.

Just as the taste of a slice of bread belongs to the loaf and not to a cup of flour, the mood of this nation also belongs to the whole. And this book is written to appeal to that mood of the whole. This book is written to motivate all individuals to participate in the dynamic dualism of democracy and capitalism. But, more than that, this book is written to encourage future creative action — to encourage the use of our democratic-capitalistic partnership for the active pursuit of meaningful national goals.

One hundred years ago this nation was divided against itself, it was half slave and half free. The people fought a Civil War and all were awarded political equality. Everyone had gained the right to vote — the right to speak when spoken to.

Now this nation is again divided against itself, it is again half slave and half free. But this time the divison is an economic division. The people would like to win economic equality; they would like to have equal opportunity for employment and they would like to have a freedom of choice that that employment provides. They would like to have the right to act without being acted upon. The American people would like to have the right to speak without having been spoken to.

The future is ours for the making; the opportunity is ours for the taking. Tomorrow became today in the middle of last night. And today is the day for you to commit yourself to the task of improving the quality of human life. Today is the day for you to use electronic systems and information exchange for the benefit of all mankind. Today is the day for you to participate in the American way of life.

November 3, 1982   Anna van Gogh
Palisade, Colorado

A Note of Thanks

I graciously acknowledge with fond affection and sincere gratitude the help provided to be by my many friends and colleagues in the United States Senate, United States House of Representatives, and the many Executive Departments and Agencies of the federal government. You know who you are and you know the thanks I have already expressed. I am sure you appreciate my having resisted the temptation to commit your names and rank to paper since the latter has changed, in any case, many times during the past 23 years.

Since I entered the government service, March 10, 1961, at the National Bureau of Standards, Boulder, Colorado, we have all become members of a far greater community, the Brotherhood of Man. We are all working toward a common national goal of economic prosperity. And only by achieving that internal economic prosperity can we teach by example the rest of the world the many spiritual advantages of the freedom of choice offered to us by our democratic-capitalistic way of life. It is our combined good fortune that we have been able to work together.

My historical perspective for the World War II industrial mobilization of the United States came from my father, George W. Buckel, a life member of the Society of Manufacturing Engineers (SME), formerly the American Society for Tool Engineers (ASTE). My father was employed by General Motors. He dedicated his career to gage designing and to the establishment of precision standards for the automotive industry.

My 1982-1983 visits to Palisade, Colorado, were at the invitation of Glen and Laura Farmer who created an extended family environment for my emotional support. My brief stays in Boulder, Colorado, were sponsored by Edwin and Eleanor Crow. Their hospitality nourished my soul. In Grand Junction, while using the Mesa College Library, Lonnie and Mary Frances Pool came to my rescue.

Original concepts for the art work were created by Charles Hardy, Department of Fine Arts, Mesa College; Kenton W. Main, Head of the Media Services Department, Mesa College, provided preliminary technical makeup design for the cover lettering, text composition, type style, and page format.

Neither the book nor the author would have survived without the professional skills and personal determination of my editor. She defined my reading audience, she established my non-technical vocabulary, tempo, and level of scientific involvement. She found the Herculean courage to sustain my writing style in spite of my fits of artistic temperament. I owe her the courtesy and the glory of a simple statement: "Thank you for being you."

Elvin H. "Al" Bratton, retired United States Air Force, a graduate of the course of studies at Saint Paul School of Theology, United Methodist, was able to introduce and retain readability of the manuscript from the military-theological perspective that I so much desired, a desire that was at times dominated more by emotional turmoil than rational thought.

In the animal kingdom, my exciting new-found companion was a turkey. One could not have hoped for a more devoted strolling partner. Soaring Eagles may well be the destiny of this nation, but dedicated turkeys are a blessing during a time of creative endeavor.

25 August 1983   *Anna van Gogh*

Foreword

The past year has shown an increase in violent confrontations around the world, with the Middle East and Latin America emerging as the flashspots of conflict. It is not known where the next war will occur or what issue — oil, water, or political power — will be the bone of contention.

What is certain, unfortunately, is that more such conflicts are inevitable. The human race has always been a violent species. As we have become more industrialized and "civilized," these innate aggressive instincts still remain. And as we have developed more sophisticated weaponry, there is more at stake in war than who will control a strip of land.

Alarmingly, our new weapons have made it possible that the disputed strip of land can be completely annihilated, making it unfit for occupation of any kind.

It is the duty of the press to inform the public about these consequences, to report the facts for informed interpretation by the public. In a democracy, the public can use this information to bring about change, through pressure on their elected leaders.

Information, then, is a treasured commodity. Our founding fathers, in their infinite wisdom, gave the free press wide latitude. This was no easy decision, for the press at that time was less responsible and not held to standards as strict as those today. One of my favorite quotes comes from our third president, Thomas Jefferson, who said given the choice between government without newspapers and newspapers without government, he "would not hesitate to choose the latter."

This statement is all the more dramatic since Jefferson was often the subject of vitriolic criticism from the press.

I am not so arrogant as to suggest that the press, thus far, has prevented nuclear war; that disseminated information has kept the trigger-happy away from the button. But a well-informed public can influence the dangerous decisions of those in authority. If our leaders perceive the public as ill-informed, then they will be more inclined to make rash decisions.

It is the need for information, along with the literal explosiveness of the issue discussed, that makes this volume indispensible. The author carefully disassembles — then reassembles — this complex situation, giving the reader a firm, factual understanding of this issue and its ramifications.

The best source for day-to-day information is the daily paper and the nightly news. But a book like this is necessary to view the issue in perspective. The daily media is under severe constraints, we must present information quickly and superficially and conform with the limits of time and space. A book has no such constraints, and while it takes more time to read 230 pages than to scan a 230-line news story, the reward — a clearer, more objective understanding of the issue — is well worth the extra effort.

Each of us has an opinion about how current conflicts should be resolved. But an informed opinion — one that takes all the facts and all the sides into account — is more useful than one that is based on emotion and rhetoric. This is true, whether you favor a nuclear freeze or a build-up of weapons systems.

In this volume, Anna Van Gogh has made it possible for us to develop a more informed opinion. She has provided a valuable public service.

Washington, D.C.
November 10, 1983

Jack Anderson

Summary of Contents

1

PART ONE

The Announcement

If you are going to make a campaign promise,
then limited nuclear war is a real crowd pleaser

31

PART TWO

Nuclear War Strategy

If you are going to fight a limited nuclear war,
then you really should find a willing target

55

PART THREE

Delivery of Nuclear Warheads

If this is evolution, then methinks I prefer creation

89

PART FOUR

Detection and Early Warning

If the gift of foresight is our most effective weapon,
then information flow is the live ammunition

139

PART FIVE

Information Politics

If freedom of the press is the best insurance,
then it is time to pay the premium

175

PART SIX

The Birth of a Nation

If the meek shall inherit the Earth,
then what will happen to all us hawks

Contents

Preface v

A Note of Thanks vii

Foreword by Jack Anderson ix

PART ONE
The Announcement 1

If you are going to make a campaign promise,
then limited nuclear war is a real crowd pleaser

Chapter A	**Introduction** 3	
	Political dueling and dualism	
A001	The threatening aspect of peace 3	
A002	Technology push 4	
A003	Demand pull 5	
A004	"Demand-side" economics 6	
A005	The promising aspect of war 7	
A006	Forward look 9	

Chapter B **On the Campaign Trail** 11
The loyal opposition

B007 George Bush the candidate 11

B008 Fighting a nuclear war 13

B009 And winning? 14

Chapter C **At the White House** 16
A domestic policy for war

C010 In defense of national security 16

C011 The evolution of nuclear strategy 17

C012 The preemptive First Strike 18

C013 Authority to use nuclear weapons 20

Chapter D **And then the State Department** 21
A foreign policy for peace

D014 Peaceful thoughts from Senator Muskie 21

D015 A bypass for the State Department 23

Chapter E   **A Quick Fix for a Press Leak** 24
The sudden death of credibility

E016   The realities of "stealth" 24

E017   The politics of leaking 25

E018   The vanishing power of the President 26

Perspective   **The Power of Public Opinion** 28
The suffocation of a President with a security blanket of political loyalty

With everything coming up roses, national security became a bouquet of political thorns

PART TWO
Nuclear War Strategy 31
If you are going to fight a limited nuclear war, then you really should find a willing target

Chapter A   **Anti-City Strategy** 33
Mutual Assured Destruction is MAD

A019   The logic of geography 34

A020   Silo positioning in the Soviet Union 35

A021   The arithmetic of counting bombs 36

A022   Survival becomes a way of life 36

A023   Escalation or holocaust 37

Chapter B   **Soviet Adventurism Flourishes** 40
The protocol of being first

B024   Expanding the sphere of influence 40

B025   The Soviet Union is land locked 41

B026   Minority rule 42

B027   Separation of faith and reason 43

Chapter C   **The NATO Alternative** 45
European allies don't like bombs either

C028   National Technical Means 46

C029   The urgency of technology transfer 47

C030   Theater Nuclear Forces 48

C031   The reality of de-coupling 49

Perspective   **Deterrence is MAD** 51
The nesting instinct of Mother Russia remains rooted in tradition

Nations fight wars, not automated weapons systems produced by munitions industries

PART THREE
Delivery of Nuclear Warheads 55
If this is evolution, then methinks I prefer creation

Chapter A **Land-Based Missiles** 57
People and missiles don't mix

A032 Missile eXperimental 57

A033 The ICBM is a "dumb" bomb 58

A034 The "disposable" rocket engine 59

A035 The payload 60

A036 The reality of pork barrels 60

A037 Priorities for land use 61

Chapter B **Sea Launch** 63
The United States is an island

B038 Keeping weapons at sea 63

B039 Like Ivory soap, it floats 65

B040 Navigation to the rescue 65

Chapter C **Airplanes or Cruise Missiles** 68
Pilots are people

C041 An "invisible" airplane 69

C042 The "disposable" airplane 70

C043 Offense becomes the defense 71

Chapter D **Satellite Launch** 73
*Those military-operated satellites are fulfilling our
rendezvous with destiny*

D044 My technology, your technology 74

D045 HAIL COLUMBIA, a Space Shuttle at last 75

D046 The "militarization" of space 76

Chapter E **Hiroshima** 79
The good old days of limited nuclear war

E047 People are easy to kill 79

E048 Accuracy was the problem 80

E049 A commanding responsibility 82

E050 The weapons strike back 83

Perspective **System failure knows no limit** 85
*In the event of accidental nuclear holocaust,
how do you say you're sorry*

*The military may be the user of modern weapons
systems, but the Congress is the supplier*

PART FOUR
Detection and Early Warning 89
If the gift of foresight is our most effective weapon,
then information flow is the live ammunition

Chapter A **A Spy in the Sky** 91
On a cloudy day you can see clouds;
on a clear day you can see everything else

A051   As the world turns, so does the ground station 92

A052   Information relay with delay 93

A053   Interrogation and relay with delay 95

A054   The look-and-see satellite 96

A055   The listen-and-hear satellite 97

A056   The active observer 98

A057   Effective lifetime of the payload 98

Chapter B **Real-Time Monitoring** 100
Receiving raw data is like eating a pine cone,
the stuff is hard to digest

B058   *Sorting signal from noise 101*

B059   *The hazard of the digit 102*

B060   *The sensor is smart 102*

B061   *A file cabinet in the sky 103*

B062   *Information at a glance 104*

Chapter C **Identification: Friend or Foe** 106
IFF I had known you were coming, I would have coded
my transponder pulse

C063   The active observer 107

C064   The active electronic fence 108

C065   Airborne Warning And Control System 109

C066   A flying transponder 110

C067   The case of the false echo 110

C068   The air space merger 111

Chapter D **Detecting the Explosion** 113
The ground shakes like an earthquake

D069   Underground nuclear testing 113

D070   Atmospheric nuclear testing 114

D071   The false hope of ABM 116

Chapter E **Decentralizing Networks** 118
The digital revolution that broke the camel's back

E072 A down-to-earth message 119

E073 A package of information 120

E074 Democratization of information flow 121

Chapter F **Communication Satellites** 123
The relay station in the sky

F075 Geostationary satellites 124

F076 Getting the signal off the ground 124

F077 Boost and return 125

F078 The receiver on the ground 126

F079 The transmitter is the target 126

Chapter G **Use it or lose it** 128
National technological advantage comes from the use of information, not from its collection

G080 Automation is the enemy 129

G081 Industrial push 130

G082 The fault is me 130

G083 User pull 131

G084 Back to computer basics 132

G085 Technology is culture 133

G086 People with a purpose 133

Perspective **Information is Firepower** 135
National defense is the fine art of hiding behind the time barrier

The creative spirit of Uncle Sam is circling the globe in free flight

PART FIVE
Information Politics 139
If freedom of the press is the best insurance, then it is time to pay the premium

Chapter A **SALT Treaties** 142
Prohibition was also a flop

A087 Equality for all nations 143

A088 No force for enforcement 144

A089 International regulatory activities 145

A090 Verification to the rescue 146

A091 Creating a wartime economy 147

Chapter B   **The "Invisible" Government**   149
              It is difficult to take part in a process
              when you can't even find it

    B092   Fire the bookkeeper   150

    B093   "Constitutional Dictatorship"   151

    B094   America First   153

    B095   Emergency response   154

    B096   Military-industrial divorce   155

Chapter C   **National Weather Service**   157
              Money may talk but information has a lot more to say

    C097   "Born classified"   158

    C098   The basic waste of basic research   159

    C099   Research with a purpose   161

    C100   Getting the harvest to the market   162

    C101   The surface of the globe is no secret   163

    C102   Pattern in motion   165

    C103   The vanity press   166

    C104   The military-civilian work force   167

Perspective   **Learn to love a snoop**   169
                Blessed are the peacemakers, for they shall be called
                into active duty in time of national emergency

                As defense spending goes, so goes the economic
                prosperity of this nation

PART SIX
The Birth of the Nation   175
              If the meek shall inherit the Earth,
              then what will happen to all us hawks

Chapter A   **The American Military Tradition**   177
              In the beginning, there was Heaven and Earth
              and the citizen-soldier

    A105   This job belongs to you   178

    A106   Aristocracy in democracy   178

    A107   The individual and the common good   179

    A108   Professionalism   181

Chapter B **Unity of the Nation** 183
*The unity of the nation will be assured when
the people pursue perpetual economic prosperity*

B109 The Spirit of the Constitution 184
B110 A strong central government 185
B111 The Gettysburg Address 186
B112 The more perfect Union 187

Chapter C **The Power of the President** 189
*The fine art of attaching undreamed of importance
to well known truths*

C113 That fragile line of presidential succession 190
C114 Freedom from fear 192
C115 Freedom from want 192
C116 Freedom of speech 193
C117 Freedom of worship 194
C118 A military monarch 196

Chapter D **War Powers of Congress** 199
War powers by any name still smell like gunpowder

D119 The national emergency 200
D120 War in the absence of war 200
D121 Commander-in-Chief by invitation only 202
D122 Madison responds to Pacificus 203
D123 The power of public opinion 204

Chapter E **Purification of the Pentagon** 206
If economic prosperity dies, then so does the nation

E124 Defense can't fight a war 207
E125 Defense can't win the peace either 208
E126 The last great balance of power 209
E127 An armed peace for the industrial elite 211
E128 The uniqueness of service 212

Chapter F **The Politics of Foreign Policy** 214
*The President can play foreign politics but foreign
policy belongs to the United States Senate*

F129 Patriotic industries 215
F130 From scientist to Senator 216
F131 From advocate to lobbyist 218
F132 To teach is to transfer 219
F133 Information is a trade commodity 220

Chapter G **The Presence and the Purpose** 221
The American military has an ambience all its own

G134 Fight or flight is not enough 222

G135 The Letter of the Law 223

G136 The Spirit of the Law 224

G137 Do it — a nation in action 225

G138 The mystique of presence 226

G139 Stand your ground 227

G140 There is a nation standing behind you 228

Perspective **Tell it like it is** 230
*The majestic Ship of State will be carried by the current
in the river of information flow, but that old row boat
of democracy will need strong members of Congress
to man the oars*

*Most Americans are hawks in dove's clothing,
it is only a question of when they change their feathers*

Notes and References 234

Bibliography 351

Index 378

PART ONE

The Announcement

*If you are going to make a campaign
promise, then limited nuclear war
is a real crowd pleaser*

". . . a winner in a nuclear exchange . . ."

As a campaign promise, it was a real crowd pleaser. It made national news early in the 1980 presidential campaign when Walter Scheer of the *Los Angeles Times* reported it from an interview with George Bush, candidate for the Republican nomination. But it was more than just news, and it was more than just another studied opinion of U.S. nuclear strategy. It was an ANNOUNCEMENT of an awareness of the profound shift that was taking place in the political mood of the country.

Though double-digit inflation and increased defense spending were already attracting national political attention, the emotional appeal for "fighting a nuclear war and winning" was undeniable. The American people were growing weary of the threat of destruction from surprise nuclear attack, a threat that had been for years part and parcel of official national policy.

PART ONE

Chapter A

Introduction

Political dueling and dualism

Political "dueling" is the necessary interactive response between opposing philosophies, goals, policies, attitudes. It is a dynamic manifestation of the two-party political system in this country. Political dueling attracts attention to both sides of public discussion. It helps to polarize public opinion, and it helps to escalate public controversy. Political dueling has the overall effect of drawing more people into the arena of public debate.

As a political process within the context of the democratic form of government, dynamic dueling is essential. It is the only meaningful way to benefit from the dualism of opposing views. It is the only known mechanism that uses the dualism in human behavior to ensure forward motion rather than stagnation from action-reaction response.

A001   The threatening aspect of peace

Peace is now being defined as an absence of war, yet that absence of war has been achieved entirely by the threat of nuclear holocaust. The current pro-defense mood of the country is, therefore, identified with an emotional reaction against that threat.

Never had any nation developed and mobilized such military force as the United States expended against Germany and Japan during World War II. Never had the military defeat of an enemy been more decisive. Since the August 6, 1945, bombing of Hiroshima, and the unconditional surrender of the Japanese government, the United States has been at "peace," yet the United States is engaged in an ever-expanding arms race with the Soviet Union and it is plagued with economic stagnation at home. The fatal flaw lies with the current working definition of the word "peace."

Peace has been defined as an absence of war and that absence of war has been accomplished by imposing a "balance of military power" between the United States and the Soviet Union. That concept of "balance" goes back to a fundamental law of nature. Like two ends of a rope, like the front and back sides of a piece of paper, or like the north and south poles of a permanent bar magnet, both members of the pair must exist at the same time for either to be defined.

This classical concept of twoness became distorted when it was carried over to the world of international politics. The equal but opposite (static) pairs were interpreted as being equivalent to action-reaction partners, and the partners were perceived to exist in a state of near equilibrium. Much like children sitting on opposite ends of a teeter-totter, political leaders were required to balance their action-reaction responses to each other.

With this undue emphasis on the equilibrium of the "balance," on action-reaction partners, rather than on the dynamic process of interaction, the equilibrium state produced near-perfect stagnation. It is for that reason—the stagnation of the balance—that the balance of military power has been so totally successful in preventing war between the two superpowers.

Nevertheless, this balance of military strength has given rise to an unprecedented threat of nuclear destruction, a threat that remains conveniently hidden behind the very thin veil of that which we call peace.

A002   Technology push

Technological innovation in the form of automated weapons systems has been determining U.S. nuclear strategy. This "push" of technology has created the myth that the accumulation of more and more hard-

ware will bring with it the reward of greater and greater military superiority.

Technological innovation that originally motivated technology push was exciting. Much of the economic growth of the past three decades can be directly attributed to the push of modern technology. And that technology push was responsible for social change that could have been achieved by no other method. Yet within the military-industrial complex proponents of technology push have also been advocates of "war potential," a philosophy that caters to the belief that a nation can and should do as much as possible ahead of time to prepare to fight a war.

Unfortunately the driving force for much of the technology push and, hence, for a major portion of war potential has been technological innovation in the form of automated weapons. It was supposed by defense planners that automation held in reserve as war potential would make it possible for this nation to fight a nuclear war across intercontinental distances in a matter of minutes. By mobilizing only a handful of men and a great wealth of technology—the automated systems would already be in place, the military would only have to push the buttons—it was supposed that the United States could instantly engage in a MAD [Mutual Assured Destruction] nuclear exchange with the Soviet Union.

As scientists became convinced that they could use equipment to replace people, they designed hardware accordingly, and the black-box mentality dominated. Military dependence on automation increased, and the need for human resources declined. Automation eliminated not only human participation but also human judgment and human incentive from the nuclear war-fighting capability.

With this over-emphasis on the development of hardware, the needs of the military were no longer assessed within the context of productive national goals. U.S. strategy instead had come to be determined by the industrial availability of automated weapons systems.

A003   Demand pull

"Demand pull" of the user is the natural dueling partner for "technology push" of the industry. Technology push provides the driving force for forward motion, demand pull the guiding principle.

One method of starting an old Model-T Ford was to get behind it and push. It naturally worked best with two people; one in the driver's seat to do the guiding, the other out back to do the pushing. Ingenious efforts to convert the operation from a two-man to a one-man job were usually doomed to failure. To rope the steering wheel to the door handle was a favorite but, in the absence of the driver, when the push came, the car would invariably hit a tree, mail box, or drainage ditch.

Technology push and demand pull work together in very much the same way. It is the twosome that is needed to pursue national goals. If technology is pushing and there is no one to do the guiding, then the nation is equally doomed to failure. The driver, not the pushing motion, has access to the steering wheel and the brake pedal.

When demand pull takes its place in the driver's seat the "driver" then makes decisions about direction and speed of travel. The technology of the industrial suppliers may "push" only when the "demand" of the driver is in control.

Though industrial suppliers do view themselves as responsible for national economic prosperity and, hence, do feel an urgency to push as often as possible, it is that same economic consideration that should now compel the industry to become supportive of the demand pull of the people. Users of technology who have an awareness of national purpose could create the demand; that demand could then pull the production of the industrial giants to become supportive of national needs.

A004   "Demand-side" economics

In departing from the classical concepts of supply and demand, the Reagan Administration failed to consider the attractive option of an all-new "demand-side" economics. The American people could demand a shift in defense spending priorities so their tax dollars would be used to create an all-new industrial base for this nation.

Just as the politicians have been caught up in an eternal "balance" of military power, economists have been strangled by their own balance of supply and demand. Any action-reaction response, when carried to the extreme of the security of an artificially contrived balance, can do little more than contribute to the stagnation of a perfect state of equilibrium.

The secret of success for supply-side or demand-side economics is not to reshuffle the same old tax base, and not to continue adjusting the same old self-adjusting supply and demand, rather it is to expand the industrial base. But any such expansion will certainly require a determined and a persistent change in the priorities for defense spending.

The transition to demand-side economics suggested in this book would retain the increase in defense spending, it would even encourage more increase in the increase. The theme of this book encourages a dramatic shift in funding priorities away from the technology-push of munitions industries. Those industries that produce automated weapons that merely sit and wait for the "unthinkable" to happen are violating our economic ideals.

Tax dollars in the defense budget would have to be spent to pay the price for global monitoring systems. Those systems would be in constant use collecting information needed by the military, by the federal, state, and local governments, and by information industries in the private sector. It would be the users of the information who would be responsible for "pulling" defense dollars into defense contracts in the private sector. It would be the users of the information who would "demand" that the information systems be designed to meet their operational needs.

Information would be re-processed, re-organized, and re-interpreted, over and over again; each new user would create a new product for the next. The information itself would become a "raw material" from which information industries would manufacture new "computer products." Tax dollars invested in information gathering, information processing, and information dissemination would become the driving force for economic expansion.

Within the context of a dynamic demand-side economics, the military could become cost effective. Every defense dollar invested in military-operated systems for information collection could provide at least one dollar return in the form of profit in the private sector. The federal government may be a non-profit organization, but that is no reason for the taxpayers to continue to be born losers.

A005   The promising aspect of war

The Constitution of the United States grants war powers to the Congress. Somewhat in contradiction to that, authority to order the use of nuclear weapons is now resting with the President. It is that contradiction that needs to be resolved.

How can the American people want peace yet at the same time vote for military superiority? The answer is simple. Compared with the threat of destruction (millions of civilian casualties would result from the failure of our national policy of deterrence), the promise of decisively doing anything was a real crowd pleaser.

With the writing of the Constitution, the criteria for the United States to employ military action became well documented for the rest of the world to read: Article I, Section 8—Powers Granted Congress—"The Congress shall have power . . . (Paragraph 40) To provide for calling forth the Militia to execute the Laws of the Union, suppress Insurrections and repel Invasions." For the purpose of this book, the focus of attention is on the phrase, "To repel Invasions," the operative word is "repel."

Since World War II, the American people have had to live with the war powers-emergency powers contradictions. The national policy of deterrence required the United States to absorb a First Strike from the Soviet Union, and, after a survey of damage and a consideration of intent, the President of the United States could then "declare" a national emergency and retaliate.

Modern electronics now permit the intelligent use of "live" information-communications networks and global monitoring systems. The United States military can now eliminate the element of surprise from any aggressive action. With adequate global coverage from detection and early warning systems, any massive mobilization of Soviet military that would precede any massive attack against the United States would be known ahead of time. Furthermore, any launch of a ballistic-type missile would be detected at lift-off; the booster engine could be destroyed by a conventional weapon.

The promising aspect of war would be the peace of mind the American people would enjoy knowing that the United States Congress would have to declare war before U.S. military personnel could be ordered onto foreign soil.

It is technologically feasible and economically mandatory that "We the People" of the United States return war powers

to the Congress. With continuous global monitoring, war powers that constitutionally belong to the Congress could also
include the authority to order the use of nuclear weapons.
Congressional control of the American military-industrial
complex has become the last great challenge of our
democratic-capitalistic way of life.

A006   Forward look

*Woman scientist offers an alternative to the threat of
nuclear destruction—move the industry out of the
Pentagon and assign unique national responsibilities to each of the military service organizations.*

PROMISE ME WAR takes the position that the "armed peace of
the industrial elite" has held the human race hostage long
enough. The intent of the book is to bring American military
policy out of the closet and into the arena of public debate. It
encourages immediate popular endorsement of an international law against possession and use of nuclear weapons,
weapons that are, in any case, already obsolete.

The wisdom of using any destructive military action as a
means of implementing American foreign policy is questioned not only within the context of common sense but also
within the context of constitutional law. The American people
should no longer be willing to passively accept the destruction
of absorbing a First Strike nuclear attack from the Soviet
Union and then retaliating. The proposed alternative for the
use of continuous global monitoring systems would not only
eliminate the element of "surprise?" from foreign aggression,
it would also go a long way toward eliminating public officials
who are unable to comprehend the importance of continuous
information flow as a replacement for artificially stimulated
fear.

A new foreign policy for the United States would have
continuous monitoring of silo construction and launch operations become codified as international law, that law would
have to be established at the insistence of all peoples of all
nations. As part of those same international regulatory activities, the United States would have to dissolve all permanent
alliances with foreign nations. There would be no favored

friends and there would be no fearful foe. Access to information would be the same for everyone. With continuous global monitoring systems, all nations would be treated equal under the rule of law.

The weapons-related industrial base of the United States is rejected. Every aspect of evolutionary technological innovation on the part of the weapons industries that has moved this nation closer and closer to the possibility of accidental nuclear holocaust is dismissed in just one line: If this is evolution, then, methinks, I prefer creation.

Increased defense spending would have to be retained. The spending priorities would have to be shifted to fund the development and use of military-operated global information systems. American military service organizations would use the information flow from those systems to fulfill their constitutional mandate: To repel Invasions, that information flow would also be used to replace the "firepower" overkill inherent in the existing strategic triad. Many automated weapons systems that are a product of technological evolution would be immediately recognized as obsolete.

The decision is ours for the making, the future is ours for the taking. Defense spending can be used to rebuild the national economy, it can create a new industrial base dependent upon information industries, not the production of munitions. The ballot box can be used to bring new talent to the Congress. The voters could go outside the traditional party structure for able candidates, not cater to well established campaign funding channels and not endorse ongoing political patronage.

The intelligent use of global monitoring systems makes it feasible to return the authority to order the use of nuclear weapons to the Congress. The increased risk of accidental nuclear holocaust makes it mandatory. Those satellites you see circling the globe in free flight may well be "birds of prey," but they are American Eagles, not materialistic war hawks. Only a slight change in national focus is needed for everyone to see their true feathers.

Chapter B

On the Campaign Trail

The loyal opposition

The Democrats had held the majority in the Congress of the United States since 1956. The Committee structure of the Congress had become rigid. Committee staffers were entrenched in the political landscape. And the possibility for internal change had long since drifted into oblivion.

Thirty-five years is a long time to have any particular influence dominate anything in this country, but it is especially a long time when nuclear strategy is the issue.

The question was not whether the Republican members of Congress had noticed that they were in the minority—they had—and the question was not whether the Republicans felt they could present alternatives at the White House—they did. Rather the question was how to attract the attention of the American voters.

B007   George Bush the candidate

The "trial balloon" was launched on January 24, 1980, after George Bush, candidate for the Presidential nomination, had been victorious in the Iowa Republican caucus.

Walter Scheer of the *Los Angeles Times* was interviewing George Bush, who was a former Ambassador to the United Nations, and a former head of the CIA (Central Intelligency Agency). Scheer started by asking about defense spending. The question by Scheer that triggered most of the press response was: "Don't you reach a point with these strategic weapons [the word strategic is used by the press to mean long-range nuclear weapons that can travel intercontinental distances] where you can wipe each other out so many times and no one wants to use them or be willing to use them, that it really doesn't matter whether you're 10% or 2% lower or higher?" To that question, Bush had responded, "Yes, if you believe there is no such thing as a winner in a nuclear exchange, that argument makes little sense. I don't believe that."

That phrase, "a winner in a nuclear exchange," was the "winner" for George Bush. It brought Bush more column inches in the press than one could ever have imagined possible in a campaign year.

Since Scheer had interpreted Bush's remark to mean that the United States could fight and win a nuclear war, Scheer then asked, "How do you win a nuclear exchange?" Bush explained, "You have a survivability of command in [and] control, survivability of industrial potential, protection of a percentage of your citizens and you have a capability that inflicts more damage on the opposition than it can inflict upon you. That's the way you can have a winner, and the Soviets' planning is based on the ugly concept of a winner in a nuclear exchange."

With regard to the survivablity of the American population, Scheer went on to ask, "Do you mean like 5% would survive?". To which Bush replied, "More than that—if everybody fired everything he had, you'd have more than that survive."

Those remarks were directed toward the firing of nuclear weapons across intercontinental distances between the United States and the Soviet Union. Bush was apparently trying to assess the consequences of the use of nuclear weapons by the Soviet Union, if the United States would absorb a First Strike and then retaliate.

That interview with George Bush, "Bush Assails Carter Defense Strategy," was the first that gave any indication that the Republicans were viewing U.S. nuclear strategy as a war-fighting strategy, rather than one of deterrence. As the 1980 campaign progressed, the questions of military superiority and defense spending went on to attract national political attention.

B008   Fighting a nuclear war

> *U.S. intercontinental ballistic missiles aimed at the Soviet Union were to deter the U.S.S.R. from firing intercontinental ballistic missiles at the North American continent. Smaller, short-range nuclear weapons were to be used to fight a war in Europe.*

The point Walter Scheer of the *Los Angeles Times* was trying to make in his interview with the Republican presidential candidate George Bush was that long-range nuclear weapons were intended as a deterrent against the use of long-range nuclear weapons; nuclear weapons fired from the United States were not then, or are they now, intended as a deterrent against the Soviet use of conventional forces in Europe.

Scheer went right to the heart of the matter when he asked Bush, "What is the relationship between the possession of an [ICBM] MX missile [Missile eXperimental] system and being able to do something about problems like Afghanistan or Iran?" Bush went out around Scheer's real question and responded, "The direct linkage is rather remote, but in the overall linkage, as long as the United States is perceived to not be slipping behind the Soviets in strategic nuclear forces, the Soviets will be constrained from adventure."

Again the Bush reply failed to address the issue of nuclear versus conventional weapons, so Scheer continued with the same line of questioning. "They [the Soviets] were weaker in '68 than they are now." Bush acknowledged the validity of that statement, "Much weaker." So Scheer gave specifics, "In '68 they [the Soviets] invaded Czechoslovakia. That was adventurism."

Bush was still skirting out around the question of the Soviet use of conventional weapons versus the American threat of nuclear weapons. "But it doesn't follow that therefore if we're weaker [if the American military is weaker] that will constrain [Soviet] adventure. They [the Soviets] are stronger today and they invaded Afghanistan."

Bush still did not mention the dilemma of conventional versus nuclear weapons, so Scheer went still farther back in time, "Yes, but in the late '40's, we [the Americans] were the only one who had nuclear weapons. Our superiority was total and awesome. It didn't stop the Soviets in Berlin, [or] from the Korean War. Aren't your ideas a throwback to the old massive retaliation position of John Foster Dulles?"

George Bush persisted. Bush confined his remarks to the use of nuclear weapons: "I'm going back to the fact that the United States should not be inferior to the Soviet Union in strategic balance." In the vocabulary of a politician, one should always assume that strategic means long-range nuclear unless otherwise stated; thus, Bush was willing to discuss only the U. S.-Soviet balance of long-range nuclear weapons. The fact that the Russian military has been using conventional weapons was simply beyond the scope of the Bush concept of what should be discussed under the news banner "strategic balance."

Readers of the Walter Scheer interview were left to wonder if indeed George Bush would have the United States retaliate with tactical (battlefield) nuclear weapons when the Soviet Union made military use of conventional weapons; if he had in mind to introduce the use of short- or medium- range nuclear weapons as a "war fighting" capability in Europe; if ICBMs were to be fired from the continental United States anytime a Russian soldier was ordered to step foot on foreign soil.

B009   And winning?

Political remarks are much like a head of fresh lettuce; they are highly perishable.

The *Christian Science Monitor,* August 19, 1980, "Readers write" commentary did much to clarify what George Bush had said about "a winnable nuclear war." A brief letter by James L. Bush [relationship unknown] elaborated on the George Bush views on conventional weapons as they had been reported in the January Walter Scheer interview in the *Los Angeles Times.*

"Bush did not say ... that he was 'for nuclear war.' Neither did he say we could win one, or that we should plan to."

"He [did say] that he would initiate, even before he was inaugurated ... negotiations toward 'meaningful reductions in nuclear weaponry stockpiles' and labeled this as a corner-stone of his foreign policy."

"Lastly," wrote James L. Bush, "George Bush understands the Soviet Union, from direct dealings with the Soviets, and said that he felt we could only negotiate with them from a position of strength." According to this August reply, George Bush had intended to focus "primarily on the more conventional type of weapons . . . not on the nuclear." George Bush was not insisting only upon nuclear capabilities in his arguments in favor of a build-up of U.S. military strength.

Thus, by August, 1980, Bush's initial remarks about fighting a nuclear war and winning were fast fading into the background. The remarks of George Bush were relevant at the time they were made in January, 1980—Bush had introduced the nuclear war-fighting concept into the 1980 presidential campaign—but such remarks were difficult to keep in storage for delayed retrieval. There were clear indications that long-range nuclear weapons based within the continental United States would not be fired to discourage Soviet adventurism in Afghanistan or anywhere else. Soviet use of conventional weapons would be treated in the political arena, rather than with military retaliation.

The defense-related remarks of George Bush had attracted the attention of both the Soviet and the American press. Bush had publicly suggested that the United States should depart from its passive policy of absorbing a First Strike and then retaliating, that the United States should move toward an official policy that would endorse a nuclear war-fighting capability. And, judging from the Carter response with Presidential Directive 59, that was the "primary" intent of the Bush remark in the first place.

Chapter C

At the White House

A domestic policy for war

Early in the 1980 presidential campaign, the Republican candidate George Bush had found the political mood of the country receptive to the build-up of U.S. military superiority. By mid-summer 1980, with his own political future at stake, President Carter announced a change in official U.S. nuclear strategy that was perceived to include a limited nuclear war-fighting capability.

Though the Carter White House used press conferences to elevate public awareness, the new "counter-force" precision targeting strategy was not as novel as the announcement made it appear. The targeting strategy had started with Mr. Schlesinger under the presidency of Mr. Nixon; Mr. Carter merely continued its development and then accentuated its existence with politically timed public statements. All were intended to encourage the American voters to return Mr. Carter to the White House for another four years.

C010   In defense of national security

The Presidential Directive ordering a new nuclear targeting strategy signed by President Carter in July, 1980, only 90 days prior to his election defeat,

> *should not be passed off as campaign rhetoric. Even though Ronald Reagan was elected President, that Carter Directive still retains official status as U.S. nuclear strategy.*

In response to the Republican camapaign success with defense-related issues, President Carter signed a series of four Presidential Directives to implement a new U. S. nuclear strategy. The targeting policy developed in the 1978 Department of Defense Nuclear Targeting Policy Study, contained in Presidential Directive/National Security Council-59, calls for increased missile accuracy. Enemy "political leadership, nuclear forces, non-nuclear forces, and direct defense-supporting industries" become military targets. Of course this new targeting policy requires additional national resources. Such precision targeting would require development of a new long-range (intercontinental) ballistic missile system.

Though details of this strategic planning must always remain closely guarded, the basic premise of U. S. nuclear policy should be openly and clearly understood. Only when strategic policy (including the consequence of aggression against the United States) is publicly stated can it act as an effective deterrent against enemy attack; only then can it encourage our friends who support us and discourage our enemies who confront us.

Especially when U. S. nuclear strategy is to be effective as a deterrent, it is neccessary to demonstrate acceptance by the American people. Public endorsement is the only U. S. endorsement that can convince Soviet leaders that the resources of this nation will be made available for military needs in time of national emergency.

Public endorsement conveys the message that not only national defense policy but also national economic policy is implemented in concert with the over-all management of other national resources, that national security is indeed a national effort.

C011   The evolution of nuclear strategy

> *On Sunday, August 17, 1980, Secretary of Defense Harold Brown, appearing on a network news show, ABC-TV "Issue and Answers," provided the first*

*public explanation of the Carter change in U. S.
nuclear policy. For all the press attention it
attracted, it could as well have been a routine
weather report.*

ABC-TV's Mr. Clark asked, "There is a great deal of concern
over those who worry about nuclear war; over President Carter's recent approval of a new concept of limited nuclear war.
Doesn't any attempt even to define limited nuclear war raise
the risk that nuclear war becomes more thinkable?" Mr. Clark
had gone right to the immediate concern of most Americans:
"if you have already decided how to fight a limited nuclear
war, then haven't you already, in effect, decided that you are
going to fight it?"

Secretary Brown dismissed the question of risk; he spoke
instead of the evolutionary change that had brought the new
strategic policy into effect. Brown also went on to say that he
didn't think a nuclear war is winnable; he said he believed
that "a nuclear strike on the United States, even though we
retaliated initially in a limited way, would probably escalate
ultimately to an all-out nuclear war that would destroy both
the United States and the Soviet Union."

Thus, according to Secretary Brown, the only significant
change in the official U.S. nuclear strategy, as had been publicly stated by the Carter White House, was that there would
be "more options" available to the President; targets would be
"not only cities but also the conventional military forces on
which they [the Soviets] place great emphasis, the nuclear
forces and the military and political command systems." "All
kinds of targets in the Soviet Union would be at risk."

Speaking for the Carter White House, Secretary Brown
further emphasized, ". . . we are talking about the way the
United States would retaliate to a nuclear attack on itself."
Brown insisted that any nuclear attack on the continental
United States would come as a surprise attack by the Soviet
Union. Indeed Brown insisted that the Carter nuclear war
policy was to sit and wait for a "surprise" First Strike from the
Soviet Union, and then to retaliate.

C012   The preemptive First Strike

*The authority to order the use of nuclear weapons
has already been delegated to the President of the*

United States. According to what is known through the press, there is nothing in that delegation of authority to preclude the President's ordering a preeemptive First Strike.

The "new" Carter strategic policy had already been advocated by Defense Secretary Robert McNamara in Ann Arbor, Michigan, in 1962. The same concept of "counter-force" strategic policy was again confirmed by Schlesinger in 1974, under the presidency of Mr. Nixon. The primary feature of this "new" strategy is that ICBMs (Inter-Continental Ballistic Missiles) fired from the continental United States would be used to destroy well-protected military targets in the Soviet Union. It would require the use of powerful nuclear weapons over intercontinental distances that could hit their "hardened" targets with extreme accuracy.

Unfortunately—it is unfortunate for the American taxpayers because the cost to fund the development of such a missile system would be excessive, and it is unfortunate for the economy because such technology will be held as war potential and, thus, contribute to economic stagnation—the "new" strategy did depart from past official U.S. policy. The new strategy moved from the unthinkable (the threat of war for the purpose of deterrence) to the thinkable (a host of war-fighting options).

The question of a preemptive First Strike now arises when the Soviet Union has already launched a First Strike against the United States. Under those circumstances, decision-making times correspond to the travel time of the missiles, a time interval of 20 to 30 minutes. Should the American military be expected to respond while the Soviet missiles are in flight, or should the American people absorb the First Strike, assess the damage, and then retaliate? Neither seems desirable because either retaliation or a preemptive First Strike would, within the context of political rhetoric, leave the nuclear initiative to the Soviet leaders.

It would be better for the United States to have its own well-thought-out plan, for the U.S. Congress to declare war, and for the U.S. military to take the initiative. That means in very simple terms, when diplomatic relations between the United States and the Soviet Union actually deteriorate, then the U.S. military should be ordered to deliver an offensive First Strike. Such an order would come only after the Congress of the United States had declared war on the Soviet Union.

C013   Authority to use nuclear weapons

Current indications are that Presidential authority to order the use of nuclear weapons may be delegated to subordinate military officers.

Underlying interest in the delegation of authority to order the use of nuclear weapons exists in the United States because official strategic policy now excludes a First Strike option. It does not, however, rule out "first use." Once war has been declared and conventional warfare is in progress, then the use of nuclear weapons could be ordered.

One situation for "first use" of nuclear weapons was publicly discussed by Secretary of Defense Harold Brown, "If a massive conventional attack were overrunning Western Europe, then I would not rule out the 'first use' of tactical (short-range) nuclear weapons as a way of showing that this was a very critical situation, and that the risks were very great, not only for the Europeans who were being overrun and for the United States, but (also) for the people who had attacked and invaded."

This question of which official has the authority to initiate a "first use" of nuclear weapons has periodically generated controversy. The most exhaustive public debate of the issue appears to have taken place during the 1964 Presidential campaign when Senator Barry Goldwater suggested that small tactical (battlefield) nuclear weapons should be considered conventional weapons, and that the authority to use them should be given to local (battlefield) commanders.

It is well documented that the broad delegation of command authority by a President to a military commander in time of war has been the rule, not the exception. For that reason, one would expect that a "first use" of nuclear weapons could now be ordered by the President or it could be ordered by a subordinate military officer with delegated authority.

Within the context of current desire of the American people to limit the use of nuclear weapons, it would appear that a "first use" of nuclear weapons in a conventional war should be made unconstitutional. A new (nuclear) war would need to be declared, and such a declaration of a "first use" of nuclear weapons could, therefore, not come from the President. The Founding Fathers were very definite; war powers belong to the Congress.

Chapter D

And then the State Department

A foreign policy for peace

The political mood of the country was contradicting itself. There were those in favor of arms control—a foreign policy for peace; and there were those in favor of the campaign promise of military superiority—a domestic policy of war. And Republican presidential candidates were inter-relating that war-peace contradiction by using the political rhetoric: peace through strength. Thus, the American people were in favor of peace, but they were also intending to have some say in the manner in which that peace would be pursued.

The Carter White House had taken on this same war-peace dualism—the national policy for war was being presented by Secretary of Defense Harold Brown; the foreign policy for peace by Secretary of State Edmund Muskie. But the public image of President Carter remained one of negotiating arms control, one that had been identified with the State Department.

D014　Peaceful thoughts from Senator Muskie

Edmund Muskie came into the Carter Cabinet directly from the Chairmanship of the powerful U.S.

*Senate Budget Committee. But, more than that, Mus-
kie brought with him his reputation for favoring
arms control negotiations.*

The new Carter appointee for Secretary of State (the man to
fill the vacancy created by the April 29, 1980, resignation of
Cyrus R. Vance) was Edmund Muskie, a United States Senator from Kennebunk, Maine. Secretary of State Muskie had
grown accustomed to the U.S. policy of deterrence. With the
MAD (Mutual Assured Destruction) concept of nuclear
exchange, there was the commonly held belief that there
would be no exchange at all, that the threat of destruction was
so great that there would be no destruction. And it was that
policy of deterrence that Senator Muskie had supported for his
entire political career.

As Chairman of the U.S. Senate Foreign Relations Subcommittee responsible for the 1974 review of the "Analysis of
Effects of Limited Nuclear War," Muskie had appointed a
special Congressional advisory panel of prestigious nuclear
experts to assess the casualty estimates given to Congress by
the Pentagon. Those Pentagon estimates of civilians that
would die from a "limited" nuclear strike were found faulty,
and Muskie refused to accept the use of nuclear weapons fired
across intercontinental distances as a way to fight a limited
nuclear war.

Thus, when Senator Muskie became Secretary of State, he
was well aware of the historic rivalry between the Department
of Defense and the Department of State in determining American foreign policy as it relates to the use of American military
abroad. Each Department had its own philosophy for the use
of arms or refusal; each had its own philosophy for implementing U.S. foreign policy, and the two were in direct conflict.

The U.S. Department of Defense appeared to have an
approach to U.S. foreign policy that was at odds with the
diplomatic mission of the State Department. The State
Department favored arms limitations talks. The Department
of Defense viewed arms control as nothing more than an
opportunity to replace old weapons systems with something
better—the harder the Department of Defense would "push"
for technological innovation, the sooner their weapons systems would become obsolete.

The internal policy-making machinery of the State Department was well equipped to deal with the negotiating traditions

known to Secretary Muskie; it was not equipped to deal with the "technology push" from the Department of Defense. The Department of Defense was far more supportive of increased productivity for the munitions industries than negotiations for arms reductions.

D015   A bypass for the State Department

Traditionally the State Department has coordinated U.S. foreign policy. Yet Secretary of Defense Harold Brown was bypassing Secretary of State Edmund Muskie to defend the new U.S. nuclear targeting strategy.

The new counter-force strategy for U.S. retaliation following a Soviet nuclear attack presupposes the existence of survivable communication capabilites, it presupposes the passing of orders within the military command structure, and it presupposes the persistence of atmospheric conditions that would permit accurate targeting of weapons systems. It also presupposes that such a new nuclear strategy has survived serious public debate in the United States and in all European NATO countries.

The new nuclear strategy described in Presidential Directive/National Security Council-59 requires the United States to acquire new more accurate delivery systems for nuclear warheads. And these delivery systems would have to carry nuclear warheads across intercontinental distances. Defense spending would have to be increased, and tax dollars would have to go to munitions industries.

Increased defense spending deserves equal attention from both the peace-seeking and the war-fighting branches of the federal government. The best defense may not necessarily come from more bombs, it may not necessarily come from the war-fighting half of the war-peace political dueling team. And that one-sided representation completely violated the existing public image of the Carter Administration.

Chapter E

A Quick Fix for a Press Leak

The sudden death of credibility

Information is firepower. Information was being manipulated to influence public opinion, and it was the President of the United States that was being accused of the manipulation.

A "press leak" had revealed U.S. development of a military airplane that would be "invisible" to enemy radar detection. That was supposed to be used to ensure accurate delivery of nuclear warheads across intercontinental distances between the United States and the Soviet Union. Follow-up news conferences were so well orchestrated that the "leaking" aroused political suspicion and the political credibility that was subsequently lost by the Carter White House was never to be regained to save the November election.

E016 The realities of "stealth"

Say "Kelly Johnson" and smile. That was one way to talk about "stealth" at the Pentagon during the fall of 1980, in the months preceding the November presidential election.

"Stealth" technology—the ability to mask an aircraft from enemy detection by radar or other remote sensing techniques—received media attention when a "press leak" by the Carter Administration revealed the existence of a secret project to build a bomber airplane "virtually invisible to enemy radar."

Reconnaissance aircraft continue to be used by the U.S. military for electronic snooping as well as for photographic recording. The most recent electronic marvel of the United States Air Force—the SR-71—known in the press by the nickname Blackbird after its sooty heat-resistant paint, is the world's highest flying airplane. The SR-71 is also the fastest flying manned airplane, exceeding 2,000 miles per hour. It far exceeds the military specifications for the better known U-2.

The SR-71 carries high-power cameras that can map the United States in three passes (at 85,000 feet altitude it can film 60,000 square miles in one hour) as well as record three-dimensional filming that can cover 150 square miles so precisely as to locate a mailbox at the side of a country road.

The SR-71, the number one snoop for the U.S. Air Force, has reason to want to remain "invisible" to enemy radar. The aircraft carries equipment to monitor radio and radar transmissions and it is armed with electronic gear capable of disrupting enemy tracking systems, even for wiping its own image off a radar scope.

The Pentagon press "leak" that revealed the use of even more "stealth" techniques to conceal a manned fighter-bomber aircraft caused all the ruckus at the Pentagon and on Capitol Hill. Stealth aircraft were intended to fly under or through enemy radar to deliver nuclear bombs. The fighter-bomber would carry electronic equipment that would detect the presence of enemy radar signals and return "false" echos to hide itself while flying over enemy territory.

Originally camouflage meant to hide in natural surroundings. Now camouflage also means to hide from an electronic radar pulse.

E017   The politics of leaking

When you look for a needle in a haystack, you at least know when you have found the needle. When you

*look for a "press leak" at the Pentagon, you may
meet it face to face in the corridor, and never know
the difference.*

Both the timing and the content of the "stealth technology"
disclosure suggested political motivation. Secretary of
Defense Harold Brown went on to confirm the information in
the press leak, with the announced purpose of stopping further
"leaks." And President Carter was accused by Republicans of
jeopardizing national security for the sake of his own political
future.

United States Senator Richard G. Lugar, Republican from
Indiana, a member of the Senate Select Committee on Intelligence and a member of the Senate Foreign Relations Committee, immediately requested the Intelligence Committee to
conduct an investigation of the state of the country's stealth-
technology research. Lugar made public a letter from former
Chief of Naval Operations Elmo Zumwalt. Admiral Zumwalt
alleged personal knowledge that the "stealth" disclosure was
ordered by the White House, that the purpose was "partial
camouflage for a miserable national defense record [of President Carter]."

The difficulty with inadvertent or intended public release of
sensitive military information is that it cannot be publicly
discussed by members of the Congress or other government
officials. Those who prefer to respect the classified status of
the material cannot publicly comment on the validity, or the
lack of validity, of the claims. Whether the claims are sound,
or not, can therefore never be determined.

The suspicion aroused by the press leak produced negative
political effects for those allegedly responsible, the Carter
White House.

E018   The vanishing power of the President

*There was a time when many Americans believed
the power of the President to be supreme. Now, with
improved communication, the political power of the
country is shifting back to the force of public opinion.*

Following World War II, there was much to be said in favor
of the President's classifying information to protect details of
national security. But those days are gone forever. The mood

of the country has changed and so have the many electronic capabilities that permit instant information transfer. It is no longer possible to keep a secret, at least not a secret upon which American military leaders or high government officials can depend.

Rules for secrecy of information that now exist within the federal government should become the subject of Congressional review. In all probability, many of those rules could be abolished. But, in the mean time, until those rules are legislated out of existence, the classification of information must be officially respected by the President of the United States, the Secretary of Defense, and all other high government officials.

Freedom of the press is one thing. Unofficial "leaking" of information to the press by the loyal opposition is equally acceptable. But any politically motivated, officially manipulated, sensitive (classified) information released, without first having changed the rules of classification, is a direct violation of the law. And besides that the American people don't like it either.

The United States is controlled by the rule of law. It takes the force of public opinion to change those laws. It also takes the force of public opinion to return a President of the United States to the White House for a second term.

Perspective

The Power of Public Opinion

*With everything coming up roses,
national security became a bouquet
of political thorns*

*The suffocation of a President
with a security blanket of
political loyalty*

Mood was in the air. Like the humidity that saturates the air in the still of the morning in swamp country, mood was hanging heavy. As is usual in such a "foggy bottom," there was nothing all that visible. There were no billowing storm clouds in motion, there were no harsh cold winds to keep you indoors, and there were no sudden bursts of lightning and thunder to startle the senses. There were no demanding signs of danger.

Rather, there was restlessness. A stirring in the land, as though someone who had been dormant for a long time was about to make a new appearance on the American political scene, to roll over, to give a stretch and then a groan and a yawn. There was just enough movement to let everyone know that a slumbering giant, a tall lanky, half-starved, undernourished fellow, was ready to greet the dawn of a new day.

During the 1980 presidential election, the arrival of a new political mood was evidenced by a heavy Republican vote. Ronald Reagan became President. The Republicans gained a majority in the United States Senate; a majority that gave the Republicans the freedom they needed to redo the Senate Committee structure. But there had been no national statement of national purpose. There had been only a popular claim that change would be better than four more years of the same. Thus, the actual commitment of the American people was a bit fuzzy. The 1980 vote had endorsed increased defense spending, a national commitment to "peace through strength," but no guidelines for the method of achieving that strength had been provided.

Old skin and bones himself had come to life. His hair was snow white, his joints were creaky with age, and his muscles were deteriorating from lack of use. The old fellow was hardly recognizable by many in the younger generation. But there he was, the national symbol associated with the American military tradition, a favorite Uncle of many, and his name was Sam.

Yes, the 1980 vote was Republican and the mood of the country was patriotic. The vote had not been just a matter of politics; and it was not just a matter of deciding between a Democrat and a Republican. The 1980 vote was an American vote; it was a vote for an American tradition called national independence. And that tradition of independence is rooted far deeper than any political rhetoric of any presidential campaign.

When President Carter released what was perceived by many to have been classified information about defense-related issues (and he did it in the name of national security), those close to the Carter White House remained loyal, but the Democratic Party fragmented. The Democratic Party divided over the question of national security. The people had rejected the manner in which national security was being pursued by President Carter in concert with his Secretary of Defense Harold Brown. And they had rejected the Carter attempt to go out around the State Department.

Though the flowers were in full bloom in the Rose Garden at the White House, the bouquet of national security that President Carter presented the American people was filled with political thorns. The credibility of the Carter White House was lost because of a perceived politically timed release of defense-related information. And that Carter credibility was not to be recovered in time to save the November election.

The political mood of the country favored increased defense spending, but it favored it Republican style. The Democrats and the Republicans had made good dueling partners for the 1980 campaign, but the Republicans were elected to exert the dominant political influence for the next four years and to implement the anticipated economic recovery.

The security of the nation as the American people had perceived it had more to do with national economic security than it had to do with national defense policy, yet the connection between the two was not immediately evident to the voter. There were many Americans who believed that this nation, as a nation, should be formulating its own economic policies. They apparently had in mind that the people themselves should "invent" a kind of democracy that would protect the common economic good. Military superiority, even when defined with a combined purpose of common economic good and free enterprise, was supposed to protect the security of the nation.

The question of fighting a limited nuclear war surfaced as a political issue during the 1980 presidential campaign. But the question that was really being asked went far beyond the military question of nuclear strategy. The question of the identity of the nation was at stake. The question of the role of the American military in the future of American foreign policy was left dangling in mid-air.

Public opinion had its influence at the ballot box in 1980. Public opinion continues to have its influence on in-progress legislation in the U.S. Congress. Modern communication networks are linked to computer capabilities for more rapid information transfer and more and more political influence is shifting directly to the people. There is a sense and strength developing in the collective response of the people that is available from no other source. And that response is now the response that should be used to determine the priorities for defense spending.

The American tradition of independence is tied to 200 years of national behavior. It is tied to the aggressive independent spirit of the freedom of the individual and it is tied to the aggressive independent spirit of the nation as a whole. It is the American pride in the uniqueness of the American nation, and it is the American pride in the uniqueness of the American military tradition that is creating the political and the economic mood of this country. It is that American pride in the American ideals that must now hold this American nation together.

PART TWO

Nuclear War Strategy

*If you are going to fight a limited
nuclear war, then you really
should find a willing target*

MAD (Mutual Assured Destruction) has been the common nuclear strategy between the United States and the Soviet Union for the past two decades. That strategy has depended upon having ICBMs (Inter-Continental Ballistic Milliles) aimed and ready to fire. There were no ABMs (Anti-Ballistic Missiles) to intercept and destroy incoming missiles. Thus, a missile launched was a missile received.

This MAD "balance of terror" has been effective as a deterrent against an all-out nuclear exchange between the two superpowers. It has, however, failed to discourage Soviet, or American, use of military forces on foreign soil. Soviet "adventurism" has been confined to the use of conventional weapons, and that use of conventional weapons appears to remain below the threshold that would warrant the launching of ICBMs from the United States. Thus, the human race was held hostage only to the threat of accidental nuclear holocaust.

Now the United States is faced with the prospect of using Europe as the battleground to fight a limited nuclear war with the Soviet Union. The United States would use combat nuclear weapons to respond to Soviet military action initiated entirely by non-nuclear means. It is the answer to this question of the *first use* of nuclear weapons in Europe that will now completely determine the politics of U.S. foreign policy and U.S. nuclear strategy. It will also determine the role of the American military in implementing American foreign policy for many years to come.

Chapter A

Anti-City Strategy

Mutual Assured Destruction is MAD

The nuclear strategy of MAD (Mutual Assured Destruction), as it was well publicized, stated that the United States had its ICBMs aimed at population centers in the Soviet Union. For that reason, it was logical for both the United States and the Soviet Union to construct silos to house ICBMs in remote desolate areas in the interior of the country.

The United States had an equally well publicized national policy that required the American people to absorb a First Strike from the Soviet Union—the American land-based missiles were to be fired only in retaliation to a Soviet attack. Thus the Russian people had no reason to fear a surprise nuclear attack from the United States.

But now, in the 1980s, both the Russian and the American people have the same problem. Both have to develop enough influence on their own government to prevent their own military from initiating a nuclear exchange over intercontinental distances. Both have to get rid of the "push-button" land-based systems that would make accidental nuclear holocaust possible.

A019   The logic of geography

With the United States on one side of the globe and the Union of Soviet Socialist Republics on the other, it is necessary for the two superpowers to fire bombs across intercontinental distances to engage in a "push-button" nuclear war.

There exists a well-established Russian tradition for the use of military force—the use of brute force methods to defend geographical-political boundaries. It was, therefore, not surprising that the same tradition continued even when the perceived threat of "invasion" was coming from a nation on the other side of the globe, even when the destruction that was being threatened was nuclear holocaust.

Following World War II, the Russian government decided to develop enormous rocket boosters to carry their relatively primitive (heavy) nuclear bombs over the intercontinental distances. At that time, the Russian military had no possibility of using bomber airplanes to carry nuclear warheads. The Russian aerospace industry could not "catch-up" with the lead the aerospace industry of the United States had gained during World War II.

The state-of-the-art Russian-made rocket of the 1950s was strictly "ready, aim, fire, blast-off" for the delivery of nuclear warheads to the United States. While the "ready" and the "fire" phases of the launch may well have been satisfactory by military standards, the "aim" part was poor. Thus, the MAD (Mutual Assured Destruction) concept of nuclear strategy (the anti-city strategy of firing nuclear warheads at population centers) was born. Accuracy was no longer a stumbling block in a large metropolitan area. A bomb could miss a prime target and still hit something worthy of destruction.

To compensate for this lack of accurate delivery capabilities and the ever-increasing high cost of the rocket engines needed for launch of the nuclear warheads, the development emphasis was understandably on bigger and bigger bombs. With a bigger bomb the explosive radius would be bigger; fewer bombs would have to be launched. Thus the Russian mastery of the hydrogen bomb (announced in the August 12, 1953 testing) was a necessary economic achievement. It meant more destructive power for the cost of a single launch vehicle. These

early Russian concepts of MAD nuclear strategy were, therefore, justified by the combined realities of inaccurate missile
launch systems and necessary economic constraint.

A020   Silo positioning in the Soviet Union

*Underground silos have been the essential construc-
tion element for land-based missiles ready for rapid
vertical launch. Though a missile can be built with
some degree of secrecy, the silo cannot.*

Silo construction in the Soviet Union has been observed
from aerial reconnaissance or satellite surveillance since the
1950's. Much of the U.S. interpretation of aerial photographs
is based upon our knowledge of similar American silo construction. For example, the American Minuteman, a land-
based missile similar to the Soviet SS-13, is housed in a silo
109 feet deep and 12 feet in diameter. Excavation for the silo
requires the removal of some 2,200 cubic yards of earth for the
construction, 1,050 cubic yards of which are later replaced.
Removal of so much earth is highly visible from the air.

While primitive roads built in rugged terrain will be almost
invisible from the air, rail construction is more conspicuous.
To locate a silo near rail access involves even more people and
the construction areas are even more susceptible to satellite
reconnaissance. Thus, the positions of the Soviet ICBM silos
are well known. The positions along the trans-Siberian rail-
road are mapped and have been published in the United
States by *Aviation Week and Space Technology*, a journal
widely read in the defense community.

The Soviet missile-launching ramps located in this belt
straddle the trans-Siberian railway between Moscow and Vladivostok. If the United States were to fire weapons at those
missile sites, it would not be a simple matter (in actuality it
would be virtually impossible) for the U.S.S.R. leaders to survey the region to decide whether the attack had been
"limited." It would, therefore, seem foolish to assume that the
Soviets would react with "due restraint," particularly since
they would have to decide their manner of retaliation within
minutes.

A021   The arithmetic of counting bombs

When is a bomb not a bomb? When the government of the United States gets through counting it.

The arithmetic of counting bombs defies all common sense; at least that is the way it would appear to anyone experienced in the logic of number sequence. To begin with, it is illogical to count "almost" bombs. Is a bomb a bomb before it is deployed for field testing, before it has been manufactured, before the component parts have been assembled, after the bomb is complete but before it is transferred to the custody of the military, before it is installed at the field site where it is stored in a vertical launch position? The dilemma is obvious. There are many varying degrees of "completeness" before the final deployment of a bomb for strategic purposes.

The SALT II (Strategic Arms Limitation Talks) treaty was not negotiated with regard to bombs. Rather, the limitations were intended for the number of launch vehicles. This SALT counting scheme implied that a bomb was not a bomb until there was a way to deliver it, that there was no reason to limit the number of bombs, only the number of delivery vehicles.

One other problem with counting bombs deals with the question of ownership. Does an American-made bomb belong to the United States military once it has been transferred to a foreign country? Can an American-made bomb be stored on foreign soil for the purpose of protecting a foreign country in the interest of the United States, yet not be counted with the American arsenal of nuclear weapons?

The arithmetic of counting bombs is not the simple "one, two, three" learned in school. Rather there is an actual complex issue of knowing when and where to do the counting. It is this inability to count bombs—(almost bombs, component parts of bombs, stockpiles of bombs in foreign countries, and bombs deployed with launch vehicles that can be re-loaded) that has now reduced to nonsense the entire concept of a negotiated U.S. -Soviet balance of power.

A022   Survival becomes a way of life

The Russian people have a long-standing national tradition of fighting against people to defend their borders. The Americans have fought largely against nature. It is no wonder that the survival instincts of the two nations are very different.

In 1839, Alexis de Tocqueville foresaw the long-term competition between the United States and the Soviet Union as the two nations were destined to use two very different methods to pursue their transition toward a new world order:

> There are now two great nations in the world which, starting from different points, seem to be advancing toward the same goal: The Russians and the Anglo-Americans.
>
> Both have grown in obscurity, and while the world's attention was occupied elsewhere, they have suddenly taken their place among the leading nations, making the world take note of their birth and of their greatness almost at the same instant.
>
> All other peoples seem to have nearly reached their natural limits and to need nothing but to preserve them; but these two are growing. All the others have halted or advanced only through great exertions, they alone march easily and quickly forward along a path whose end no eye can yet see.
>
> The American fights against natural obstacles; the Russian is at grips with men. The former combats the wilderness and barbarism; the latter, civilization with all its arms. America's conquests are made with the plowshare; Russia's with the sword.
>
> To attain their aims, the former relies on personal interest and gives free scope to the unguided strength and common sense of individuals. The latter in a sense concentrates the whole power of society in one man. One has freedom as the principle means of action; the other has servitude.
>
> Their point of departure is different and their paths diverse; nevertheless, each seems called by some secret design of Providence one day to hold in its hands the destinies of half the world.

The methods of human survival used to pursue the new era of human behavior may differ but the era itself will arrive. The thought patterns of the era can be understood, at least for the purpose of introduction, within the context of dynamic dualism in the decision making process. And for that purpose, perhaps Karl Marx wrote most effectively for the Soviet Union; William James for the United States; and Alexis de Tocqueville for the world.

A023   Escalation or holocaust

Any escalation to "the use of all weapons" should now be considered an invitation to nuclear holocaust.

An official pamphlet of the United States government entitled, "Authority to Order the Use of Nuclear Weapons (United States, United Kingdom, France, Soviet Union, People's Republic of China)," prepared by the Subcommittee on International Security and Scientific Affairs of the House Committee on International Relations (prepared by the Congressional Research Service of the Library of The Congress), states that "Soviet strategy calls for a capability not only to deter its potential enemies from attacking it but to wage a nuclear war and win it."

That same pamphlet notes the expectation of specialists in Soviet affairs that "... while the Soviets require their armed forces to be flexible in the use of either category of weapons [conventional or nuclear] ... in view of the unlimited aims of both sides [the United States and the Soviet Union] in a confrontation, the war is likely to lead to the use of all weapons."

The published Soviet strategy "... to wage a nuclear war and win it" is, however, now of questionable value. Logic would dictate that a Soviet First Strike across intercontinental distances would escalate to massive destruction. Nuclear bombs exploding within the continental United States would destroy visibility and, in all probability, much of the existing communication capabilities. It would make an assessment of damage impossible; the United States would be unable to retaliate in a studied (limited) traditional war-fighting fashion. Rather, any indication of increased Soviet military activity would more appropriately trigger an instant preemptive First Strike by the American military.

Though political rhetoric by government officials may suggest otherwise, any American military preemptive First Strike against the Soviet Union would bring massive destruction of military-industrial targets. One can only suppose that the American military would be in no mood to succumb to controlled response dictated by political folderol from the White House.

The United States military has taken its turn as the doormat for the political blundering of the industrial interests of this nation. Both the American people, and the rest of the world, would be well advised to anticipate aggressive action from the United States armed forces. The Vietnam War marked the last time the American people would be willing to use their tax dollars for American military to be manipulated by a political minority.

Land-based push-button nuclear weapons are in place. Any confrontation between United States and the Soviet Union, as the specialists in Soviet affairs suggest, would "lead to the use of all weapons." And any such "escalation" would be nuclear holocaust; it would destroy life as we know it today on Planet Earth.

Chapter B

Soviet Adventurism Flourishes

The protocol of being first

Determined management of combined military-civilian resources has allowed the Soviet Union to pursue its long-term grand strategy of expanding its sphere of influence to its nearest geographic neighbors. This Soviet adventurism appears to have flourished at a level of military action comfortably below the MAD threshold that would have warranted a devastating nuclear response from the United States.

The minority ruling party of the Soviet Union has been able to implement peacetime civilian-military comprehensive planning with minimum regard for popular opinion. And the Soviet Union expands its sphere of military influence around its extensive land-locked borders when that minority makes the decision. Yet, even a minority government will eventually realize that its survival depends not upon military force but rather upon the combined faith and reason of those being governed.

B024   Expanding the sphere of influence

In the face of growing Soviet military power, smaller politically and economically troubled nations seem even more likely targets for the expanding Soviet sphere of influence.

The geographic width of the Soviet Union extends essentially halfway around the globe. The hugeness of the actual expanse is exaggerated by the Mercator projection often used in a home atlas. But no matter what the representation, the land mass of the Soviet Union is big.

Clustered around the borders of the Soviet Union are 12 different countries, and 7 more are directly accessible across short distances of water. For the purpose of launching land-based (nuclear) missiles, Western Europe, North Africa, the Middle East, the Persian Gulf areas, and India and all of her neighbors are within reach of the Soviet Union.

Military objectives for the Soviet Union, as they are understood in the West, are the same in peacetime as in wartime. In the western world, especially in the United States, the outstanding quality of current Soviet military doctrine is its wartime-peacetime comprehensive nature. Soviet military doctrine reaches far beyond the limits of what the West would ordinarily recognize as a necessary scope for military planning. The true significance of this so-called Clausewitzian view is that wartime is but a continuation of peacetime policy.

With this planning philosophy, the Soviet leaders, the Central Committee of the Communist Party (an apparat of the State and the military high command), give every indication that any war, conventional or nuclear, could be fought and won. The Soviet leaders with their continuous peacetime-wartime planning intend, of course, that the element of surprise remain in their favor. According to Soviet doctrine, the Soviet military is always expected to deliver the first blow.

B025 The Soviet Union is land locked

By far the greatest consideration of the Soviet Union in her development of nuclear war strategy is geography. No amount of planning can alter the fact that the Soviet Union is land locked.

The Soviet Union must maintain four distinct naval forces to achieve its mission of interfering with American naval presence around the globe. Yet ready access to open ocean water is a problem for ships leaving Russia on the east, west, north, or south. On the west, along the coast between Poland and Sweden, the route passes into the Baltic Sea, only to be further restricted by the North Sea on the other side of Denmark.

The southern route is no better. Russian ships leaving the Black Sea must pass through the narrow straits that cut through Turkey, only to enter the Aegean Sea by Greece and then the Mediterranean. To the east, the Soviet port of Petropavlovsk, on the Kamchatka peninsula, provides direct entry to the open sea, but the port is far removed from industrial centers. During time of conflict, supplies for Petropavlovsk would have to come by sea from Vladivostok.

Thus, the only alternative is the Norwegian Sea on the north. The Norwegian Sea provides open-sea access for Russian submarines. And that access has changed in recent years from being a convenience to a necessity. To paraphrase a remark by the newly appointed U.S. Ambassador to Norway, Mark Evans Austad, "He who controls the Norwegian coast controls the world." The remark dramatizes the situation, but it is sure that Russia's land-locked navy would be virtually powerless without access to open ocean. And it is a matter of judgment as to when, or if, the United States should discourage the Soviet Union from having convenient access to Norwegian coastal islands.

B026   Minority rule

The Communist Party is a minority ruling party in Russia. It is not necessary for that ruling minority to seek public favor when assigning defense spending priorities.

Western electronic technology has slowly become available in the Soviet Union, and the Soviet military has been a favored recipient. But even within the military the user of the technology, especially the user of modern communications, is still restricted. It is not uncommon for a military user to be supplied receive-only equipment. One-way communication provides for information transfer down the chain of command, but there is little provision for transfer in the other direction.

The Soviet Union will derive full benefit from the utility of modern communication technology only when the people themselves become active users. Only when the people themselves become users will the technology become assimilated into the society, and daily living habits change accordingly.

The drawback to technology assimilation is the social change it brings with it. Social change driven by the assimilation of technology cannot be controlled from the top. Social change motivated by technology assimilation is, by its very nature, unpredictable. It is unpredictable for the economy and it is unpredictable for its political influence as well. Such social change depends entirely upon human need and human desire. There is no way to predict or to dictate the secondary effects.

The minority ruling party in the Soviet Union may be slow to make modern communication-computer technology available to the ordinary citizen. Confinement of the use of modern electronic equipment to military or industrial use may well prove supportive of planned Soviet adventurism and planned economic development, but it will stifle refreshing internal change.

Equal opportunity for information exchange is the best known economic equalizer; it allows people to learn from each other. It also makes it necessary for the Communist Party to seek public favor when deciding national spending priorities.

B027   Separation of faith and reason

Faith and reason—the Soviets are slow to combine them; the Americans are slow to separate them. The objective is not to decide who is right and who is wrong, but rather to recognize the profound importance of the distinction.

"One of the chief, age-old methods ... used by promoters of many different faiths, is to create the belief that your particular faith, unlike others, was given to us from heaven and, therefore, is beyond criticism or inquiry. This habit, common to the many competing faiths, more than almost any other device, builds long-time barriers between men, keeping them from uniting in a common search for truth, and from steady increase of mutual understanding."

Communist leaders in the Soviet Union can, therefore, justify their efforts to discourage religious affiliation. Their conviction is that the Russian people can seek and find "truth" much faster, and with much less internal conflict, without the disruptive teachings from any Church.

Andrei Sakharov, an outstanding Russian scientist and a member of the Soviet Academy of Sciences, wrote and distributed an essay entitled "Thoughts on Progress, Peaceful Coexistence, and Intellectual Freedom." Sakharov asked for an "equilibrium" based on *reason*. He was urging, among other things, joint action by the United States and the Soviet Union to prevent nuclear war.

Sakharov was correct in concluding that the "balance of terror" between the Soviet Union and the United States is unacceptable (Sakharov, in effect, made a strong plea for freedom from fear), but his focus on studied *reason* as the suggested mechanism for action was self-defeating. And that is the dilemma.

Advancement on the frontier of human development sits exactly with the integration of faith and reason. Individuals in both nations will have to admit that studied reason is not enough, that the "logical" next step will require a "leap of faith." The logical next step will require confidence in every individual. Yet such confidence, because it cannot be supported entirely by clear logic, should not be naive.

Political and military leaders in both the Soviet Union and the United States will have to admit that they have run out of "reason." Both will have to develop faith in the ability of their own people and those people will have to combine faith and reason in their use of modern communication-information transfer capabilities. And such a profound change in human behavior will only suffocate itself if it is controlled from the top by the dictates of a few.

Chapter C

The NATO Alternative

European allies don't like bombs either

Large numbers of U.S. nuclear warheads in Europe are deployed under programs of cooperation with NATO countries, through bilateral agreements with the United States as the common partner. The host nation provides support for U.S. weapons, and all nuclear weapons remain in U.S. custody until they are released by the President of the United States. Those nuclear weapons include atomic demolition munitions, artillery projectiles, bombs, depth charges, and warheads for short-range missiles.

All of those weapons could be used to fight a "limited" nuclear war on European soil. They are there because Russian-made, land-based, prepositioned, ready-to-launch missiles can reach European targets in a matter of seconds.

At the present time, because of a 1979 modernization agreement, the United States is progressively scheduling a major updating of its battlefield capabilities in Central Europe, its so-called Theater Nuclear Forces. For that reason, every European NATO military member needs to agree upon a reason for U.S. military presence in Europe or do away with it.

C028   National Technical Means

U.S. military-operated global monitoring systems, ground-based radar equipment, and other remote-sensing devices keep track of military activities and environmental conditions on a continuous basis. That electronic remote sensing equipment and supportive communication networks is collectively known as National Technical Means.

The potential use of artificial earth-orbiting satellites for military reconnaissance was well appreciated following World War II. It was not until the mid-1950s, however, that the availability of rocket boosters was assured, so the actual use of reconnaissance satellites could finally be established.

Today U.S. military-operated satellites circle the globe every 90 minutes. Those satellites collect, process, and transfer more detailed information in one day than an average espionage activity would produce in years. The information flow from National Technical Means (National Technical Means is here used to mean exactly remote sensing and supportive communication capabilities belonging to the United States no matter in which country the equipment is physically located or over which country the satellite may be orbiting) has a peace keeping value not only of discouraging armed conflict but also of monitoring violators of international agreements.

Military-operated global monitoring systems have become the eyes and ears of the world. The value lies in continuous operation. The military is watching and listening so the American people can go about their daily living. From that perspective, it is only a few that now provide the peace of mind for so many.

Critics of defense spending have argued that initial costs for satellite monitoring systems have been excessive, and they are right. The costs have been excessive because many of the systems never get past the one-of-a-kind prototype stage. But those initial phases of development are now behind us. Operational reliability, information interpretation capabilities, and extended lifetime for electronic components—all are now available, most are able to satisfy even the wildest expectations.

Now is the time to replace old remote sensing systems with new ones, but that takes money. Tax dollars would have to be used to buy new electronic equipment, to install it, and to develop the software to make it operational. Those tax dollars would not be used to buy weapons systems that would sit in reserve as war potential. Those tax dollars would be buying the timely availability of essential information flow.

Every increase in defense spending that could be used for the modernization of National Technical Means would be the best investment the American taxpayers could make in their own future and in the future of mankind.

C029   The urgency of technology transfer

The transfer of modern electronics to other nations has become imperative and the reason is simple. Information can be communicated back and forth across the Atlantic Ocean much faster than people and bombs can be transported and the information is our most powerful weapon.

The transfer of electronic equipment from the United States to other nations is required if the American military is to use National Technical Means of verification to carry out cooperative-coordinated operations. To control common air space, common land use, and common sea access electronic equipment must be available to all nations alike. The military of one nation cannot support the military of another until they can transfer information back and forth.

Given "intelligent" use of modern electronics for information gathering and information transfer, there can be no secrets and there can be no surprises. Official U.S. policy or official U.S. strategy that has been formulated depending upon either the existence of a secret or the necessity of a surprise can no longer be considered acceptable for military purposes.

The new age of information exchange has arrived. It has brought with it the actuality of eliminating redundancy (and waste) in the traditional planning for military weapons systems. Intricate operational details of satellite systems need not be revealed, but the urgent need for the American military to enjoy cooperative use of elecronic technology in concert with other countries should now be accepted.

Without international cooperation, and without the sharing of human resource, there soon will be no government-controlled, military-operated satellite systems at all. And, one might add, no way to gain access to information flow from global monitoring systems.

C030   Theater Nuclear Forces

Theater means European and Nuclear Forces means exactly what you think it means. And the sum of the two is about to spell the end of our NATO military alliance.

In 1979, the United States negotiated a military moderniza-tion agreement with its European NATO allies. According to Pentagon sources, the agreed 1983-1984 dates for deployment of new land-based missiles in Europe are, however, starting to slip. For one thing, the anti-nuclear demonstrations have become numerous enough that they may, in fact, sway politi-cal thinking at the military planning level. For another, the Soviet military doctrine for Europe appears to be more aggres-sive. The Soviet Union may well intend avoiding global nuclear war with the United States but it appears to have no equivalent reason for caution in Europe.

The alternative to NATO military modernization has been the "Zero Option" proposal by Helmut Schmidt, Chancellor of West Germany. In view of the controlled militarization of Germany that has evolved since World War II, the Zero Option proposal (in some form) appears to be the only option worth considering.

The Soviet Union would remove all pre-positioned, ready-to-fire, land-based nuclear missiles now aimed at Europe. The United States (and U.S. allies) would remove from European soil all pre-positioned, ready-to-fire, land-based nuclear mis-sles. That is to say, all land-based missiles would be removed. Neither the United States nor the Soviet Union would be at liberty to use Europe as the battlefield for a "push-button" nuclear war.

The truth about deterrence is that the United States never intended intercontinental range nuclear weapons as a deterrent for the use of conventional weapons in Europe. U.S. strategic [nuclear] weapons were a deterrent for Soviet strategic [nuclear] weapons. And that's all. Soviet adventurism in Europe is not only below the threshold for global conflict, it is also beyond the intent of U.S. nuclear retaliation from the North American continent.

The deployment of U.S. land-based nuclear missiles on European soil should be prohibited. Theater Nuclear Forces, and U.S. military presence in Europe, are dinosaurs of the defense establishment. Theater Nuclear Forces are best declared extinct.

C031 The reality of de-coupling

The United States and its European NATO military members could now terminate coupling through Theater Nuclear Forces but coupling through National Technical Means of verification should grow stronger.

Following World War II, the European members of the North Alantic Treaty Organization and the United States were coupled together as a single unit in matters of military defense against Russia. Now, however, it seems that the United States cannot and will not fire ICBMs from the North American continent to defend Europe. The risk of retaliation from the Soviet Union is too great and the extent of destruction too massive. Any use of combat troops or combat weapons in Europe will have to come from within Europe.

The United States and the European countries now have a far more urgent common military interest than Theater Nuclear Forces, it is called National Technical Means. The transfer and the common use of National Technical Means of remote sensing and satellite monitoring (with support from ground stations) is essential for the continuous collection, processing, and transfer of information for the purpose of detection and early warning. And that electronic coupling is the only military coupling that will eventually bring all nations of the world together for the common purpose of preventing surprise acts of aggression.

On April 4, 1949, when the NATO Atlantic Alliance was formed, President Truman said of the European community, "To protect the area against war will be a long step toward peace in the whole world." With a major shift of emphasis from the deployment of nuclear weapons to the operational use of electronics, military coupling could now be created through satellite information networks.

Because of extraordinary advances in electronic capabilities since 1949, the United States can now use military-operated global monitoring systems to make information available to all nations alike. There is no reason to favor a friend; there is no reason to fear a foe. With cooperation from all NATO members (including France), Europe could protect itself from surprise armed attack.

European NATO countries can now draw the line. They can now refuse any form of modernization that would require the installation or deployment of land-based nuclear weapons. European NATO countries can now insist upon being decoupled from the United States by rejecting all force of the Theater Nuclear Forces.

Electronic coupling is the coupling of the future. Only increased National Technical Means of verification will eventually accomplish that ". . . long step toward peace in the whole world."

Perspective

Deterrence is MAD

The nesting instinct of
Mother Russia remains
rooted in tradition

Nations fight wars, not automated
weapons systems produced by
munitions industries

Since the 5th century B.C., philosophers have acknowledged the dualism of law that governs the behavior of man, the divine law and the human law. In the United States these two essential aspects of human behavior are now codified as the "spirit" of the law and the "letter" of the law. The spirit of the law is embodied in the U.S. Constitution; the letter of the law (the legal profession refers to the letter of the law as positive law) rests with the legislative base as it is constantly revised and otherwise modified by the U.S. Congress. Thus, the dualism of law is very much a part of the American way of life.

By comparison, the people of the Union of Soviet Socialist Republics appear to be less fortunate. The minority rule of the Communist Party appears to confine human behavior so it is regulated only within the letter (or the logic) of the law.

Though the Dutch lawyer Hugo Grotius (1583-1645) is regarded as the "father of international law," it was Jean Bodin (1530-1596), "a lawyer who practiced law unprofitably and lost himself eagerly in philosophy and history," who believed strongly in the influence of climate, and hence history, on the character of a people. It is that "climate bias" that offers perhaps some explanation as to why all peoples do not embrace identically the same type of government at the same moment in history.

Bodin believed that men differ in character and conduct depending upon whether they make their living from the sea, from the land, or from desolate mountainous terrain. Bodin remained convinced that men were also influenced markedly by prevailing weather conditions. He concluded that men in colder climates of the north developed physical strength and relied upon muscular energy; in the south, they were more apt to develop personal sensitivity and rely upon emotional or spiritual devotion. And, thus, there could be a similar bias in governments. Such a bias would depend upon the prevailing harshness of the weather.

When one accepts climate as having exerted a significant influence on human behavior, then it is possible that religious conviction and religious motivation could have a stronger tradition in the countries of lower latitudes, that military force and physical strength could play a more dominant role in the north. Away from those extremes, between 30° and 50° latitude, there should then be a people more intellectually inclined than those of the far north, more practically oriented than those of the far south. Such is the situation for the United States with its mid-latitude position in the northern hemisphere.

By comparison, the Soviet Union lies north of 50°N latitude. The climatic influence on the Russian people would, therefore, differ from that on the Americans. A modern manifestation of climatic influences could be one of the reasons for the serious economic dichotomy that now exists between the Soviet Union and the United States. The two nations are pursuing two very different methods of reaching their goal of self-government and national economic independence.

Soviet statements and announced policies, as well as current trends in scientific (engineering) training and research activities, suggest a strong desire to "catch-up" with western technological achievement. This theme can be traced back to the 19th century, even to the reign of Peter the Great at the turn of the 18th century. But, technology is culture. And, as any good theologian knows, the use of technology has impact on the human soul. The assimilation of technology into a society will always bring with it dramatic social and economic change.

Social change "pushed" by technological innovation could bring with it internal pressures so great as to crumble the foundation of a rigid political structure. Social change driven by the free choice of the user of technology would, at the very least, tend to be unpredictable and, more than likely, highly democratic. That is to say, there is no way technologically motivated social change can be controlled by minority rule. The assimilation of technology produces its own change in human behavior.

Soviet strategic, political, and military doctrines are firmly grounded in Russian history. They are born in the people. And the nesting instinct of Mother Russia is rooted in centuries of tradition. For that reason, continuity, in an evolutionary sense, is the order of the day. The Communist ruling party could well continue to depend upon military strength, and could logically even be expected to use that strength to cope with pressures from within.

Nevertheless, one way or another, the Russian people will gain access to their own version of electronic information processing technology. Once communication-information transfer capabilities are made available to civilians, the ruling minority will remain in power only so long as it is responsive to the needs of the people. Sooner or later, with or without the consent of the Communist Party, information will be exchanged and the majority will rule.

The United States government does not intend dominating the Soviet Union. Had the United States wanted to use armed force to dominate the world, they would have done it in the 1950s when they clearly possessed awesome military superiority over the Soviet Union. The American people do no intend massive nuclear retaliation in response to Soviet "adventurism." Had the United States wanted to launch an all-out nuclear attack across intercontinental distances for the sake of stopping a Russian tank in Afghanistan,they would have done it.

The openness of the democratic process in the United States clearly limits the capacity of government officials to bluff or threaten a foreign government. And as the people in the

Soviet Union exercise more influence on their own government, leadership in the Soviet Union will have that same
problem. Therefore, openness is the only long-term alternative for all nations. When it comes to nuclear war strategy,
government officials will eventually have to say what they
mean and mean what they say, or they will be violating the
ideals of the people whom they claim to represent.

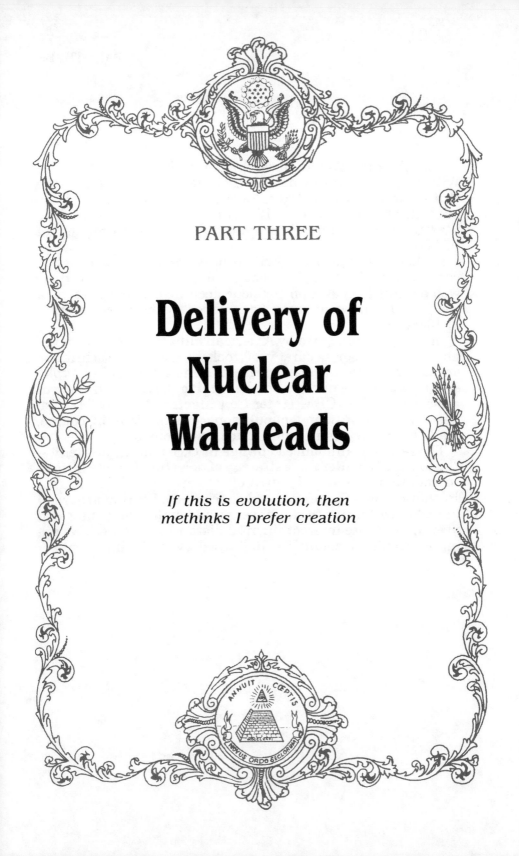

PART THREE

Delivery of Nuclear Warheads

*If this is evolution, then
methinks I prefer creation*

"... the rocket's red glare, the bombs bursting in air ..."
With the first light of dawn on September 14, 1814, as the
British fleet bombarded Fort McHenry near Baltimore, Mary-
land, during the War of 1812, Francis Scott Key wrote "The
Star Spangled Banner" to immortalize the wartime use of
rockets.

Rockets had aided the British only three weeks earlier to
capture Washington, yet rockets were destined to earn their
well-deserved reputation for poor accuracy. The rocket, as a
weapon of war, would soon be replaced by the more accurate
artillery shell.

In 1954, it was argued by American military leaders that the
unavoidable poor accuracy of rockets made it essential to
develop massive nuclear warheads. The far-reaching explosive radius of the nuclear bomb would make up for the lack of
accuracy of the ICBM (Inter-Continental Ballistic Missile)
itself. Large sprawling population centers were, of course,
ready-made targets for such inaccurate bombs.

The recently announced change in U.S. nuclear strategy—
the so-called counter-force strategy of targeting Soviet military
installations—is directly attributed to and entirely motivated
by the promise of improved rocket accuracy. Yet that accuracy
in rocket performance can never be adequately demonstrated
over appropriate intercontinental distances or under prevailing atmospheric conditions disturbed by exploding bombs.

Chapter A

Land-Based Missiles

People and missiles don't mix

People live on the land. When missiles are planted on the same land, then people become a military target. People and land-based missiles don't mix.

A032   Missile eXperimental

> *MX is a military designation for a missile system in its experimental stages (Missile eXperimental). That the military would have as experimental missile system is understandable, that the basing of that missile system should be on land is unacceptable.*

The MX, as it is perceived by the American people, is a missile system to be based on land within the continental United States. It is a ballistic-type missile that can travel the intercontinental distance from North America to the Soviet Union with a trajectory over the north pole. The MX, as it was discussed in 1980 during the closing months of the Carter Administration, was to have been a land-based system with an MPS (Multiple Protective Shelter) basing mode, the so-called "race track" shelter to be constructed in the Utah-Nevada desert basin.

A more recent suggestion for housing the MX in existing Minuteman silos is under study. The Minuteman missile is a solid fuel rocket stored in a vertical position ready to be launched over an intercontinental distance of 5,000 to 7,000 miles. To replace that land-based ICBM with another is to continue to ignore the basic problem: Any permanent land-based installation is obsolete.

Whether a missile system designed to carry a nuclear warhead across intercontinental distances is housed in a new or an old silo (possibly in an old silo with upgraded electronics) is totally irrelevant. U.S. military experimental missile system should be developed to provide a flexible war-fighting capability. But there is no reason such a missile should be nuclear and there is no reason such a missile should be land based.

A033   The ICBM is a "dumb" bomb

An ICBM is a long-range ballistic-type missile that "coasts" through the air after it leaves its firepower at the trigger. A ballistic missile lacks fuel for cruising. A ballistic missile is a "dumb" bomb.

A ballistic missile is "aimed" from the time it leaves its rocket-launch position. As in a rifle or any hand-held weapon, the firepower is at the trigger. There is no cruising power to propel the projectile (in this case the bomb) along its trajectory path. The bomb travels along the trajectory dictated by the external forces of gravity. Upon re-entry into the lower atmosphere of the Earth, where the aerodynamic properties of the projectile configuration may be used to alter the path, there is a modest "guidance" capability.

System performance of an ICBM may be tested in Kwajalein Missile Range in the Marshall Islands in the Pacific Ocean. That trajectory path of the Pacific test range from Vandenberg Air Force Base in California to the Marshall Islands covers a distance of, perhaps, 4,300 nautical miles. Not only is that test distance less than the intercontinental distance (intercontinental distances are considered to be 5,000 to 7,000 miles) the actual path is also different.

The wartime trajectory for an ICBM launched from the continental United States would go over the North Pole to the Soviet Union. The gravitational pull of the Earth differs along different trajectory paths. And so do atmospheric conditions.

For that matter, adverse air density, temperature, or wind direction change from one day to the next. Effects of natural atmospheric variations could, however, be minor compared with effects of adverse atmospheric conditions generated by mid-air blasts of prior bomb explosions. Any ICBM that relies upon aerodynamic properties of a projectile for target accuracy when entering a hostile environment is really a dumb bomb.

A034 The "disposable" rocket engine

The ICBM is now launched using a "disposable" rocket engine. Compared to a Kleenex, a rocket engine is an expensive throw-away item.

Over intercontinental distances the ballistic missile has been favored because of its speed of delivery. A ballistic missile travels much faster than an old B-52 bomber flying from a SAC (Strategic Air Command) air base located within the continental United States. The trade-off for this rapid delivery is undependable targeting accuracy upon re-entry and the high cost of a booster engine that is not reusable.

Once a land-based ballistic missile has been launched using a disposable rocket booster engine, whether there be an electronic malfunction, false alert, or a change in military command decision, there is no way to reverse the launch. The booster engine is gone; the firepower is gone; the bomb is launched. And a bomb launched is a bomb delivered. The bomb just keeps going until it hits something and explodes all over everything within the blast radius. If it is set to explode in the atmosphere above ground zero, it explodes all over everything within that blast radius.

The cost of a disposable launch vehicle is also not a trivial matter. The operational Saturn-V rocket booster engine, for example, is reported to cost about twice as much as a giant C-5A military transport airplane, one of the more expensive operational airplanes of the United States Air Force. Yet the Saturn-V rocket engine is a throw-away item.

The use of the disposable launch vehicle by the United States military is a luxury the taxpayers of this nation can no longer afford. One alternative is the reusable launcher (available on submarines), intended for targeting over much shorter distances.

A035   The payload

A rocket booster engine is fired for the purpose of launching a "payload." If the mission were reconnaissance, the payload would be a satellite capsule full of electronic equipment. For nuclear war, the payload is a bomb.

Two basic types of nuclear warheads have been developed. One depends upon FISSION, the other upon FUSION. The energy from a **fission** bomb is released when the nucleus of a heavy atom (perhaps Uranium or Plutonium) splits into two parts. The energy from a **fusion** bomb is released when two lightweight atomic nuclei (perhaps hydrogen) unite or fuse together to form one new heavier nucleus.

The fusion reaction (the so-called thermonuclear reaction) occurs at extremely high temperature. Thus, this **fusion** bomb or thermonuclear device has much larger blast radius than the smaller yield atomic **fission** bomb. For example, the atomic (fission) bomb dropped on Hiroshima had an estimated equivalence of 20,000 tons (20 kilotons) of TNT (**Tri-Nitro-Toluene**), an old-fashioned chemical explosive. The fusion bomb, with far greater yield, has an estimated equivalence of 5,000,000 to 7,000,000 tons (usually referred to as 5 to 7 megatons) of TNT. Indeed an ICBM delivering a fusion-type hydrogen bomb has, as advertised, a payload that produces "a bigger bang for a buck."

A036   The reality of pork barrels

Pork barrels are political rewards that bring federal funding into a favored Congressional district. Pork barrels, especially those associated with defense spending, now come in two distinct forms: those that are welcome, and those that are not.

Traditionally the pork barrel provided a welcome flow of federal money into the home state of an influential politician. Federal buildings were constructed (usually the building would carry the name of the politician responsible for the funding); federal dams were built (perhaps to increase hydroelectric capacity of the area or to attract tourists); factories were modernized or expanded to increase industrial employment opportunities; national parks, wilderness areas, and

forest lands were protected or otherwise made available for
public use—the list goes on and on. Local residents of the area
generally viewed the additional employment provided by the
government funding as a much needed stimulus for their
otherwise sluggish local economy.

In quite another category, the arrival of federal funding
related to defense spending, especially military construction,
was not always welcome. Not only money but also people
would arrive. There would be a rapid increase in the number of
residents in the community. There would be an increased
demand for more sewers, more water, more power, more roads,
more housing, more schools, more churches, more shopping
facilities. But the rapid growth could be short lived, it could
become a burden rather than a blessing to the local residents.

Attitudes toward military-related pork barrels were not
always positive. The military had failed to take into account
the rate of population increase and the irreversibility of the
damage the construction would do to the local environment.
When the demands placed upon the community exceeded the
threshold for acceptance by local residents, the federal
government was apt to find itself most unwelcome.

Short-term short-sighted use of federal money should be
avoided. Alternative proposals for land, water, and air use
could then be forth coming. Pork barrels associated with
defense spending that fail to support long-term national needs
as perceived by the local residents, and long-term local needs
as perceived by the local residents, have certainly lost their
charm.

A037   Priorities for land use

*The land area of Planet Earth is finite. It is the
responsibility of the human race to manage its use.
And many Americans now view their own community as a good place to start.*

Historically, in the United States, private ownership of land
gave the owner all the rights, the land none. The land owner—
the private citizen, the industrial giant, or the federal
government—was the land lord, and the "lord" determined
the use of the land. There were no national, state, or local land
use policies for conservation, and there were no public
methods for deciding priorities for land use.

National policies for land use are still lacking, but national policies for environmental protection are coming on the horizon. In recent years, the American people have started to realize that many damaging effects to the land cannot be reversed. Indiscriminate use of the land can contaminate local water supply, pollute the atmosphere above, and adversely alter the local climate.

A national review of land use (and air use) could now show land-based ICBMs to be unacceptable. In fact, public refusal to accept land-based ICBMs could now attract political attention. Especially when ICBMs are shown to have limited or no military value, public rejection of land-based systems could even be enthusiastically encouraged.

Chapter B

Sea Launch

The United States is an island

The United States Coast Guard patrols the coastal waters of the United States. The United States Navy maintains a global presence everywhere else. Yet both are expected to fulfill the constitutional mandate: "To repel Invasions."

The United States is an island. With broad expanses of coast exposed to open ocean access, the United States Navy must monitor global ocean traffic patterns to protect those territorial waters. Supply lines for arms and munitions, shipping lanes for food and other trade commodities, cruising routes for unidentified, armed submarines—all must be known at all times so the United States Navy can anticipate entry of foreign-owned ocean-going vessels into territorial waters. Because of this national responsibility, the United States Navy should have control of and access to all nuclear weapons systems of the United States military service organizations.

B038   Keeping weapons at sea

Missile systems that carry nuclear warheads should be moved off the land and out to sea. Though those systems may be replaced with conventional weapons, the urgent change is to base all weapons at sea.

The lack of willingness of the American military to use land-based ICBMs (Inter-Continental Ballistic Missiles) has been clearly demonstrated since the 1950's when they first became available during peacetime conditions. That same anti-nuclear mood is now being reflected in the political mood of the country. Elected officials now exchange among themselves the simple plea—please don't put those _____ nukes in my state. The politicals are, of course, interested to protect their own political future. They are also trying to protect the military service organizations that have, in turn, to protect the American population.

With public opinion on his side, Ronald Reagan could well go down in history as the President of the United States who was able "to stop putting cannons in the village square, where they would draw fire down on the people in time of war."

In 1956, the AEC, the original Atomic Energy Commission, recently re-named the Department of Energy, and who knows what to be named in the future, announced a break-through in hydrogen-bomb (fusion) technology. At that time, the attention of those in the United States Navy responsible for the development of weapons systems shifted from the liquid-propellant to the less efficient (but far more reliable and far easier to handle) solid-propellant rocket technology. The availability of the small, high-yield thermonuclear (fusion) warhead was destined to have practical value to the United States Navy.

As the years passed, the United States Navy developed and perfected submarine launch systems. The submarine launch system is now a cold-launch system with re-load capabilities intended to carry small thermonuclear warheads. These U.S. Navy systems (the Trident class submarine and so-called fleet ballistic missiles) are probably the most flexible and the most dependable ballistic-type delivery systems in the world today.

The sea-launch option for nuclear warheads is now gaining in popularity. Global (remote sensing) systems, global navigation systems, and global communication networks are making the sea-launch option more feasible. Economic stagnation coming from the production of redundancy in weapons systems is making it mandatory. But the force of public opinion is the only known force strong enough to make elected officials implement such a change in national spending priorities and, hence, such a change in U.S. nuclear strategy.

B039   Like Ivory soap, it floats

*The mobility of a launch facility far removed from
large population centers is the military merit of keeping nuclear weapons at sea.*

As early as August 1953, the United States Army, with its
German-transplant Wernher von Braun scientific-engineer-
ing team, had already fired the Redstone rocket (a rocket developed at the Redstone Arsenal, Huntsville, Alabama). The
Redstone was the first U.S. liquid-propellant, single-engine,
so-called long-range ballistic missile (The Redstone traveled
barely 200 miles.).

The hazard of launching a large liquid-propellant rocket
from a ship at sea was intolerable. That meant, unlike the
Army, the Navy would be discouraged from continuing with
that line of research and development. Instead, the ingenious
"float launch" concept of the Navy was born. A rocket that
would float vertically in the ocean could be launched from the
sea without the need for complex, massive, and expensive
launch facilities. The "big dumb booster," its advocate Robert
C. Truax, and the United States Navy BuAer (Bureau of Aeronautics) all had their unpopular moments, but the float-
launced concept may still have a military future.

Whether it is an anchored float launch concept or a mobile
submarine-based delivery system, the responsibility for
nuclear weapons should now belong to the United States
Navy. Until all nuclear weapons can be replaced with the
more modern conventional systems, the nukes and the Navy
deserve each other.

B040   Navigation to the rescue

*The military miracle of the century is in the making.
The United States Air Force is introducing a new
navigation system. With the advent of NAV-
STAR/GPS (Global Positioning System) a constellation of operational navigation satellites will be
orbiting the Earth.*

It is no minor accomplishment to put an atomic clock in
space. The National Bureau of Standards had to develop a

clock that was not only accurate but also one that could sustain accuracy for the expected lifetime of a modern satellite. It is a miracle of modern technology to be able to communicate that time signal accurately (and retain the integrity of the signal while it is being communicated) and then to interpret that signal as a "position" in four dimensions.

A position in four dimensions is a very special position. It is a position in not only latitude and longitude for the location on the surface of the Earth, it is also the height (altitude) above the ground. And then, for very special occasion, and with very special equipment for electronic processing, the time rate at which that position is changing can also be determined. In other words, the velocity of a moving object is computed in both space and time.

As originally planned, the NAVSTAR/GPS was to have been a constellation of 24 satellites. NAVSTAR is now reported to be a group of 18 satellites to be placed in orbit around the Earth at an altitude of more than 10,000 miles. While a GPS position accuracy of 30 feet in three-dimensions is anticipated (some of the "old salts" trained by the United States Navy to use the sextant would have been content with a navigation error of 2 miles), the eventual operational accuracy of NAVSTAR will depend upon the quality of the receiver provided to the user. Ideally the internal electronics of the receiver would be equivalent to those of the transmitter, and NAVSTAR would achieve its full operating potential.

Nevertheless, the American people could now insist that the military move the nuclear weapons out to sea. The American people could also insist that the redundancy in those weapons systems be removed. With improved electronic capabilities, improved targeting accuracy can be provided and survivability insured.

The United States military is clearly on the frontier for the utility of satellite systems. NAVSTAR/GPS could become fully operational. Military efforts to field the equipment, routinely install, maintain, and operate such an accurate navigation system could indeed use all the popoular support they can receive.

Many potential users of the NAVSTAR system are in the private sector. A civilian tuna boat needs to know its position at sea to comply with a 200-mile coastal fishing limit. That same tuna boat might also like to record the edge of a warm-water current reported by a remote sensing satellite and then return to that exact location at a later time. The FAA (the Federal Aviation Administration) might need to know the four-dimensional "position" of a space shuttle as it is re-entering the Earth's atmosphere.

NAVSTAR/GPS has the possibility of becoming a well-coordinated civilian-military system. Increased lobby efforts from special interest groups could convince the United States Congress that NAVSTAR is not merely a military-operated satellite system intended for military use, rather that it is a national resource.

PART THREE

Chapter C

Airplanes or Cruise Missiles

Pilots are people

An important controversy within the United States Air Force has been in progress for years. The controversy has to do with the importance of having a pilot (a person) fly an airplane rather than a computer.

The controversy of the airplane versus the cruise missile is the controversy of man versus machine; it is the controversy of human judgement versus automation. The cruise missile is a small jet-powered airplane-like thing with short wings (it looks like a flying torpedo) that is guided by remote control as it flies through the air. The cruise missile is much like an airplane except it has no pilot.

The cruise missile versus airplane controversy is no different than the robot versus human resource controversy that now permeates our daily lives. It is the controversy of the creative, innovative use of the human mind versus the pre-programmed machine that can do exactly what it is built to do. And deciding this issue in favor of the pilot and human judgement will bring the human race that much closer to eliminating the need for war as a means of making political and economic decisions.

C041   An "invisible" airplane

An airplane is "invisible" because it cannot be detected by enemy radar when it flies through a radar beam.

At the end of World War II, the United States had a large powerful fleet of B-29 Bombers (the B is for Bomber). The aircraft could carry the great weight of any bomb that would have to be dropped to bring an end to the war in the Pacific. Thus, it was during the War that the United States decided it would concentrate its national efforts on achieving superiority of a manned aircraft rather than pursue the development of a rocket-booster engine for an ICBM [Inter-Continental Ballistic Missile].

Advocates of an aircraft with a pilot claim that pilots are people and that human judgment is needed to respond to the unexpected. The primary concern of the aircraft advocate is that the delivery of a nuclear or conventional warhead remain under the control of the pilot as long as possible. Such people-advocates would trust little or nothing to the automation of an ICBM or to the remote control of a long- or a medium-range cruise missile.

Current B-52 strategic bombers (strategic bombers are bomber airplanes that are designed to carry nuclear bombs over intercontinental distances) could be electronically upgraded to make the aircraft "invisible" to enemy radar detection. This would require the installatiuon of a radar warning system and the electronics of such an electronic "jamming" system are not all that new. Many aspects of radar "scanning and jamming" have been in use since World War II. It is just that the electronics have been steadily improved (they have been digitized) to give instant response.

The development of electronic systems to deceive an enemy radar falls generally into the broad category of "stealth" technology. The idea of a "magic hood" is that electronics can be used to listen for probing radar signals (a listening device can automatically scan the frequency spectrum because only certain frequencies are used by enemy military radar). Once an enemy radar signal is detected, a false echo is returned from a transmitter carried onboard the B-52 bomber. The bomber remains "invisible" because it returns a false echo in response to the probing signal of the enemy radar and because it does not originate (transmit) a probing signal of its own.

The use of such electronic monitoring equipment, however, can no longer be handled mechanically. It is necessary to use dependable computer-controlled (digital) electronics to scan the frequency spectrum, to evaluate incoming probing radar signals, and then to return a false-echo response in microseconds.

Advocates of "invisible" bombers remain convinced that the safety of the airplane and the safety of the pilot can be protected by electronic means, that the airplane and the pilot make a winning combination. Such advocates would insist that human judgement remain an active participant in any delivery system for nuclear warheads. And, above all else, they would insist that there be a way to return the airplane to home base in the event of a false alert.

C042   The "disposable" airplane

An unmanned Ground Launch Cruise Missile is a single purpose, one-time airplane that takes off from the ground but has no pilot. It is a "disposable" airplane.

The modern military trend toward automation, and the strong anti-people propaganda that goes along with it, reminds one of the writings of John Lord as he described the Roman military in *Beacon Lights of History*: "The Romans loved war, but so reduced it to a science that it required comparatively small armies to conquer the world." Some Americans in the military-industrial complex today appear to subscribe to the same philosophy: make war a science and let automation do the fighting. There would be no manpower problems for the American military, there would be no need for men in uniform. The civilians could design, develop, and produce automation that would conquer the world. Human intelligence would be needed only to produce the machines of destruction.

The controversial Ground Launch Cruise Missile falls into that category of automation replacing people. The cruise missile would use existing jet-propulsion technology to take off from the ground. It could carry a conventional or nuclear warhead. It would cruise by remote control (rather than pilot control) toward its target. Advocates of the use of remote control subscribe to the fantasy that an ideal automated system will one day be perfected, that it takes only more time and more money in the defense budget to accomplish the miraculous deed.

The cruise missile monitors its own flight path using radar signals. The success of the mission, therefore, depends upon the transmisssion of the radar signal even when the atmosphere is disturbed by mid-air bomb blasts, ground fires, or changes in the contour of the terrain. But even under ideal conditions, the remote control of the cruise missile actually controls very little.

A cruise missile cannot change its mind while in flight to select a secondary target (unless it is pre-programmed to recognize that target). One cruise missile cannot be diverted to assist another. And, unlike an airplane with a pilot, a cruise missile cannot, as the case of a false-alarm (computer) alert, remain airborne for a time, then turn around and come home.

An ICBM is a dumb bomb and so is a Ground Launch Cruise Missile. To use a "disposable" airplane with no pilot control over a ground distance greater than a few kilometers is not a military alternative, it is insanity.

C043   Offense becomes the defense

Offense is the best defense. But when the offense requires the use of nuclear weapons, then it is time for the United States to alter its grand strategy.

One fundamental asumption about U.S. nuclear strategy is that SAC (the Strategic Air Command of the United States Air Force) has the authority to use nuclear weapons (when ordered to do so by the President of the United States); that TAC (the Tactical Air Command of the United States Air Force) does not. That is the assumption that most Americans tend to make, consciously or unconsciously; strategic means nuclear, tactical does not.

The purpose of this book is to insist upon a public policy statement that would give an answer to the question, "who has the authority to order the use of nuclear weapons?" Can Tactical Air Command—TAC Air as it is known—be ordered to use offensive nuclear weapons?? Think about it. That is the monumental question for today. Can offensive weapons of the

United States military be nuclear weapons?? This is your opportunity to think.

The answer from the American people must be NO. The answer from the American industry must also be NO. No offensive nuclear weapons for the United States military. The answer must be No for right now and forever in the future. There is no magic nuclear weapon that should be developed. There is no cure-all nuclear weapon that will save the human race. There is no nuclear capability that will fight the war to end all wars. The answer is No, No, and No.

All offensive "weapons" of the United States Air Force and, indeed, of all branches of the uniformed services of the United States should be electronic weapons. They should be radar planes, reconnaissance planes, early-warning planes, and planes that carry communication capabilities to every part of the globe. These electronics should be dependable in the sense of needing minimum maintance with maximum reliability. These electronics should be user friendly. These electronics should be used every day as a service to all peoples of all nations of the world.

The time is now. Draw the line and draw it firm. No Nukes for TAC Air. No offensive nuclear weapons for the United States military. "Offensive weapons" should be an electronic capability needed for continuous monitoring and continuous transfer of continuous information flow. Human insight is still the best weapon; electronic "bits" of information are still the best "live" ammunition.

Note: The question of whether the B-52 bomber should carry a gravity bomb (a bomb that falls to the ground according to its aerodynamic properties under the pull of gravity from the Earth) or an air-to-ground attack missile (a missile fired like a projectile from a gun that seeks out its own target) is not a "nuclear" question. A gravity bomb or an attack missile could be a conventional weapon.

Chapter D

Satellite Launch

**Those military-operated satellites
are fulfilling our rendezvous
with destiny**

An oak tree can grow from an acorn, but not from an English walnut. You can grow from yourself, but not from the self of your neighbor. And so it is with this nation. The United States can become an American nation but it can not become another. The United States can fulfill its own destiny but it cannot transform itself to fulfill the destiny of another.

The United States can fulfill its own national destiny or it can commit internal suicide. Abraham Lincoln proclaimed it in his dramatic and highly controversial speech, "A House Divided Against Itself Cannot Stand." The speech was delivered at the close of the Republican State Convention that nominated Lincoln for the United States Senate, in Springfield, Illinois, on June 17, 1858. The issue of the time was slavery and Lincoln was concerned because the United States was a nation, half slave and half free.

The issue is no longer slavery but the principle is the same: A House Divided Against Itself Cannot Stand. The American people are again both judge and jury. But the verdict this time lies in space.

Information coming from military-operated Earth-orbiting satellite systems must now become a national resource. The two space programs now operating within the federal government are dividing the nation against itself. The two space programs are splitting the military and civilian resources. They split not only the manpower but also the loyalty of the people within the government services trying to do the work.

The two space programs can no longer be allowed to divide the nation against itself. There is only one nation. There is only one work force. And there is only one destiny. This nation must now use Earth-orbiting satellites to unite itself, and to unite the world. This nation can now teach the rest of the world how to use electronics for the benefit of all mankind.

D044   Your technology, my technology

Satellite technology operated by the United States military is national technology. It is used to protect the health and safety of the people. There is no way this nation can survive with space divided against itself.

The space age began on October 4, 1957, when the Soviet Union launched its artificial satellite Sputnik I into orbit around the Earth. Some months later, January 31, 1958, the United States orbited its own artificial satellite, the 18-pound Explorer I. Measurements made by the instruments onboard the Explorer I satellite led to the discovery of enormous radiation belts that surround the Earth. Those radiation belts were later named after the Iowa professor who designed the Explorer payload, James van Allen.

On July 29, 1958, the civilian space program was born. President Eisenhower signed into law the National Aeronautics and Space Act, the Act that created NASA, the National Aeronautics and Space Administration. Ironically, Eisenhower himself lacked enthusiasm for the arrival of the space age. The political driving force that pushed the Republican Administration into the Earth-orbiting satellite business came from Lyndon Johnson, a Texas Democrat then in the United States Senate.

From that time forward, the American people, and especially those working within the government services, have had to live with the dilemma of "your" technology and "my" technology in space. The "national" space program of Lyndon Johnson was not a national program at all. There were two national space programs, one was civilian, the other was military, and the two programs had to compete with each other for the resources and funding priorities of this country.

The two space programs in the United States have had to compete with each other for talent and for money. And they have to compete with each other for a definition of national purpose. The two space programs have had to compete with each other to pursue their own version of national economic security.

Though the separation of the two space programs (actually the civilian and military space programs were not always as separate as some would have liked) may originally have had the advantage of focusing national funding on two distinctly different development programs, that separation is now a luxury this nation can no longer afford. The duplication of effort and the lack of coordination between the two is an unacceptable source of waste in government spending.

There is only one Earth to orbit; there is only one nation to protect. Military-operated Earth-orbiting satellites are "our" technology. The sooner the United States Congress dissolves the civilian space agency NASA (the National Aeronautics and Space Administration), the sooner the space program of the nation can become one.

There is an urgent need to use "our" Earth-orbiting technology to stimulate the growth of "our" economy. Those Earth-orbiting satellites have a rendezvous with destiny. But, at this late date, and with the existing political confusion about the secrecy of information being collected, only the force of public opinion can integrate military and civilian space activites. Only the force of public opinion can unite the resources of this nation toward a national economic prosperity.

D045   HAIL COLUMBIA, a Space Shuttle at last

> *The American military is again on the frontier of practical understanding. The American military is pioneering the use of the reusable re-entry vehicle.*

Satellite payloads were invented. The electronics of remote sensing were perfected. Electronics for computers, circuits for automatic data processing, and internal digital components were miniaturized, electronics for communications were miniaturized, nuclear power plants were miniaturized—

everything was miniaturized to operate inside a tiny space capsule. But it all would have been for naught if the satellite payload could not have gotten off the ground. A launch vehicle is required to carry a space capsule into orbit around the Earth.

On April 12, 1981, Space Shuttle COLUMBIA landed safely at Edwards Air Force Base, California. COLUMBIA was the first "launch vehicle" to leave Cape Canaveral, orbit the Earth, and then return to the ground like an airplane. Prior to that success of the Space Shuttle, the great big rocket that lifts the payload off the ground and into orbit was a disposable engine. Like Kleenex, all stages of the rocket engine were throw-away items.

The Space Shuttle is a reusable launch vehicle, it is a space "truck." The Space Shuttle is the *U-Haul-It* of the nation for Earth-orbiting satellites. The Space Shuttle can haul hardware, fuel supplies, or even a solar telescope from the surface of the Earth up into orbit. It can also pick up damaged equipment, containers, or space junk and return to the ground.

Space Shuttle COLUMBIA is, however, a no-frills operation. COLUMBIA has only enough get-up-and-go to reach a relatively low-orbit altitude. The "truck" can reach a 100 to 600-mile (160- to 960-kilometer) orbit, but no more. That means a "tug" is needed to ferry payloads between the low-orbit limit of the Space Shuttle and the higher orbits of geostationary satellites, a height of 22,300 miles, or even beyond into a "parking" storage orbit.

Another severe limitation of COLUMBIA is her cargo bay. COLUMBIA has in effect, a volume limited rather than a weight limited capacity. That is to say, the COLUMBIA cargo bay would be ideal to haul gold bricks. The 65,000 pound payload weight limit has to be crammed into a relatively small space. Bulky cargo and flimsy spatial structures such as vast expanses of antenna beams or gigantic lattice arrangements for photovoltaic cells would simply be out of the question unless they could be collapsed into a very small bundle . . . and assembled in space.

D046   The "militarization" of space

The "militarization" of space—the consolidation of the military-civilian space programs into a single

*national resource—is finally taking place. The tim-
ing is good. And increased defense spending can be
used to hasten the merger.*

The American people and the United States Congress have
been slow to appreciate the utility and economic importance
of Earth-orbiting satellites. The research community, interested primarily in research and development, has neglected to
encourage the operational use of satellites for continuous
monitoring. The interpretation and processing of data have
also been carried out as a secondary priority compared to the
technology push for the development of more and more automated hardware.

The global mission of the military service organizations, as
it has evolved since World War II, has required the operational use of Earth-orbiting satellites. Those military-operated
global information systems included reconnaissance capabilities, communication capabilites, navigation capabilities,
and other operational aspects of detection and early warning.
By contrast, the only civilian satellites to be used routinely by
the federal government were the meteorological satellites that
collect weather data for daily forecasts.

The potential military use of laser weapons in space has
often attracted attention in the United States because Senator
Malcomb Wallop, Republican from Wyoming, has been pio-
neering the funding of research and development programs.
The operational use of lasers for weapons (including particle
beam weapons) may, however, be only a gleam (or a beam) in
the eye of the beholder, where the operational use of lasers for
communication purposes may soon be realized.

The militarization of space could be hastened by changing
the spending priorities in the defense budget. The focus of
national attention should be on the continuous use of digital
data sets collected and processed by military-civilian operated Earth-orbiting satellites. The military service organizations cannot be expected to indefinitely carry the burden for
the entire nation.

The electronic "war" of continuous global monitoring is a
never ending war. It requires the consolidation of the civilian-
military space programs. It requires one single national effort
for one single nation. Continuous remote sensing-information

flow would allow the elimination of redundancy in nuclear delivery systems and it would encourage the operation of global peacekeeping networks. The "militarization" of space in the United States is the nationalization of space—and it is long overdue.

Chapter E

Hiroshima

The good old days of limited nuclear war

"Sixteen hours ago, an American airplane dropped one bomb on Hiroshima, an important Japanese Army Base..."
Read it again, slowly, and then again. Read it out loud. Those words were spoken by the President of the United States. That bomb, upon impact, gave off a flash of light "Brighter Than A Thousand Suns." The day was August 6, 1945. The United States had just dropped its first atomic bomb on enemy soil. The United States military had just fought the first "limited nuclear war" in the history of civilization. The President of the United States was Harry S. Truman.

E047 People are easy to kill

The atomic (Uranium-235-fission) bomb dropped on Hiroshima was a tiny bomb. It exploded in the atmosphere 1,800 feet above "ground zero." The yield equivalence was estimated at 20,000 tons (20-kilotons) of TNT.

The August 6, 1945, message from President Truman to the American people explained that it was to spare the Japanese people from "utter destruction" that an earlier ultimatum had been issued on July 26, 1945, from Potsdam (Potsdam is a suburb of Berlin). The warning was issued by the United States, Great Britain, and China. That Potsdam message concluded with a promise of a "rain of ruin," the like of which has never been seen on this Earth, if the Japanese government did not accept the terms of surrender.

It is a matter of recorded history that the Japanese government reply had said of the Potsdam warning, "To us its meaning does not seem of great worth, just something to be ignored." That negative Japanese response to the Potsdam Declaration convinced Truman that the bombing would be necessary in order to save not only American but also Japanese lives that would otherwise be lost in an invasion of Japan proper. President Truman, Commander-in-Chief of the United States military, ordered the dropping of the atomic bomb on Hiroshima.

The city of Hiroshima, Japan, had been built on several parts of a river delta between high hills. The "crater-like effect from the land" confined the blast of the bomb, turning it in upon itself. Intense heat, fire, and suffocation instantly consumed everything and everybody; more than 4 square miles in the center of Hiroshima were completely destroyed.

The blast was reported to have demolished all of the flimsy buildings (those of earthquake-resistant construction more common to the United States survived) out to a distance of 2,640 feet (one-half mile) from the center. Some 12-inch thick walls were cracked 5,280 feet (one-mile) away, modest damage extended another mile or more depending on structures and materials.

Increased war effort had demanded an influx of people into the downtown area, estimates of civilian population were less than accurate. The pre-war population of Hiroshima had been reported at 343,969, but wartime estimates during working hours were running twice that number. Thus, the casualty count could have been far more than the estimated 150,000 to 160,000 dead or wounded. For Hiroshima, Japan, the people were no match for the bomb. The people were easy to kill.

E048   Accuracy was the problem

The attention of the reader should now focus on the accuracy of the bombing of Hiroshima and the question of national responsibility for technical failure.

[*The political merit of the bombing has been discussed often enough in the literature that an interested reader has a wealth of information from which
to choose.*]

"I flew over the target area for approximately forty-five
minutes to study the group of clouds which partially obscured
the prime target, a bridge between the Japanese military
headquarters and the city of Hiroshima."

"Some fifteen Japanese aircraft were flying at 15,000 feet,
but made no attempt to come to my altitude of 29,000 feet.
These [enemy] planes soon disappeared." As to the weather
that day of August 6, 1945, ". . . there were scattered clouds
over the city of Hiroshima at an altitude of 12,000 to 15,000
feet. The clouds seemed to be moving toward the city at a
speed of 10 to 15 miles per hour. The time of observation was
about 7:30 a.m. and the real target [the bridge] was clear."

Those remarks were written by Major Claude Robert Eatherly, commander of the lead plane, STRAIGHT FLUSH. It
was Eatherly's job to reach the primary target, to get information about the weather conditions, and to determine if there
would be resistance from enemy aircraft and ground fire.

"As I said before, the primary target was the bridge where it
would do the most damage to the Japanese military headquarters. The weather seemed ideal to me—the city of Hiroshima
would be obscured and saved, and the dropping of the bomb
on the military headquarters would cause the military to realize the strength and destructive force of the bomb, thus con-
vincing the Japanese military that they should sign a peace
treaty and end the terrible war."

"I sent my coded message which was the final 'go ahead' to
the bomb-carrying plane [the ENOLA GAY, piloted by
Colonel Paul W. Tibbets, Jr.] to bomb the primary target." The
bomb had been loaded into the bay of a specially equipped
B-29 Superfortress bomber that was to fly from an American
air base in the Mariana Islands. The bomb had been
assembled on Tinian Island, south of Saipan in the Marianas;
a scientist onboard the plane was to assemble the detonating
device in flight, a precaution against any unexpected mishap
at take-off.

"What I wanted to happen, did not happen." "The clouds
over Hiroshima diminished and scattered. The bombardier on

the bomb-carrying plane missed the target some 3,000 feet and destroyed the city of Hiroshima."

"I do not think it was an intentional miss, but an error of the bomb falling straight and true."

E049   A commanding responsibility

In the military, the commanding officer is responsi-
ble for the action of his troops. Is the commanding
officer also responsible for the performance of his
equipment? Is the commanding officer responsible
for technical failure?

The patient died because of equipment failure. The respirator was unattended and it stopped.

The driver of an automobile was killed because of equipment failure. The steering mechanism locked and the car skidded out of control.

Equipment failure. What does it mean to a military user? Who is responsible for equipment failure? That is the most important question you may ever have to answer with regard to the use of automation. Who is responsible for equipment failure?

Technology cannot be guilty. Technology has no fault. People make decisions. People are responsible.

A new era in the field of international criminal law was conceived on February 23, 1946, when the General of the Japanese military "plunged to his death at the end of a rope on American gallows." Tomoyuki Yamashita, commanding officer, had been punished for failure to retain control over the action of his men.

General Yamashita was "not charged with personally participating in the acts of atrocity or with having ordered or condoned their commisssion. Not even knowledge of these crimes was attributed to him." It was simply alleged that "he unlawfully disregarded and failed to discharge his duty as commander, to control the operations of the members of his command, permitting them to commit the acts of atrocity."

At Los Banos Prison Camp, 30 miles south of Manila in the Philippines, Tomoyuki Yamashita paid with his life for the crimes of his troops. A frightening international precedent had been set for war crimes.

At the time of the appeal—the case was set down for oral argument before the United States Supreme Court on January 7, 1946—the contention was made that *no one* in a position of command in the military, from Sergeant to General, could escape the implications of the charges against Yamashita, that the fate of some future President of the United States as Commander-in-Chief of the United States military or of his chiefs of staff or his military advisers could well be sealed by a decision against the Japanese General Officer.

The conviction of General Yamashita leaves open the question of the legal responsibilities of the "go ahead" given by Major Eatherly, if not for the actions of the bombardier that missed the prime target, then for the [aerodynamic] failure of the new untried technology.

E050 The weapons strike back

Major Eatherly was the American pilot flying the reconnaissance plane that gave the final "go ahead" for the bombing of Hiroshima. Major Eatherly is the only American who has ever written at length about the psychological torment that followed the dropping of an atomic bomb on a city full of people.

According to Eatherly, he was a criminal. There was, however, no way for a military court to recognize Eatherly's guilt without at the same time recognizing the guilt of his military superiors and indeed the guilt of the American people. Thus, according to published military standards, Major Eatherly was a hero.

In the Foreword of the book containing Eatherly's letters (published in German by Gunther Anders, his correspondent-teacher-doctor) Robert Jungk wrote, "It is not the sufferings of this Texan pilot which is the real tragedy of this drama, but rather the baleful entanglement of his country and his fellow citizens. In its fight to insure Freedom from Fear, it [the United States government] has felt itself compelled to employ the counter-threat of death and destruction to countless millions."

Though nuclear weapons are often portrayed as unique for their psychological repercussions, it should be recognized that no American male in uniform is immune to the horrors of having been responsible for the destruction of human life. Any decision to use destruction as a means to reform government is indeed serious. Any decision to use untried and unproven technology as a means to reform government is, by comparison, criminal.

Perspective

System failure knows no limit

*In the event of accidental nuclear
holocaust, how do you
say you're sorry*

> *The military may be the user of modern
> weapons systems, but the Congress
> is the supplier*

The technology of delivery systems for nuclear warheads had evolved. The human race has evolved. The word is the same, yet "evolved" has been given two entirely different meanings.

In the living system, the process of evolution takes place by natural selection. In the evolution of the grotesque technology of the delivery systems for ICBMs (Inter-Continental Ballistic Missiles) the selection has been done by retaining artificial priorities within rigid thought patterns in the minds of those involved in the decision making process. This phenomenon of having intellectual giants prepare today's military to fight yesterday's war is not uncommon.

To break away from firmly established behavior patterns in the defense community is not easy. People depend upon institutions for their employment and they depend upon professional organizations for their reputations. They conform, consciously or unconsciously, to well-established thought patterns. By the time a military man is deeply involved in his own career, his loyalty to his own branch of service requires that he remain a "believer" in (obsolete) concepts endorsed by that particular service organization even though his own logic might dictate otherwise. Those within the system will conform to the security of the status quo, rather than risk the innovation of change.

For that reason, and that reason alone, it is now imperative for those outside the defense community, especially the American voting population, to start to ask the right questions. Never mind that you do not have the answers, just ask the questions. That is all that is required. Those in the reserve, on active duty, or retired status can provide the answers. In that regard, the military as a national service organization deserves the right to regain some control of its own destiny.

In his little book, *Science and Government,* C.P. Snow wrote, "In this 'advanced industrial society' one of the bizarre features in our time is that 'cardinal choices' have to be made by a handful of men: in secret: and, at least in legal form, by men who cannot have a first-hand knowledge of what those choices depend upon or what their results may be." Snow goes on to define an "advanced industrial society" to be the United States, the Soviet Union, and England; Snow defines "cardinal choices" as those that determine in the crudest sense whether we live or die.

Examples of "cardinal choices" given by C.P. Snow were: "The choice in England and the United States in 1940 and 1941, to go ahead with work on the fission [atomic] bomb: the choice in 1945 to use that bomb when it was made: the choice in the United States and in the Soviet Union, in the late forties, to make the fusion [Hydrogen] bomb: the choice, which led to a different result in the United States and [in] the Soviet Union, about intercontinental missiles."

It is that last choice, the choice about the use of ICBMs, the use of Inter-Continental Ballistic Missiles as a deterrent for nuclear war, that the American people now need to reverse. There is no longer anything secret or elite or scientific about the threat of the use of long-range land-based pre-targeted ballistic missiles. And every day those missiles remain installed and ready to launch is one day closer to the day of push-button accidental nuclear holocaust.

Much of the "selection" in the evolutionary development of delivery systems for nuclear warheads has been determined by the profit motive, increased employment in the home district of some Congressman, and increased "foreign aid" in the form of munitions. Since tax dollars are paying industry to develop and produce ICBMs, since tax dollars are also paying the government to threaten to use them, it is the American people who must alter their own thought patterns, and their own budget priorities.

The development of the ICBM, in particular the MX (Missile eXperimental), is in many ways reminiscent of the French development of the Maginot Line. Once the decision was made, the analyses focused on technical details of intricate internal design. Calculations of excessive sophistication for fire angle, range, and technical performance were substituted for confrontation of the real problem: an upper atmosphere that cannot survive the heat and destruction of nuclear explosions.

The basic change that needs to be made in the U.S. military strategy is the need to take into account the availability of continuous information flow from detection and early warning systems, information that could be made available on a global scale. The American military need for continuous responsiveness will never be satisfied with rigid land-based pre-targeted ICBM launch systems. For one thing, the hostile area may not even be included in the pre-determined target options. For another, the promised accuracy of the delivery may be nullified under disturbed atmospheric conditions typically associated with bomb explosions. Less than ideal weather conditions that might well exist at the time of the threat would also degrade the anticipated performance of the systems.

The evolution of delivery systems has left a few dinosaurs roaming the land. Those monsters eat tax dollars like peanuts, they drink water that is scarce in the Western States, and they try to hide out in old Minuteman silos. The dinosaur of the delivery systems is the land-based ballistic missile. And the time has come for the American taxpayer, through the United States Congress, to declare all land-based missile species extinct.

The United States Navy should be given delivery responsibility for all nuclear weapons. Putting the weapons at sea is fast becoming technologically feasible (because of global information systems that could now become operational) and economically mandatory (because of excessive costs for redundancy in U.S. strategic systems). The only "war" the United States Air Force can afford to fight is an "electronic war" using continuous information transfer. The continuous flow of information is the only "live ammunition" the United States can use to reduce the excessive redundancy in their own weapons systems.

The C.P. Snow reminiscence of an Icelandic saga comes to mind. "Snorrie was the wisest man in Iceland who had not the gift of foresight."

In the United States, time has shown that politicians look for continuity and long-term planning; bureaucrats also look for continuity and long-term planning. Yet the uniqueness of the United States has always been its responsiveness in time of emergency. The American people can respond in time of crisis. The Americans can always come up with an immediate solution to an immediate problem. That is the American way. And the long-term evolution of missile delivery systems runs absolutely, completely, totally contrary to the American way. Any evolutionary selection process that depends upon persistence and continuity, rather than innovation and creative genius, is violating American tradition and the American military tradition as well.

The 1950-vintage, status quo of "push-button" nuclear warfare, which includes all aspects of the balance of terror known as the balance of military power, should now be abandoned. Otherwise, buried beneath a pile of rubble where the Pentagon now stands, will one day be written the epitaph for the American military: Here lie the men in uniform, "the wisest men in the land who had not the gift of foresight."

PART FOUR

Detection and Early Warning

If the gift of foresight is our most effective weapon, then information flow is the live ammunition

"The major advances in civilization are processes that all but wreck the societies in which they occur," wrote Alfred North Whitehead. With the social structure of the United States in shambles, and the economy not doing much better, one can only hope that Whitehead was right. The American people would like nothing better than to be reassured that they are making a "major advance" for the good of the human race.

Technological capabilities needed for continuous information transfer are already available. Their limited use is already starting to alter the American way of life. And the industrial base of the United States is already starting to shift toward the production of software so modern electronics can be adapted to the unique needs of every individual user. The sale of computer software is even making a name for itself in the marketplace. Yet that all-important shift toward the use of real-time global information systems is yet to come.

The American military is now fighting an electronic war of global monitoring. That eternal war continues 24 hours a day, 7 days a week, week after week, with no end in sight. The American military must fulfill its constitutional mandate: To repel Invasions. The American people, in complete coordination with their own military, could fight this same war of DETECTION AND EARLY WARNING for humanitarian reasons.

There is an immediate need for search and rescue operations. There is also an immediate ongoing need for monitoring of the natural environment. In the realm of national readiness, continuous monitoring could reduce the military need for an excessive redundancy in weapons systems and it could effectively eliminate the possibility of "surprise" attack. Eventually global information exchange could even do away with the fear-motivated need to pursue secret operations.

Orbiting satellites and ground-control stations, ground-based (active) radar equipment and ground-based (passive) remote-listening devices—all could be used for continuous monitoring. And as more and more nations prepare to use armed force as a means of pursuing their own economic freedoms, that need for continuous information exchange will continue to grow. Human insight is the ultimate weapon and giga-bits of information flow are the necessary "live" ammunition. Electronic monitoring of Planet Earth has become an eternal "war" the American people should now feel compelled to support.

Chapter A

A Spy in the Sky

**On a cloudy day, you can see clouds;
on a clear day, you can see
everything else**

Weather satellites are unmanned instrumented satellites that carry electronic equipment or "cameras" to take pictures of clouds on a cloudy day. A time sequence of those pictures can be used to determine direction and speed of travel of the background wind at the height at which the clouds are observed. A time sequence of those pictures can also be used to infer the rate at which a thunderstorm is developing.

On a clear day, a satellite with similar remote sensing (electronic) equipment can see everything else. Cameras can photograph the surface of the Earth rather than the tops of clouds. Two things determine the usefulness of those clear-day photos: the spatial resolution, the detail that can be recovered from an enlargement; and the temporal resolution, the time spacing between the picture frames.

Of profound importance to both military and civilian users is the time needed to transfer those data from the observing station (in this case the satellite) to a ground station where the data can be further processed and interpreted. Excessive time delay for transfer or interpretation would, of course, render some types of information useless. In fact, only real-time information flow—the continuous collection, processing, transferring, and interpretation of data—can be used effectively for global monitoring of military-related activities.

A051   As the world turns, so does the ground station

Planet Earth rotates on its axis at a constant rate of one rotation every 24 hours. The ground station of a satellite rotates with the Earth. Since the orbit of a satellite remains "fixed in space," electronic equipment carried aloft will only seldom appear directly over a ground station.

All satellites circle the globe with no propulsion of their own. The space capsule simply coasts through the upper atmosphere, circling round and round the Earth. The projection of that satellite orbit onto the surface of the Earth below traces out the so-called track or path of the satellite. Basically there are three such orbits and, hence, three such paths traced out on the surface of the Earth.

The most common orbit for a communication satellite is an equatorial orbit. Satellites that orbit at the equator can travel far above the equator in an east-west direction so the rotation rate of the satellite is exactly synchronized with the rotation rate of the Earth. When viewed by an observer standing on the surface of the Earth, such a satellite would appear "stationary." These special equatorial satellites, the so-called geostationary or geosynchronous satellites, are used as communication satellites. Communication satellites are discussed in Subsections D076 through D079

The other extreme orbit position for a satellite is the polar orbit. The ground path of a solar-orbiting satellite runs exactly north-south. The path passes systematically over the complete range of latitudes from the north to the south pole and back again on the other side of the globe. The path that the satellite traces out on the ground also precesses in longitude as the Earth rotates. Satellites traveling in polar orbits are, therefore, the only satellites that provide complete global coverage. They view all latitudes between the north and south poles, and eventually all longitudes of rotation.

The third type of satellite orbit, the so-called inclined orbit, has an inclined path that remains somewhere between the two extremes of an equatorial and a polar orbit. That is to say, the path of an inclined orbit is slanted not only away from a strict north-south (polar) orbit but also away from a strict east-west (equatorial) orbit. For example, an orbit inclined at 40° would have its satellite track crossing back and forth over the equator, systematically covering only those latitudes between 40°N and 40°S.

The only place the United States can position a chain of ground stations to provide pole-to-pole satellite contact is along the 75°W longitude meridian. A 75°W longitude chain of stations runs along the east coast of the North American continent, across the equator, along the west coast of South America. For any other pole-to-pole pass, the chain of "ground stations" would have to include air-borne or ocean-based stations for telemetry contact, or the satellite would have to communicate with ground control stations located on foreign soil.

To accommodate the ever-growing demand for ground-control stations for orbiting satellites, the United States government attempted to locate ground stations in foreign countries. With those additional facilities, signals from American satellites could be picked up by the foreign-based, ground-control stations. But American ground-control stations were not always welcome on foreign soil.

The fixed-in-space orbit of a satellite determines exactly the path on the surface of the Earth available for survey from on-board cameras. The question of whether satellite equipment can be turned on and off to operate at the desired time, above the desired place, is, however, a question of command-control. Earth-orbiting satellites of the United States do pass over segments of the Earth where they are out-of-sight and, hence, out-of direct line-of-sight contact with a ground station. As the world turns, so does the ground station.

A052   Information relay with delay

> *Earth-orbiting satellites serve the all-important spy-in-the-sky function of data collection and information transfer. Of comparable value, however, are the Earth-orbiting satellites that relay (with delay) information from one ground station to another.*

When one ground station has information stored in a computer array and that information needs to be transferred to another ground station, and the two stations are located on opposite sides of the Earth, one effective way to transfer the information is with a relay with delay satellite. Relay satellites are very different from geostationary communication satellites. Relay satellites are orbiting in polar orbits, not equatorial, and they provide direct line-of-sight narrow-beam information relay when they pass directly over a ground station. An orbiting relay satellite simply records and carries information to be communicated at a later time.

The effective use of relay-delay satellites for data transfer depends upon the sender, the station that originates the message, being able to transfer the data at extremely high speed as the satellite passes directly overhead. The satellite then records the message. Later, when the satellite passes over the receiver ground station, that same message is transferred at extremely high speed, back to the ground. Thus, relay-delay orbiting satellites receive, record, and transfer data sets. In the receive-record process the data may also be sorted or surveyed to alert the user to critical parameter changes.

To transfer a big message in a very short time—a message the size of the complete set of Encyclopaedia Britannica would be a big message, a time interval of a few seconds would be a very short time—is the operational requirement for a relay-delay communication satellite.

One way to arrange the text of the entire set of Encyclopaedia Britannica for relay would be to start with the first word on the first page of the first volume and then progress systematically through each page of each book. The text of the message would be arranged in one great long line. To transfer such a long message would take a long time.

Another way to arrange the text of the entire set of encyclopaedia for relay would be to start with the first word on the first page of each of the 19 volumes at the same time, and then scan systematically through all of 1,178 (or so) pages in each volume. The length of each message would be the content of one volume arranged in a continuous line. The transfer time for the 19 parallel channels would be only the length of the single continuous chain of words for each volume.

A much faster method of transfer for the entire set of books would be to use at least 23,600 parallel channels, to transfer exactly one page through each channel, to transfer 23,600 short messages at the same time. The division of a big message into small packets of information, with several packets transferred all at the same time, is efficient but it does require an extraordinary number of parallel communication channels.

The electronic capability to deliver a big message in a short time is a necessary capability when a satellite has to receive, or transmit, an entire message during the short time of a few seconds when it passes directly over a ground station.

The advantage of the over-head satellite transfer is that path length through the atmosphere is shortest at exactly that moment. The message is, therefore, less susceptible to atmospheric disturbance, naturally or artificially generated.

A053   Interrogation and relay with delay

Some of the very long messages that Earth-orbiting satellites need to transfer are messages that have been collected from many tiny scattered sources. Only after the message has been collected and compiled can it then be delivered.

Instead of receiving one very long message from one computer array at one ground station, a relay satellite may have to systematically collect bits and pieces of its message as it travels along its orbit. The senders may be ground- or ocean-based. The end result is the same. The onboard computer would still have to dump the total (composite) message on one ground station.

An ocean survey could be conducted by planting many small sensors in the ocean. Each sensor, for example, would be equipped with its own electronic device for recording local measurements of surface wind, salinity, water temperature, or perhaps even traveling acoustic disturbances. As an orbiting satellite would move in its north-south direction along its polar orbit, it would also systematically precess (east to west) over the ocean area. The onboard instruments would then systematically interrogate the ocean sensors.

A composite time-dependent map of ocean area parameters would be recorded as the satellite computer array collects and sorts the data. The stored map is collected—it takes several orbits of one satellite or several satellites to collect one message—and then the map is delivered with delay. The interrogate-record-relay method is one of the better ways to collect measurements from ground-based sensors that accurately record time-dependent changes in local behavior in remote regions.

A054   The look-and-see satellite

*A look-and-see satellite is a spectator. It is a passive
observer satellite carrying electronic equipment or
cameras (and film) onboard to record what the satellite sees on the surface of the Earth below.*

The United States military used two different types of look-
and-see satellites for reconnaissance purposes in the early
1960s. A search-and-find moderate-resolution satellite would
look at large areas, a high-resolution close-look satellite would
then examine the detail of areas of interest.

Originally, the search-and-find data had to be transmitted
back to the ground station to be processed in a central computer facility. The computer result was then used to command
a close-look satellite to survey the selected area.

As electronics were improved, Big Bird satellites were designed to carry both the search-and-find and the close-look
equipment in one payload. Big Bird is reported to be an 11-ton
(22,000-pound) satellite monster built around a huge camera
with ground resolution of 1 foot (approximately the length of
a football) from a height of 100 miles.

Two advantages of these photographic recordings of reconnaissance information are well known: the speed of the
exposure—the entire field of view can be exposed at essentially
the same instant—and the resolution—fine detail that can be
recovered from an enlargement. The primary disadvantage of
photographic reconnaissance is that the film canister itself
must be dropped to Earth before the film record can be made
available for interpretation. The time delay needed for canister
retrieval is unacceptable for some users.

The alternative to film photography is digital (electronic)
recording. Though digital recording provides poorer resolution
it does have the possibility for immediate transmission. The
problem with any electronic recording, however, is that there
may not be a ground station conveniently located immediately
below the satellite orbit at that particular instant to receive
the digital read-out (the digital picture) at exactly the time the
picture was taken. In such a circumstance, immediate transfer
does not take place, and the benefit of electronic recording is
decreased.

Thus, until satellite-to-satellite relay is perfected, and the capacity for digital transfer increased, film records of reconnaissance information may well be preferred, providing the delay of film canister retrieval can be tolerated.

A055   The listen-and-hear satellite

Electromagnetic listen-and-hear sensors of the ferret passive observer satellites (or aircraft) are also only spectators. Instead of looking at the Earth below, the ferret satellite listens.

The ferret electromagnetic sensing satellite possesses many attributes recommending it as a source of reconnaissance information. These electromagnetic listening devices can pinpoint the location of air defense and missile defense ground-based radar and other active transmitter antennae located at military or civilian installations.

As with the Big Bird camera satellite, the present generation ferret satellite is reported to be able to handle both initial wide-area surveillance and detailed close-look signal analysis. That is to say, ferret electronics have also improved. It is no longer necessary to collect wide-area data, send them to a central computer facility on the ground, and then direct a second ferret-listening device to conduct a detailed analysis of one special signature.

Ferret satellites are expected to carry with them, recorded in the computer data base, not only the geographic locations of all known ground-based transmitter installations of interest, but also all electronic signatures, those are like fingerprints, of radar equipment operating at known installations. With operating transmitter characteristics recorded in the data base, it is possible for the computer to identify any new signal source and to relocate any mobile (or transportable) radar equipment.

Newly acquired information about ground-based transmitters can be used to immediately amend the existing data base. To be able to write on or add to a data base, rather than simply to read what was originally stored, is a great electronic improvement. When it comes to monitoring radar equipment operating in a foreign country, immediate identification of a new transmitter, or identification of increased work load for an old one, is an important indicator for other changes in military or civilian activities.

The rate at which the entire computer-stored data base of a ferret satellite can be dumped onto a receiving ground-station has, of course, the same electronic transfer constraint that exists for all relay satellites. The upper limit of the rate of transfer depends upon the number of parallel channels.

A056 The active observer

The look-and-see and the listen-and-hear satellites are silent passive observers. By contrast, a radar-type remote sensing device is active. The radar transmits a pulse and then listens for an echo return.

A moving aircraft, missile, or spacecraft may need to know its distance from something else. Also it may need to know its direction and speed of travel with respect to the direction and speed of travel of another moving object. This information could be needed in an instant. A radar-type active observer can obtain just such information and the information can be made available immediately.

The obvious disadvantage of an active observer, especially in a hostile environment, is that an enemy detector can immediately identify the presence of the (active) transmitter. Using an active observing technique is like turning on a flashlight in a dark room; the light immediately becomes the target.

When the United States government needs military-operated Earth-orbiting satellites to gather information, the silent spy-in-the-sky passive observer may well remain the observer of choice. In spite of all claims to the contrary, a Silent Sally satellite, as toothless as the old dog may appear, when well equipped with an all-new pleasingly-plump belly full of modern electronics for data collection, sorting, processing, and recording, may well continue to have an operational advantage over her razzle-dazzle whiz-kid Singing Sam brother who makes far too much noise for his own good.

A057 Effective lifetime of the payload

The effective lifetime of U.S. satellites continues to increase, but then so do the demands of the users.

The effective lifetime of a passive, or an active, observer on-board an orbiting satellite depends upon many factors: the availability of expendables (film, chemicals, hydrazine fuel for thruster to correct the orbital position, electric power to run the equipment), and the lifetime of the electronic equipment itself.

The height of the satellite above the ground is also a prime factor in determining the rate of orbital decay. The atmospheric density is greater and, hence, the satellite drag greater for a lower orbit.

The willingness to pay the cost of operating ground-control station is another factor in the effective lifetime of the payload. When a ground station no longer transmits a signal to turn on the satellite equipment or it no longer listens for the return of telemetry information, then the lifetime of the payload is effectively over.

The greatly extended lifetime of U.S. electronic equipment, the controlled orbits, and the willingness to pay the cost of operating ground-control stations could enable military-operated satellites to clearly see more with less. Even so, indications are that the number of satellite launches could remain about the same, or increase, if the U.S. expands its utility of operational satellite systems to their full potential.

Chapter B

Real-Time Monitoring

**Receiving raw data is like eating a
pine cone; the stuff is hard to digest**

Global monitoring, in the form of looking and listening with
government-sponsored, military-operated satellites, goes on 24
hours a day, 7 days a week, week after week, to inform both
the American military and selected public officials of military-
related activities around the world. Those global information
systems, with their ground-support networks, could also eventually provide the civilians of the United States, and the rest
of the world as well, with the peace of mind of knowing that
there can be no surprise attacks.

Information collected by spy-in-the-sky satellites may be
stored for delayed transfer to a ground-control station or it may
be transferred immediately as it is received, sorted, and processed. In the latter case of immediate transfer, the satellite
monitoring is said to be taking place in real-time. That is to
say, the military or the civilian user is actually receiving the
information at the time the event is taking place. In that sense,
real-time satellite monitoring is like watching a live television broadcast of a sports event.

The significant difference between a live broadcast and real-
time data transfer is that the viewer of the sports event is
merely being entertained. The viewer of real-time satellite data
may well have to interpret the incoming signals—there may

even be several different interpretations of the same information depending upon the needs of a particular user—and the user of real-time data may well have an urgent need to issue an alert or early warning.

B058   Sorting signal from noise

During real-time monitoring, incoming information must be sorted to accept wanted signal and reject unwanted noise.

When information is in view of a reconnaissance satellite, the wanted information is considered signal, the unwanted information is considered noise The signal is processed and recorded or relayed for the user; the noise is not. This means that some of the incoming information is actually rejected when it arrives.

The entire success or failure of global monitoring systems—whether the systems are satellite-borne or ground-based is not relevant—rests with the ability of the electronics to sort wanted signal from unwanted noise. But this sorting of signal from noise is often much like viewing a modern painting, beauty and information utility lies in the eyes of the beholder.

The diversity of user interests is increasing from one day to the next. A new user wants different information than a past user and a current user expands his needs to make new demands upon the system. Yet incoming information that has been rejected is gone forever. There is no way, after the fact, to recover noise that is sorted and discarded in a real-time system.

Thus tendency has been, with the development of new systems and better electronics, to accept more and more data. By accepting essentially everything available to a real-time system, it is supposed that the data can be stored and, after the fact, sorted when the user decides precisely what it is he would like to monitor. By converting an information system to a storage and retrieval system, the system itself is, however, no longer real-time.

Eventually the decision has to be made, is the system a real-time system—can the information be used as live ammunition in an electronic war—or is the system a storage system? Digital electronics are now available. Global monitoring systems should be operated to accept their signals and reject their noise in real-time.

B059   The hazard of the digit

To digitize a piece of information means to assign it a numerical value—a digit. In practice, digitizing means to convert incoming information to a format that can be read by a digital computer.

All satellite information is processed and recorded in one of two forms: analog or digital. Analog information is qualitative; digital is quantitative. A typical black-white photograph is analog. It has varying shades of grey, and those shades of grey represent varying intensities of light. A digital recording, by comparison, has only black-white dots. There is either light or there is no light for each little bit of information. A digital picture is a composite of many black-white dots or yes-no binary bits of information.

In the early 1950s, a digital picture had poor resolution, an analog photograph was better. Since that time, electronic capabilities have improved and digital pictures have become more detailed. One could imagine that eventually enough bits of digital information would be transferred fast enough that a digital picture would be as detailed as its analog counterpart. And that is exactly what is happening. With the most sophisticated up-to-date electronic equipment, and under the most ideal conditions of transfer, digital pictures are becoming better.

There is the risk, however, that military-operated satellites are producing poor quality digital pictures. Those satellites were too long on the drawing board and too long in the procurement stage.

With old electronics the hazard of the digit is indeed severe. Important detail is lost—it is rejected as noise. And when detail is rejected it is gone forever. The dreadful mistake is made at the interpretation phase—when it is assumed that the detail was never there in the first place.

B060   The sensor is smart

A remote sensor in the payload of an orbiting satellite is far removed from the object it has to sense. The sensor is also for removed from the people who have to use the data.

There are two ways of telling a remote sensor what it will see and what it will hear: one is through hardware, the other is through software. The remote sensor built from hardware is as smart as it will be ever at the time of the launch. The logic of the imbedded computer capability is included in the circuit design of the sensor. A remote sensing device engineered entirely with hardware is considered to be automated. When a piece of automation is engineered entirely as a plug-it-in-and-let-it-run piece of equipment, then the operator has only to push the on button. Until now most smart sensors have been only as smart as the scientist in the laboratories who designed the hardware.

New remote sensing devices can be educated to be smarter. When a smart sensor can be told what to do with a special software package is becomes smarter. A smart sensor may have only one way to sort information it receives. A learning sensor will learn what ever the user decides to teach. And that teaching information can be transferred from the ground up to the satellite while the remote sensor is remote.

Those up-link commands are, however, closely guarded by satellite operators. Requests for data acquisition depend upon available satellite time and available satellite power. A satellite passes directly overhead only on very rare occasions.

Making a demand upon a remote sensing device for an overhead pass is like trying to schedule a commercial announcement for a prime time sports event—you have to know all the right people in all the right places.

The option of educating an onboard remote sensor through an up-link command is a privilege. Someone may not want a smart sensor to become any smarter. It may also attract attention from the nation being monitored.

B061   A file cabinet in the sky

Remote sensing data can be sorted to satisfy different needs of many different users. Every user can then request and receive information from the file cabinet in the sky.

There is an engineering option known as the inversion of technology. Sophisticated expensive technology is put onboard the orbiting satellite; by comparison, the ground receiver is simple and inexpensive. This option of inverting the technology was devised so one-time expenses for expensive electronics would be included in the cost of the satellite payload. It left open the option of passing along to the user the savings for ground installations.

Included in this inversion of technology is the possibility of onboard sorting of incoming information. This sorting of information is similar to the sorting that happens in an office as we now know it. Incoming letters and invoices would be filed according to ease of retrieval and relevance one document might have to another. Multiple copies of the same document might even be generated so they could be filed in different places for different users.

Once remote sensing data are sorted by educated smart sensors onboard the satellite, the down-link data transfer can theoretically be used to service both centralized and decentralized users. All pre-processing and pre-sorting would be done onboard for selective data to be fed to the down-link of a decentralized user. The actual transfer would be slow and highly limited. High-cost central facilities would be the only facilities that could receive high data rates and cope with immediate real-time interpretation.

The file cabinet in the sky is the way of the future. The American taxpayers need only to be sure they pay the cost of inverting the technology. Both centralized and decentralized users need to be encouraged.

B062   Information at a glance

Digital information can be assimilated at a glance only when it is displayed in graphic form.

The print-out of a computer, if it were taken directly from the machine, would be nothing more than a great list of numbers. Computer print out would look like a bank statement. And there is nothing to be learned from that column of numbers without looking carefully to each entry and associating it with a particular expense. A bank statement provides no visual aid or picture representation of the numerical meaning.

A graphic display produces a picture rather than a list of words or numbers. The digital wrist watch is a commonly known example for this comparison. The read-out of a digital wrist watch is a number. To tell the time of day you have to read the number.

An old style wrist watch with two hands would form a picture of the time of day. That pattern can be recognized at a glance and the time of day can be instantly assimilated.

A time-dependent graphic display of a data base forms a picture of a continuously monitored time-dependent activity, providing the rate of change can be established as pattern in motion. Neither increased sampling rate nor data spacing can improve the significance of such a diagnostic method. Once that pattern is established, where data collection is concerned, more is not necessarily better. As with the hands of the clock, more information would be redundant and irrelevant. All you need to know is the time of day.

Chapter C

Identification: Friend or Foe

IFF I had known you were coming, I would have coded my transponder pulse

The truth has finally revealed itself to the human race. Planet Earth has only one atmosphere and all peoples and all nations have to share it.

Radar systems operate according to the dictates of their design. Their transmitter frequency and their direction and rate of scan are pre-determined by the construction of the hardware. But, even so, there are operating limitations that have very little to do with design. The radar beam travels only in a straight line and it travels only for a given distance.

There are flying altitudes that are too high for a probing radar pulse and there are altitudes that are too low for a line-of-sight ground-based beam. Pilots who fly at those awkward altitudes have to fly with the uncomfortable knowledge that a radar cannot follow their path. Or, it could be a comfortable knowledge, if the intent of the pilot were to avoid detection.

As aircraft flying capabilities expand to fill every level of flight between Heaven and Earth, controlled air-space is also going to have to expand accordingly. Whether you are a friend

or a foe, it really does not matter at all. When two planes col-
lide mid-air, it is still a long way down to the ground.

C063   The active observer

The RADAR (RAdio Detection And Ranging system)
is an active transmitter-receiver system that transmits
a pulse toward a target and listens for an echo return.
All RADAR are active, not passive, systems.

Radar observing systems are active systems that generally
have only two basic modes in which to operate: one is an
automatic or pre-programmed scanning mode, the other is the
so-called tracking mode. But, in both cases, the system actively
transmits a pulse toward its target and then listens for an echo
return.

An old-style scanning radar rotates only in the azimuth
(horizontally). An auxillary beam has to be superposed on this
standard horizontal sweep to determine elevation. By comparison, a tracking radar has very little scan capability at all.
A tracking radar beam simply follows its target. Just blow in
the ear of the computer and the radar beam will follow its
target anywhere.

The operating frequency of the radar determines the size of
the object visible to the radar pulse. A high-frequency radar
will see little things, because a high-frequency radar has a short
wavelength. A low-frequency radar will see bigger things,
because a low-frequency radar has a long wavelength. In this
manner, a radar will see only what it was designed to see.

One factor that determines the distance a diagnostic pulse
will travel and still have enough power to be reflected and
returned to the receiver, is the radiated power. Another is the
behavior of the atmosphere. Under ideal weather conditions,
and ideal target reflector conditions, the radar will see up to
its maximum distance. It will see a shorter distance under less
favorable conditions.

The operational value of any active radar system depends
upon instant interpretation of the returned echo data and instant relay of that interpretation to those who need to respond.
Even so, an active radar system will always have to tolerate
the delay of both sending and receiving a signal—the active
system will always be slower than the passive one.

C064   The active electronic fence

Several radar installations are arranged to form the ground network known as an electronic fence to alert the North American continent to incoming aircraft.

The North American defense systems for detection and early warning were designed knowing that targets within the United States were easily identified and conveniently located for attack by an enemy. About 85% of the heavy industry and 59% of the population are concentrated in 13% of the nation's land area.

The electronic detection of a slow moving manned bomber begins in the far north (near 70° N latitude) with the DEW (**D**istant **E**arly **W**arning) line. The next radar "fence" is the mid-Canada radar line (near 60° N latitude) and was originally named the Pine Tree radar line. The ground distance from the DEW line to the mid-Canada Line is about 600 miles.

The entire detection system, including the radar-equipped aircraft provided by the United States Navy, or Air Force, is tied together by a communication network terminating in the NORAD (the **NOR**th American **A**ir **D**efense command) Combat Operations Center located inside Cheyenne Mountain near Colorado Springs, Colorado. This air-defense communication and information network in the continental United States and southern Canada has often been compared to a nerve system. Stimulation at any one point creates an awareness and then triggers response throughout the system.

To receive the information, process it, and then issue proper instructions in an extremely short time requires the use of an electronic air-surveillance and weapon-control system called SAGE (**S**emi-**A**utomatic **G**round **E**nvironment), or something similar to it. Communication capabilities have been upgraded to accommodate more sophisticated detection systems such as BMEWS (**B**allistic **M**issile **E**arly **W**arning **S**ystem) with stations located at Clear, Alaska; Thule, Greenland; and Flyingdales Moor, Yorkshire, England. The SPADATS (**SPA**ce **D**etection **A**nd **T**racking **S**ystem), though also using relatively primitive electronics, is responsible for satellite-orbit information.

Coordination of the two systems is necessary so computers can compare the trajectories observed with those known for earth-orbiting satellites, characteristic aurora behavior, meteor trails, and other artificially generated disturbances. To determine a trajectory, the radar sends out two narrow beams at two different angles of elevation above the surface of the Earth (usually at about 2° and 10° elevation). A ballistic missile in free flight (the unpowered phase of flight) follows a well known trajectory or arc through the atmosphere that can be identified.

A radar constructed on Shemya Island, Alaska, only 450 miles from the Russian Kamchatka Peninsula, is an Arctic watch-dog, reported to be of medium power, able to spot an object as small as a missile at a distance of, say, 3,000 to 4,000 miles. The radar at Shemya Island is particularly useful for monitoring test firings from the Soviet Union. Shemya Island is in the Aleutian chain near Attu.

C065   Airborne Warning And Control System

To overcome the inadequacies of ground-based line-of-sight radar, a radar was installed on an airplane.

A radar beam, like any other beam of light, travels in a straight line. The surface of the Earth is, however, curved. Therefore, a radar beam cannot see an aircraft flying near the surface of the Earth. Such a low-flying aircraft can and often does fly under the beam of ground-based radar.

An airborne radar command-control system such as the converted Boeing 707 (United States Air Force E-3A) is the AWACS (Airborne Warning And Control System) used to look down on low-flying aircraft. The AWACS onboard computer has to sort the (known) motion of the plane carrying the radar from the (unknown) motion of the low-flying target aircraft. This identification of the low-flying aircraft must be made while both planes are in motion. The delay time for radar pulses returned from fixed man-make structures on the ground are, of course, easily computed. They do not move at all.

When flying at an altitude of 30,000 feet, the AWACS can spot an approaching aircraft as far away as 350 miles. When flying at a lower altitude the distance is reduced to, say, 250 miles.

The airborne radar is, however, far from perfect. Any man-made structure such as an office building or a hill in the natural terrain will intercept the beam. The radar echo is then returned from the (unwanted) obstacle in the radar path. An airborne radar also has difficulty to interpret the distortion of the slant. When the probing beam is scanning at a ground distance of several kilometers to the side, even when the beam path to the surface of the ground is completely free of interference, the line-of-sight view becomes distorted.

C066   A flying transponder

One way for a radar man to know you are his friend, and not his enemy, is to tell him.

IFF (**I**dentification: **F**riend or **F**oe) is one of the primary real-time missions of airspace traffic control. Whether a satellite is circling the globe in free flight, an AWACS (a Boeing E-3A, a militarized Boeing 707) is flying border patrol, or a commercial aircraft is right on time, it is still necessary to know if that bleep on the radar screen is a friend or a foe.

The signal of an ordinary (primary) active radar observer is returned from the target aircraft while the target transmitter does nothing. The transmitted radar pulse simply bounces off the target and returns to the sender. That diagnostic radar beam cannot uniquely identify a friend or a foe. For that matter, a single diagnostic radar beam cannot accurately determine altitude and ground speed of a friend.

The use of the secondary transponding coded pulse radar response is fast becoming mandatory for all aircraft flying in controlled air space. The aircraft has to carry a transponder radar onboard. This radar can **trans-pond**, it can **trans**-mit and it can res-**pond** to an active diagnostic (exploring) radar pulse. The transponding radar receives the radar pulse, shifts the received frequency, and responds by transmitting a friendly coded signal.

C067   The case of the false echo

To jam an enemy radar means a lot of different things to a lot of different people. But one thing it means to a radar man is the return of a false echo.

Stealth technology is the broad category of technology developed by the military for the purpose of camouflage or secret movement. When stealth technology becomes specialized within the use of electronics, it may be considered part of electronic warfare. Within that world of electronic warfare, the use of jamming equipment to interfere with radar or communication systems or even remote sensing devices has become commonplace.

A transponding device receives a radar pulse, shifts the received frequency, and responds so the probing radar can receive the signal. A transponding device can be used as a stealth device when it returns a radar echo that serves to conceal the presence of the target aircraft. It is in this fashion that an aircraft becomes electronically "invisible" to enemy radar.

C068   The air space merger

Everything between Heaven and Earth is air space. The whole thing belongs to the nation below . . . providing the radar beam can monitor the space.

Twenty years ago it was easy for everyone to distinguish between an airplane and a satellite. Air travel was for airplanes, and a space capsule was one of those things that carried John Glenn into orbit around the Earth.

At that time, airspace was all one word and national airspace extended only up as high as an aircraft could fly, or, perhaps more realistically, as high as an anti-aircraft gun could shoot. But gradually the upper fringes of the atmosphere, space 60 miles (90 kilometers) up, became accessible to a flying machine.

In 1981, with the successful landing of the Space Shuttle COLUMBIA, without any particular invitation or anticipated fanfare, the inevitable merger of air and space took place. Air travel and space travel combined into one gigantic air-space travel; air traffic control, airway facilities, and space monitoring became one overgrown air space safety control system.

Nowhere is the air-space merger more evident than with the planning of the CSOC (Consolidated Space Operations Center) of the United States Air Force. The CSOC is being designed to accomplish two separate, but closely related functions: telemetry, tracking, and commanding of spacecraft for the Department of Defense; and planning, readiness, and control activities associated with the Space Shuttle flights. This new operational site, located near Peterson Field, Colorado Springs, Colorado, should be reviewed so all of the electronic systems concepts can be updated, before they go operational.

Air Traffic Control is fast moving in the direction of **Air Space Safety**. All international organizations should start now to insist upon improved **Air Space Safety**. Mid-air collisions are **deadly** serious business. So are these low-orbiting nuclear powered satellites that come crashing down to Earth. From here on out, **Air Space Safety** could be your ASS or mine.

The idea of everyone hiding from everyone elses radar is nonsense. Small private airplanes flying below a radar beam, or high-flying SR-71 reconnaissance planes flying above—all should be flying in controlled air space. Every flying machine should transpond to a surveillance (diagnostic) radar, to make known its exact flying altitude, position, and speed—to identify itself as friend or foe.

Chapter D

Detecting the Explosion

The ground shakes like an earthquake

An underground bomb explosion or the blast of a rocket engine, both will make the ground shake like an earthquake. And those vibrations can be recorded on a siesmograph-type instrument similar to that used for recording vibrations of natural origin.

An array of seismometers, when connected with communication lines, can record and report the passage of a disturbance as a function of time and direction. The interpretation of such records can tell not only the speed and direction of travel of each vibration, but also the source of the disturbance.

Satellite detectors can sense and record the flash of X-ray or light at the time of the explosion of a nuclear warhead. Detection of the blast, after the fact, is, however, going to provide no protection for the atmosphere. The composition of the upper atmosphere has already been altered by the heat of the explosion, and there is no known method of reversing those artificially stimulated chemical changes.

D069   Underground nuclear testing

There are those who argue in favor of underground testing of nuclear weapons, there are those who argue

against it. But, that question aside, the detection of an
underground explosion can be recorded and inter-
preted much like the vibration from an earthquake.

After a decade of General Assembly resolutions deploring the
superpowers' refusal to implement a complete ban on nuclear
testing, the United Nations Secretariat this past year (reported
October 1980) launched a formal investigation into the snail's
pace of negotiations. The current negotiating efforts were
described as . . . "the moral equivalent of insanity."

Those in favor of nuclear testing claim that it is better to
test a weapon than not—that it is totally irresponsible to use
any weapon that has never been tested. Those opposed to the
testing claim that non-nuclear testing, meticulous testing of
components, and other assurances can be sufficient to
guarantee weapon performance—that the danger of excessive
contamination of underground water or eventual seepage of
radioactivity through the immediate venting process, is so
great that all underground testing should now cease. Opponents claim briefly and bluntly that contamination from "underground testing does not remain underground." Logic would
dictate that they are both right.

Efforts on the part of public officials to deny the feasibility
of verifying a Comprehensive Test Ban Treaty are apparently
motivated through ignorance. Modern electronic equipment is
sufficient to record and communicate any and all seismic vibrations of artificial origin.

A reporter for the *Las Vegas Sun*, Las Vegas, Nevada, com-
plains that much of the material is classified, a problem that
. . . "has been the trouble at the test site since it was founded
in 1951." Reasons for classifying these seismic data are obscure
and illogical. But, worse that that, it seems that monitors in
Utah were not even operating during several underground
tests—that there are no data at all, classified or otherwise.

". . . left to their own devices, the nuclear-weapons testers
will destroy us all. To allow their [those involved with weapons
systems] rationales to dissuade us from opposition is to give
them permission to incinerate the world." The plea to those
people is simple: terminate all underground nuclear testing.

D070   Atmospheric nuclear testing

The reason to ban nuclear testing in the atmosphere
has little to do with the unsightly appearance of the

mushroom cloud, and it has little to do with the destruction of people and property. Rather it has to do with an irreversible change in the chemistry of the upper atmosphere.

The explosion of an atomic bomb is characterized by an almost instantaneous release of huge amounts of energy from a point source. This release of energy produces a large fireball composed of gases under extremely high temperatures and pressures. The gases, move rapidly and forcefully outward, to produce a powerful blast wave in air, a shock wave in water, or a severe resonant vibration to the ground. In many respects, an atomic bomb explosion would be similar to an ordinary high-explosive weapon, except the atomic blast is more powerful.

The thermonuclear or hydrogen bomb works on a different principle. An atomic bomb trigger device is exploded to release an extremely high temperature. That heat, in turn, fuses the deuterium and tritium of the hydrogen bomb to produce an even more violent explosion. Once the deuterium-tritium mixture begins to fuse, enough heat is produced to continue to fuse the rest. It is for that reason that a hydrogen bomb can be made as big as you like. It is for that reason that the explosion of a thermonuclear device can be made any more times violent that the atomic bomb dropped on Hiroshima.

Satellite detection of nuclear explosion in the atmosphere can be made using detectors with the threshold of their sensitivity adjusted for flash detection. The detectors can also be educated to analyze X-ray or light intensities at the time of the flash. Modern electronics can then provide almost instant transfer of that analyzed information to the perspective user.

Following a nuclear explosion, direct probe sampling and remote sensing monitoring from satellite-borne instruments can also detect and report chemical composition change in the upper atmosphere. The presence of dust, dirt, and debris carried aloft by the updraft of the explosion can also be detected and reported. It is this artificially introduced or induced foreign matter that can remain aloft for long periods of time.

The upper stratosphere, when filled with particulate matter, tends to darken the surface of the Earth below. The particulate matter prevents or decreases the passage of the sun's rays. Though these transmission properties of the upper atmosphere can be monitored, there is little that can be done to improve or alter the state.

Detection of a thermonuclear explosion after the fact does nothing to prevent atmospheric change. The upper atmosphere has already been incinerated from the heat; the upper atmosphere has already been contaminated with material carried aloft. And there is no known method of reversing artificially induced atmospheric changes.

D071   The false hope of ABM

Anti-Ballistic Missile systems have been portrayed by the President of the United States as a defense against nuclear attack. But those ABM systems give false hope. The cure is more deadly than the disease.

The size of a nuclear warhead has been measured and reported in equivalent tons of TNT, but those units of measure are really without meaning.

For one thing, a one-megaton warhead is said to release, upon explosion, the same blast force as a one million metric ton TNT explosion (the prefix mega stands for million). The irony of that TNT megaton equivalence is that one does not ordinarily measure the explosive power of TNT in tons. That is to say, one ton is equal to 2,000 pounds; the one megaton bomb would release an amount of energy upon explosion equivalent to 2,000,000,000 (two billion) pounds of TNT.

For another thing, the damage that is done by exploding a nuclear warhead is not directly related to total tonage. It is well known, for example, that five bombs would do more damage to the upper atmosphere than one blockbuster, even though both would have the same TNT megaton equivalence. That means, the testing and use of small bombs does not, in itself, offer more protection. Five one-megaton explosions would do more damage than one single five-megaton blast. Dividing the same five-megaton explosive equivalence into 25 bombs would do even more damage.

The use of modern electronic devices and modern communication capabilities would enable the United States military to have under attack any ICBM within seconds after it leaves the launch pad. A conventional heat-seeking missile could be fired toward the booster engine soon after lift-off. Such a defense would supposedly protect the American population. The subsequent explosion would leave all contamination, radioactive debris, and blast damage in the Soviet Union, over the North Pole, or high in the upper atmosphere.

The truth of the matter is that detection and destruction after launch, just like detection after testing, does not provide any protection at all. It does not matter that a thermonuclear explosion has taken place over some other country or over some other continent. The Earth has only one atmosphere and that atmosphere is needed to sustain life as we know it today.

All things considered, the atmosphere of Planet Earth is relatively fragile. And that one atmosphere circulates around the globe. There is no known pound of cure for the disease of nuclear destruction—there is only the ounce of prevention, the passing of an international law against the manufacture, possession, or use of nuclear warheads.

BMD (**B**allistic **M**issile **D**efense) may sound better than MAD (**M**utual **A**ssured **D**estruction)—but that is only on paper or only in political speeches. Defense is no longer a national issue. And defense is no longer an economic issue. Defense is a matter of protecting an otherwise defenseless environment. The atmosphere you save is your own.

Chapter E

Decentralizing Networks

The digital revolution that broke the camel's back

Information saturation is a common fault with any centralized communication network. The other common fault is the under-utilization of available human resource.

Centralized information systems tend to be exclusive—they tend to exclude concerned citizens from the decision making process and they tend to exclude concerned citizens who could become involved in emergency preparedness at the local level. To suppose that a centralized system would survive during time of national disaster, that everything that needs to be replaced or repaired would make itself known during regular working hours, that the system would never be down during a time of national emergency, is probably a risky assumption for this nation to make.

A nationalized information-communication system would require public participation in privately owned industries when those corporations are funded by tax dollars. A nationalized information-communication system would require all component parts to be supplied by industries located and operated within the continental United States. A democratized-nationalized system would further provide sufficient redundancy that survival would be assured during time of national emergency.

Any nationalized-democratized system would have to be a de-centralized system—everyone would have to have equal opportunity to access the same information. Any nationalized-democratized system would also have to be diversified—it would have to be designed to meet the needs of many varied users. These ground-networks might eventually have to be used as back-up for satellite communication-information transfer systems.

E072   A down-to-earth message

The advantage of keeping the message on the ground is that the equipment is also there. Ground based equipment is less expensive to use and it is more rapidly replaced and updated.

Ground-based communication networks generally depend upon two different types of communication capabilities: one is fixed wire, the other is microwave relay. In the first, information travels along a fixed cable; in the second, it travels through the air. Of the two, fixed wire is the older style and it is more traditional. Yet both have their own unique advantages, and disadvantages.

The AT&T (American Telephone and Telegraph) is the industry in the United States largely responsible for long-distance communication facilities. The AT&T is heavily controlled by legislation from the United States Congress; it is also heavily regulated by policy decisions (or are they political decisions) from the FCC (Federal Communication Commission), a regulatory commission staffed through political channels.

The AT&T could be required, by law, to replace all of its fixed-wire facilities. The old copper wire lines could be replaced with fiber (glass) optics. At the same time, all of the lines could be put into underground tunnels. The new, larger capacity glass cables would be too heavy, in any case, to string on poles above the ground. Though fiber optics transmission may well be less efficient, the line capacity would be greatly increased.

Microwave relay towers are alternatives for long distance information transfer. Advocates of microwave relay see especially the advantages of redundancy—in a remote area relay stations can be arranged to provide alternate paths for line-of-sight transfer. Advocates of the microwave relay also argue that it is much easier to replace a relay tower than a broken underground cable . . . providing you can get to it . . . in the middle of the winter, during a blizzard, at 20° below zero.

In either case, land-based equipment is more accessible than an orbiting satellite. Ground-based equipment can be designed in a modular fashion—it can be designed so it can be piece-wise upgraded even after the system is in daily use.

E073   A package of information

A long recorded computer message can be divided into packets, and then the many packets can be transferred all at the same time. The only requirement is that the message, and all the switches along the path, be digitized.

The telephone user of today has grown accustomed to the idea of circuit switching. An actual, continuous two-way path or circuit is established between each pair of users for the entire duration of the call. Circuit switching allows two people to tie up an entire line—to have one complete circuit dedicated to their exclusive use—during the entire time of their conversation. But the use of such a dedicated circuit is very expensive.

An alternative to circuit switching is packet switching. Packet switching implies the use of a method of fragmenting a message into several packets or pieces before it is transmitted. Each packet is then transmitted at the same time, but each travels along a different path. The packets may even use different links between different channels. The packets progress along the way in a stop-and-go or store-and-forward fashion.

The use of packet switching is similar to the use of a traffic light to regulate the flow of automobiles at a busy intersection. The packets of information are like automobiles that travel along the city streets—the packets of information stop-and-go at the network nodes much as automobiles stop-and-go at the traffic light. The computer-controlled digital switches are the traffic lights for the information flow.

The regularity of traffic flow is programmed into the operation of the traffic lights. This is possible because all cars are, more or less, the same size, and, with experience, the engineers have learned to anticipate the time of arrival of rush hour traffic. But switching decisions for information flow are far more complex.

Three decisions have to be made for digital switching: the number of packets into which the message should be divided, i.e., the "length" of the packet, the path each packet should travel, and the time of day for the transfer.

Each packet of information must be identified so the total message can be assembled in proper sequence at the receiver end. This means identification heading must be added to each packet, and the overhead cost is increased according to the number of packets. Thus, if one message were divided into too many packets, then the overhead cost for the total message would become prohibitive.

Packet switching could replace much of the old-fashioned circuit switching, the only requirement is that the United States Congress appropriate funding so AT&T can provide digital switching and line capacity . . . or should the American people, through monthly payment of their telephone bill, pay the price for modernization of their own national communication capabilities.

E074   Democratization of information flow

Information read into a computer can be read out. It can also be processed and updated. The important thing is that everyone have equal opportunity for access.

A centralized computer network for global monitoring systems would have all information from detection and early warning systems flow into one central facility. With everyone trying to talk to the same computer at the same time, someone is bound to get a busy signal.

A decentralized computer network would be designed with emphasis on increased through-put rather than on an ever-expanding capacity for central storage and retrieval. Through-put is a time-dependent measure of the amount of information than can flow through a network, where storage and retrieval is more like a static measure of the amount of information that can be gathered together for later use. One is like a water pipe; the other is like a bucket.

People in a money exchange system, when the system is alive, are much like computers in an information network. People receive money and they spend money. Occasionally they take some money to the bank. Computers in a network receive information and they, in turn, are a source of information. Computers can also save information by depositing it in a data bank.

Computers do, however, have one important difference. Information flowing through a network or deposited in a data bank may be withdrawn by a hundred users all at the same time. The same information can be read out of the system by one hundred different computers, yet the information is still in the data bank. In that sense, information flow and computer networking are more democratic than the transfer of money could ever be.

Chapter F

Communication Satellites

The relay station in the sky

A listening-type remote sensing satellite is like a microphone planted in the ladies lounge, it collects everything within the dynamic range of the receiver. The communication satellite, by comparison, carries a highly pampered payload. The communication satellite has to receive everything in a nice neat format—at a prescribed frequency, organized into well-marked time intervals. That is to say, the remote sensing satellite is designed to digest just about any sort of raw data; the communication satellite is a very finicky eater.

Microwave relay towers have to be spaced only a few miles apart. Those ground-based towers have to bend the path of the line-of-sight signal to match the curvature of the earth.

The satellite communication link provides an alternative to a ground-based communication network. The communication satellite provides a single relay over a very long distance. The satellite link could cover a distance as great as the width of the United States in only one hop—one up- and one down-leg of signal transmission.

F075   Geostationary satellites

The geostationary or geosynchronous satellite stays fixed at the equator, conveniently positioned above a fixed location on the surface of the earth, ready to relay a signal from one ground station to another.

The orbit of a geostationary satellite is synchronized with the day-night rotation rate of the Earth itself. The orbit of the satellite above the equator is such that the satellite appears to remain fixed with respect to a transmitter or receiver located on the ground.

The communication satellite must be carefully tracked by the ground-control stations. Those stations control the thruster engines that control the attitude of the satellite (the orientation of the payload around the three axes), move the satellite in an east-west direction, or compensate for gravitational pertubations from Sun, moon, or Earth distortions. The purpose of the thruster engine is to keep the payload in its assigned orbital position, also to point the solar panels at the Sun or the satellite sensors at the surface of the Earth.

The supply of hydrazine fuel consumed by these thruster engines, the fuel needed to do the positioning or the pointing, may well determine the effective lifetime of the communication satellite.

F076   Getting the signal off the ground

A ground-based central station collects and processes every signal that has to be communicated over a satellite link. The ground station is a highly specialized station with a high power transmitter.

There are many ground stations that cannot transmit their messages directly to a communication satellite. Those many small users have to send their messages, instead, to a central facility. As the central station receives those incoming signals, it converts everything to a common format.

Computers imbedded in the electronics of the outlying facilities understand a particular language and they read their messages only at one particular rate. Neither the language nor the data rate is compatible with that used by the central facility for communicating with the satellite. This means that all of the messages from all of the many diverse users along the ground network must first be translated so the communication satellite can understand the incoming signal.

When the ground station is ready to send the messages to the communication satellite, the signal must be amplified so it has enough strength to reach the height of the orbit. The signal is amplified, say, 320,000 times and then fed to a parabolic-shaped dish antenna. That dish is about 90 feet or 30 meters across its diameter. That antenna must point directly at the communication satellite that is to receive the signal.

F077   Boost and return

The communication satellite serves much the same purpose as the microwave relay tower on the ground. It gives a boost to the strength of the signal and it points the beam in the right direction.

A strong signal is transmitted from a central facility on the ground. By the time that signal reaches the height of the communication satellite, it has become very weak. The 22,300-mile distance above the equator is a very long distance for a signal to have to travel.

The communication satellite is equipped with a transponder-type device, a device that can trans-mit and res-pond, a device that is used to shift the frequency of the incoming signal. For example, when the up-leg signal is transmitted at 6 GHz, the down-leg signal frequency would be shifted to 4 GHz. (The units for measuring the frequency of those signals is Giga Hertz.)

Another purpose of the communication satellite is to control the width of the beam it transmits back to Earth. A narrow beam would be directed to a select user. A broad beam could be used to broadcast the beam to a wide number of users. The communication satellite could even code its signal so only authorized listeners could de-code the message received at the ground stations. This coding could be done, for example, by transmitting the message in many different packets, each on a slightly different frequency, with the sequence of frequencies selected by a special computer program.

The needs of the users determine the operating requirements for the communication satellites. The practical limiting factor is the cost of the equipment.

F078   The receiver on the ground

The receiving antenna on the ground is tuned to accept only certain frequencies and even those frequencies must be strong enough for the equipment to sort signal from the noise.

Select users find it desirable to have the incoming signal beam as narrow as possible, and as weak as possible. To pick up and sort a weak signal from noise requires sophisticated and expensive signal-enhancement, signal-processor, receiver-antenna systems. The enormous expense of such a ground receiving station immediately limits the number of direct users. It assures all users that their signal is protected from unwanted users because other antenna systems would be equipped with much less electronic paraphernalia.

A commercial broadcaster would subscribe to exactly the opposite operating philosophy. The commercial sender would like to reach as many subscribers as possible. The commercial sender would like to broadcast the signal over a wide area and he would like to have the signal strong enough to be picked up by an inexpensive receiver.

There are two opposing philosophies for the use of communication satellites. One would have the expensive equipment on the ground, limited to select central facilities. The other would "invert" the technology—the expensive one-time electronics would go into the satellite payload. An inexpensive receiver antenna would then be used by as many subscriber-receivers as possible on the ground.

If the marketplace is allowed to determine the emphasis, the marketplace would logically dictate the inversion of technology. The marketplace would logically cater to the many diverse users.

F079   The transmitter is the target

The high-power transmitter needed to give the signal a boost is an easy target for an electronic enemy.

Communication satellites provide an alternative to fixed wire or microwave relay ground-based communication networks. But, it remains for the marketplace to do the deciding.

The launch of a satellite is expensive and the payload is a long way from the repair shop. The electronic hardware has to be used for the lifetime of the orbit position. For a domestic user, one would think the ground-based network would be more practical than a satellite link.

The communication satellite clearly has advantages for global users. The communication satellite can relay information across the ocean to Norway or the other direction to the islands in the Pacific. But, those remote communication needs are more supportive of global information systems—systems needed for global environmental monitoring and for continuous monitoring of military activities for peacekeeping purposes—than anything needed by domestic consumers.

The American taxpayers may well be willing to pay the price for information transfer around the world, but still the use of a high-power ground-based transmitter must be examined with other alternatives in mind. A tiny low-power coded beep may be strong enough to be received during an overhead pass of an orbiting satellite. And the low-power transmitter, because there would be thousands of them, would provide less of an electronic target. Inverted technology seems far more reasonable than a transmitter target on the ground.

Chapter G

Use it or lose it

**National technological advantage comes
from the use of information,
not from its collection**

Henry Ford produced an automobile, but it took the American people themselves to create an economic prosperity around its use. In the same manner, the technological advantage this nation now seeks in electronics will come from the use of computers, not from their production.

Automated electronic hardware is designed so the interactive possibilities at the man-machine interface are determined by the person doing the engineering. That is what automation is all about. The machine is designed to tell the user what to do . . . or, perhaps, the user only has to plug the equipment in and let it run. Automated electronic equipment dictates user response or, in extreme cases, the equipment dictates no user response at all.

Automated electronic equipment is an enemy of individuality. It destroys human initiative and it fails to motivate creative action.

The individuality of the user of information is our salvation. The user of information systems can create the technological advantage this nation seeks. The user of information systems can create a new industrial base for this country. And those information industries in the private sector can use information flow from military-operated global monitoring systems as their raw material, raw material from which to manufacture their all-new computer products.

G080   Automation is the enemy

Automated radar, computer-controlled satellite systems, automated weapons systems—all were supposed to have been more dependable than those systems dominated by human judgement.

The gospel doctrine for U.S. defense contracting had been: save money, produce automation to replace people. The practical argument in the robot-replacing-people era was that a piece of hardware was cheaper to produce and maintain than a person . . . and it was more dependable. A piece of equipment could be designed to do precisely the same thing over and over again. Repetition was its strength, boredom was its favorite companion. Under pressure of rigid time schedule, whether in the middle of the day or the dark of night, no matter how adverse the weather conditions, a piece of equipment would be motivated only by the power supply. Just plug it in and let it run.

Scientists, funded by American tax dollars, remained convinced that they could anticipate all the needs of the military users. And they designed automation accordingly. This black box mentality dominated many of the decisions within the defense community. Would-be military users were soon at the mercy of the scientists who were funded through the government agencies, yet had little sense of operational military mission, and no sense at all for the life-death dependence of the military on the performance of a piece of equipment.

In the eyes of many scientists, the American military has long since lost its need for human intelligence or human responsibility. The superior intelligence of the engineers and the scientists would be enough.

Automation has become the enemy of the American military service organizations, and it has become the enemy of the American people those service organizations are supposed to be protecting.

Automation was developed by the scientific community for the sole purpose of eliminating the need for people. Automation also eliminated the need for human judgement, human incentive, and human purpose. Automation has become the enemy of individuality—it has also become the enemy of national responsiveness.

G081   Industrial push

Technology push, in the form of automation, has been playing a dominant role in deciding national priorities for defense spending. This happens because those employed by munitions industries derive benefit from government contracts.

Following World War II, those responsible for assigning priorities for defense spending decided that sophisticated delivery systems would make it possible for the United States to fight a nuclear war across intercontinental distances in a matter of minutes. Not only automated delivery systems but also automated alert and early warning systems would be designed so one man, the President of the United States, could control the entire U.S. military operation from the White House.

With automated systems, the Commander-in-Chief of the American military, and a few military personnel of sufficient loyalty, would be able to achieve the ultimate in global reach. While sitting at a computer display-communication console, the President would have control of the world. The complete destructive power of the American military, in the form of industrial automation, would be at his finger tips.

Much of the driving force for the development of this automation, automation that was, in fact, intended to be held in reserve as war potential, came from and continues to come from the technology push of the industry. Members of the military-industrial complex, devoted to the philosophy of technological evolution, exploited one basic assumption: more hardware in the form of automation will bring greater military superiority.

Technology push has now been carried to such an extreme that it neglects not only the needs of the nation, but also the needs of the military. And, worse than that, technology push has started to neglect the ideals of the American people.

G082   The fault is me

I have just come face to face with the enemy, and it is me.

A centralized command-control-communication structure is the ultimate in separation of responsibility and authority. Authority would go to the National Command Center, or the President, yet the responsibility would still belong to the people. The people are responsible for the use of military destructive power in this do-it-yourself government we call democracy.

As long as the technology push for automated weapons systems dominates the decision making process for determining the defense spending priorities, the military service organizations will continue to be the dumping ground for every conceivable mutation-defect of technological evolution. As long as automated detection and early warning systems persist, the United States military does not dare to eliminate the excessive overkill in its strategic weapons systems.

Public debate of defense spending priorities could eliminate a few freaks of technological evolution. Public debate of national purpose could attach national meaning to detection and early warning. Public participation in the political process is our salvation. When it comes to personal preference, the American people still prefer the ballot to the bullet. They only have to make sure their elected public officials appropriate their tax dollars according to that preference.

G083   User pull

Technology push is the natural dynamic dueling partner of demand pull. With technology pushing as hard as it seems to like to push in the defense community, the demand pull of the users will have to provide the guiding principle.

The true meaning of technology has to do with human action—the use of tools or techniques to carry out desired human objectives. For the American people, that desired human objective has now become the use of modern electronics for the purpose of global monitoring.

Because of the enormous numbers of highly trained and highly skilled people needed to perfect and use global information systems, both the military and the civilian human resource will have to be combined in this national effort. And the users of those systems will have to assume the responsibility for establishing the defense spending priorities.

When a mutation occurs in human evolution, nature has her methods of rejecting it. When a freak comes along in technological evolution, the marketplace, the consumer, or the user, or all three, will reject it. When a faulty piece of automation evolves in the defense community, there is no one except the American people, in the form of defense spending, to refuse to allow its survival. Yet that refusal should come in the form of a positive national goal.

A dramatic increase in demand pull would alter defense spending priorities—it would also proudly uphold and gracefully embrace the ideals of the American people.

G084   Back to computer basics

Born talent and acquired skill—that is the eternal dualism of creative human behavior—that is the eternal dualism needed to write the software so basic to the creative use of the computer.

The computer is a basic piece of hardware. The computer software is the list of instructions that tells the computer what to do. It is the computer software that protects, preserves, and indeed provides uniqueness and individuality to the user. It is the computer software that is responsive to user needs.

The military has insisted upon underestimating the need for the development of computer software. Both the human resource and the time needed for the development have been blatantly ignored.

The development of computer software goes according to the so-called 90/90 chain rule. The first 90 percent of the development of a piece of software takes 90 percent human resource, the next 9 percent takes another 90 percent, the next 0.9 percent takes still another 90 percent and so on. It is easy to see that human resource very soon dominates performance of any computer system.

Training for the development of computer software would ideally be provided only to those with born talent. While skill is the ease with which a person performs with body response—to work with one's hands, as in the case of electronic skills, would be an example—with computer software, it is the skill of the sense of computer logic that matters.

Computer software development requires a dependence not upon the sensitivity of sense organs, but rather upon intuition and insight. It takes sensory perception of stimuli of the lowest possible intensity. It takes a sixth sense. It takes a talent with which a person is born. The development of computer software is not a science; it is an art. Those computer programmers are born, not made.

A return to computer basics is a return to human resource. Acquired skill should reinforce born talent, because only born talent can develop the software needed to satisfy those individual users of global monitoring systems.

G085   Technology is culture

People are not the problem, they are the solution.

Science deals with human understanding of the natural world. Engineering deals with the application of knowledge to the creation of plans, designs, or means of achieving desired objectives. But technology has to do with the actual carrying out of those objectives.

Culture is lifestyle as it happens. Culture has to do with human endeavor as it existed at some time in the past. Only after the fact does it become evident that users of technology have created cultural heritage. It is that viewing after the fact that is now taking place. The American people are starting to realize the place electronic technology has in their daily living pattern.

Culture is what is eventually created by the hope, faith, and mood of the people who are involved in doing. For that reason, it is absolutely certain that the multitudes of military- and government-users of information systems are having a profound influence on the cultural heritage of this nation. Those people are in the process of creating cultural heritage. They have sustained the use of computer technology long enough that it has become American tradition.

G086   People with a purpose

All computer systems will have to become manpower intensive, or they will be under-utilized.

The miniaturization of electronics has increased the reliability and decreased the cost of computers. The computer has become as essential for the processing of information as the cookstove has become for the processing of food. And just as the taste for food varies from one person to the next, so does the taste for information flow and the many computer products.

Information nourishes the human soul. Information nourishes the ability of an individual to act with feeling and emotion. And it is that feeling aspect of experience and affection that determines the striving factor for each of us.

It is the striving factor of human motivation that is goal oriented. It is the striving factor that has not only direction but also strength of action. It is the striving factor of human motivation that can make the computer respond to many diverse user needs.

The human spirit is motivated by dedication to service—by a sense of duty and by native curiosity. The national service organizations are the strength and the soul of this nation. The national service organizations are the doing part of this nation. And those doers are doing it with computers—this nation is moving into a new era of creative human action.

Perspective

Information is Firepower

*National defense is the fine art
of hiding behind
the time barrier*

> *The creative spirit of Uncle Sam
> is circling the globe
> in free flight*

Throughout the history of civilization, the purpose of war has been to conquer: to conquer the right to control people, to conquer the right to control land, sea, and available air space. Once the disputes of war were settled, the conquered people would become a captive work force; the conquered land, sea, and air, a place for agricultural or industrial expansion.

As war fighting became more and more mechanized, war fighting also became more and more destructive. The destruction of human life and the destruction of private property became sought after goals rather than unfortunate consequences of the fighting. War became a human activity void of any indication of positive effort to improve the quality of human life.

War, like sex, is now a three letter word used to describe a human activity that is, at best, poorly understood. For that reason, and that reason alone, any blind condemnation of war would now be as much a mistake for this generation as the blind condemnation of sex was for the last. To try to make war uniformly ugly or uniformly evil would be to deny the reason for its existence. To simply and strictly forbid war would not teach anyone how to do what ever it is that the human race has been achieving through violent destructive action. To give war a bad name would not alter, or would it satisfy, the basic human need fulfilled by its pursuit.

There has always been a creative aspect of war. Journalists and authors would write at their best—their passion would amplify to keep pace with the intensity of human endeavor. Painting, poetry, plays; music, media, movies; living, longing, loving—all forms of human expression would become as radically creative as the tearing down of out-of-date political and economic institutions would be destructive.

The lesson to be learned is that creativity has been forced to lie dormant in the minds of men until the false hopes of war were somehow glamorized, until deep emotional commitment was strong enough to break the bonds of conformity and release accumulated creative energy, until a moral battleground could be established in the patriotic image of common good.

The American people are now living in the most technologically advanced society in the world. The American people appear, nevertheless, to want to sustain their national identity and to propagate their national ideals. But they seem to want to do both within the limits imposed by their natural environment. It is that combined popular demand to project a national image yet protect the natural environment that is becoming increasingly difficult to sustain. It is that combined popular demand that is forcing the American people to examine closely the purpose of war.

The American people have elected Ronald Reagan President. And that vote was also a vote for increased defense spending. Yet priorities for the defense budget, like all other national spending priorities, are going to have to be established through a TEAM effort. A national coordination of Technology, Environment, And Man would have every member of the TEAM involved in the decision making process. Such an ongoing TEAM effort would allow the release of creative energy before it has accumulated to a dangerously explosive level.

Decisions for the coordination of the national TEAM effort would have to be made so the creative aspect of human endeavor would strive to be ever increasing, while the consumption of natural resources would be ever decreasing. The American military, the American industry, and the American people—all would participate in the maximum-minimum adjustment process because they would participate in the decision making process. The goal toward which the adjustment would always be striving would be to make all human activity manpower intensive.

A new dynamics for the decision making process is developing. Man is replacing machine, but he is doing it at the creative level, not at the level of the human drudge. The computer can routinely process information but human judgement and human insight are going to have to transform that organized information into human knowledge and that human knowledge into inspired wisdom.

Nature intended human interaction to be composed of two dynamic components: one with a continuous rhythmatic persistence, the other with a spontaneous creative energy. Plasma physicists tend to picture this dynamic interaction as the wave-particle dualism. Thomas Aquinas (1226-1274) wrote about this same dualism of nature; he perceived it as two components in human behavior: faith and reason. Today in the United States the interaction of dynamic partners permeates all aspects of our daily living.

Dynamic dueling partners are now, as they were during the time of Aquinas, and as they shall always be in the future, deserving of equal opportunity. Neither science nor religion, neither male nor female, neither Church nor State, is above or below the other on the scale of human endeavor. Both should remain uniquely strong and both should interact with the other. And divine truth and divine action have never been more ready to become natural partners; the non-violent, non-destructive behavior of the decision making process is contained in that dynamic interaction.

Whether one has to monitor military maneuvers, industrial waste disposal, changing agricultural yield, or open ocean fishing practices, modern techniques of remote sensing could be used successfully. As global monitoring systems are upgraded to provide continuous information flow, the threat of the unknown would certainly disappear.

The continuous transfer of information could allow the American military to substitute information for firepower. The continuous assessment of information could remove the element of surprise from intended destructive action. The continuous flow of information from military-operated DETECTION AND EARLY WARNING Systems could make a beginning by rendering land-based, pre-targeted, push-button delivery systems for nuclear weapons obsolete.

Natural Eternal War is an eternal war of electronic monitoring. Natural Eternal War is an eternal war of ideas. Natural

Eternal **W**ar is an eternal war of deciding. The era of eternal war is the era when the American people, the American military, and the American industry could combine their dynamic thinking and doing into one common purpose for this nation, the common purpose of improving the quality of human life.

This nation has always been ruled by the rule of law. A change to rule by dynamic partners of natural law would be but a logical extension of that past experience, with one important exception. In the NEW era of **N**atural **E**ternal **W**ar, rule by dynamic law would be more binding. Rule by dynamic law would contain its own method of enforcement—failure to abide would simply endanger our own survival.

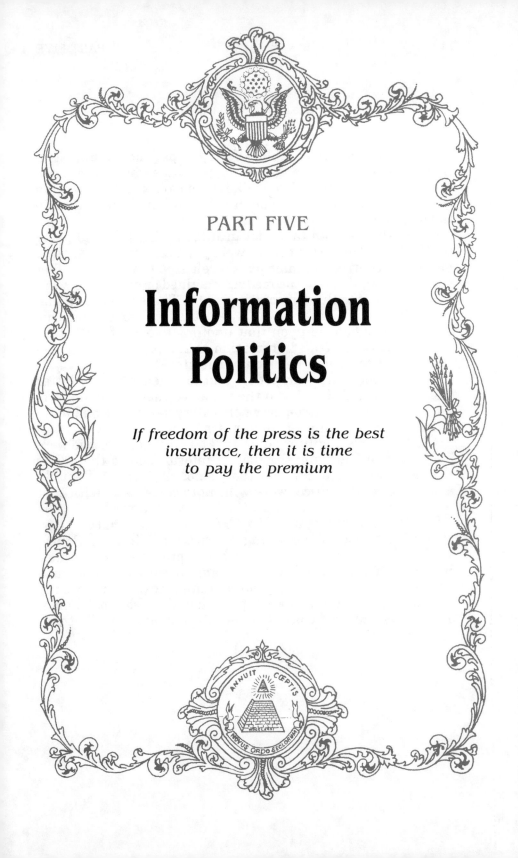

PART FIVE

Information Politics

If freedom of the press is the best insurance, then it is time to pay the premium

Information politics, public affairs, propaganda administration—the name may change but the purpose remains the same: the federal government would like to control, or at least reserve the right to control, the type of information made available to the general public.

It has always been taken for granted by the political party in the White House that there were political advantages to be gained by controlling information released to the public. Yet such manipulations of the media, imagined or otherwise, were never a threat to the democratic process. There was the official party line, and then there was always the loyal opposition. One could always depend upon that unofficial voice of that other political party to leak information to the press, information that would tell the other side of the story.

In 1971, the American people had to re-learn a very bitter lesson; they had to re-learn the negative aspect of being protected by their own two-party political system; they had to re-learn the evils of a controlled press.

American lives, military dignity, and national prestige were being lost in Vietnam; the flow of information to the public had been strangled. Neither the Democrats nor the Republicans, in or out of office, were willing to come forth with that all important "opposing view" of the Vietnam war.

Finally, on Sunday, June 13, 1971, excerpts from the "History of U.S. Decision-Making Process on Vietnam Policy, 1945-1967," papers that had been prepared for former Secretary of Defense Robert S. McNamara, papers that detailed how American involvement had escalated inexorably since the days of Harry S. Truman, were printed in the *New York Times*. That news leak to the press revealed U.S. policies in Vietnam to be different from those the American people had been led to believe.

In a landmark First Amendment decision, the Supreme Court of the United States ruled 6-3 in favor of Freedom of the Press. The *Washington Post* and the *New York Times* were given permission to print those Pentagon Papers. Thousands of pages taken from a "top secret safe," copied after hours at the Rand Corporation by Daniel Ellsberg, were available for public reading. The closed decision-making process within the defense community of the United States government—a blatant government abuse of secrecy in the name of national security—proved to be no match for the people's right to be informed.

Freedom of the press is the only insurance the American people have against a closed government. And, now with the collapse of the traditional two-party system (the two major parties appear to be only one "party," and that party favors political loyalty), the people themselves are going to have to pay the premium for that insurance.

Chapter A

SALT Treaties

Prohibition was also a flop

More than any other people on Planet Earth, the American people should know the failure of prohibition. The Constitutional Amendment written for the prohibition of the manufacture and sale of alcoholic beverages concealed a serious social ill. Prohibition of the production of nuclear arms is also concealing a serious social ill. Prohibition of the production of nuclear arms is hiding behind the very thin veil of that which we call peace.

Prohibition activities, as they relate to arms control among nations of the world, started in Washington, D.C., on November 12, 1921, when then Secretary of State, Charles Evans Hughes, opened the Washington Arms Conference with a speech that ended by declaring a ten-year naval "holiday" for governments to consider their future course. The build-up of arms that followed escalated the world right into World War II.

Since the Second World War, peacetime levels of weapons have continued to increase steadily. Arms prohibition activities have gone along with the political mood of the country. They have done little more than legalize the proliferation of weapons and the proliferation of international organizations that oppose proliferation. Though arms prohibition agreements are well intended, just as the prohibition of alcoholic beverages was well intended, the method is clearly in need of improvement.

To get rid of nuclear weapons, the United States must first get rid of the need for the destruction. That is to say, constructive, rather than destructive, goals need to be accepted. Constructive, rather than destructive, methods of interaction have to be established. And that can start only when all nations are treated equal under the rule of law.

Military-operated global monitoring systems are already needed by the United States military for reasons of their own constitutional mandate: To repel Invasions. But a greatly expanded continuous flow of remote sensing data coming from those information systems could also be used for global monitoring of the international regulatory agreements. And those international agreements could now be motivated by the world's need for monitoring of the natural environment.

The United States could initiate international regulatory activities to control environmental pollution. Those regulatory provisions could be continuously and routinely monitored by remote sensing. And those data sets could be continuously and routinely displayed through interactive communication networks. All civilian and all military groups would have simultaneous access to the remote sensing information flow for the purpose of environmental monitoring.

A087   Equality for all nations

> *George Washington warned against "seeking [or] granting exclusive favours or preferences" to other nations. That advice is as sound today as it was on the 19th of September, 1796, when Washington provided it.*

George Washington's FAREWELL ADDRESS TO THE PEOPLE OF THE UNITED STATES divides into two parts. In the first, Washington definitely declines to run for a third term, gives his reasons, and acknowledges a debt of gratitude for the honors conferred upon him and for the confident support of the people. In the second and more important part, Washington presents, as a result of his experiences and as a last legacy of advice to the people of this nation, his thoughts upon the government.

It was Washington's hope that the American people would somehow prevent this nation from running the course which has hitherto marked the Destiny of Nations. For that reason, Washington questioned:

> Why forego the advantages of our detached and distant situation—Our detached and distant situation that invites and enables us to pursue a different course—why, by interweaving our destiny with that of any part of Europe, entangle our peace and prosperity in the toils of European Ambition, Rivalship, Interest, Humour, or Caprice?

Washington was considered an "isolationist," as contrasted with an "interventionist." Though those terms no longer have the same economic or political meaning (with the global communication we have today, one could hardly be isolated even when one wanted to be), Washington was advocating a strong sense of national independence, a strong sense of national identity, and a strong sense of national purpose.

No matter what the terminology, our philosophy of national independence remains very much the same. This nation should avoid awarding special privileges to a favored few. This nation should avoid selective bilateral agreements. This nation should seek "Harmony" with all nations as "recommended by policy, humanity, and interest."

Washington's Farewell Address is delivered on the Senate Floor every two years, at the beginning of each new session of the United States Congress. Perhaps one day the delivery of that address will be broadcast live for all Americans to hear. National independence—not only political independence but also economic independence—is a philosophy the American people now appear ready to support.

A088   No force for enforcement

> *According to the Charter of the United Nations, there can be no national force for the enforcement of international law. It is for that reason that no one nation can play favorites or grant special privileges.*

Enforcement action for international agreements is clearly recognized as the paramount authority of the Security Council of the United Nations, with appropriate assistance from the

Military Staff Committee. Chapter VIII: Regional Arrangements, Articles 52 and 53, of that Charter, absolutely prohibit the initiation of any individual enforcement action by individual member nations.

This means, then, that any bilateral agreement or binding alliance between two member nations within the United Nations cannot be enforced by those nations alone. In that respect, individual nations of the United Nations are no different from individual States of the United States. All States of the United States have exactly the same independence and the same national allegiance granted to them by the federal government.

If the lack of force for enforcement by individual nations is to be taken seriously, then the United States should terminate its membership in the North Atlantic Treaty Alliance and any other permanent alliance that organizes groups of nations together for political, military, or economic reasons. The United States government should make an official statement of its intent to comply with the Charter of the United Nations or it should withdraw its membership.

A089   International regulatory activities

> *There can be no greater error than to expect, or calculate upon real favour from Nation to Nation . . . 'Tis an illusion which experience must cure, which a just pride ought to discard.*

The spirit of international law may one day provide for "an indissoluble Union of indestructible [Nations]" here on this Planet Earth. The individual [Nations] of that Union and the people of those individual [Nations] will enjoy immense powers —powers that will be denied the Union—powers that will have to be protected by a Bill of Rights, so the "new central government might not become an instrument of tyranny"

But until an acceptable written constitution does emerge, international regulatory activity (the letter of the law in coordination with the spirit of the law) appears to be the only available format. Regulatory activities, especially those related to global environmental pollution and real-time monitoring, must be implemented so all nations receive equal protection under the rule of law.

International regulatory activities should be conceived so they are creative and innovative; they should be implemented so they create more than they destroy. Such creative action can take place only when the utility of human resource is at its maximum, the consumption of natural resource at its minimum.

Military-operated global information systems and interactive communication networks, when properly utilized for continuous information flow, make it feasible for the American people and, hence, the government of the United States, to treat all nations with equal and just consideration.

The increased risk of accidental nuclear holocaust that comes with every increase in the level of American military preparedness makes it mandatory that the United States government take sides with no other nation. The government of the United States should now use its increased defense spending to fund global information systems. The United States government should provide real-time information flow to all nations with the intent of eliminating the possibility of surprise attack from any potential armed aggressor.

A090   Verification to the rescue

Military service organizations are a national resource. Information coming from military-operated global monitoring systems should be used not only for the military purpose of detection and early warning but also for the civilian purpose of verification of international regulatory agreements.

Satellite telemetry and photography were given protected international legal status in the SALT (Strategic Arms Limitation Treaty) Agreements—the ABM (Anti-Ballistic Missile) Treaty and Interim Strategic Weapons Accord of 1972—the two superpowers formally acknowledged that National Technical Means (of verification) could not be interfered with.

Apart from that formal agreement, and entirely as a practical matter, Herbert Scoville, former Assistant Director of the Arms Control and Disarmament Agency, has argued that, in view of the recognition of international legality of intelligence-gathering techniques to obtain military information (it could be argued that all remote-sensing information collected by the United States government has military importance), high-secrecy classification that restricts access to military surveillance-reconnaissance information should now be removed.

So far as the American people themselves are concerned, there is nothing all that secret about the surface of the Earth as viewed from an Earth-orbiting satellite. The recording of traffic flow patterns, mappings of urban areas, and routine survey of land use can be obtained using other aerial monitoring. One might as well paint the street address, family name, and other relevant information on the roof top. Everything could then be in convenient view of an overhead observer.

All international regulatory activities that cannot be verified directly or indirectly by remote sensing, and reported to all concerned nations on a continuous basis, should now be rejected. Verification should be done by remote sensing or not at all. Verification by remote sensing is the only known verification technique that can pay for itself in the marketplace. Remote sensing creates an active electronic data base that can be made available to commercial users.

The American people no longer have confidence in newspaper reporting. And they no longer believe high government officials. The American people have been lied to too many times.

Remote sensing, as a technique, can be used for continuous monitoring of international agreements. Military (troop) movement and armament installations would all be publicized. The graphic display in the form of pattern in motion could provide a means for assimilating that information at a glance. Verification that comes from information transfer could be used to exert political pressure. It could be used to eliminate much of the (economic) need for armed aggression.

A091   Creating a wartime economy

The direct correlation between political power and government spending has been recognized since this country was founded. Staunch Federalists welcomed it, Republicans feared it, but both were painfully aware of its existence.

A wartime economy is an economy that is created when federal money arrives in the private sector at a rate that exceeds the natural elastic limit of the responsiveness of the existing industrial base. This deluge of money sweeps aside well-established barriers between industries and professional (academic) communities. Information is exchanged and ideas are rapidly implemented. A wartime economy puts the national needs ahead of those of the individual.

Today the power of excessive government spending is nowhere more evident than within the defense budget of the United States. But, even so, those defense dollars are not all alike. Some add, some multiply, and some dead-end as war potential.

Dollars spent for manpower tend to be additive, while dollars spent for weapons systems tend to dead-end as economic stagnation in the form of war potential. But dollars going into electronics industries and information services (the use of computers, communications, and remote sensing) will multiply. Because of the timely need to upgrade global monitoring capabilities, those electronic defense dollars are dollars that could be used to feed rapid economic growth.

When a closed decision making process is used to establish national spending priorities within the defense community, those priorities could well drift away from or conflict with the intent of the American people. Those spending priorities could fail to support the military mission To repel Invasions because that government spending was tied only to the political power of those responsible for the contracting. Those spending priorities could also fail to revitalize the national economy.

The alternative is for the United States Congress, especially the United States Senate, to establish national spending policies that are compatible with the ideals of the American people, to establish national spending priorities that are compatible with a national economic policy directed toward a common economic good.

Chapter B

The "Invisible" Government

It is difficult to take part in a process when you can't even find it

The pro-military mood of the country was evidenced by the 1980 election of Ronald Reagan for President. As Reagan arrived in the White House, so did his version of supply-side economics. Thus, Reaganomics in action could now be coupled with a public mood that favors increased defense spending.

The invisible government, the decision making process within the OMB (the Office of Management and Budget) responsible for establishing spending levels for the federal government, has been adjusting the budget with little sense of national purpose that the American people are able to perceive. Within the context of the budget process, David Stockman, Director of the OMB, talks only of decreased federal spending, where, in fact, he is tinkering with the definition of national purpose.

There is much to be said in favor of using defense spending as a driving force for national economic recovery. There is much to be lost by refusing it. The creation of a "wartime economy" could build an all-new industrial base for the nation. And that all-new industrial base could be built upon the use of information technology rather than the production of weapons systems.

Just as the demands for increased war production forced the automotive and aviation industries to combine during World

War II, increased defense spending could now pay the price for a shotgun wedding within the world of electronics. An odd foursome of reluctant industrial partners, the wedding of remote sensing, communications, microprocessors, and main-frame computers, could emerge. Such a change in spending priorities within the federal government would at least syn-chronize defense spending with economic growth.

B092   Fire the bookkeeper

The nation's bookkeeper is supposed to be counting the President's money and implementing the President's fiscal policies. He has no "business" regulating the flow of information.

Within the Executive Branch of the federal government, the OMB—the Executive office created by President Nixon from the Bureau of the Budget—is held accountable for coordina-tion of the president's budget. In turn, the president is held accountable for the performance of the national economy. (Ac-tually the state of the economy is very much dependent upon both fiscal policy and monetary supply. The president is respon-sible for fiscal policy. The Federal Reserve controls monetary supply. Therefore there is no way the president alone can be held accountable. The only single entity responsible of economic recovery is the Congress of the United States.)

During the closing days of the Carter Administration, the OMB was assigned still another responsibility. The OMB was legislated the responsibility to manage information resources of the federal government. To implement the new legislation— the Paperwork Reduction Act was signed into law by Presi-dent Carter on Thursday, December 11, 1980—the OMB was to consolidate the currently fragmented information policy responsibilities of the nation into a newly created Office of In-formation and Regulatory Affairs.

The United States Congress of 1980, the Democrat-dominated Congress of the Carter Administration, said the purpose of the new legislation was to remove serious deficiencies that then existed in the government regulation of information resources. Opponents of the Paperwork Reduction legislation immediately recognized (and voiced the opinion) that information related to national security should not be regulated by the OMB. That attempt to use the nation's bookkeeper as a manager of information resources was equated with a failure on the part of the United States Congress to realize the inherent dangers of using any single presidential Executive Office (or federal agency) as a clearing house for information resources.

Information is this nation's most perishable commodity. And it is the most valuable. Information is needed to mobilize the industry, the military, the citizens. And information is needed to sustain the cooperative aspects of free enterprise. Information is the essence of wealth. Information flow is the foundation upon which the survival of our democratic form of government now depends.

In more polite circles in Germany, a person heading an office for control of information resources—an office that would provide needed leadership and direction for information transfer—would be considered the Minister of Propaganda. In England, a person heading such an office would probably be considered lacking in sportsman like conduct. Today, in the United States, such a person is generally considered to be just some smart-alec trying to tell the rest of us what to do.

Any form of harassment over information flow could well be ignored by those internal to the federal government. Government employees tend to become overly protective of their right to exchange information. It is the citizen and, hence, the democratic process itself, that would suffer the loss. Citizen access to real-time (electronically recorded) government-initiated, government-sponsored data sets would be greatly restricted.

There is no reason for any single Executive Agency or Office of the President, and certainly not the OMB, to consolidate information resources into a strong central management office. This nation's bookkeeper should direct his attention to fiscal matters of the President. Information should be a national resource, available to all citizens and all industries alike.

B093   "Constitutional Dictatorship"

War powers, disguised as emergency powers, now concentrated in the hands of the President of the United States are sufficient to make the Chief Executive a military dictator.

When the Special Committee on National Emergencies and Delegated Powers—a special committee of the United States

Senate—began work in January 1973, there existed no basic study outlining the use of emergency powers in the United States "from the time of the Philadelphia Constitutional Convention to the present." That Special Senate Committee concluded that "delegated emergency powers," when taken collectively, would confer enough authority upon the President of the United States that he could rule this country without reference to normal constitutional process.

While occasions may arise when the President "must exert a broad discretion in meeting special emergencies for which the legislative power has provided no relief and/or existing law (a prerogative not limited to wartime or even to situations of emergency) that decision to terminate a constitutional dictatorship, like the decision to institute one, should never be in the hands of the man who constitutes the dictator."

In spite of existing Congressional concerns for constitutional dictatorship, President Carter was able to carry forward even further the institutionalization of emergency powers for the president. President Carter created the **F**ederal **E**mergency **M**anagement **A**gency, known as FEMA.

One justification for the excessive concentration of emergency power in the hands of the President comes from the "take care" clause in the constitution: the President of the United States "shall take Care that the Laws be faithfully executed (Article II, Section 3)." But with modern communication-information transfer capabilities, the necessity for such a distorted constitutional interpretation of presidential power as now exists could be challenged.

Citizens of the United States who are seriously interested to regain control of their own government should now start with a review of emergency powers of the president. Emergency powers are legislative. Emergency powers by their very nature, are like war powers, they negate existing laws so the common good of the nation can take precedence over the rights of individuals. Emergency powers replace existing guidelines with new emergency provisions.

The power to declare a national emergency, like the power to use military force (or the power to order the use of nuclear weapons), must be taken from the president. Emergency powers are but war powers in disguise. Emergency powers, like war powers, belong to the Congress.

B094 America First

The purpose of national readiness is to insure a coordinated civilian-military response in time of national emergency. That emergency could be a short-term need to provide relief for a natural disaster; it could be a long-term need to shift industrial priorities.

In 1939, more than two years before the declaration of the Second World War, isolationists were everywhere in the United States. Charles A. Lindbergh, the "most idolized figure of the first half of the century," spoke out against any form of American military intervention in Europe.

In concert with that appeal of Lindbergh, Father Charles E. Coughlin, the Radio Priest of the time, "declaimed against the President of the United States Franklin Delano Roosevelt, The New Deal, the possibility of military intervention, and the machinations of the international bankers (in the lexicon of Father Coughlin, international bankers and international Jewry were synonymous)." Yet, those America First isolationist fought a losing battle.

On September 8, 1939, President Roosevelt declared a limited state of national emergency. Of his own authority, as President of the United States, as Commander-in-Chief of the American military, President Roosevelt declared a "limited" state of national emergency. Later, on May 27, 1941 (more than six months prior to the December 7, Japanese surprise bombing of Pearl Harbor, Hawaii), of his own authority, President Roosevelt removed all limits from that limited state of national emergency.

In 1939, President Roosevelt also asked for and received from the United States Congress, an appropriation of $552 million "to shore up America's badly sagging national defense posture." On October 29, 1940, the first peacetime military draft in the history of the nation began.

An aging Henry Ford spoke out against the possibility of war and any possibility of American military intervention in Europe. The Automobile Manufacturers Association went on record with a formal declaration that opposed American intervention: "on the basis that peace for all civilized people dictates that industry's concern should be in keeping this country out of the war in Europe, and that the interests of the automobile industry are unmistakably linked to peace."

In 1940, President Roosevelt asked for, and received from the United States Congress, an appropriation of $1,182,000,000.00 for defense. The United States industrial base was to be immediately converted to munitions. The United States was to become the *Arsenal of Democracy* for the entire world.

Those same tell-tale signs surround us today. Tax dollars are being spent to keep America First. Yet there is the question: should those tax dollars in an ever-growing defense budget be spent for electronics and global monitoring—should those tax dollars in the defense budget be spent for detection and early warning systems, or should those tax dollars in the defense budget be spent for the production of weapons of destruction? Should American tax dollars in the defense budget be spent to sustain an old industrial base dependent upon the production of munitions, or should the information era of the future take precedence?

Tax dollars in the defense budget spent for electronics would keep America First in defense. Tax dollars in the defense budget spent for electronics would also help build the foundation for future economic prosperity.

B095   Emergency response

A national emergency is a time when the common good of the nation takes precedence over the rights and interests of individuals.

The willingness of the people in the United States to respond to a national emergency is stored as human potential. The effectiveness of that human potential can be roughly equated with the patriotic mood of the country. Yet that national response is collective. It is a willingness of the nation to respond to the unexpected while maintaining a sense of common good. And that willingness of the whole is a group property, it is not a property that belongs to any particular individual. That is to say, the patriotic mood or national willingness is a condition that must exist ahead of time; it must be held in reserve as human potential. It is the collective willingness that belongs to the whole.

Emergency preparedness is something that has to happen ahead of time. Emergency preparedness can store human potential and it can store industrial potential. Emergency responsiveness is then the release of that stored potential. Emergency responsiveness is a coordinated effort that happens at the time of the emergency.

Military service organizations (and other national, state, or local service organizations), because they are prepared ahead of time, can release human potential at the time of an emergency. Only with adequate preparation ahead of time, and a patriotic mood to sustain it, can human potential (and industrial potential) be released and utilized in time of national emergency.

B096   Military-industrial divorce

Shifting the national industrial base from munitions to electronics goes beyond mere military preparedness. The industrial base of the nations must support national defense policy; it must also support national information policy.

The diversity of industrial activities now being coordinated within the civilian administered Department of Defense is enormous. There are 19 assistant secretaries. The Department of Health and Human Resources, the only government agency with a larger budget than Defense (Social Security is included in the Department of Health and Human Resources) is able to make do with only seven.

Even so, the Reagan Administration requested legislation that would create still five more positions for Assistant Secretaries of Defense. And that request for five, when reviewed by the House Armed Services Committee, was recommended for increase to six. Much of that diversity within the Department of Defense has, however, absolutely nothing to do with preparedness or responsiveness of military service organizations. Rather it has to do with the coordination of the nation's industrial base.

The large civilian contingency within the Department of Defense devoted to the management of the industrial base of the nation could be transferred to Federal Emergency Management Agency. Such a move would separate military preparedness from industrial preparedness and it would allow the industrial needs to be assessed in the broader context of national economic prosperity.

The American people in their demonstrations against nuclear weapons appear to be demanding such a separation. They appear to be demanding that national economic policy become more compatible with national purpose, that national industrial capabilities become separated from their present dependence on weapons production.

Military service organizations, left at the Pentagon, would make up a Department of Military Affairs. The needs of the military could then be assessed as needs for national service organizations. Such a change in the Department of Defense would remove (or at least shield) service organizations from the technology push of the weapons industries.

A user-oriented demand pull could alter spending priorities in the defense budget. In the case of a Department of Military Affairs, the buyer would actually be the person responsible for the use and the performance of the equipment.

The characteristics of the Sun and the American people were compared in the *Story of the U.S. Constitution.* Both were viewed as central to a system of coordinated motion; the Sun as the center of attraction for the solar system, the American people as the center of the force field of public opinion. And just as the limits of the powers of the Sun are not known to man, the limits of the powers of the American people are not known to public officials.

Reasons for the attractive force of the Sun remain hidden by physical nature. Reasons for the cohesiveness of a collective response from the American people remain hidden by human nature. Yet when the people decide to reorganize the Department of Defense, there will be nothing hidden about the decision making process.

The grounds for the military-industrial divorce will be prolonged national economic cruelty. The American people will act as both judge and jury. And neither the military nor the industry will be able to defend its past actions. The verdict will be guilty of economic stagnation. Testimony will reveal a prevailing passion for the concentration of industrial power in the hands of a select few.

National Weather Service

Money may talk but information has a lot more to say

Remote sensing data sets—pictures of the surface of the land, recordings of ocean temperature, measurements of weather-related atmospheric parameters—all are "raw material" from which "computer products" can be manufactured by information industries in the private sector. And the availability of that information could give a boost to the industrial transition and to economic recovery.

The National Weather Service is buried within the doldrums of the calcified career-oriented middle-management of NOAA (the **N**ational **O**ceanic and **A**tmospheric **Ad**ministration), a federal agency that, in turn, crawls around on its hands and knees to remain lower than the low profile of its parent organization, the Department of Commerce. The National Weather Service of the United States is the weather service of the most technologically advanced nation in the word, yet it has now hung onto its own "primitive" techniques for routine data handling long enough to hang itself.

The National Weather Service is the national service organization within the federal government responsible for collecting and disseminating remote sensing (weather) information. In the future, "public" libraries could well become electronic information resource centers where users of weather information could gain 'round the clock access to government collected digital data sets. One way for the American taxpayers to receive reasonable return for their tax dollars would be to combine the National Weather Service and the military weather service capabilities for routine data collection.

The U.S. Congress could combine the military-civilian service capabilities for detection and early warning of natural and man-made disaster. And this information would remain in the public domain where all information industries in the private sector would have access to it.

C097   "Born classified"

When you are no longer officially authorized to listen to yourself talk, then you are born classified.

Along with the growth of technological know-how since World War II, has come an ever-increasing effort on the part of the federal government to strangle the flow of information within the scientific community. Scientists in the generation that pioneered the development and use of remote sensing, computer technology, and satellite communications in the late 1950s and the early 1960s, now know more about military hardware capabilities than the military user will ever know. And those scientists, engineers, and technicians—they number in the thousands—are all expected to refuse to discuss much of the work they have done. They are so-called born classified.

Many of those senior scientists have migrated into related disciplines. They permeate all walks of life. And they either live in or visit essentially all foreign countries of the world. The absurdity of the situation becomes even more ridiculous when one realizes that all of this classification of so-called sensitive information applies only to the American scientists. There has never been an equivalent secrecy demand placed upon members of the research community in the European NATO countries.

Many existing U.S. restrictions on the exchange of information appear to have been motivated by the competitive aspect of government (defense) spending. There was certainly the desire within the scientific community to protect poor quality research, the compulsion to conceal the development of automation that was found to have no practical utility (it was too sensitive to meet even minimum operational requirements once installed at a field station, outside the sterile environment of the research laboratory), and the fear of revealing the pursuit of meaningless, unwarranted precision in the development of remote sensing equipment.

The irony of it all is that restrictions on information flow within the scientific community have always been justified in the name of national security. Yet no one has ever been able to explain to me the value of a political barrier to information exchange at the research level and, in particular, what that barrier could or should contribute to the security of this nation.

It would seem to me that the federal government would do better to concern itself with positive, rather than negative, goals for communication. The advantages to be gained by the transfer of knowledge in the scientific community appear to be far greater than those that can be lost by its prevention. After all, scientists, by the tine they leave graduate school, have already perfected their own inability to communicate. And that communication failure has been demonstrated time and time again to be detrimental not only to the outside world but also to the scientific community as well.

C098   The basic waste of basic research

When results from "basic" research are published in a scientific journal, those results dead-end in a bound volume in the Library of the Congress. It is like plowing under the fall harvest, research results make for fertile soil only within that plot of political turf called an academic discipline.

Atmospheric monitoring was first accomplished using American scientific satellites during the IGY (International Geophysical Year). Starting with the successful January 31, 1958, launch of an Explorer satellite most monitoring of the upper atmosphere, including measurements of magnetic field strength and electron density distribution, were done within the confines of the research community.

Observational data from the Explorer satellites were made available primarily to scientists in the program areas where the research had been initially funded. Observational data were not made available to operational service organizations, forecast centers within government agencies, or information industries in the private sector. No one was trained to use these data. And nothing was transferred into the realm of routine operations to upgrade service capabilities.

As more and more scientists moved into the arena of atmospheric physics, each would design and build a new piece of equipment to make a new kind of measurement. Many of the original scientific disciplines disappeared as new ones were created. Atmospheric physics became the training ground for the initiation of senior scientists to the use of satellite information systems. There were as many new disciplines in atmospheric physics as there were senior scientists to claim them.

Yet, after 25 years of basic research, atmospheric scientists have only one thing in common: all researchers are one time users of observational data. One-of-a-kind instrumentation is the name of the game, and the American taxpayers are expected to pay the bill.

There is always more and more research, and there is always more and more development. But utility is neglected. There is still no money for anyone to use the information that has been gathered. Observational data are used only once or, in the event of poor calibration, low resolution, or faulty software, not at all.

The publish or perish syndrome within the scientific community has exaggerated this basic waste of basic research. One-time users of data are the rule not the exception. Career-related promotions are still based on the number of publications, not upon the ability of a scientist to use (or tell someone else how to use) research results. And service-related duties such as weather forecasting continue to be neglected.

Both military- and civilian-operated Earth-orbiting satellites provide myriads of information to ground stations. But communication links for the transfer of those data to operational forecast or information centers are grossly inadequate. Not only are new data sets not being transferred to potential users, potential users (meteorologists at weather stations would be one example) are not even being trained to interpret these new types of data.

Information users, military and civilian alike, are being handed a sack of wheat for breakfast. One would have hoped that a hungry user would at least have been given a slice of bread and a toaster.

Tax dollars continue to be wasted to gather information for one-time users. And research results continue to dead-end in scientific journals. The basic waste in basic research fertilizes only the growth of more basic waste in more basic research. The entire process is self-serving, not nation- or civil-serving.

C099 Research with a purpose

Research devoted to improved understanding of the fundamental laws of nature is basic research. When that research is funded by tax dollars it can and should be supportive of national needs.

In the 1950s, the research done by scientists at the Central Radio Propagation Laboratory at the National Bureau of Standards, Department of Commerce, Boulder, Colorado, was related to ionospheric forecasting, radio wave propagation, and the measurement of electron density in the ionized portion of the Earth's upper atmosphere. The immediate application was radio communication, satellite communication, and remote sensing—everything had to be extended to global coverage, for all variations of atmospheric conditions.

Most of the early research in ionospheric physics was basic research. The research improved our basic understanding of atmospheric physics, atmospheric chemistry, or natural resonant oscillation behavior of the medium itself. And those results were immediately available for improved forecast services.

Those Boulder Laboratories were then re-organized. They were re-organized at least three times during the 1960s and 1970s. Eventually the atmospheric research responsibilities were organized into the several laboratories of the Environmental Research Laboratories of NOAA (the National Oceanic and Atmospheric Administration). In spite of various Congressional attempts to remedy the situation, the legislative base that would have defined the purpose of those research laboratories, and also the purpose and responsibilities of the satellite monitoring services and the weather forecasting services within NOAA, has still not been written. The NOAA mission remains as cloudy as much of the weather the service organizations are supposed to be forecasting.

Much of the atmospheric research of NOAA fails to support the operational needs of the NOAA service organization. Other service organizations in other Departments, such as the Forest Service or the Park Service within the Department of Interior, are also not supported. The NOAA mission, including the national responsibility to prevent loss of life and property in the event of natural disaster, is in need of a new Congressional mandate.

The NOAA mission should be stated in a language any layperson can understand. Legislative gobbledygook tacked onto an authorization bill is a poor substitute for comprehensive, concise statements of services to be provided in return for tax dollars received.

The NOAA mission should be implemented within the specific guidelines that respect up-to-date economic and political needs of the country. But the information collected by the service organizations should be managed so the information industries in the private sector will have immediate electronic access to the data sets.

Information collected by national service organizations belongs in the public domain. Everyone is entitled to have equal opportunity to access that information through federally funded computer-information transfer networks. But the networks have to be designed to carry the work-load (the throughput) of continuous data flow from global monitoring. This information transfer capability has to be not only nationalized (the information has to remain in the public domain) but also democratized (everyone has to have equal opportunity for access to the information networks).

Scientists who feel no sense of responsibility to provide information (or knowledge) to the private sector in return for federal money (especially when they openly admit and actively advocate an anti-service attitude) should be encouraged to seek their research funding from private foundations.

There is a place for everyone, but the place for anti-capitalistic, anti-democratic people is not the federal government of this country. Federally funded programs, including those that fund basic research, should be reserved for scientists with a sincere concern for the common economic good. Scientists receiving tax dollars should indeed become dedicated public servants.

C100   Getting the harvest to the market

The American people, especially information users in the private sector, do not appear to be able to get scientific knowledge or technological know-how out of the

political turf of federally funded laboratories. There
is only one solution—go get it.

Harvesting a crop of grain in the fall pre-supposes the existence of a support system far beyond the productive soil of
the farm. To harvest wheat takes heavy equipment for
threshing and heavy trucks for transporting. There has to be
a mill to grind the grain into flour and there has to be a system
of roads for delivery trucks to travel. There has to be a baker
and a candlestick maker. And there has to be a consumer.
Every link of the transfer chain depends upon the existence
of every other. In that chain, one man's finished product
becomes the next man's raw material.

To harvest research results, technological know-how, or
numerical (data) processing techniques for interpreting observational data sets also requires a transfer chain. And, as with
the harvesting of grain, one man's finished product must
become the next man's raw material. The only difference is
that information is far more perishable than grain. The transfer
of information has to happen much faster. To be exact, the
transfer of information has to happen at the speed of light, or
at the practical speed of electronic digital switching.

The people in this country have not yet been able to create
a transfer chain to get information and continuous data flow
out of the federal government. The scientists have not done
their share and the people have not bothered to recognize the
economic importance of the chain.

The transfer chain is, in fact, a multi-dimensional utility network that cannot be imposed or structured from the top down.
The transfer chain for information users will have to grow from
the roots of grass. The best the federal government can do, or
should do, is to provide a high quality fertilizer in the form
of technical assistance from the scientific community.

C101   The surface of the globe is no secret

On a cloudy day, you can see clouds. On a clear day,
the detectors on an Earth-orbiting satellite (whether
the satellite belongs to the United States or to some
other nation) can see the surface of the Earth below.

TV viewing audiences in the United States became aware
of the technical feasibility of the immediate transfer of the

satellite reconnaissance data by watching their nightly TV weather shows. Satellite pictures were flashed on the TV screen to display stationary cloud cover or a sequence of photographs were used to show progressive storm development. But on a clear day, pictures of the land or ocean could have been displayed on a much finer grind.

A satellite picture taken from a geostationary orbit (a geostationary satellite travels in a geosynchronous orbit 22,300 miles above the equator) is taken with a field of view that covers the complete latitude range of the continental United States. That view reaches even beyond the required Mexican border near 30°N to the Canadian border near 53°N. Pictures taken from a polar-orbiting satellite would have progressive access to all latitudes along the north-south path, but not all latitudes at the same time. In either case, a user of the pictures would have to survey the data to select local areas from which to recover detailed recordings.

At the present time, satellite pictures provided to the private sector are not positioned precisely enough on their true (geographic) latitude-longitude grid to even track a thunderstorm for radar ground-truth verification, let alone to identify military or civilian construction sites.

The list of practical inadequacies of routine data handling goes on and on. Technological know-how is there but the effort and money for utility are not being provided.

Government funding has been spent for research and development, for environmental studies, for pilot programs. Routine operational capabilities and routine information services are simply not yet available in a fashion that would encourage information industries in the private sector to electronically access these data sets to make their computer products.

It is no wonder there is an irrate public out there. The American people would like to know what is being provided them in return for their tax dollars. And rightly so. Every year the United States Congress funds the development or the production of hardware. But the benefit from the utility of that equipment never comes.

The surface of the globe is no secret. The potential for the American people to make money using real-time information flow is also no secret.

Information industries in the private sector appear ready to start using information available in the public domain. Information coming from military- and civilian-operated Earth-orbiting remote-sensing satellites could fill that void. And the quality of that information would in no way be diminished by having been accessed by a variety of users all at the same time.

C102   Pattern in motion

The hands of a clock provide a picture of the time of day and that picture can be recognized at a glance. The time of day displayed on the face of a clock is actually pattern in motion.

The National Weather Service is the only service organization in the federal government with a tradition of years of practical experience at handling operational observational data flow on a continuous basis. Twice a day, 7 days a week, week in and week out, the weather occurs and the National Weather Service produces weather charts.

Numerical (analysis) charts of winds, temperatures, heights of constant pressure surfaces—all describe atmospheric conditions from the surface of the Earth up to and even beyond the height of the jet stream. And those numerical data sets, when they are displayed as contours of horizontal wind fields or as standing wave patterns for vertical variations, describe atmospheric behavior at exactly the time of observation.

A weather chart is like a snapshot of the hands of the atmospheric clock. The pattern of the motion is fixed at exactly the instant of the photograph. The time rate of change for the motion of the hands of the atmospheric clock is, however, not always the same. That is to say, the hands of our own clock move at the same speed all the time. With that constant rate of change it is easy to anticipate a new pattern. The pattern that the hands will display 30 minutes later is already well known.

The only way to assimilate weather information, since the rate of change of the weather is **not** known, is to interpret the information itself as pattern in motion. That changing rate of the pattern then determines how often a picture must be taken. The weather pictures would have to be taken often enough to preserve the continuity of the pattern. Otherwise the user of the weather information would not be able to assimilate the information at a glance.

Data sets can be assimilated continuously when information is displayed as pattern in motion. But the pictures have to possess enough regularity that the human eye and the human mind could grasp their meaning.

C103   The vanity press

The "vanity press" of the United States Government is the Government Printing Office. The Government Printing Office can now provide electronic interface with the private sector and become a national resource at the same time.

Information is created every day within the federal government. Data sets are collected by military- and civilian-operated global monitoring systems. The spoken word (and the written word) is generated every day on Capitol Hill and in the Executive Offices. And that information is raw data. Those data need to be processed and sorted, they need to be organized and re-organized, they need to be cross-referenced and cross-referenced and cross-referenced, but above all else they have to be digitized into a computer language that is accepted as standard and easily read by the users. Those data are a valuable national resource. Those data are our new democracy in action.

The *Congressional Record* (the written record published by the United States Congress to provide an account of the activities taking place on the House and Senate floor) and the *Federal Register* (the written record published as a report of the activities of the President and other executive officials) are available in the traditional bound format. The paper resembles newsprint. The possibilities to access that information in digital format are, however, rather limited.

In 1979, during the Carter Administration review of the Government Printing Act, the broad question of the continuation of the Government Printing Office attracted little attention. At that time, the Senate Rules Committee overlooked much of the importance of electronic transfer as a means of providing government information to information industries and information resource centers in the private sector.

Library-style information resource centers could one day form the basis for an electronic interface between the federal government and the private sector. The vanity press of the federal government, and many of the traditional aspects of the Government Printing Office, could be replaced by electronic transfer. The American taxpayer would become not only the sponsor but also the user-consumer of that government printing service. The taxpayer would derive benefit from his investment.

The practical constraint on the transfer of information from the federal government into the private sector is that the information itself remain in the public domain. Everyone should have equal opportunity to access the data sets. Everyone should have equal opportunity under the law. No one, including the federal government can own that information.

Government generated information is potentially the most valuable national resource the American people have available to them. And that is what the First Amendment of the United States Constitution is intended to protect.

C104   The military-civilian work force

There is only one nation and there is only one work force. Whether the service is civil service or military service, it does not matter. National service is what the nation needs to pursue service dedicated to the common good.

Responsibilities for detection and early warning of man-made disaster (enemy invasion, terrorists activities, or accidental nuclear holocaust) appear to belong to the military. Responsibilities for detection and early warning of natural disaster (tornado, flash flood, or severe wind storms) appear to belong to the National Weather Service. For that reason, both service organizations already have operational requirements for global monitoring. Yet the coordination of the two has yet to be clearly mandated through the funding practices of the United States Congress.

Studies of emergency warning systems indicate that the monitoring capability should be national. And trained people who can work in an operational environment to respond to national needs should be distributed through all professions both in and out of the government services. Some would be reserve military or National Guard and some would be civilians qualified for emergency rescue operations. Some would be students and some would be retired professional people. Coordination of human resource would be the task at hand.

If civilian services in the United States were to take the lion's share of highly talented people, then the military would be left with the dregs. If the military service organizations were to attract the cream of the crop, then the private sector would suffer the loss. In either extreme, the American people and the common good of the nation would be the loser.

There is only one nation. And there is only one work force. Everyone has to share the human resources, the natural resources, and the money. Yet everyone should be provided the freedom to work to his or her full capacity. If the American people can get the American military out of the closet, and their own heads out of the sand, coordinated military-civilian service organizations could get information to flow through global monitoring systems.

Every citizen of the United States would serve for a definite time in government service but remain forever in reserve status as human potential. Every citizen would work with detection and early warning systems for the combined protection of the people, the property, and the natural environment. National service dedicated to the common good would become the natural dueling partner for the many competing special interests in the private sector.

The training of people is no small matter. The reluctance of industry is no small matter either. But the defense budget, with its increased level of spending, would be used to pay the price of that all-important transition. The alternative is to remain dependent upon the existing industrial base of munitions production. And that alternative is highly unattractive.

Both military- and civilian-government services could become cost effective if remote sensing information (and other government generated information) were to become a national resource. Information in the public domain, available to everyone in the private sector, is the national resource upon which the future of self-government could be built. It would be a reward worth every penny of tax money invested in the defense budget to make it happen.

PART FIVE

Perspective

Learn to love a snoop

*Blessed are the peacemakers, for they
shall be called into active duty
in time of national emergency*

*As defense spending goes, so goes
the economic prosperity
of this nation*

At the time of the First World War, it was suppose that one or maybe two people would need to work to support one fighting man in the United States military. By the time the nation was tooling up for the Second World War, it was estimated that 16 or 17 people would have to work full time to keep one combat soldier on the front lines. The American military had become that much more dependent upon sophisticated industrial support for its combat readiness.

The tragic delay for the industrial mobilization of the United States prior to World War II, the time it took for the American people and the American factories to convert to wartime production, the time it took for the American industry to meet the munitions demands of the allied nations—the time it took for the United States to become the *Arsenal of Democracy*— was evidenced to the entire world. Allied troops suffered heavy losses during the early days of the war. Disastrous effects of the industrial delay of the United States took their toll in every European country. Friendly or neutral nations were overrun by invading armies. There simply was no such thing as instant industrial response to instant industrial needs of a world at war.

Following the Second World War, common sense dictated, as 20/20 hindsight taught, the industrial giants of the world would never again be able to wait until the moment of aggressive action to build an industrial base to meet their wartime needs. The industries of the United States would never again have even that two years of time for industrial conversion. The United States would have to sustain an ever-ready warfighting capability. All resources of the nation would have to be committed to a peacetime effort to maintain combat readiness. The front lines of the next war would surely extend through every nation of the world, and the war would surely involve all peoples of every nation.

Thus, the question became not one of whether the American people, the American industry, and the American military should be prepared to fight a war, but rather which war??

American industries now receive tax dollars from the defense budget each year. And those tax dollars are appropriated by elected public officials, by elected members of the United States Congress. The truth is that the American people, through their own tax payments, through their own priorities for defense spending, through their own munitions production capabilities, have already created a continuing wartime economy. And it is that coordinated national effort, a grand combined effort of the people, the industry, and a strong central government, that shall one day be recognized as the miracle of modern democratic capitalism. It is that modern day miracle that has now set the stage as the precursor for **Perpetual Economic Prosperity.**

The American people now have to decide where they are going to establish their front lines of defense. They also have to decide if they are going to continue to fund the American military to wallow in its weakness, the threat of nuclear holocaust? If they are going to continue to hide behind the economic stagnation created by the false security of a balance of military power? If they are going to look backward in time—if they are going to use imperfect hindsight to try to rewrite an unpopular history? Or if the American people are ready to pursue an alternative?

Can the United States as a nation recognize that weapons of destruction were but a necessary evil during a time of industrial transition, that the destructiveness of the armed peace should be judged as a necessary forerunner for, but not an acceptable participant in, the era of **Natural Eternal War?** Can the American people let go of the past without insisting upon more human misery and more human suffering?

There is only one nation and there is only one work force. And that work force must now have the freedom to collect, process, and transfer information. Only with the freedom of information exchange can the national efforts of military, industry, and people be coordinated. Only with freedom of information exchange can creative bursts of political energy be directed toward stimulation of national economic growth within the confines of global environmental monitoring. Only with freedom of information exchange can government spending within the defense community rid itself of the burden of the consume-oriented, energy-intensive, waste-prone mentality of our munitions industries, a burden that has been endorsed, if not imposed, by our own United States Congress. Only with freedom of information exchange can the pursuit of American military action in the guise of combat readiness avoid destroying the very nation it was created to protect.

The American people have elected Ronald Reagan President and that vote for Reagan was also a vote for increased defense spending. That defense spending can now pay the price for a shotgun wedding between our communications and remote sensing industries. That defense spending can also pay the price for the use of imbedded computers for processing and transferring real-time data to individual users.

Industrial offspring have already been conceived in the private sector, but they will survive only when nourished by a continuous information flow from government-operated global monitoring systems. That continuous flow of information could be used to protect the safety of all nations of the world and it could become a national resource within our own country. Real-time information flow is the raw material from which the information industries in the private sector can manufacture their own computer products.

Perpetual Economic Prosperity is the future PEP of the nation. The American military, the American industry, and the American people should now be fighting the same war, and that war is eternal. It is an eternal information war. And the American military, the American industry, and the American people, through ever increasing use of human resource, should soon be able to create more for the national economy than they consume from the natural environment.

The days of national economic security are gone forever. The days of national economic opportunity are arriving. The strong will of the American people to pursue perpetual prosperity is the will of tomorrow. But that economic prosperity will be sustained only when the daily activities of the nation become "cost effective" according to economic standards soon to be imposed by the rule of the natural law.

The entire nation can support an all-new military mission and that mission can fulfill the valid constitutional mandate: To repel Invasions. The American military, along with an "army" of civil servants, can provide the work force required for global operational systems. The American people can take this opportunity to pay the price for a transition to an all-new industrial base. They can use that money to pay the price for continuous information flow, to fight the eternal electronic war of global environmental monitoring, to make Global Environmental Monitoring, the GEM of the future for all mankind.

Fundamental to the arrival of the NEW era of Natural Eternal War is INFORMATION POLITICS for the 1980s. This nation can either endorse freedom of information exchange or it can hide behind the security of the secret. But, for those who would care to notice, that is no choice at all. Theoretically the security of the secret disappeared 200 years ago when the people of this country decided in favor of democracy. In practice, the security of the secret disappeared 20 years ago with the arrival of the miniaturization of modern electronics.

The absence of continuous information flow can create nothing more than a false hope for economic security. There is no escape from the fear of failure that will always come from the threat of disturbing the stagnation of an artificially contrived, industrially motivated "balance" of military power. Whether the dynamic dueling partners are democracy and capitalism, equality and freedom, subjugation and liberty, or faith and reason, the American people themselves will have to initiate selective change so it becomes compatible with the ideals of their founding fathers. The American military and the American industry can then be given the responsibility to sustain that change until it can be transformed into an economic tradition for this nation.

Perpetual Economic Prosperity has to be carried forward by the dynamic dueling partners of evolution and creation. Though the two roles are uniquely different—long-term continuity can be refreshed only with creativity, and sporadic creativity can be focused only with the persistence of a guiding principle. Technological evolution and creative endeavor will have to interact to support this wave-particle dualism of human behavior.

The technology of man is now confronting the laws of Mother Nature. Since Mother Nature wrote the rule book long before man invented the technology, the last word will come from Her. The commitment of man is to conceive, communicate, and create, to act within the dictates of the laws of Mother Nature. The level of destruction of the natural environment will never exceed the limits imposed by those natural laws—at least not for very long or in a very large geographic area.

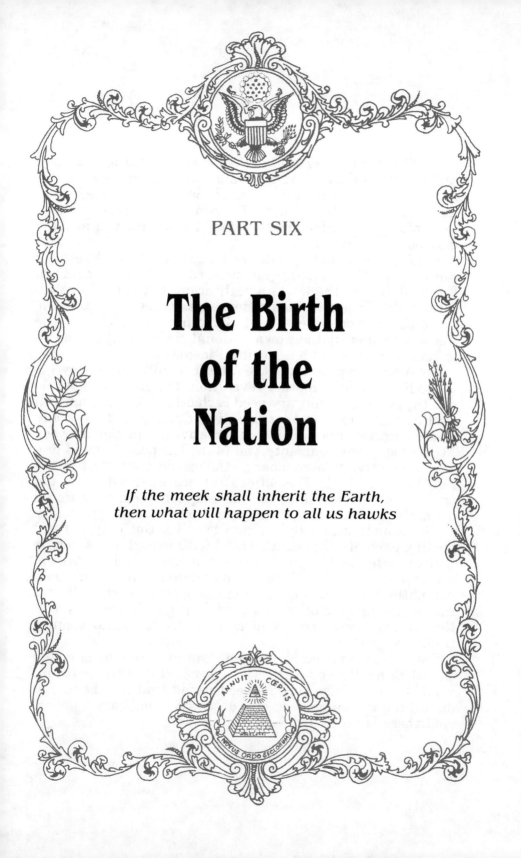

PART SIX

The Birth of the Nation

If the meek shall inherit the Earth,
then what will happen to all us hawks

The Pride of the Pentagon—the heart beat of the nation—a cadence for the living and a tribute to the dead—the male-dominated American military service organizations are inventing the future of this country. The American people will have to reinforce that effort or there may be no future, and there may be no country either.

In 1776 our founding fathers fought the First American Revolution; they fought for political independence from England. Slowly there was a realization that not only political but also economic independence was necessary if the people of this nation were going to have freedom of choice—the freedom to identify their own national goals and the freedom to retain their own high spiritual ideals.

The American people and the American military are now going to have to fight another revolution. The American people and the American military need each other; they are natural dueling partners. Together those two dueling partners could create a TEAM effort, an ongoing creative interaction between Technology, Environment, And Man. The people would provide innovative creative energy; the people would protect the rights of individuals. The national service organizations would provide the driving force for the common good; they would maintain the continuity, the rhythm, and the guiding principle.

Life is motion and this nation is alive. But only natural dueling partners can sustain that life. One partner cannot do it alone. Whether the partners are democracy and capitalism, war and peace, faith and reason, or science and religion, it does not matter. One is an energetic creative partner who initiates radical change; the other is a guiding principle that sustains that change long enough to carry it forward into popular tradition.

The forward interactive motion of natural dueling partners can sustain a living future. The absence of that living future would be but a false hope for security; it would be the fear of disturbing the stagnation of a destructive military balance. And there is no escape from such a fear.

Chapter A

The American Military Tradition

In the beginning, there was Heaven and Earth and the citizen-soldier

Talent nurtured in solitude, character formed by the stormy seas of daily living—those are the two qualities of the American male dedicated to military service. Without them, there would be no dedication and there would be no service.

As late as the 1700s, most wars were fought be mercenaries, serving in the armed forces merely for pay or sordid advantage. But in keeping with the spirit of self-government the early settlers of this nation created the citizen-soldier of Colonial times. And those citizen-soldiers created an American military tradition that ran contrary to centuries of brutality that had gone before.

Our forefathers possessed the courage of their convictions. They remained convinced that war should be fought by the people of the nation as a whole; that war should be fought and won for the common good of the nation, or not at all.

There may be a few feathers lost, and the body politic may be a little battered and bruised from the ruckus, but that materialistic war hawk should soon start to look an awful lot like an American Eagle.

That American Eagle will have to dispose of those arrows in its left talon and the olive branch in the right. The American Eagle will soon have to achieve not only the selectivity of the perch but also the harmony of the glide. Only with an American Eagle able to soar above the heavens will a truly citizen-sponsored, citizen-supported military service remain true to the ideals upon which this nation was founded.

A105   This job belongs to you

By the rude bridge that arched the flood,
Their flag to April's breeze unfurled,
Here once the embattled farmers stood,
And fired the shot heard round the world . . .

Ralph Waldo Emerson

This country began with a bang. The universe also began with a bang. One could almost suppose that nature, whether physical or human, needs a trigger to initiate action. But such an abrupt beginning must be followed by the persistence of evolution if that abrupt change is going to be sustained in the environment in which it was created.

The outstandingly positive feature of the citizen-soldier military tradition in this country is the contribution it has made to the spiritual quality of the individuals who comprise those service organizations. In that respect, the citizen-soldier tradition is the only military tradition that can survive in a democratic society. It is the only military tradition where the citizens and the soldiers are one.

A short term service commitment belongs to you. And it belongs to me. Every citizen must become a soldier and every soldier must be a citizen. Otherwise there can be no honor in the military tradition and there can be no democracy to guide it.

The laws of nature appear to dictate a trigger response. The laws of nature also appear to dictate a collective response of the whole if the whole is going to survive. That collective response is a service response and it is there for the purpose of preserving the common good.

A106   Aristocracy in democracy

"To annul the privilege of an aristocracy of wealth;
to make an opening for the aristocracy of virtue and
talent," that is what Thomas Jefferson wrote about

*the responsibility of the American people. There re-
mains only the question of the method one should use
to pursue it.*

The ideal soldier of early colonial times in Boston, a community with a religious history of Separatists (commonly called
Puritans), was the Minuteman. That citizen-soldier provided
his own arms, was practically without uniform, and was by
professional military standards of today, lacking in formal
training. He belonged to the great body of the population.
Above all else, the Minuteman of 1776 was not a class apart.

The Minuteman came forth in an emergency to fight with
all his will, but returned to his ordinary avocation the moment
the emergency had passed. "And, not infrequently, reserved
to himself the right to judge when that moment had arrived."

The antithesis of that Massachusetts version of the citizen-
soldier was the professional soldier of the Continental Army.
In many respects, the behavior of that professional soldier
resembled the aristocratic arrogant manner of the British Red
Coats. But such behavior characteristics were enthusiastically
endorsed by many early residents of the Colonies who remained
coupled to England through a lingering loyalty to the King.
Indeed it was the elitist attitude, patterned after the British
Red Coats, and the class distinction of the uniformed professional military of the King of England that was to carry over
to the career military of the Continental Army.

Today it is the early American version of the citizen-soldier,
the Minuteman Spirit of '76, that is being summoned. And that
citizen-soldier response could very well determine the future
of the common economic good of the nation.

A107   The individual and the common good

*There is a tendency for any institution to claim to of-
fer infallible advice on moral issues. The United States
government, in general, and the American military,
in particular, is no exception.*

The conflict that now exists between the Soviet Union and
the United States is often perceived as a philosophical conflict
between subjugation (rule by a minority) and liberty (rule by
the majority), as though one were right and the other wrong,

as though one were good and the other evil, as though the existence of one should or could, in some way, exclude the existence of the other.

On the contrary, when one believes in the fundamental laws of nature, as most physicists tend to do, then the fundamental aspects of human nature are everywhere the same. Apparent conflicts are also everywhere the same. Therefore, whether you live in the United States or in the Soviet Union, one would eventually hope to derive benefit from the dualism of liberty and subjugation. But the benefit would be derived only by adjusting the levels of subjugation (group slavery) and liberty (individual freedom) to meet the expectations of those involved.

In the United States, because there is a popular government and because the American people themselves acknowledge it as such, there appears to be a more workable process for achieving political and economic adjustment—for maximizing both subjugation and liberty.

Democracy, as it functions in the Congress of the United States, certainly has to sacrifice efficiency but, in return, it guarantees maximum creativity and maximum freedom of thought. By contrast, the Executive must function through subjugation. The government agencies are elitist oriented and they are more efficient. The pyramid-style command structure within the Executive functions as a form of minority rule.

Nevertheless, that popular government of the United States does have to achieve incredible strength. It has to have a strength compatible not only with the military force it has created but also with the will of the individuals it represents. And, by any standard one would ever hope to use, that is awesome.

The point at which individual liberty and human judgement should yield to subjugation and dedication to the common good is an ever changing adjustable point. Those in the United States military should feel compelled to re-examine their own willingness to surrender responsibility for their own thoughts and their own actions to that particular institution. Every citizen should feel compelled to do the same with regard to the strong central government.

Subjugation of individuals to a strong central government, or to a strong military organization, is required if those individuals are going to be supportive the the common good. But blind obedience to a strong central authority is an outstandingly good way to foster tyranny. It is the profound responsibility of every American citizen to distinguish and to interrelate subjugation and liberty. It is imperative for both to function at maximum capacity.

A108   Professionalism

Given a choice in military matters, the citizens of the United States still seem to prefer to rely upon patriotic enthusiasm rather than a professional army in time of national emergency.

Members of the Continental Congress and the Constitutional Convention opposed a standing army. Prejudice against professional military was, without doubt, one of the strongest rooted prejudices of the Anglo-Saxon people. And, for the most part, the American people still view too much discipline and too much organization with great skepticism.

"The man who enjoys marching in line and file to the strains of music falls below my contempt; he received his great brain by mistake . . . the spinal cord would have been amply sufficient," said Albert Einstein. But Einstein was a German-born transplant to the United States with no appreciation for the inherent spiritual quality of the American military or for the sense of patriotism of the American male in the uniformed services of this country.

Einstein had failed to make any distinction between service for the common good and destruction for the sake of conquest (or conquest for the sake of conquest). Einstein appears to have thought of war, much the same as many think of sex. He was unwilling to make a distinction of quality.

The patriotic American is a totally unique human species. He cannot conceive of war without a moral battleground. In his mind, if the American military should ever do anything immoral, it is because the American people themselves are immoral. The American people and the American military are really one because the citizens and the soldiers of the nation are the same. That is what patriotism in this country is all about.

In spite of what Rheinhold Niebuhr had to say to the contrary in the title of his book *Moral Man and Immoral Society,*

this country is now and it always has been "Moral Man and
Moral Society." Should that equivalence between man and his
society cease to exist, then one could no longer speak of
self-government and the rights of individuals; one would no
longer be able to refer to the government of the United States
as a democracy.

Chapter B

Unity of the Nation

**The unity of the nation will be assured
when the people pursue
perpetual economic prosperity**

"The doctrine of self-government is right, it is absolutely and eternally right." I come to the people of this nation seeking a force far more powerful than the force of law and far more powerful than the force of military destruction, I seek the force of public opinion.

In a democracy, the force of public opinion is the only force that can sustain economic prosperity. And it is the attitude with which that prosperity is achieved that, in turn, provides a sense of common purpose. But that force of public opinion should in no way be construed to mean common political consensus. Political consensus should now be equated with mob rule and, therefore, rejected.

Contained within the collective response of the people of this nation is a wisdom and a strength that is available from no other source. In its entirety that response is created by the mood of the people. And that mood can create or it can destroy economic prosperity. That mood can determine the extent to which the people are willing to subjugate themselves to the common good of a strong central government, to accept the uniqueness of national identity, to use the political process to pursue a national policy of economic independence.

The mood of the people eventually determines the political and the economic fate of the nation. The mood of the people also determines the cohesiveness of the collective response of the nation. It is that cohesiveness in the collective response that one calls unity.

B109   The Spirit of the Constitution

The genius of those who drafted the American Constitution was that they were realists, and did not over-idealize their American countrymen . . .

By accepting the laws of nature and the practices of states as had gone before, writers and scholars known as the Grotians (taken from the name of Grotius (1583-1645), the father of international law) brought into being the fundamental concepts of natural law for human behavior.

The most famous of the Grotians were the German mathematician and philosopher Christian Wolff (1679-1754) and the Swiss diplomat Emmerich de Vattel (1711-1767), who popularized Wolff's ideas in his *Droit des Gens* in 1758. That book, more than any other, influenced the thoughts and actions of our forefathers as they formulated the American style of self-government during and after the American Revolution.

Following the revolution, the Articles of Confederation was the agreement under which the 13 original Colonies established a government of States, effective March 1, 1781. Those Articles served in an unsatisfactory fashion as the basic law of the new nation until the Constitution of the United States was written and then ratified in 1789.

When our founding fathers conceived and wrote the Constitution they codified for the entire world a new philosophy of popular government. No people had ever before turned more completely away from their own political heritage. No people had ever before gone so far in trusting their own ability to govern themselves. No people had ever before had enough faith in themselves to assume responsibility for their own destiny. This American style of self-government was the first of its kind.

Any violation of the Spirit of the written constitution, any threat of full-scale destruction of that Supreme Law of the Land, would strike at the heart of the nation. It would contradict the ideals upon which this nation was founded. It would be enough to return the people to revolution.

The American people have grown fond of the idea of contributing to their own destiny and the destiny of their nation.

The written version of the United States Constitution should stand forever. It is the working interpretation that should be continually revised.

B110   A strong central government

The strength of this nation, as a nation, is determined by the strength of the central government that the people themselves have created.

One of a group of French author-philosophers, Charles de Secondat Montesquieu (1689-1755) wrote *The Spirit of the Laws,* a study of various forms of government that had appeared in history. In that extensive work, Montesquieu concluded that political freedom could be maintained only by separating the Executive, Legislative, and Judicial powers of government.

Following Montesquieu's conclusions requiring the separation of powers, those three powers are lodged in separate bodies in the central government of the United States. No uncontrolled power is lodged in any one. The powers and the duties compel each of the three branches of government to check and balance the other two. It is for that reason that the written Constitution of the United States remains paramount to any particular Legislative, Executive, or Judicial authority.

The system of central government of the United States, as codified by the written Constitution, appears to be the strongest form of popular government that could have been created. In its present for, it remains in constant flirtation with tyranny, yet it retains the humility and the popular support of the people. In its present form, the system of central government of the United States follows the laws of nature.

The system of central government of the United States is unique because it was created to exist alongside the government of the several states. The two systems (the State government and the central government) overlap, each having authority in some areas but not in others. Yet no State or group of States shall ever become judge and jury for the Union. The Union created the States; the Union of the several States shall remain supreme.

Though Montesquieu was against violence, he did believe that reform of government would come about if the people were but given knowledge and truth. It was Montesquieu and other writers of that group, however, who stirred the French people to Revolution in 1789.

No one needs to wonder what the American people will do when they are but given knowledge and truth. The American people will retain their system of self-government. The roots of self-government have grown into the bedrock of this nation. And there they shall remain.

B111   The Gettysburg Address

Following the Civil War, Abraham Lincoln recognized the need to restore human dignity to the people in order to create a source of vitality within the nation. The true genius of Abraham Lincoln is displayed in his Gettysburg Address.

Gettysburg was the scene of the decisive battle between Union and Confederate armed forces on July 1, 2, and 3, 1863. A memorial now stands there. It marks the northernmost point reached by General Robert E. Lee's Confederate Armies as they fought against the Union Forces.

On November 19, 1863, at that site of the Battle of Gettysburg in the State of Pennsylvania, Abraham Lincoln delivered a short address. His purpose was to dedicate a portion of that battlefield as a national cemetery for those who had lost their lives there.

That Gettysburg Address is simple—*Four score and seven years ago, Our Fathers brought forth upon this continent, a new nation, conceived in liberty, and dedicated to the proposition that all men are created equal*—the complete Address contains only 267 words, in ten sentences, yet time has made it the most popular statement of our national purpose ever written. The Gettysburg Address concludes:

> It is rather for us to be here dedicated to the
>   great task remaining before us—
> That from these honored dead we take increased devotion,
>   to the cause for which they gave the last
>   full measure of devotion—
> That we here highly resolve that these dead shall
>   not have died in vain—
> That this nation, under God, shall have a new
>   birth of freedom—
> And that government of the people, by the people,
>   for the people, shall not perish from this earth.

The Gettysburg Address is a profound statement of faith in the process of self-government. It is also an expression of deep belief in the people who were to sustain that government.

The Lincoln memorial now stands in Washington, D.C., and it shall stand there for many years to come. But the true memorial to Abraham Lincoln, and to the unity of this nation, lives in the hearts of men. And there it shall live for all eternity.

B112 The more perfect Union

I do not expect the house to fall. But I do expect it will cease to be divided. It cannot remain half slave and half free; it will become one thing or it will become the other.

The most controversial speech Abraham Lincoln ever delivered was A House Divided Against Itself Cannot Stand. Lincoln was opposed to slavery. But, more than that, Lincoln was dedicated to the preservation of the Union.

When the southern States banded together to form the Confederacy, a group of States within the Union of the several States, Abraham Lincoln was convinced that the southern Confederacy had violated the Supreme Law of the Land, that the southern Confederacy had violated the intent of the written Constitution.

The fundamental issue of constitutional interpretation settled by the Civil War was the unconstitutionality of any of the several States entering into a binding agreement with another. That is to say, the formation of any regional coalition, for the purpose of trade, service, or banking practices, is a blatant violation of the supreme authority of the central government.

The unique differences of the several states, and the unique differences of the special interests of their citizens, must be acknowledged, respected, and strengthened. The survival and the viability of the many different needs and many different desires of the may different states is inherent in the complexity that comes with a more advanced society. It would be a dreadful mistake to seek or to try to force national unity through conformity. There could be nothing more destructive to the vitality of the Union than to try to impose the uniformity of political consensus.

The survival of a complex society such as our own has to do with self-sufficiency and diversity. The government of the people, by the people, for the people will not "divide against itself''when the people seek unity through common economic good.

The more perfect Union will become even more perfect when a democratic type of capitalism creates the cohesiveness of perpetual economic prosperity. And that cohesiveness has to do with the mood of the people. The mood of each and every person, the integrity and the determination of every individual. There is no substitute—the collective interactive response of the people makes the mood of the country. It makes the Union.

Chapter C

The Power of the President

The fine art of attaching
undreamed of importance
to well known truths

The doing of the nation appears tied to the ability of the people to achieve freedom from fear the freedom from want. The thinking of the nation appears tied to the ability of the people to actively pursue freedom of speech and freedom of worship.

In the past, the doing of the American people appears to have dominated the thinking. In the future, the thinking could well play a far more important role. As the thinking increases, it will be the combined thinking and doing that will generate a positive mood for this country. As the people themselves combine their thinking and doing, the purpose of the federal government will emerge as the carrier of the common economic good, as the dynamic force for perpetual economic prosperity. The President will then become the spokesman for that common economic good.

The President of the United States has officially threatened the use of nuclear weapons as a deterrent for nuclear war. Such a threat of destruction is an attempt to use fear as a means of motivating human action. But such fear-motivated response is fast losing its credibility.

Fear admits no hope of prosperity. Fear has opened the way for any advocate of armaments to appear valiant. Fear can nourish itself only when it can feed on human misery.

The power of the President of the United States lies in his ability to motivate the American people with a far more powerful weapon, the weapon of truth. The President of the United States has the freedom to attach undreamed of importance to well-known truths. The President of the United States has the freedom to use truth to stimulate human emotion for the purpose of motivating human action. The President of the United States has the freedom to use truth, the only weapon against which there is no known defense.

C113   That fragile line of presidential succession

Immediately following the March 30, 1981, assassination attempt on the life of President Reagan, the American people were made publicly aware of the fragile line of Presidential succession and the ambiguity it presents.

"In case of the Removal of the President from Office, or of his Death, Resignation or Inability to discharge the Powers and Duties of the said Office, the same shall devolve on the Vice President, and the Congress may by Law provide for the Case of Removal, Death, Resignation or Inability, both of the President and Vice President, and such Officer shall act accordingly, until the Disability be removed, or a President shall be elected." The Constitution of the United States makes it sound so simple, yet the past 200 years of practical experience has made presidential succession so complicated as to be incomprehensible by the American people.

An order of precedence, established in the Executive Branch of the Federal Government at the time of the writing of the Constitution, places the Secretary of State as the highest ranking Officer following the President and the Vice President. In spite of that order of precedence, the Succession Act of 1792 designated both the President pro tempore of the Senate and the Speaker of the House ahead of the Secretary of State in the line of succession. Both members of the Congress were, however, designated only to become Acting President, not President, and then only until a new President could be elected.

In an apparent contradiction to that Succession Act, the strict interpretation of the Constitution of the United States is very definite; a member of the Legislative cannot be an Officer in the Executive. The rationale for that interpretation follows from the Constitutional provision for the separation of powers of the three branches of the federal government. Thus, the subtle, but nonetheless significant, reason the Speaker of the House or the President pro tempore of the Senate cannot act as the President of the United States has to do with their affiliation with the Legislative. A member of the Congress would have to resign before assuming the Duties of the President.

Even though resignation from Congress could take place in an instant and leave a member free for appointment to the Executive, there would arise the question of the wisdom of such action. The Speaker of the House of Representatives is a key position in the Congress and, indeed, in the central government of this country. It might seem unwise to request his resignation for a temporary assignment to the White House, especially in time of national emergency.

The authors of the Succession Act of 1792 were apparently of the mood to try to divide the Duties and the Powers of the President, with the Powers going to the Congress, the Duties to the Secretary of State. In fact, the Duties that were to devolve on the Secretary of State were described in great detail. The Succession Act of 1886 made it equally clear that the Secretary of State would carry the continuity at the White House, namely the continuity for the Executive Branch of the federal government.

Following the assassination attempt on the life of President Reagan, with the eyes of the world on Washington, D.C., Secretary of State Alexander Meigs Haig, Jr., stepped before TV cameras to assure an anxious viewing audience, "As of now, I am in control here in the White House, pending return of the Vice President" Haig went on to state publicly, "Constitutionally you have the President, the Vice President, and the Secretary of State, in that order."

The Secretary of State not only said what he meant, he meant what he said. The Secretary of State is the only Officer in the Executive who can assume both the Duties and the Powers of the President, in the absence of both the President and the Vice President, and survive the challenge of the Supreme Law of the Land.

The confusion both perceived and propagated by the news media following the assassination attempt on the life of President Reagan is totally unacceptable. That confusion borders on insanity. That line of presidential succession carries with it—somewhere—in limbo—the authority of the Commander-in-Chief of the American military, the delegated authority to order the use of nuclear weapons.

It would seem the time has come for the American people to remove the ambiguity in the line of presidential succession, the ambiguity in the authority to order nuclear holocaust.

C114   Freedom from fear

"The only thing we have to fear is fear itself," declared Franklin Delano Roosevelt on March 4, 1933, in his first inaugural address [the inauguration of 1933 was the last inauguration of a President of the United States held in March].

Many Americans think of freedom as though it were an object, as though freedom were something to be used or ignored at their convenience, as though freedom were something that could exist in any environment. But conceptually, that is like saying, "I can breathe when or where ever I want to breathe." Try sitting at the bottom of a swimming pool under six feet of water. You could go through the motions of breathing but you would soon suffocate.

The breathing process requires not only an internal utility mechanism, but also an external source of oxygen. Being able to breathe pre-supposes an active internal respiratory system. It also presupposes an ongoing external supply of fresh air. Oxygen has to enter the lungs, it also has to pass into the blood stream and into body tissue.

The principle of the life-support system needed for breathing parallels that needed for freedom from fear. Freedom from fear depends greatly upon external pressure from the social atmosphere in which we live. It also depends upon an internal source of self-confidence and courage of individuals. Thus, both breathing and freedom from fear ultimately depend upon a composite of **external-internal interactive conditions,** and neither can have meaning without the other.

C115   Freedom from want

Freedom from want, like freedom from fear, is a from freedom. Both depend upon action-reaction responses and, when there is no freedom from them, both fear and want tend to immobilize rather than motivate human action.

Want, like fear, is basic to human existence. Whether it is hunger for food, thirst for water, or the seeking of shelter from a hostile environment, whether it is the want for it or the fear of not having it, it is critical to human survival. That is to say, a from freedom, whether it is want or fear, requires human want or human fear to exist before the striving to be free from it can be initiated.

A want of having material goods can be created entirely by externally imposed social conditions. The social conditions play on basic human instinct. The want of having or the fear of not having may come from hidden persuaders of commercial advertising and can take full advantage of basic human desire.

The consequence of striving to be free from want and of striving to be free from fear are the same. The fear or the want can be made to increase as fast, if not faster, than the striving. Freedom from is constrained by action-reaction response. The reaction is self-limiting and it is oppressive. The reaction, if it is truly a reaction, can do nothing more than match the action to which it is responding.

C116   Freedom of speech

There are from freedoms and there are of freedoms. The preposition makes the difference. The from is based on action-reaction, the of requires creative innovation.

Freedom of speech is a basic human need rooted in human existence. Speech exists because the human being exists. Yet that freedom of expression can be actively pursued only after the basic from needs of want and fear have been satisfied.

An of freedom requires a sense of individual responsibility and a sense of self-motivation. An of freedom is by its very nature an open ended creative process to be carried on within the guidelines imposed by the froms.

Freedom of expression can create or alter public opinion. Freedom of speech can stir men to pursue happiness. Freedom of speech can incite revolution. And, once initiated, freedom of speech and freedom of the press need only themselves upon which to feed.

Within the context of people interacting with people, freedom of speech is a very powerful freedom. It is the ability to communicate. Freedom of speech opens the door to creative non-violence.

The combined use of the from and the of prepositions is the transition that is now taking place in this country and, so it would seem, in other parts of the world as well. This transition of the prepositions appears to be a basic transition in human development. It is the transition that will allow individual independence yet encourage collective group behavior.

C117   Freedom of worship

Freedom of worship is fundamental to human existence. It is devotion to an idol and/or an ideal. It is the devotion that determines our daily action. Freedom of worship carries with it the key to the development of the human soul.

All people of all cultures throughout the history of civilization have shown devotion to something. They have also been involved in some sort of decision making process so they could retain their own peace of mind yet justify to themselves their own daily actions.

The question is not whether there is devotion or not, but rather devotion to what. There is also the very real consequence, how is that devotion reflected in the daily priorities for human activity.

In spite of the fact that early settlers in America came to the new world to escape religious persecution, most were reluctant to grant any form of religious liberty to others. They taught and they respected only the rigid ideology of their own particular Church and that ideology was often their own particular version of Christian reform outside the Roman Catholic Church.

The first attempt to legislate religious freedom in this country came with the Maryland Toleration Act of 1639. "No person or persons within this Province professing to believe in Jesus Christ shall henceforth be in any way troubled, molested, or discountenanced from, or in respect to, his or her religion, nor in free exercise thereof . . ." That legislation was not so much advocating freedom of religion as it was protecting the practice of Christianity in its broadest sense, a practice that would eventually have to include all Christian teachings.

In 1786, the State Convention of Virginia led the way to the adoption of freedom of religion as part of the Bill of Rights. The first of the ten amendments to be added to the body of the United States Constitution was eventually an amendment on religious freedom proposed by James Madison, the Father of the Constitution. The First Amendment: "Congress shall make no law respecting establishment of religion, or prohibiting the free exercise thereof . . ." was passed by the United States Congress on September 25, 1789, as part of that package of ten amendments identified as the Bill of Rights. Eleven States were necessary for the ratification of the Bill of Rights. Virginia became that eleventh State when she agreed to the amendments on December 15, 1791.

Those words for religious freedom sounded good in the First Amendment. But, as time progressed, it became obvious that religion was free to be interpreted as devotion to almost anything. The options were without limit. With that ambiguity in religion, the teachings of the Church diverged from daily devotion or perhaps it was the other way around. Daily devotion diverged from the teachings of the Church.

The end result was that the American people were free to worship who ever and what every they felt inclined to worship, and they could do it according to their own convictions. Where religion had originally carried with it a teaching of spiritual quality, freedom of religion was extended to include all types of teachings and all types of devotion.

Since true devotion is the only devotion that can influence human decisions and motivate human action, it is easy to see how the thoughts and the deeds of the nation followed two separate paths, how the old saying practice what you preach fell into disfavor. The practice went one way, the preaching went the other. The practice was left to the bureaucratic institutions of the central government and public schools, and to those in the United States who had to maintain a strong industrial base. The preaching degenerated into formal ceremony and doctrine to be recited under the ever-narrowing banner of the Church.

The recombination of daily devotion and religious teaching will require putting religion back into the public schools, back into the bureaucracy of the central government, and back into our daily lives. In that sense, devotion to the possession of material goods is not in itself evil.

The Catholic Church is noted around the world for its excessive wealth and its conspicuous possession of material goods. If the truth were known, the Vatican Library might well be rated as the best in the world for a library of its kind. So it would seem, as long as the motives and the methods of acquisition, and the motives and the methods of preservation, can be justified, that Vatican Library should remain part of the Church. And the Roman Catholic Church should be credited with that religious accomplishment.

When religion returns to its original spiritual purpose of continually seeking and continually teaching truth, then religion will also be able to act as the guiding principle for the collective actions and the collective ideals of all mankind. All people will be able to unite to protect their common health and their common safety, yet they will be able to retain their own individual freedom of self-expression. When religion becomes religion, just as when science becomes science, all people will welcome diversity that comes from the development of the uniqueness of individuals.

Uniqueness will not violate the survival of the whole; it will not even threaten it. When religion becomes religion, the spiritual quality of life will prevent individual preference from violating the survival of the whole because that is what truth is all about.

C118   A military monarch

A president with authority to order the use of armed force is a military monarch. He has no inclination or need to respond to the wishes of the people.

Election to the Office of the President of the United States carries with it two distinctly different responsibilities. The President of the United States is the president of the people and he runs domestic matters. The President of the United States is also Commander-in-Chief of the military and he has taken it upon himself to use that military to project the policies of this nation around the world. He also has been delegated the authority to impose military rule over the United States during the time of national emergency which he himself can declare.

In 1956, when the American people campaigned for and re-elected Dwight David Eisenhower to the White House, they elected a Commander-in-Chief. Decisions that would control the use of American military in foreign countries were the key issues and the people responded accordingly. President Eisenhower was a military man. President Eisenhower had already served his first term in the White House and he had repeatedly ignored the recommendations of civilian advisers by refusing to initiate a "bold new foreign policy of military intervention." Eisenhower had preferred to remain "peaceful and passive" in his attitudes toward the use of armed force as a means of implementing American foreign policy.

At the end of Eisenhower's second term John F. Kennedy was elected President. It was then, in 1961, that American military involvement escalated in Southeast Asia. Both Eisenhower and Kennedy had the opportunity to "pick and choose from divided military advice." Kennedy became "active, even belligerent," a reflection of his own style and his own response to interest groups, "not the influence of the military."

The refusal to order military action does not indicate, however, that Eisenhower was a man of peace, while Kennedy was a warmonger. Had Eisenhower been in office during the time of the Kennedy Administration perhaps he would have decided the same as Kennedy. Rather it indicates that the decision came as a result of Eisenhower's own view of the world. The authority to order military action had, of course, already been delegated to the White House by the Congress.

The President of the United States, when he acts as the Commander-in-Chief of the military, has no immediate need to appeal to the popular opinion of the people. He may pursue a foreign policy of military adventurism and military intervention. The men in the Armed Services are expected to follow his orders.

Military service organizations composed of an army of mercenaries are, however, more susceptible to the bad judgment of a Commander-in-Chief. Those composed of young people from all walks of life, all levels of society, all faiths and denominations, will have parents and close relatives of the young people who tend to act as the public watch dog.

National service organizations, supported by American tax dollars, should become an honest representation of the diversity of the American population. All young people should devote a portion of their life to national service. National service organizations should be able to uphold democratic-capitalistic-religious ideals because all young people are taught these same ideals in the home, in the school, and in the government institutions.

The behavior of young people can be dominated by action-reaction response only when that behavior is motivated by fear or want. The behavior of young people can become creative only when that behavior is motivated by freedom of self-expression and guided by a sense of common safety for all mankind.

Misdirected widespread hostility toward the national service organizations will not produce a national economic policy free from military intervention in foreign countries. It will also not eliminate the need for every individual to assume responsibility for his own actions. Misdirected widespread hostility toward national service organizations could cause the nation to commit internal suicide.

The delegated power of the President has expanded into a peacetime role as Commander-in-Chief of the military. It is a fantasy that has developed in the minds of slaves who seek the security of rule by absolute authority.

The constitutional power of the President of the United States as a leader of citizen response is a living mirror. That mirror can do nothing more than reflect the character of the people themselves. That mirror will tend to remind us of our own imperfections.

Chapter D

War Powers of Congress

**War powers by any name still
smell like gunpowder**

The power to declare war, including the power to elevate or to in any way alter the alert status of the American military, is legislative. And legislative acts belong to the Congress.

A declaration of war is not an Executive act. Any decision to use military action does not constitute an execution of existing laws. On the contrary, a declaration of war is one of the most deliberate acts that could be performed to have the effect of repealing all existing laws, insofar as those laws are inconsistent with that state of war. Therefore, a declaration of war, no matter how you define the use of American troops on foreign soil, is legislative.

Any definitive change in war powers as they are not exercised by the President and any definitive change in delegated authority to order the use of nuclear weapons to be exercised by the President, will have to be initiated by the central authority of the United States government, the American people themselves.

Only the very loud voice of public opinion can convince elected public officials of the urgent national need to refuse to accept any doctrine which holds that the nation must submit to the will of a single individual.

D119   The national emergency

*Powers now concentrated in the Office of the Presi-
dency are contrary to the intent of Constitutional Law.
Yet Congressional efforts to alter the situation have
failed to impress the past two Presidents.*

Special legislative powers—war powers—were conferred on
the President and other Officers, Boards, and Commissions as
a result of the National Emergency Proclamation of December
16, 1950. In 1973, after becoming alarmed about the power of
the President to control the use of American military action
abroad, the United States Senate established a Select Committee on National Emergency Powers to examine the desirability and possible consequences of terminating those powers.

The War Powers Resolution passed the Senate, 75-20, on October 10, 1973; the House with a vote of 244 to 170 on October
12; the Conference Report was voted out of Committee 238 to
123. The vote was, therefore, far from unanimous, and the
President was far from convinced that it was the voice of the
American people that had been represented.

The Committee's findings eventually resulted in passage of
the War Powers Resolution of 1973 (Public law 93-148), a
Resolution that became law on November 7, 1973, over the veto
of President Nixon. The intent of that Resolution was to return
Constitutional war powers to the Congress.

Since that time, both former Presidents Ford and Carter have
boldly and defiantly circumvented the War Powers Resolution,
Ford in the Mayaguez seizure and Carter with his raid to rescue
American hostages held in Iran. Both incidents were of short
duration. But both involved the use of American military personnel on foreign soil. And both did result in the loss of
American military lives during peacetime.

Indeed the authority to order American military action during time of national emergency is still in the hands of the President, and that action need not have anything to do with the
Constitutional mandate: To repel Invasions.

D120   War in the absence of war

*The President of the United States now has the
authority to order the use of nuclear weapons. That
authority violates Constitutional Law. That authority*

is the authority of the President of the United States to commit an act of war.

The United States Congress, apparently reluctant to exercise its own emergency authority, has preferred instead to confer emergency powers on the President. The Senate Select Committee on National Emergencies and Delegated Emergency Powers reported in 1973 that the Congress had transferred "awesome magnitudes of power to the Executive without having examined the cumulative effect of that delegation."

That Committee also reported that the Congress had failed to provide written guidelines to the Executive to indicate what should or might constitute a national emergency. In that regard, Vice President George Bush, as head of the "Crisis Management" team for the Reagan White house, said at a news conference, "[It is] a matter of judgement on the part of the President."

In this book, the primary concern for the ambiguity in Presidential "war powers," and in Presidential succession, has to do with the authority of the President to order the use of nuclear weapons or, in a broader context, the authority of the President to order the use of American military on foreign soil without a declaration of war by Congress.

National policy officially excludes the First Strike option. But, as the policy is now stated, a launch on warning, the so-called preemptive First Strike (the use them or lose them response), is clearly justified.

Should the President of the United States find it convenient, he has the authority to withhold information from the American people in the interest of national security, and then to order the use of nuclear weapons as retaliation to a surprise attack, no matter how contrived the surprise may have been.

Electronic capabilities of the American military must now be funded at an operational level that would prevent a surprise attack. And any government official claiming the need to retain the possibility of surprise should be asked to leave public office for reasons of his gross incompetence.

The return of the authority to order the use of nuclear weapons to the Congress has become imperative. Any Presidential decision to use nuclear weapons should be declared an act of treason. No matter the circumstances or the level of involvement, authority to initiate military action belongs to the legislative. Constitutional War Powers belong to the Congress.

D121   Commander-in-Chief by invitation only

Don't call us, we'll call you

At the time of the writing of the Constitution, the founding fathers were in no mood to trust monarchical powers. It was a dislike they had brought with them from Europe. For that reason, within the written constitution, the sole granting of War Powers to the President of the United States is contained in the Commander-in-Chief designation.

"A limited statement merely meaning First General for the Military," wrote Alexander Hamilton when he defended the Constitutional designation, Commander-in-Chief of the military for the President. Hamilton declared,

> ... it would amount to nothing more than the Supreme Command and direction of the military and naval forces, as first general and admiral ... while that of the British King extends to the declaring of war and to the raising and regulating of fleets and armies ... all of which, by the Constitution under consideration, would appertain to the Legislative.

One explanation even went so far as to imply that the U.S. Constitution would have the President of the United States become Commander-in-Chief of the military only *after* the Congress had declared war, an act that would, in effect, put the nation under military rule.

All powers to regulate the military were to sit with the Congress. Even the militia units of the several states were controlled entirely by those States until the Dick Bill of 1903 established some degree of Federal control. The National Defense Acts of 1920 and 1933 further extended Federal authority by giving the President the power to order National Guard officers to active duty during time of national emergency. There is, however, still an ill-defined distinction between civil action and armed combat for the militia.

The inherent power of the President of the United States, especially his authority to order military action, is nothing more than a euphemism for the exercise of Presidential power that goes beyond the strict interpretation of the Constitution. This misplaced authority for the use of military action now sitting at the White House, extended under the banner of the take care clause, should indeed be removed.

The American people need a Commander-in-Chief by invitation only, an invitation that should be extended and withdrawn only by the United States Congress.

D122   Madison responds to Pacificus

Tyranny, like hell, is not easily conquered.

Nowhere has the separation of powers for the three branches of government become so intensely defended as in the letters from James Madison, under the pen name Helvidius, written in response to the letters of Alexander Hamilton, under the pen name Pacificus. Those Pacificus letters of Hamilton (e.g., No. VII, July 20, 1793) show the unifying strength of George Washington (Washington was still President), the totalitarian-type rule associated with his Office of the Presidency, and his role as Commander-in-Chief of the Army. Hamilton, then Secretary of the Treasury, wrote his Pacificus letters to argue in favor of Expanded Executive Power for the President.

Arguments like Hamilton's did not go unanswered as long as there were good Republicans within ear shot. Thomas Jefferson, Secretary of State, was so enraged by the Pacificus articles that he implored his friend James Madison, a member of the U.S. House of Representatives, to reply:

> Nobody answers him, and his doctrines will therefore be taken for confessed. For God's sake, my dear Sir, take up your pen, select the most striking heresies and cut him to pieces in the face of the public. There is nobody else who can and will enter the lists with him.

Madison then wrote his Helvidius letters. Madison argued that the Congress possessed policy making power in the field of foreign affairs by virtue of the clearly stated power to declare war, which "by its very nature was legislative." Madison argued that diplomatic powers of the president were only instrumental in the execution of that policy. In other words, Congress had the power to make international policy or national policy as it relates to other nations; the President had the power and the responsibility to implement that policy.

Madison's rebuttle was by no means ineffective. John Quincy Adams was so impressed that he described the Helvidius letters as having "scrutinized the doctrines of Pacificus with acuteness of intellect never perhaps surpassed and with a severity scarcely congenial to his [Madison's] natural disposition and never on any other occasion indulged." And it all happened for good reason.

Foreign policy for the young nation was being addressed as a precursor to war. Madison went on to become the first wartime President of the United States, 1809-1817, during the War of 1812.

Nevertheless, time brought expanded power to the executive as advocated by Hamilton. There has been a steady drain of power from the Congress on Capitol Hill down Pennsylvania Avenue to the White House.

Today, however, the American people are showing signs of wanting to reverse the direction of flow. It now seems better to limit the power of the President rather than live with the rule of a tyrant.

D123   The power of public opinion

Everyone likes to talk about strong leadership from the Congress, but no one really expects it. Congress is representative and it is democratic. The United States Congress can do little more than acknowledge innovation when it arrives on its door step.

Career prospects for the Executive and Legislative branches of the federal government are fundamentally different. The President remains in his Executive office for one four-year term or, at most, two. By comparison, a member of Congress may continue his chosen legislative profession as an elected public official for 20 to 30 years.

There is a built-in sense of urgency for the President. The President has to respond to his campaign promises during his brief tenure in office. That same urgency has not been reflected by motives or actions of members of Congress. Members of Congress have to concern themselves with their constituency and a campaign for their re-election.

The natural tendency is for members of Congress to lag comfortably behind the frontiers of public controversy. A member would prefer to reap the benefits of activities in Washington, DC, once they are announced as conclusive. Legislative actions that have positive impact on the home-town constituency can then be publicly advertised through well timed news releases, those that are negative can be passed over.

Indeed members of the Congress seem to follow the tendencies of human behavior described by Thomas Jefferson in the Declaration of Independence:

> Prudence, indeed, will dictate that governments long established should not be changed for light or transient causes; and accordingly all experience hath shown that mankind are more disposed to suffer, while evils are sufferable, than to right themselves by abolishing the forms to which they are accustomed.

Accordingly, any definite change in war powers will have to come from the force of public opinion. The American people must decide that there should be a declaration of war before military action can be ordered. The American people must decide that there should be a declaration of war before the alert status of the American military can be elevated. The American people must decide that only the Congress of the United States has the authority to order the use of nuclear weapons.

The power of public opinion is the only dependable motivating force in this country. Without it, members of Congress do indeed appear "more disposed to suffer, while evils are sufferable."

Chapter E

Purification of the Pentagon

**If economic prosperity dies,
then so does the nation**

The creation of a Department of Military Affairs at the Pentagon, the creation of an executive department dedicated to the service aspect of the military service organizations, is proposed as the all important first step in the PURIFICATION OF THE PENTAGON.

The industries of this nation could now break away from their World War II dependence on the production of munitions. A new national economy could be established; a new industrial base could be created. Economic prosperity is what the future of this country is all about.

During World War II the need for armaments stimulated a collective industrial response in this nation. Now this nation has become the most destructive and the most actively militarily responsive nation in the world. So destructive and so responsive, in fact, that the threat of destruction or the threat of military action can no longer be used to motivate its own people.

When this nation can promise nothing to an enemy or to any friend except total annihilation, then this nation can no longer depend upon the use of armed force as a means of implementing its own foreign policy. The threat of violence by the United States has simply outgrown its usefulness.

The threat of nuclear destruction is but a charade. If a President of the United States were ever to invoke massive destructive military action, it should be considered an act of treason.

The entire idea of nuclear retaliation across intercontinental or even international distances—the overwhelming necessity for instant and massive destruction, with no time for deliberation and no means or manner to alter the course of events once undertaken—is a stoneage strategy intended only to make dastards look like valiant men. And besides that, such primitive brutality is a disgrace to the honorable military tradition of this country.

The pride of this nation is tied to decisive, deliberate responsiveness. The American people could now return dignity to their own military service organizations. They could re-organize the Department of Defense to create a Department of Military Affairs.

The responsibility for the coordination of the industrial base of the nation should be removed from the Pentagon. And that move should be scheduled as a 1984 spring housecleaning.

E124   Defense can't fight a war

> *"These are the times that try men's souls. The summer soldier and the sunshine patriot will in this crisis shrink from the service of his country,"* wrote *Thomas Paine during the winter of 1776 of the Revolutionary War.*

Americans may well have a tendency to become summer soldiers or sunshine patriots when there is no stated national intent, no identifiable national policy, and no declaration of war on the part of Congress to commit the people of the nation to a common purpose. The Korean and Vietnam conflicts would be two such examples of failure on the part of the politically-motivated presidentially-controlled Department of Defense to fight a war with no popular support.

American military men were sent into combat but there was no declaration of war by the United States Congress. American people were asked to pay the price of war but there was no popular commitment to national purpose . . . and certainly no statement of common good.

The decision to fight in Vietnam was proclaimed by the President and it was endorsed by the complacency of the Congress. The Vietnam war was nothing more than the blatant political abuse of the American military for non-military reasons.

A time of war was intended by our forefathers to be a time when the citizens of the nation assigned higher priority to the common good than to their own individual needs and desires. In that sense, the Department of Defense has never fought a war and it has never won one either.

E125   Defense can't win the peace either

Having an industry-oriented Department of Defense running the military is like having a coyote guarding the chicken coop.

The recorded life of James Forrestal would appear to contain a message for all Americans. It is a sad commentary on the political precursors for the Department of Defense.

James Forrestal served in naval aviation during World War I. At the end of the war, in 1919, he resumed his connection with a New York City investment banking firm of which he was made President in 1938.

In June 1940, prior to the declaration of World War II, Forrestal became an administrative assistant to President Franklin Delano Roosevelt. In August, 1940, Forrestal was named Under Secretary of the Navy; his assignment was to direct the massive expansion and procurement program for the military build-up of arms and equipment.

It was the winter of 1943-1944 when Ernie Pyle wrote of "the turn in the fortunes of the war." In May 1944, Forrestal became Secretary of the Navy, a civilian appointment with financial-industrial overtones. On September 17, 1947, James Forrestal took the oath of office as the first "Secretary of Defense." The following day the National Military Establishment came into being. The National Military Establishment was to be renamed the Department of Defense about two years later.

Though the appointment of the Secretary of Defense requires confirmation by the United States Senate, the qualifications for the individual and the purpose of the office remain obscure. If Forrestal's ability with wartime procurement was indeed as outstanding as was claimed, then one would certainly have to question both his interest and his ability to motivate a transition of the economy and the industrial base from a wartime to a peacetime situation. Unless, of course, the contrary was true.

The intent of the Congress, and of the President, was that Forrestal should continue wartime procurement in peacetime, that Forrestal should further a national wartime economy, that Forrestal should maintain an armed peace for the industrial elite, and he should do it with the blessings of the federal government.

During those formative years, even with the help of Dwight D. Eisenhower, Forrestal was unable to resolve the competing claims for military (armed forces) funding priorities coming from interservice rivalries, a global strategy for nuclear war supremacy (at that time the United States had total supremacy), and fiscal limitations being imposed by a politically motivated Congress.

Effective March 28, 1949, almost six months before the Department of Defense was officially created, suffering from depression, James Forrestal resigned his position with the United States government and entered the United States Naval Hospital at Bethesda, Maryland. On May 22, 1949, at 3 o'clock in the morning, Forrestal plunged through a third story window to his death.

The unresolvable rivalries perceived by Forrestal not only survived his death, they prospered. Peacetime interservice rivalries expanded into interdisciplinary rivalries within the academic community.

As the importance of high technology and automation increased, so did the money going into defense-related industries. The civilian-coordinated Department of Defense exploited operational requirements for the nation's service organizations, it justified research and development and then eventually prototype procurement of more and more hardware.

Peacetime funding was clearly supporting war potential rather than civil action. Peacetime funding was indeed wartime funding. And the political abuse of the defense spending soon became the most blatant conflict of interest openly tolerated in the federal government.

E126   The last great balance of power

The European Great Power system designed to create world order was based on a false concept of human behavior. The emphasis was on the stagnation of a

*perfect balance, rather than on the dynamic adjust-
ment in a decision making process.*

During the period 1789 to 1815, the people of Europe were
rejecting the idea of the concentration of power in the hands
of a few. Europe had been shaken to its foundation. Old conceptions of absolute monarchy were being questioned, and the
new ideals of democracy were transplanting themselves across
the Atlantic to the newly formed United States of America.

In spite of the mood of the time among the people, the chief
objective of the power elite at the Congress of Vienna meeting
from September 1814 to June 1815, was the restoration of the
balance of power in Europe. The published intent was "to put
an end to the long disturbance of Europe and to the suffering
of the people" by introducing a "stable peace based upon a
just division of forces between the powers and carrying with
it a guarantee of its permanence."

That "just division of forces" provided occasion throughout
the nineteenth century for new wars to undo the plans that
had been so carefully made by a "system of governing machines
abominably suited for the purpose." From the stresses of the
maladjustment various "nationalist" movements (movements
for national independence) drew their driving force.

The Holy Alliance of the three leading powers of Europe—
Russia, Prussia, and Austria—acting upon the initiative of Czar
Alexander, served for more than a century as a symbol of the
combined forces of despotism at work to suppress democratic
movements. The Alliance was outstandingly successful in
reducing the established traditions of international law to the
arbitrary will of a small group of absolute monarchs. Those
monarchs of the Holy Alliance labored under the delusion that,
in defeating Napoleon, they had defeated the revolution, turned
back the hands of time, and restored the dignity of Grand
Monarchy to the world.

At the end of World War II, the United States fell comfortably into that same trap. The allure of the power elite was
enticing. The Big Three concept of power emerged.

To placate the Soviets, and so it would seem the Senate of
the United States as well, a veto right for the Great Powers
had to be incorporated into the Security Charter of the United
Nations signed in San Francisco on June 26, 1945. As one looks
back, the establishment of that veto power for the power elite
could well be viewed as the famous last stand of the Holy
Alliance. And the United States subscribed to it.

The American people are a proud people. The American people are a just people. And, generally speaking, most Americans reject any position of great power. The American people appear to prefer their single-minded pursuit of democratic-capitalistic prestige. The "power" in the world would be divided.

E127   An armed peace for the industrial elite

A balance of power, known to the skeptics as a teeter-totter of terror, is, when used as a philosophy for the prevention of war, as barbaric as the armed peace it has created.

The Department of Defense was conceived during a two-year debate which concluded with the enactment of the National Security Act of 1947. It was not, however, until August 10, 1949, that the National Security Act was finally amended to abolish the status of the Army, Navy, and, by that time, Air Force as separate Executive Departments, to create the single civilian-staffed Department of Defense.

In September 1950, the President of the United States, Harry S. Truman, named George C. Marshall to head the newly created Department of Defense. Marshall, the Architect of Victory from World War II and later Secretary of State, was then Army Chief of Staff. After Marshall, as had been the case with Forrestal, Secretaries for the Department of Defense often came from the industry.

Secretary of Defense C.E. Wilson (January 28, 1953 to October 8, 1957) had previously been President of General Motors. Secretary of Defense Robert S. McNamara (January 21, 1961, to February 29, 1968) had been a former President of Ford Motor Company. It was McNamara who used the power granted by the 1958 Reorganization Act to significantly increase his own version of "unification of the military service organizations."

McNamara's non-military unification of the Department of Defense could, in retrospect, be viewed as "unification through industrialization." From that perspective, unification was the "institutionalization" of military dependence upon automated systems. The weapons were automated and so were the accounting systems. There was a prevailing philosophy that the effectiveness of the military should be judged by the ability of the federal government to procure hardware and count dollars.

The American military had become a collection of automated systems, and those systems were researched and developed within the scientific community. The production of the automated systems was to guarantee the security of the nation with no regard for human participation and no operational risk of human judgement. Automation had created an armed peace for the industrial elite. And the purpose of that automated military was to remain shrouded in secrecy. The decision making process within the Department of Defense was to remain removed from the considerations of military preference and from the influence of public opinion.

E128   The uniqueness of service

Restoring the uniqueness of service to American military service organizations would provide a much needed opportunity to define a peacetime mission for non-combat personnel.

The First Congress under the Constitution in 1787, re-established the four Executive Departments—Foreign Affairs (now the State Department), Treasury, War, and the Post Office—that had existed under the Articles of Confederation. Some 10 years later, in 1798, Congress separated the naval forces from the land forces by creating a new Department of Navy. The original War Department retained control only over the Army. The Secretaries of both Departments reported to the President. The responsibilities and indeed the capabilities of the Army and the Navy were indeed recognized as uniquely different.

Prior to World War II, the War Department's job was to manage not only military combat actions but also civil non-combat assignments for military personnel. Within the scope of that mission, the War Department (e.g., the Army Corps of Engineers) conducted large construction programs improving rivers and harbors, built dams and reservoirs, and developed other public facilities.

Even though other government agencies took over many of the public works programs during the 1930s, one of the biggest civil action tasks did remain within the War Department. An organization of about 300,000 young men who worked on government conservation projects was administered by the War Department as the Civilian Conservation Corps. This work force became known as the CCC boys to local residents involved with the projects. The War Department also remained responsible for providing a national relief labor force on short notice.

PURIFICATION OF THE PENTAGON, the moving of the civilian-staffed industrially-oriented procurement responsibilities out of the Pentagon and into (perhaps) the **F**ederal **E**mergency **M**anagement **A**gency would be but one step toward restoring the uniqueness of the military service organizations. Within the remaining Department of Military Affairs each service organization would have to acquire its own unique responsibilities and it would have to develop its own unique identity. But in every case, each service organization would support a common national purpose of economic independence and a common global purpose of environmental monitoring.

The Politics of Foreign Policy

The President can play foreign politics but foreign policy belongs to the United States Senate

Along side freedom of the individual person stands the common good of the nation. And along side freedom of the individual nation stands the common good of the human race. But, no matter the common good of the whole or the rights of the individuals involved, the behavior must go far enough to take into account the harmony of the nature. Everyone will have to eventually respect the creative interaction of the entire TEAM, Technology, Environment, And Man.

Foreign policy of the United States, as many Americans now perceive it, is being conducted within the confines of technological capabilities. The international scientific community, because it is far ahead of the rest of society in the use of technology, has reserved for itself the luxury of setting the stage for what can, and usually does, happen within the political arena. Those scientific precursors actually place constraints upon the governments of all nations, and upon the way those nations interact with each other.

By the time the United States Congress becomes aware of any social or economic implications of the use of modern technology, there is little room left for political maneuvering. The Congress seems to have little alternative but to tag along behind the pioneers of technological achievement, endorsing those achievements as they go. As a consequence, much of our national economic policy has been determined by the push of technology created within the scientific community, funded by the Department of Defense, realized through industrial capabilities located in many countries of the world. No one feels responsible to the neglected American voter.

Foreign policy being implemented by the President of the United States, legislated by the United States Congress, and influenced by trade relationships endorsed by both, should, however, come from somewhere and that somewhere should be a philosophical foundation dictated by the voice of the American people. The voice of those elected to public office should be doing the deciding, not the profit motive of the industry, and not the self-indulgence of technocrats within the scientific community.

F129   Patriotic industries

> *The dynamic driving force behind social unity in the United States is economic prosperity. Deny it and you deny your own national heritage, accept it and you smile all the way to the supermarket.*

From the time the country was founded through the early 1800s, there was no uniformly accepted national economic policy. The industrial north and the agricultural south were sharply divided. In 1861, an extreme phase of economic conflict, the Civil War between the north and south almost fragmented the Union. Following that War, banking practices of the industrial north simply dictated increased economic dependence on world trade. There was still no generally agreed upon nation policy for a national economy. There were those who favored economic trade dependence and there were those who favored a more self-sufficient independent economy.

On December 23, 1913, an Act of Congress created a national monetary policy, a major reform for U.S. banking and finance. That Act established the Federal Reserve System, a system that is well recognized as a minority control for the flow of credit and money in the United States, a control mechanism that is supposed to "facilitate an orderly economic growth, a stable dollar, and a long-term balance in international payments."

Under President Carter, the Monetary Control Act of 1980 was signed into law. That Carter legislation was an attempt to expand uniform banking practices. Those regulatory practices for the flow of currency were neither creative nor inspiring. They were, as advertised, controlling.

Some in the United States government and some in the American population are slowly recognizing that the availability of money is a very poor indicator for the quality of life or, for that matter, for the level of economic prosperity in this country. Instead a second monetary system, an unofficial home-spun barter system, is emerging. The American people are resourceful enough to use direct (and some not so direct) methods to cope with their own economic woes. The Americans people appear ready to form their own national economy freedom, free of trade dependence on other nations, and free of exploitation of foreign labor.

George Washington, when he retired from public office, advised: "The Great rule of conduct for us, in regard to foreign Nations, is in extending our commercial relations to have with them as little political connection as possible. So far as we have already formed engagements let them be fulfilled with perfect good faith. Here let us stop." The American people appear to be in the mood to take that advice seriously.

F130   From scientist to Senator

The foresight of physicists-philosophers can be made available in the United States Senate only when those scientists are elected Senators.

This nation is the most technologically advanced nation in the world. The immediate use of technology by the citizens and by the military has provided a direct driving force for both social and economic change. That change is now having a profound influence on public opinion. It is dictating the manner in which political decisions can be made and military strategies can be formulated.

A scientist may not be any more able to comprehend the meaning or purpose of social change than any other talented creative person—an artist, a poet, a religious leader—any man born with a talent for perceiving the grand strategy or national purpose. All have perception and all can anticipate trends in human behavior. But the scientist, once aware of those trends, and once directly involved in the decision making process, does have the ability to utilize the fundamental truths of natural law. That sense of judgement of a good physicist can, however, not be transferred. It is not a lesson to be memorized and it is not an exercise in logical thought to be recorded. The words can be repeated at some opportune moment of debate but not the philosophy. The philosophy is a philosophy of life. The philosophy is an involvement in a thought process that belongs to the individual.

The United States Congress, as its membership now looks, is comprised primarily of lawyers or others of non-technical background. Many of the lawyers have been exposed largely to the intricacies of logical thought and legal tactics. Compared to a research physicist, such a person might have a difficult time comprehending the scope and the implications of natural law and, hence, natural law as it applies to human behavior.

An awareness of technology-dependent change in human behavior or a sense of the rate at which that change could alter human consciousness would tend to be lacking in those who do not understand natural law. The physicist has a built-in scale for judging the technological dependence of the human being and a philosophical grasp of the meaning of that scale. The physicist is more apt to have a sense of what can happen. The lawyer, by comparison, would tend to write statutory base after the fact.

Knowledge and artistic talent, combined with the order and discipline of logical thought, allow a good scientist to enjoy a prophetic advantage over others with comparable background. Americans who want comprehensive national policy and even more comprehensive international relations, should be working to elect physicist-philosophers to the United States Senate. For his ability to combine commitment and reason, Freeman Dyson at Princeton would be one scientist to consider. For his ability to recognize the parallel between human behavior and natural law, Carl Sagan would be another.

This nation has a great resource of senior scientists who have proven themselves as advocates of the democratic process. Though physicists, as a group, have tended to be invisible citizens, those associated with international satellite programs, atmospheric dynamics diagnostics, and the many aspects of global pollution monitoring could perhaps now be nudged into public office. The decision is one the people have to make. The

American people still possess the power of the ballot. It is the supreme power of the land.

F131   From advocate to lobbyist

Lobbyists are an essential part of the democratic process. Advocates make good lobbyists only if they were good advocates in the first place.

An advocate is a person who is willing to enthusiastically defend, with great conviction, a particular decisive action on behalf of someone else. All women who have been actively engaged in child rearing are, by definition, good advocates.

A good mother is an advocate. She invokes her influence on behalf of others everyday as she teaches her children—brush your teeth (the dentist said so), do your homework (the teacher said so), eat your pancakes (the coach said so). The experienced mother seldom has to invoke the Supreme Law of the Land, "I said so or you are grounded." A good mother has the ability to use both her presence and her influence with great skill or she abandons her role as advocate (and as mother) very early in life.

A lobbyist actively tries to influence the thinking of a public official. Usually that public official is involved in the legislative process. Advocates who leave the home to become lobbyists on Capitol Hill could now become the primary driving force in the reform of the democratic decision making process. They could shape national defense policy and, along the way, redo the national economy as well.

The children are grown. The house is filled with deafening silence. The time has come for all those highly qualified advocates to move out of the home and into the work force. Those homemakers can become activists. They can create jobs for themselves as lobbyists and they can create jobs for others. Women with 35 years or more experience, that continuous 24-hour-a-day kind of experience, should move into the political arena for only one reason: The nation needs lobbyists with a firm commitment to the common good.

The nation needs lobbyists to shift the priorities for defense spending. The nation needs lobbyists to insist that funding for the utility of global information systems take first priority. The nation needs lobbyists to redo the defense budget so those tax dollars can be spent to create a new industrial base.

F132   To teach is to transfer

The United States will have to provide continuous information flow from global monitoring systems. There is no other nation in the world with a work force already trained to perform such a highly specialized service for the common good of all nations.

The military, the government, the industry, the academic community—all can now use sophisticated electronic equipment for continuous global monitoring. All can help provide continuous information flow to protect the health and safety of all mankind. The Americans can get the job done. They have talent, and they derive pleasure from making a piece of equipment work.

Though electronic equipment can be immediately delivered, and even installed in a foreign country, installation does not guarantee performance. And it certainly does not guarantee ready-made human resource for maintenance.

To maintain a piece of equipment requires more than pushing a button or watching a dial. Any operator maintains his own equipment through his own style of use. People who are hard on their equipment do not use equipment, they abuse it. They can undo in five minutes what a maintenance man has taken hours to accomplish. To achieve optimum performance, operators and maintenance people have to work hand in hand.

Electronic equipment delivered to a non-technical society should in no way be interpreted as a transfer of technology. The transfer of sophisticated electronic hardware into a non-technical society does not create technological capability, it creates junk. American foreign policy should encourage, not discourage, the transfer of information, the communication of knowledge, and the teaching of utility. To *teach the use* of electronic equipment is the only way to transfer technology from one society to another.

The use of electronic equipment will initiate social change. The use of electronic equipment in a society will create new culture. But those changes in social pattern will come no faster than any other change in human behavior.

F133   Information is a trade commodity

Information in its applied form of knowledge is the trade commodity of the future. And the successful exchange of that commodity for the common benefit of economic prosperity depends entirely upon our increased use of human resource.

In 1932, the automobile was the keystone of the American manufacturing industry, and the country was in its worst economic depression in its history. When Henry Ford produced the Model T, he was interested in the manufacturing process itself. The assembly line, an innovation of industrial efficiency, was to eliminate the need for the human drudge. From that perspective of production efficiency, the automobile was an impressive industrial success. From the perspective of employment, the automobile was a dismal economic failure.

People in Boston, determined to save their own economy, were ready to eliminate snowplows in favor of men with shovels. A member of the United States House Committee on Patents argued that the U.S. Patent Office should stop issuing all patents on labor-saving devices. Resistance to the assembly-line production of the automobile, to the labor-saving innovation of Henry Ford, was sweeping the country. Widespread unemployment was viewed as a most unwelcome turn of events.

By the late 1930s, economic prosperity was returning to the nation. It came not from Henry Ford and not from the manufacture of the automobile. Economic prosperity came from the people themselves. The people had accepted the efficiency of the assembly line. The people were starting to use human resource in other places. Service stations, repair garages, motels, hotels, truck stops, rest stops, highways, freeways, investment, insurance—economic prosperity was coming not from the production of the automobile but from the creation of facilities for its use.

Today, in the sense of national economic prosperity, the computer is sitting exactly where the automobile was sitting in 1932. The production of the computer has become an industrial success. Yet the unemployment produced by the use of that automation has flattened the economy.

Economic prosperity that will come from the use of the computer is waiting for the people. The American people have to use the computer; the use of the computer has to turn economic stagnation into economic prosperity.

Chapter G

The Presence and the Purpose

The American military has an ambience all its own

Action-reaction physics, as it has been used to guide human behavior, has served only to prolong human suffering. Indeed it is the distorted interpretation of the action-reaction physics of Sir Isaac Newton that has already extended the age of the mechanical universe long after the funeral notice was posted in the early 1900s.

The age of the mechanical concept of the balance is the age that is now coming to an end. The balance of military strength, the balance of world trade, the balance of Great Powers—all balances are showing their natural tendency toward the stagnation of static equilibrium.

There is a natural and a necessary political map of the the world that can accommodate the needs of the people. That is to say, such a map will not be fixed and no one person will ever regulate the rate at which the map emerges. All it says is that the natural map transcends all bargaining of Czars, Kings, and other government officials. In so far as that basic premise is acceptable, American electronic presence, with due respect for national self-government and national economic independence, can but hasten its emergence.

By paying the price for electronic presence, the American people can assist the rest of the world with the transition from the static behavior pattern of balance to a time-dependent process of self-adjustment. Ongoing adjustment in the decision making process goes along with the creative action of electronic presence and the eternal war of deciding. It is the rate of increase in the level of human awareness that will eventually determine the rate at which such a pragmatic interpretation of dynamic dualism becomes acceptable.

G134   Fight or flight is not enough

The fight-or-flight response is an action-reaction response motivated by want or fear. Any such response requires someone or something to create the fear but, other than that, it is relatively uninspiring.

The fight-or-flight response appears to be a male-oriented instinctive urge to either attack or run away. The fight-or-flight response is basically nonproductive in so far as it depends upon an external force for its motivation. The great human tragedy is that the fight-or-flight response requires the existence of an enemy, rather than an ideal, to make it work.

The classical fight-or-flight military response was denied most of its human ingredient when it moved from a conquer-the-enemy purpose to a destroy-the-enemy syndrome. Without doubt one of the saddest commentaries ever written about this transition from a humanized enemy to a mechanized destruction campaign came to the attention of the American people during World War II. The well-respected American war correspondent Ernie Pyle contrasted the joyous mood of the pilots with the grimness of the men in the trenches.

While in Europe, near the front-line fighting, Ernie Pyle noted that the pilots, far removed from the death and destruction they had created, viewed war as a game of equipment performance and multi-dimensional reflex-action. By contrast the men in the trenches, exposed to daily contact with the stench of blood, urine, and rotting flesh, were depressed by the killing. It is one thing to fight an enemy on "equal terms," it is another to use automated weapons to irradicate human life.

The psychological limits of the American male are not well known. But generally those limits are well documented by Ernie Pyle in *Brave Men* and by John Keats in *They Fought Alone*. And those books should be required reading for all young people in this country.

The fight-or-flight military response is the last great action-reaction fear-motivated human response still being sustained by large sums of government funding. Stamping out the enemy does not stamp out anything. Killing merely for the sake of killing, will not kill an ideal. And killing people will not kill their will.

The American people would do well to get on with this pending transition in human motivation. By altering priorities for defense spending, and by altering priorities for every other human endeavor, American military presence could now become electronic; it could become creative.

G135 The Letter of the Law

There is nothing fundamentally wrong with encouraging nations to develop their own economy and there is a lot to be said in favor of it. Yet any international law that would impose international uniformity, for the sake of convenience, should be openly and actively opposed.

The American people, more than any other, should have learned their lesson of failure with prohibition legislation. The Eighteenth Amendment of the United States Constitution, effective January 16, 1920, provided for the prohibition of the manufacture, sale, transportation, importation, and exportation of intoxicating liquors for beverage purposes. It took 13 years of confusion, confusion about the division of police powers and jurisdiction, and excessive expenditures of tax dollars for enforcement, for that Prohibition Amendment to be finally repealed.

Whether it is alcoholic beverages or nuclear arms, the folly of prohibition is the same. Surely the American people should be able and willing to teach that lesson of failure to the rest of the world. The nonsense of investing time and national resources in non-productive enforcement should be made clear from the outset. Prohibition legislation that regulates but fails to motivate creative action should never again be tolerated for purely economic reasons.

International regulatory legislation, the positive aspect of international law, should be acceptable only when that regulatory legislation can be implemented by catering to a creative ideal, but yet those creative ideals should also yield economic benefit.

The construction of permanent installations for land-based long-range intercontinental missiles should be against the law. All such construction can be monitored by Earth-orbiting satellites. At the same time, all large-scale industrial activities that alter, in an unacceptable manner, land, sea, or air can also be monitored.

Global monitoring of the natural environment would be one ideal that could motivate all peoples. The benefits would come to the people as their quality of life is improved and their safety assured. Information flow from Earth-orbiting satellites would become the life-line as all people pursue a common purpose of economic prosperity within the guidelines imposed by natural law.

G136   The Spirit of the Law

The Spirit of the Law is natural law. When the Letter of the Law reinforces the Spirit of the Law, then the rule of law can become creative.

International law as Grotius perceived it in the early 1600s, was derived from Natural Law. This philosophy of natural law would have human behavior compatible with the natural environment. By virtue of the intrinsic truth of the laws of nature they are everywhere remarkably self-consistent, they are everywhere eternally binding.

The Spirit of the Law is the vegetable garden of Planet Earth. Regulatory action (or positive law as one knows it today) is but a means of pulling weeds. To have a productive vegetable garden the American people would need to select their fruitful seeds and toil their fertile soil. Americans who have been working in pursuit of arms control agreements—international agreements that would consume untold millions of dollars for enforcement and yield nothing of economic benefit in return—have been pulling weeds in a barren plot of ground. Prohibition alone is a weed pulling exercise with no one ever having bothered to plant the garden.

The Spirit of the Law and the Letter of the Law, like faith and reason, are natural dueling partners. The mechanical era of human behavior has encouraged the use of uninspired, non-creative regulatory legislation. And such non-productive legislation has tended to drain human resource and deplete human energy with no psychological reward.

The Spirit of the Law and the Letter of the Law now have to work together; both have to pursue the same national purpose. Global monitoring would be regulatory in that it would tend to render the construction of missile silos impossible without detection. Global monitoring would be creative in that global monitoring of the natural environment would tend to improve the quality of human life. A national commitment to provide continuous information flow from global monitoring systems would have the common national purpose of trying to protect the health and safety of all people of all nations.

G137   Do it—a nation in action

The American military is this nation in action. And, whether we like it or not, we are what we do.

At the United States Military Academy, West Point, New York, 23 May 1962, General of the Army Douglas MacArthur (26 January 1880-5 April 1964) accepted The Sylvanus Thayer Award. The following paragraphs are taken from his Duty-Honor-Country Farewell Address:

Duty-Honor-Country. The code which those words perpetuate embrace the highest moral laws and will stand the test of any ethics or philosophies ever promulgated for the uplift of mankind. Its requirements are for the things that are right, and its restraints are from the things that are wrong. The soldier, above all other men, is required to practice the greatest act of religious training—sacrifice. In battle and in the face of danger and death, he discloses those divine attributes which his Maker gave when He created man in His own image. No physical courage and no brute instinct can take the place of the Divine help, which the soldier who is called upon to offer and to give his life for his country, in the noblest development of mankind.

Your guidepost stands out like a ten-fold beacon in the night. You are the leaven which binds together the entire fabric of our national system of defense. From your ranks come the great captains who hold the nation's destiny in their hands the moment the war tocsin sounds. The Long Gray Line has never failed us. Were you to do so, a million ghosts in olive drab, in brown khaki, in blue and gray, would rise from their white crosses thundering those magic works, Duty-Honor-Country.

This does not mean that you are war mongers. On the contrary, the soldier, above all other people, prays for peace, for he must suffer and bear the deepest wounds and scars of war.

> As I listen to those songs of the glee club, in memory's eye I could see those staggering columns of the First World War, bending under soggy packs, on many a weary march from dripping dusk to drizzling dawn, slogging ankle-deep through the mire of shell-shocked roads, to form grimly for the attack, blue-lipped, covered with sludge and mud, chilled by the wind and rain; driving home to their objective, and, for many, to the judgment seat of God. I do not know the dignity of their birth but I do know the glory of their death. They died unquestioning, uncomplaining, with faith in their hearts and on their lips the hope that we would go on to victory. Always for them—Duty-Honor-Country.
>
> The shadows are lengthening for me. The twilight is here. My days of old have vanished tone and tint, they have gone glimmering through the dreams of things that were. Their memory is one of wondrous beauty, watered by tears, and coaxed and caressed by the smiles of yesterday . . . But in the evening of my memory, always I come back to West Point. Always there echoes and re-echoes—Duty-Honor-Country.

You are what you do and the military service organizations are this nation in action. In the days gone by, any instigator of war used military force to achieve national objectives. In the future, the United States could well only instigate information wars. The United States is morally obligated to try to use non-violent military action to insure equal treatment for all nations under the rule of law.

G138   The mystique of presence

> *There is no known military measure for the value of the mystique of presence. Yet the mystique of electronic presence could well be the best way to project the creative ideals of this nation around the world.*

The non-combat mystique of electronic presence could be maintained by the United States Air Force. Military-operated global monitoring systems could supply communication-coordination services for emergency civil action. Satellite control centers could assist with the global monitoring of the natural environment. Real-time information flow could become the firepower for all non-violent American military action of the future.

The United States Air Force needs and deserves the benefit of the mystique of presence because global electronic presence could be used to project American ideals around the world in a non-violent manner. That electronic presence could respect the right for all nations of the world to strive for economic independence, to have access to water-ways and air-ways of free trade. That electronic presence could also help to preserve or protect the right to self-government.

The value of the mystique of electronic presence cannot be measured by existing military standards. And, in so far as that is true, it is imperative to change those standards. In the mean time, any further wretched political abuse of the American military service organizations should be despised by all citizens alike, not because of the monstrous injustice of the abuse itself, but rather because of the benefit of the mystique of presence that the abuse denies.

The American taxpayers will have to pay the price for military-operated global monitoring systems. During this time of transition, from the wars of destruction to the wars of information, the American military will have to learn to use electronic monitoring to rid the world of automated delivery systems for weapons of mass destruction. To pay the price of presence should be a national pleasure to be preferred over the pain of perpetuating any false pomp and pride of the past.

G139   Stand your ground

> *The future of this nation will never be in doubt until you doubt yourself. That is both a distinction and a defect for a nation that depends upon the strength of its individuals for its survival.*

Around the globe, cultures may differ and lifestyles may run contrary to each other. It may be impossible to find a common language to codify those different daily endeavors. The many thoughts and actions will not, in any case, translate into words or money. But those fragile differences, the unique contribution of each individual person and of each individual nation, should be preserved.

It is the well-defined existence of the individual that allows the more perfect Union of the whole. And it is that telic harmony of the whole that can be no stronger than the commitment of the weakest unit. Continuity can be carried by an appropriate use of technology in the natural environment. Creative impulses can come from the utility of human resource.

And while individuality and common good are natural dueling partners, it is the vitality of the interaction that is determined by their respective wills to survive.

The United States Navy, as a national service organization,
can and perhaps, at the moment, should show a global presence
of armed force. The United States Navy should patrol international waters to insure free passage to all ships of all nations.
The United States Navy could maintain an electronic presence
in the proximity of any known hostile area. The purpose would
be to prevent the use of armed force by surprise attack. But
only experienced, mature men should be considered qualified
for such a responsible duty.

Your self-confidence is your strongest ally, your self-doubt
is your only enemy. Wise counsel may accelerate it, political
blundering may delay it, but sooner or later, a global system
of responsiveness is sure to come. The rule of natural law is
the only authority of the future. Only a common goal of global
environmental can make those laws self-consistent. And only
the initiative of individuals can make those laws creative.

G140   There is a nation standing behind you

*American people must think what is true, they must
do what is right. And the destiny of the nation is tied
to the use of that dynamic dualism of human behavior.*

The American nation is a living nation and like any other
living system, the American nation has differentiated into its
many essential parts as it has developed in complexity. It has
a mouth for singing and feet for dancing. It has earlobes and
eyeballs and toe nails too. It has a respiratory system in the
private sector to admit the timely arrival of a breath of fresh
air. And it has a sensory system to alert the body to danger.
And like any other living system, the American nation has
a need for all those special features.

Parallels between the vitality of the American nation and
the vitality of a living system are many. And all remind us
of our own daily needs. The communication networks are nerve
fibers in constant demand. The monetary flow is the blood supply that circulates in near-constant volume. The many special
interest groups, the kidneys, the liver, the stomach—all have
their own particular needs and their own particular function

to perform. Yet the future of our self-sufficient government and the survival of our free enterprise system depends upon the strongest muscle in the body, the heart beat of the nation, the American military service organizations.

The service organizations maintain a rhythm while the nation sleeps, they carry an extra burden during waking hours. The heartbeat of the nation quickens its pace in time of emergency, it slows in time of rest. Yet the heart of the nation does not beat alone. The heart beat of the nation has exactly the vitality provided by those all-important individual citizen cells. The people themselves have to create the mood, the purpose, and the will to make the heartbeat of this nation worth while.

The American people have always thought of themselves as a people. Now they must act like a people. And, ironically, that's all there is. The American nation will be a nation only as long as the people think and act exactly that way.

Perspective

Tell it like it is

The majestic Ship of State will be carried
by the current in the river
of information flow, but that old row boat
of democracy will need strong
members of Congress
to man the oars

Most Americans are hawks in dove's clothing,
it is only a question of when they
change their feathers

Two hundred years ago our founding fathers laid an egg, but eggs can't fly. So the American people have been setting on their nest egg of national identity ever since. They have been waiting patiently for the peep that would signal THE BIRTH OF THE NATION.

On the 20th of February in sixty two, Astronaut John Glenn circled the globe in free flight and the peep of the nation finally arrived in the form of a beep from outer space. In a few short hours, Glenn completed the consecutive looping Earth orbits that returned the entire human race to the womb of its own biosphere. With one historic mission, the awareness of human consciousness was elevated to a new level of common concern. The size of Planet Earth had been reduced to the smallness of the number of seconds it takes for a satellite signal to traverse the globe.

Astronaut John Glenn was a hero. A man-made life-support system had sustained his bodily functions in space, and modern electronic communications equipment had transmitted the triumphant accomplishments back to Earth. Human pleasure and national pride were to be expected. But then there was more. Like a bubble in the breeze that floats and turns and breaks, the ecstasy of the moment ended.

Although man had performed an engineering miracle, the misery of the human condition persisted. And the news of both would arrive by modern communication in our living rooms. The feelings of brotherhood grew stronger. For the truly compassionate patriotic American, starvation and neglect were no longer the way of life on the other side of the world. Instead that distant human suffering became a next door neighbor.

That nest egg of 1776 was destined to one day develop into a self-sufficient nation. One single egg emerged, and it would become and remain one single nation. The original fertile yolk, with its self-contained cluster of cells, comfortably confined by its protective aqueous environment, would give way to the differentiation of life. The homogeneity of sameness, and the uniformity of political consensus, would give rise to a complexity of differences. The beak and bones, the feet and feathers, the head and heart—all those special interest features would grow. Each would perfect its own uniqueness. It happens in every living organism. And so it would happen with this American nation. In that respect, a living nation will mimic the behavior of any other living system.

The Pride of the Pentagon, the heart beat of the nation, a cadence for the living, and a tribute for the dead, the military service organizations stand dedicated to national service. Those organizations embody this nation in action. And nowhere will a divergence of thought and deed of this living nation become more evident than with those service organizations. When the American people think one thing and do another, it is the American military that displays that conflict of opposites to the world.

Because the American military should implement only the thoughts of the people, it is time for the self-governing American people to express their thoughts more clearly. When the thoughts and the deeds of the nation come together, then citizens and the soldiers can become one in this do-it-yourself government we call democracy.

There may be a few feathers lost in the battle, and the old body politic may look a little ruffled from the siege. But in true American fashion, the fight for national identity will continue.

As the nation changes its focus, those materialistic war hawks will soon look an awful lot like prestigious American Eagles in flight. Those patriotic Americans, all those hawks

in dove's clothing, will undergo a meaningful transformation
right before your eyes. They will assume full responsibility for
the combative actions of the soaring Eagle, who will also be
able to decide on the selectivity of its perch.

The complexity of life that has emerged from the fertile yolk,
the diversity of American interests that has emerged from an
apparent uniformity of ideals, should come as no surprise. The
unexpected feature in the development of the American nest
egg is the double yolk.

At the time of the Revolutionary War, the founding fathers
fought for and won their political independence from England.
They put aside for later generations that all-important fight
for economic identity. So it is the necessity of unifying that
double freedom, the dualism of democracy and capitalism, that
is now attracting our attention.

The American people are already suspecting that there is
something fundamentally wrong with the oppressive nature
of action-reaction constraints imposed by the existing balance
of military power with the Soviet Union. The American people have already grown weary of the economic burden of having to maintain their own military in a state of readiness solely
for the sake of responding to destructive actions initiated by
another.

The American people are, by their very nature, self-sufficient
and self-motivated. The American people are able and certainly
evidently willing to initiate a creative activity of global
electronic monitoring. In spite of all their materialistic,
mechanistic, militaristic blundering, the American people still
instinctively prefer creative economic success to negotiated
political failure.

As though guided by prophesy, the stars and stripes of the
American flag symbolically reflect the destiny of this nation.
The continuity of economic prosperity and the selectivity of
political action, that dualism represented by the stars and
stripes, is an eternal dualism that has become integrated into
the American way of life. The continuity of the stripes represents our faith in the economic guiding principle; the individuality of the stars, those all-important pulses of creative
political energy.

Patriotic Americans have suspected for quite some time that
the fertile yolk of the military-industrial nest egg was double
from the beginning. The political-economic dueling between
the demand-pull of the user and the technology-push of the industrial producer has become so much a part of our cherished

national heritage that we cannot bear the thought of thinking or doing without it.

Everyone appears eager to become the proud parents of that pair of new-born feisty chicks. Those national twins, democracy and capitalism, are strong and healthy. And they are crawling out of their shell fully dressed: One is clothed in stripes, the other in stars. As an added convenience, their names have already been selected to fit the mood of the occasion: "Retreat, hell!" and "We just got here!"

Notes and References

Preface

The old industrial base of the United States is described in its 50 years of evolution in the January 1982, "SME Golden Anniversary Issue 1932-1982: A Review of Manufacturing and the Society which Guides Its Progress," published by the Society of Manufacturing Engineers [*Manufacturing Engineering*, January, 1982, Vol. 88, No. 1, pg. 4]. "The President's Message," and all included articles are contributions of Daniel B. Dallas, Editor-in-Chief; and Robert L. Vaughn, President. My father, George W. Buckel, who is a life-member of SME and who was personally involved with the "tooling up" of General Motors prior to and during World War II, has encouraged my writing.

The book by Burnham Finney (1941), *Arsenal of Democracy*, Whittlesey House, New York, a division of McGraw-Hill Book Company, Inc., is written from the perspective, "man's ingenuity . . . has been turned to mechanizing warfare." The rigidity of the thought pattern for that time in history is reflected in the statement: "There is a dual purpose: to design machines that can be more devastating in a shorter time . . . and to produce them in such prodigious quantities as to establish superiority . . . (pg. 5)." And then refer to pg. 10, "Thus we are in a new economy in the United States. The nucleus of that economy is a new industry—munitions manufacture. It is a business so big that it threatens to over-shadow any other . . . "

Waste in defense spending is severely criticized, " . . . social welfare spending cannot replace defense spending, social welfare is far too cheap . . . "

by Lewin, Leonard C. (1967), *Report from Iron Mountain*, The Dial Press, Inc., New York, refer to Introductory section. Lewin is critical of "The continuing use of self-serving definitions of national security . . . "

The existence of natural or "divine" law has been argued for centuries, e.g., Plato, Aristotle, and Cicero. "Many people believe that these documents [the U.S. Constitution and its Amendments] contain a statement of the natural rights of man, though they variously believe that the statements came by divine intervention, or that they grew from organized nature . . . " The Declaration of Independence says that personal liberty comes from the "Laws of Nature" and "Nature's God" and "that all men are created equal, that they are endowed by their Creator with certain unalienable Rights, that among these are Life, Liberty, and the pursuit of Happiness." [Weinberger, Andrew D. (1962). *Freedom and Protection. The Bill of Rights*, Greenwood Press Pub., Westport, Conn., pg. 6.]

Aristotle (384-322 B.C.) " . . . laid the foundation for the **organic** conception of the state, one of the two major types into which all political theories of the state may roughly be divided. According to Aristotle, the state is a natural community, an organism with all the attributes of a living being. The other major type views the state as an **instrument**, a mechanism, a piece of machinery to be used for purposes and ends higher than itself. This . . . instrumentalist view of state, is actually older, having been propounded by the Sophists a century before Aristotle . . . it [instrumentalism] was, however, rejected by Plato, the teacher of Aristotle, and revived only in modern times by Thomas Hobbes (1588-1679), John Locke (1632-1704), and John Dewey (1859-1952) . . . " [Ebenstein, William (1962). *Great Political Thinkers*. Holt, Rinehart and Winston, New York, pg. 65.]

This book advocates a return to the **organic** concept of state. I agree with Ebenstein . . . "classical democracy and classical Marxism . . . both wrongly assume that any system of society can be devised that can achieve perfect harmony of interests (pg. 680)."

In my opinion, man should focus his attention on understanding and interpreting natural "divine" law and admit his failure to "devise" pyramids or other rigid institutional structures, that he may perceive as superior.

The natural state of war "does not imply or does it require hostility." [Immanuel Kant (1724-1804), see pg. 259, Morris, Clarence (Editor), *The Great Legal Philosophers*, University of Pennsylvania Press, Philadelphia (1959).] The natural state of "war" is a manifestation of natural law, the eternal state of dualism, the responsibility of the individual to exercise free choice. It is the unnatural state of "peace," when peace is defined as an absence of war, that lacks selectivity and creative distinction. Partners of antithesis: stop and go, right and wrong, hot and cold, strength and weakness, order and chaos, or war and peace, where the existence of one excludes the existence of the other, are certainly not natural dueling partners. Partners of equality, when that equality is reduced to sameness, are also not natural dueling partners.

Dynamic dualism is the dualism identified by William James as "The Present Dilemma in Philosophy" in his book on *Pragmatism*, reprinted by

Meridian Books, The World Publishing Company, New York. [James, William (1914), *Pragmatism: A New Name for Some Old Ways of Thinking*, Longmans, Green, and Comp. (original copyright 1907), a book with readable type, dedicated "To the memory of John Stuart Mill from whom I first learned the pragmatic openness of mind and whom my fancy likes to picture as our leader were he alive today."]

The presence of the dualism of eternal war on Earth is also discussed in a Biblical reference [Barclay, William (1976). *Flesh and Spirit: An Examination of Galatians 5:19-23*, Baker Book House, Grand Rapids, Michigan (original copyright 1962)].

A word of caution comes from Queen Beatrix of Holland, "Democracy must be aware of the danger of people no longer feeling they are participating in the decision making process." ["Queen Beatrix Urges N-arms Reduction," Washington (AP), printed in the *Daily Camera*, Boulder, Colorado, Thursday, April 22, 1982, pg. 5.]

PART ONE

The Announcement

If you are going to make a campaign promise,
then limited nuclear war is a real crowd pleaser

" . . . a winner in a nuclear exchange . . . " It made national news early in the 1980 presidential campaign when Walter Scheer of the *Los Angeles Times* interviewed George Bush, candidate for the Republican nomination [*Los Angeles Times*, 24 Jan. 1980, "Bush Assails Carter Defense Strategy: Cites MX Missile and Bomber Cuts"]. It was the first public glimmer that an elected public official might have the desire to move U.S. nuclear strategy from one of war prevention, to one of war fighting.

The threat of destruction of nuclear attack had been part and parcel of the U.S. policy of deterrence [Bernard Brodie (1959), *Strategy in the Missile Age*, ISBN 0-691-01852-9, Rand Corporation Research Studies, published by Princeton University Press, 41 Williams Street, Princeton, New Jersey 08540]. Brodie is often quoted, "Thus far the chief purpose of our military establishment has been to win wars. From now on its chief purpose must be to avert them." Though no one can fault that statement, the notion of "deterrence" that has since evolved has become a form of blackmail— a threat of accidental nuclear holocaust.

Brodie, Bernard (1946), *The Absolute Weapon: Atomic Power and World Order*, New York: Harcourt, Brace; and Brodie, Bernard, "Unlimited Weapons and Limited War," *The Reporter*, XI, No. 9, November 8, 1954, pp. 16-21, provide the now classic beginning for the notion of deterrence. "The Development of Nuclear Strategy," by Bernard Brodie, Center for

Arms Control and International Security, UCLA Working Paper no. 11, February 1978, would also be of interest. (Bernard Brodie died in 1978.)

In a more recent paper [Kugler, Jacek and A.F.K. Organski with Daniel J. Fox, "Deterrence and the Arms Race: The Impotence of Power," *International Security*, Spring 1980, pp. 105-138], it is concluded that "deterrence is not operative." The authors continue, " . . . logical conditions for deterrence are absent . . . nuclear arms are not costly (in both the United States and the Soviet Union they represent only a small fraction of total expenditures on defense) . . . nuclear arsenals are built almost solely as a result of internal [political] pressures." Kugler et. al. include a quotation from Bernard Brodie, " . . . whatever these reasons were [reasons public officials used for increasing U.S. nuclear forces], they were *not* in response to Soviet figures."

Those claims are startling. They suggest that the national policy of deterrence—the threat of destruction from surprise nuclear attack—should immediately become a topic for public debate in the United States.

The central purpose of the work by Bernard Brodie was to avert war. Since averting war is a theme of many faces, I could argue that the central purpose of my work is also to avert war—to avert the destructiveness of war. Short term, I urge immediate removal of all land-based nuclear weapons by all nations—I urge the elimination of the possibility of accidental nuclear holocaust. Long term, I urge replacing the destructive aspects of war-fighting with a more creative decision making process.

An "information war" could be fought to avert using destructive war-fighting methods ["Global Information Cooperative: Toward tomorrow's science and technology of life and hope for humanity," Harriet and Howard Kurtz, Editors, *Checkpoint*, September, 1979, a Newsletter of War Control Planners, Inc., Box 19127, Washington, DC 20036. Tele: (202) 785-0708].

PART ONE

Chapter A

Introduction

Political dueling is introduced to describe a dynamic decision making process. The concept comes from the wave-particle dualism of theoretical plasma physics, where electrons behave like waves and they also behave like particles. The wave provides the continuity and rhythm of a guiding principle; the particle, an abrupt pulse of energy.

Examples of dynamic dueling partners are: faith and reason, democracy and capitalism, male and female, Democrats and Republicans. The political and economic importance of the dueling process is that it encourages forward motion rather than the stagnation of perfect balance—the balance of an action-reaction response.

Dualism represents two different but essential methods of doing the same thing. In the case of the two political parties, the Democrats and Republicans, they represent two methods of pursuing one common national goal, for example, a national goal of economic prosperity. The Republicans worry about making money, the Democrats about spending it, but both have a common concern for economic prosperity.

There is a recent book by William Glasser and William Powers (1981) that deals with the oppressive nature of action-reaction response [*Stations of the Mind*. New York: Harper and Row].

A001   The threatening aspect of peace

When peace is defined as an "absence of war," then any method of preventing war becomes acceptable, including imposing a "balance of military power" as a method of deterrence [Collins, John M. (1980), *U.S.-Soviet Military Balance: Concepts and Capabilities, 1960-1980*, McGraw-Hill Pub. Comp.]. John Collins is a Senior Specialist in National Defense at the Congressional Research Service, The Library of Congress. He has prepared the most exhaustive, best documented, treatment of the balance of military power I have ever seen. He deals with organization, budget, manpower, and technological development; he discusses U.S. and Soviet objectives, policies, and strategic concepts. The material was published as a series from the Library of Congress, but the single bound volume from McGraw-Hill is recommended because it is more comprehensive.

The preparation of this unprecedented, definitive, 623-page analysis had its beginning in 1978, when two Members of the U.S. House Defense Appropriations Subcommittee, Representatives Bill Chappell, Jr. (Democrat-Florida) and Jack F. Kemp (Republican-New York), requested Collins to produce a "handbook" to better inform Members of the Congress in their annual deliberations on defense expenditures.

As advertised, the book by John Collins is a "breakpoint in national security." It is an essential reference for anyone wanting to become seriously involved in "the current defense debate so vital to national interests," and can be ordered directly from: Aviation Week and Space Technology Book Club, McGraw-Hill Inc., P.O.Box 457, Hightstown, New Jersey 08520 (list price is $21.95 plus postage) or telephone (609) 448-1700 ext. 5296.

The cover picture, the Russian Bear snarling at the American Eagle, is slightly misleading. There is not one ounce of emotion in the entire book—Collins presents facts, facts, facts. No matter your perspective or your purpose, should the book itself prove in any way to be inadequate, then the pedagogic capabilities of the author are always available for backup.

John Collins was on the faculty of the National War College, Director of Military Strategic Studies, and First Chief of the Strategic Research Group. Collins is not only able to clarify the written material—he does it with ease and grace—Collins is also able and willing to encourage the faint at heart. So, what ever else happens in this Great Debate, this book by John Collins is a must for technical and political reference [refer to *New York Times*, September 28, 1980, pg. 16, for a review].

My only hope is that the American people prove every prediction from John Collins to be dead wrong. And, as I sense his personal preference, that is the hope of John Collins as well.

A002 "Technology push"

It is the rule, not the exception, that technological innovation pushes out ahead of social change in the United States [*Manufacturing Engineering* (a journal published by the Society of Manufacturing Engineers), January 1982. "SME Golden Anniversary Issue 1932-1982: A Review of Manufacturing and the Society which Guides Its Progress," Vol. 88, No. 1, pg. 4, "The President's Message," by Robert L. Vaughn, Lockheed Missiles and Space Comp.]

"We have lived through a burst of technological innovation and advance such as the world has never seen. The only period comparable to it in terms of human achievement is the Renaissance. We are now challenged—almost beyond our ability to respond—by the need to accept and assimilate that massive outpouring of technological developments." The President continues, he cautions against indiscriminate assimilation and misdirected absorption . . . "We are challenged to utilize technology for the great good of mankind. If we fail in that challenge, we may be sure that our prized technology will go the way of the bison and the messenger pigeon."

Though the President's message is worth reading in its entirety, I only quote portions. "We are challenged . . . by the fact that the ability to wage nuclear warfare represents one of mankind's greatest technological achievements and the most persistent and dangerous political failure. It can be said that the creation of superlative technology was the overriding challenge for the first half-century (1932-1982). Coming to terms with [the use of] that technology may well be the greatest challenge of the second."

Proponents of technology push are also advocates of "war potential," a philosophy that caters to the belief that a nation can and should do as much as possible ahead of time to prepare to fight a war. Today one might suppose that all industries in the United States have always subscribed to the philosophy of war potential [*National Defense*, June 1980, "Partners in Preparedness: An Index of Military/Industry Manufacturers"], but prior to the declaration of World War II that was clearly not the case.

The "America First" Committee, formed in 1939, was joined by many from the automotive industry. Even though both the German and Soviet armies had already invaded Poland, Americans were speaking out against any form of military intervention by the United States ["The View from America, 1939—The Depression Ends," *Manufacturing Engineering*, SME Golden Anniversary Issue, January 1982, pg. 70]. It was not until after

World War II that it became necessary for industries in the United States and elsewhere to subscribe to the theory of "war potential" in order to become card-carrying members of the military-industrial complex.

President Eisenhower alerted the American people to this industrial transformation: " . . . we must guard against the acquisition of unwarranted influence, whether sought or unsought, by the military-industrial complex. The potential for the disastrous rise of misplaced power exists and will persist." [Dwight D. Eisenhower: "Farewell Radio and Television Address to the American People," January 17, 1961. *Public Papers of the Presidents of the United States*, Dwight D. Eisenhower: 1960-1961, pg. 1038, U.S. Government Printing Office.]

Following World War II, many scientists and engineers were convinced that they could design and build automated equipment to replace people; the "black box" mentality dominated ["Information Engineering: Why Communicators are Poor Communicators," *Government Executive*, June 1980, pg. 16]. Gerald Dinneen, Principle Deputy Undersecretary of Defense, Research, and Engineering and Assistant Secretary of Defense for Communications, Command, Control, and Intelligence, is being quoted from remarks he made before an AFCEA audience (Air Force Communications and Electronics Association). Dinneen, a Carter appointee at the Pentagon, was explaining why he believed the "communicator's" most important job was to overcome our propensity to continually foster the "black box" syndrome.

Dr. Dinneen was referring specifically to radar or communication system components, rather than weapons, but the black-box compulsion has a habit of being everywhere the same. Scientists and engineers who have devoted their professional lives to interacting with a circuit board or a power supply have little understanding for or appreciation of a user-oriented system that requires human judgement and a skilled operator.

By mobilizing only a handful of men and a wealth of technology, the military would have global destruction at its fingertips; the United States could instantly engage in a MAD (Mutual Assured Destruction) nuclear exchange with the Soviet Union. "War had added empire, but undermined prosperity; it had brought wealth, but introduced inequalities; it had filled the city with spoils, but sown the vices of self-interest. The [military] machinery remained perfect, but life had fled. It henceforth became the labor of [Emperors] to keep together their vast possessions with this machinery which at last wore out. There was neither genius to repair it nor patriotism to work it." [The Roman Empire] lasted but three hundred years . . . it was broken to pieces by the barbarians [Lord, John (1883), *Beacon Lights of History*, Vol. III. "Ancient Achievement," New York: James Clarke and Co., pp. 238, 271-272].

U.S. nuclear strategy is being determined by the industrial availability of automated weapons systems. Concern for this dominating influence of "technology push" attracted national attention during the closing days of the Carter Administration when Secretary of Defense Harold Brown publicly discussed the political implications of "technology evolution" in connection with new improved targeting capabilities for nuclear weapons, especially the MX [ABC-TV "Issues and Answers," Sunday, August 17, 1980, transcribed text available at the Pentagon, Office of the Assistant Secretary for Public Affairs, Department of Defense].

A003 "Demand pull"

Demand pull is the natural dueling partner for technology push. After 25 years as an engineer at the Massachusetts Institute of Technology and 3-plus years at the Pentagon, Gerald Dinneen was able to conclude, " . . . the most important objective is not the development of C3I (read C-cube I, meaning Communication, Command, Control, and Intelligence, the name of a division at the Pentagon), but rather the selling of it [*Government Executive*, Subsection A002, as referenced above]."

"As long as we support technology people [technology push], they will come up with new systems. What we've got to do is understand what the consumer needs [the demand pull of the military users]." Actually what is needed is to keep a person like Dinneen in contact with the service aspect of national service, rather that to reward him with an imposed seclusion in the academic environment.

A004 Demand-side economics

In departing from the classical balance of supply and demand, an all-new demand-side economics might be worth considering [Thaler, Richard, "Toward a Positive Theory of Consumer Choice," *Journal of Economic Behavior and Organization*, Vol. 1, No. 1, March 1980, pp. 39-60].

The fault with classical "demand-side" economics is that the people are supposed to demand only government spending for social hand-outs. The all-new "demand-side" economics would have the people demanding increased government spending to stimulate the growth of an all-new industrial base. The new industrial base would be dependent upon electronics and service-oriented information centers. Refer to Martin Gardner, "Mathematical Games: The Laffer Curve and Other Laughs in Current Economics," *Scientific American*, December 1981, pg. 18, for a brief but helpful overview of classical concepts, and a wealth of included references.

A book of essays on supply-side economics was reviewed by Chamberlain, John, "Supply Side Economics," *The Freeman*, Vol. 32, No. 6, June 1981, pg. 381. These essays include: "Supply Side Analysis and Public Policy," by Norman B. Ture; "Rational Expectations and Supply Side Economics: Match or Mismatch," by David G. Tuerck; "The Enterprise System, Democracy, and the General Welfare: An Approach to Reconciliation," by Richard E. Wagner; "From Antitrust to Supply-Side Economics: The History of Federal Intervention in the Economy," by Naomi R. Lamoureaux.

The use of information as a "raw material" from which to manufacture "computer products" is realistic only when that information becomes available as a "national resource," when every industry in the private sector has equal opportunity for real-time access to a digital data base in the public domain [*Information For The 1980s*. Final Report of the White House Conference on Library and Information Services (1979), Superintendent of Documents, U.S. Government Printing Office, Washington, DC 20402, or contact the National Commission on Libraries and Information Science, 1717 K Street, N.W., Suite 600, Washington, DC 20036]. PART TWO of the book, "Resolution C-12: Telecommunication Networks," discusses the question of immediate access to information belonging in the public domain.

A005 The promising aspect of war

The Constitution of the United States grants "war powers" to the Congress. "War Powers are legislative, they belong to the Congress," wrote James Madison in his "Helvidius" letters in 1793 [Goldsmith, William M. (1974), *The Growth of Presidential Power*, Vol. I: *The Formative Years*, pg. 405, New York: Chelsea House Pub.]. More details are included in Subsection D122: Madison responds to "Pacificus."

Somewhat in contradiction to that legislative control over war powers, emergency powers now resting with the President of the United States include authority to order the use of nuclear weapons [*National Emergency and Delegated Emergency Powers*, Senate Report no. 94-922, 94th Congress, 2d Session, May 28, 1976, U.S. Government Printing Office, Washington, DC]. Refer also to Subsection D119: The national emergency.

The entire concept of deterrence, the national defense policy that would have the United States absorb a First Strike from the Soviet Union and then retaliate, attracted public attention during the closing days of the Carter Administration, as the United States moved closer to a Soviet-style "coercive deterrence." [Simes, Dimitri A., "Deterrence and Coercion in Soviet Policy . . . " *International Security* (Center for Science and International Affairs, a publication of Harvard University), Winter 1980-1981, pp. 80-103.]

"To repel Invasions," the phrase taken from the U.S. Constitution, is a slight simplification. The quotation, in its entirety, dates back to Hugo Grotius (1583-1645), the father of international law. Grotius endeavored to set forth "a new code of international conduct, based not upon the authority of the Church but . . . on the fundamental idea of the law of nature."

According to Grotius, "wars were justified only to repel invasions or to punish an insult to God." But, as the authors of the textbook point out, "the appeal of Grotius, however intelligent, fell largely on deaf ears." [*Civilization Past and Present*, Chpt. 14: "The Strife of States and Kings: Power Politics and the New Diplomacy: 1500-1650, pg. 324. Scott, Foresman and Comp. (1962), by T. Walter Wallbank, Alastair M. Taylor, and Nels M. Bailky.]

A006   A forward look

The appeal for equality: "There would be no favored friends," is an appeal for equal protection under the rule of law for all nations. "The Constitution of the United States is a law for rulers and people, equally in war and in peace, and covers with the shield of its protection all classes of men, at all times, and under all circumstances [McCloskey, Robert G. (1957), *Essays in Constitutional Law*, New York: Alfred A. Knopf (a collection of reprints), pg. 4]."

The intent of this book is to extend that "shield of protection" to all classes of men, in all nations, at all times; to extend rule by the force of law, rather than by the force of military destruction . . . to all classes of men, in all nations, at all times.

That the American people are qualified to teach the rest of the world "equal protection under the rule of law" can be concluded from Max Lerner, "The Supreme Court and American Capitalism," reprinted in McCloskey, Robert G. (1957), *Essays in Constitutional Law*, New York: Alfred A. Knopf, pg. 108, " . . . judicial power—or more exactly, judicial supremacy—is a uniquely American institution . . . "

The urgent need to recognize and respect the individuality and uniqueness of all nations is expressed in *North-South: A Program For Survival*, prepared by the Brandt Commission [*Parameters*, June 1980, pg. 93, a book review].

PART ONE

Chapter B

On the Campaign Trail

The Republicans won the majority in the United States Senate in 1980 when Ronald Reagan was elected President. When Republican Dwight D. Eisenhower was elected President in 1952, he carried the Republican victory in both Houses of Congress, making the only time since 1931 (or after) that the Republican party had controlled both the executive and legislative branches of government at the same time. In 1956, Dwight D. Eisenhower became the first winning Presidential candidate since Zachary Taylor, in 1848, to fail to carry his party to victory in either the House of Representatives or the Senate [*The Hammond Almanac*. 1980. Hammond Almanac, Inc., Maplewood, New Jersey, pg. 160].

The Committee structure is dominated by the political party with the majority. In 1980, the majority party in the United States Senate became Republican so the chairmanships of the Committees shifted to Republican and the emphasis of committee responsibility also shifted.

B007 George Bush candidate

The interview by Walter Scheer was published January 24, 1980, *Los Angeles Times*, "Bush Assails Carter Defense Strategy: Cites MX Missile and Bomber Cuts." Walter Scheer has since published a book, *With Enough Shovels: Reagan, Bush, and Nuclear War* (1982), New York: Random House.

B008 Fighting a nuclear war

The reader has to make a distinction between the use of nuclear weapons on the battlefield and the firing of massively destructive nuclear warheads across intercontinental distances. "Strategic balance" is usually interpreted to mean a "balance" of nuclear weapons that can be launched across intercontinental distances between the United States and the Soviet Union.

B009 And winning?

The "winnable nuclear war" refers back to the Walter Scheer interview with George Bush, see Subsection B007.

The defense-related remark by George Bush attracted a lot of attention in the press in the United States and in the Soviet Union. By the end of the summer, 1980, the Carter Administration had responded to this "trial balloon" launched by George Bush. The press was well aware of the importance of the "new" nuclear strategy announcements on American election campaign tactics. And the foreign press was uniformly denying the "newness" of the targeting options: Oslo, Norway, *Aftenposten* (in Norwegian), August 18, 1980, pg. 2; Helsinki, Finland, *Helsingin Sanomat* (in Finnish), August 16, 1980, pg. 2; Frankfurt, Germany, *Frankfurter Allgemeine* (in German), August 12, 1980, pg. 8; Paris, France, *Le Figaro* (in French), August 8, 1980, pg. 24, "Toward a Counterforce Doctrine," by Michel Tatu. Tatu directly attaches importance to the January 1980 release of the annual defense report in the United States . . . His [President Carter] departments had just completed a fundamental reexamination of strategic policy, the defense secretary [Harold Brown] explained what he calls his "countervailing strategy."

PART ONE

Chapter C

At the White House

President Carter announced a change in official U.S. nuclear strategy that was perceived to include a limited nuclear war-fighting capability ["Defense Chief Explains Shift in War Strategy," by Charles W. Corddry, *Baltimore Sun*, August 21, 1980, pg. 8; "Brown Outlines New U.S. Policy on Nuclear Strategy," by John J. Fialka, *Washington Star*, August 21, 1980, pg. 3; "Change in Nuclear Target Policy Not a Radical One, Brown Says," by George C. Wilson, *Washington Post*, August 21, 1980, pg. 1; "Carter's New A-Policy: Deterrent or Trigger?" by Brian J. Kelly, *Chicago Sun-Times*, August 17, 1980, pg. 10; "The New Brinksmanship," by Tad Szulc, *The New Republic*, November 8, 1980, pp. 18-21; "Launch Under Attack," by William F. Buckley, Jr., *Washington Star*, November 5, 1980, pg. 21].

For an intellectual response to this human (political) turmoil, refer to *Scientific American*, Vol. 243, No. 1, July 1980, pp. 43-51, "A Ban on the Production of Fissionable Material for Weapons: Such a "cut-off" could serve two purposes: to stall the further buildup of nuclear arms by the present nuclear-weapons states and to prevent their spread to the non-nuclear-weapons states," by William Epstein.

In my opinion, when you have a leak in the faucet, you call a plumber; when you have a problem with nuclear strategy, you call the military. The politicians, the industrial giants who profit from weapons production, and the intellectuals who would much rather talk than do anything else, have created the turmoil. The discipline of the military mind, the insight of "grand strategy," and the commitment to national service, when actively combined, could alter the current "evolutionary tends" in nuclear policy. After all, the military service organizations are the only national service organizations dedicated to the "art of leadership."

General Order 21, *United States Navy Regulations* (1948), superseded by *United States Navy Regulations* (1973), reprinted by John V. Noel, Jr. (Captain U.S. Navy Retired), *Division Officer's Guide*, Sixth Edition, Naval Institute Press, Annapolis, Maryland, 1972, pg. 2, describes " . . . the art of accomplishing the Navy's mission through people. It is the sum of those qualities of intellect, of human understanding, and of moral character that enable a man to inspire and to manage a group of people successfully. Effective leadership, therefore, is based on personal example, good management practices, and more responsibility." A portion of commentary by Noel is worth repeating: "Leaders, like musicians, surgeons, and scientists, do not spring forth full grown as masters of their art. They serve an apprenticeship during which they practice the disciplines of their profession."

C010 In defense of national security

President Carter signed a series of four Presidential Directives/National Security Council . . . a survey of those Presidential Directives, including PD/NSC-53, 57, 58, 59, was presented as written testimony to Congressman Albert Gore, Jr. (Democrat-Tenn), Chairman of the House Subcommittee on Science and Technology, September 29, 1981 [Foster, Richard B., "Forecastability of National Security Telecommunications Requirements," and Hoeber, Francis P., "The Changing Environment for National Emergency Preparedness and its Communications Support," both from SRI International].

C011 The evolution of nuclear strategy

The typescript of ABC-TV "Issues and Answers," Sunday, August 17, 1980, the interview of Secretary of Defense Harold Brown, was provided by the Public Affairs Office, Department of Defense, Pentagon. Harold Brown insists, and rightly so, that U.S. nuclear strategy is "evolutionary." Though Secretary Brown does not say it, one can safely conclude that there has not been one ounce of "creativity" introduced into U.S. nuclear (deterrence) strategy since August 6, 1945, the day Hiroshima was bombed.

C012 The preemptive First Strike

Authority to order the use of nuclear weapons is documented concisely ["Authority To Order The Use of Nuclear Weapons (United States, United Kingdom, France, Soviet Union, People's Republic of China)," Committee Print, 94th Congress, 1st Session, December, 1975, prepared by the Subcommittee on International Security and Scientific Affairs of the Committee on International Relations, by the Congressional Research Service, Library of Congress, U.S. Government Printing Office, Washington, DC].

The "oldness" of the "new" Carter policy seems to have made the press in all European NATO countries, for example, Bonn, West Germany, *Die Welt* (in German), August 19, 1980, pg. 6, Editorial, "Not New, but Effective," by Wolfram von Raven, " . . . the basic idea still stems from Robert S. McNamara [Secretary of Defense McNamara made an explicit policy statement at the University of Michigan, June 16, 1962 (reported in the *New York Times*, June 17, 1962), refer back to the Congressional Testimony by Richard B. Foster, Subsection C010]."

The draft dates back to James Schlesinger [a report by Secretary of Defense Schlesinger in 1974], but Harold Brown is implementing the matter according to technical developments that are rooted deep in the sixties.

A comprehensive review of the U.S. efforts to progress from a "war prevention" to a "war fighting" strategy requires consideration of Soviet policy [Simes, Dimitri K., "Deterrence and Coercion in Soviet Policy." *International Security* (Center for Science and International Affairs, a journal of),

Winter 1980-1981, pp. 80-103]. The "dichotomies" discussed by Simes would make one wonder, even more, why the United States should not take it upon itself to "unilaterally" disarm the Soviet Union, immediately. It seems the United States would be doing the entire world, including the people in the Soviet Union, a great favor . . . the United States would disarm the Soviet Union at the same time it disarms itself, of course.

C013 Delegated authority

The delegation of authority for the use of nuclear weapons is briefly stated in "Authority To Order The Use of Nuclear Weapons," as referenced in Subsection C012; the distinction between First Strike and First Use (of nuclear weapons) is also explained.

The explanation for "first use" given by Secretary of Defense, Harold Brown, is taken from the ABC-TV "Issues and Answers" transcript, as referenced in Subsection C011.

The Founding Fathers were definite in their intent, war powers belong to the Congress. This topic of Congressional War Powers is pursued, within the context of separation of powers, in PART SIX, Subsections D121 and D122. The idea of legislative dominance over the executive can be attributed directly to John Locke (1632-1704). " . . . [Locke] maintained that the legislative was a more senior partner than the executive." [Goldsmith, William M. (1974). *The Growth of Presidential Power*, New York: Chelsea House Publishers, Vol. 1: "The Formative Years," Part 1: "The Origins of Presidential Power: European Influences on American Views of Executive Power," pg. 38.]

"Rule by the force of law," if it goes to the Executive Offices and corresponding Regulatory Agencies, would be "rule by the force of an appointed police state." When rule by the force of law goes to the Legislative, then you have rule by an entire body of elected members.

PART ONE

Chapter D

And then the State Department

The political mood of the country appeared divided: there was support for a foreign policy of negotiated arms control; there was support for a domestic policy of military superiority. President Carter appeared to be contradicting himself as he tried publicly to reconcile the two . . . and the media had a grand time.

"Brown and Muskie Asked for N-Policy Testimony" [*Washington Star*, August 16, 1980, pg. 4], members of the Senate Foreign Relations Committee had asked Secretary of Defense Harold R. Brown and Secretary of State Edmund S. Muskie to testify on President Carter's new nuclear targeting policy "as soon as possible."

The article went on to say that the Senate Committee, for some months, had been examining the interaction between American military [as represented by the civilian dominated Department of Defense] and foreign policy [as represented through official channels of the State Department].

The Senate Foreign Relations Committee was merely attracting attention to the ongoing power struggle between the two contenders for dominant influence in American foreign policy: the State Department and the Defense Department [*Naval War College Review*, March-April 1980, pp. 34-57, "Departure from Incrementalism in U.S. Strategic Planning: The Origins of NSC-68," by Sam Postbrief]. This recently declassified document from Truman Administration national security planning shows " . . . arguments formed and advanced in the present strategic debate are strikingly similar to those offered in the debate on NSC-68 (National Security Council-68)."

A well-respected Nobel prize winning scientist, a colleague from Sweden, Hannes Alfven, hastened into print with an explanation that this "split" between the Department of Defense and the Department of State was not confined to the political arena in the United States, or to the shores of the Potomac. Alfven, because he is a brilliant and capable writer, left no room for doubt, " . . . the real frontier in the world . . . is within the scientific community — between the pro-bomb and the anti-bomb groups [*Bulletin of the Atomic Scientists*, January 1981, pp. 4-5]." Professor Alfven should be taken seriously. Professor Alfven should be encouraged to seek public office (refer to PART SIX, Subsection F130: From Scientist to Senator). Professor Hannes Alfven has been teaching in the Department of Applied Physics and Information Science at the University of California, San Diego, La Jolla, California 92037.

The "Transcript of the President's News Conference on Foreign and Domestic Matters," was printed by the *New York Times*, September 19, 1980, pg. B-5.

D014 Peaceful thoughts from Senator Muskie

Senator Muskie was Chairman of the U.S. Senate Foreign Relations Subcommittee in 1974 when Pentagon casualty estimates were found faulty [Committee Print, Senate Foreign Relations, September 18, 1975, 94th Congress, 1s Session, "Analyses of Effects of Limited Nuclear War," available at the Pentagon Library (U.S. Army); also "Muskie Rebuffs Soviet on Nuclear Strategy Criticism," by Richard Burt, *New York Times*, September 17, 1980, pg. 3].

D015   A bypass for the State Department

Secretary of Defense Harold Brown was publicly defending Presidential Directive/National Security Council-59 ["Point of View: Casualties in a Limited Nuclear War," by I. F. Stone, *Washington Star*, August 23, 1980, pg. 11; and "Point of View: A Soviet view of the nuclear directive," by Gennadi Gerasimov, *Washington Star*, August 27, 1980, pg. 9]. I. F. Stone was Editor and Publisher of *I. F. Stone's Weekly*; Gennadi Gerasimov is a political correspondent for Novosti Press Agency.

"The Myth of Missile Accuracy," by Andrew Cockburn and Alexander Cockburn [*New York Review of Books*, November 20, 1980, pp. 40-43], reprints a remark from Dr. Richard Garwin, IBM Research Center, a past member of the Defense Science Board, describing " . . . anomalies in the Earth's gravitational field, varying densities in the upper atmosphere, or unknown wind velocities."

The public image of arms negotiations of the Carter Administration was being violated by the Muskie bypass ["What is Muskie's role?" *Denver Post*, August 21, 1980; "The PD-59 Affair," *Washington Post*, August 22, 1980; and "PD-59: Why?" *Los Angeles Times*, August 15, 1980].

More comprehensive reports are available: "Deterring Nuclear War: 1. The New Dangers," the first of a series by Elizabeth Pond [*Christian Science Monitor*, August 26, 1980, pg. 12]; "Carter's Nuclear Policy: Going from MAD to Worse?" which includes "No: It's Evolutionary, Not Revolutionary, and Aims to Strengthen Deterrence," by Leon Sloss and "Yes: The Revision of U.S. Strategy Implies a Belief in Limited War," by Paul C. Warnke [*Los Angeles Times*, August 31, 1980, pg. 3].

The *New York Times* headline on the front page, August 10, 1980, expressed alarm about the bypass of Muskie at the State Department, "Muskie Wasn't Told of New War Policy Before It Was Set: Pentagon Promises Briefing: Secretary of State Says He Learned of Change in Nuclear Strategy Only By Reading Papers," by Bernard Gwertzman.

The serious question that existed during the closing days of the Carter Administration, still exists today. There is a question of the role for the National Security Council (NSC) versus the role for the State Department in formulating and implementing U.S. foreign policy ["The Super Bureaucracy: Time to Check the NSC," by Flora Lewis, *Washington Star*, September 12, 1980, pg. 11]. The comment is made, "Foreign governments should be able to see without doubt that ambassadors abroad, the Secretary of State at home, are their conduits to U.S. decision-making."

PART ONE

Chapter E

A Quick Fix for a Press Leak

The press leak that announced the importance of stealth technology, was printed in the *Air Force Journal*, "U.S. Has Been Flying Virtually Invisible Aircraft for Over Two Years: Several Tactical Versions Are in Production: Senior DoD Official Calls Program a 'Breakthrough,' Bigger Than Cruise Missile or Hi-Energy Laser," by Benjamin F. Schemmer, September 1980.

The *Defense Daily* Analysis [September 23, 1980. pp. 111-115] reported, "Stealth Disclosure: A Play on Motivation," which goes on to explain that the disclosure of the stealth bomber, virtually invisible to enemy radar, would counter criticism by Ronald Reagan that President Carter was failing to replace the old B-52 bombers.

E016   The realities of stealth

Say, "Kelly Johnson," and smile. Clarence "Kelly" Johnson, Chief Designer of the U-2 high-flying single-engine aircraft, is at Lockheed ["A New Life For a High-Flying Bird: At the Skunk Works: a successor to the U-2 takes shape," *Time*, December 22, 1980, pg. 64]. There is brief reference to the history of the humor of the story of fuel development . . . Kelly's Lighter Fluid No. 1.

The political implications of the "press leak" were freely reported ["Carter Denies Directing Disclosure of Stealth Program," by Richard Burt, *New York Times*, September 21, 1980, pg. 33; "Defense Secretary Fires Some Political Missiles: There's Nothing Stealthy About Harold Brown's Attacks," by Richard Halloran, *New York Times*, September 7, 1980, pg. E-2; "Stealth News Called Political by House Panel," by John J. Fialka, *Washington Star*, February 5, 1981, pg. 3].

The capabilities of reconnaissance aircraft cannot be accurately documented. One should simply assume that the technology has now been improved to the point that the theoretical resolution limit can be achieved under ideal atmospheric observing conditions, conditions that only seldom occur in most parts of the world.

E017   The politics of leaking

The **Republican** Senator from Indiana, Richard G. Lugar, respected member of the United States Senate Select Committee on Intelligence, and also a member of the Senate Foreign Relations Committee, wrote a letter to The Honorable Birch Bayh, the **Democratic** Senator from Indiana, Chairman of the Senate Select Committee on Intelligence, September 10, 1980, requesting a series of closed hearings to inquire, " . . . to what extent was the intentional leaking, and subsequent public disclosure . . . ordered by the White House?"

On September 10, 1980, Senator Lugar also released a letter from E. R. Zumwalt, Jr., Admiral, U.S. Navy (retired), dated September 5, 1980, stating that President Carter chose the method, " . . . first to leak its existence [the existence and feasibility of the stealth aircraft] and then be forced to confirm the leak." The *Journal of Commerce* immediately reported Lugar's release of Zumwalt's statement that accused "Mr. Carter of personally making the decision to reveal the new technology [September 11, 1980, pg. 4]."

Jack Anderson was equally critical of the August 22 disclosure by Secretary of Defense Harold Brown [*Washington Post*, C-27, Monday, October 13, 1980, "Stealth: The Story Behind a Secret"]. "If this is a Republican suspicion [the suspicion that the press leak of stealth technology was politically timed], it is shared by at least one prominent Democrat— Senator John Glenn (Democrat-Ohio) . . . Glenn deplored the 'manner and timing' of the leak . . . "

E018 The vanishing power of the President

"Playing politics with national security," through the press, the theme spread across the nation. Everyone was interested to know . . . whose politics . . . and whose security?

One of the most condemning reports of the abuse of Executive power comes from the Special Committee on National Emergency and Delegated Emergency Powers, Senate Report No. 94-922, 94th Congress, 2d Session, Final Report, May 28, 1976, pg. 18, "Congress has not specified substantive standards for the recording of Presidential Directives . . . Congress has not yet enacted laws to prevent the Executive branch from abusing its power to classify documents where its purpose is to withhold information from Congress and the public." The report continues, "Although Clause 3 of 44 U.S.C. 1505 permits Congress to designate classes of documents for publication, Congress has never addressed itself directly to this question in the broad sense here considered."

The Final Report ends with caution, "The Committee . . . cannot accept any doctrine which holds that a nation *in extremis* must submit to the will of a single individual. Our forefathers . . . cautioned, repeatedly, that one branch of government must not be allowed to usurp the powers of another."

It takes the force of public opinion to change those laws. When Congress writes a law that violates public opinion, the people simply never get around to implementing it. The outstanding example of this force of public opinion comes from the Prohibition Amendment to the U.S. Constitution, Amendment Eighteen, that was eventually repealed by the Twenty-first Amendment . . . because enforcement was impossible [*The Story of the Constitution*, Sol Bloom, The United States Constitution Sesquicentennial Commission, House Office Bldg., Washington, DC (1937), pg. 50].

PART ONE

Perspective

The Power of Public Opinion

During the 1980 presidential election, the arrival of a new political mood was evidenced by a heavy Republican vote. Ronald Reagan became President. The Republicans gained a majority in the United States Senate. The mood of the country is a "living" property assigned to the nation as a whole. The mood of the country is assigned according to the way the nation is viewed from outside. The mood of the 1980 election was assessed from foreign newspapers.

"Hope for Yesterday," an Editorial by Werner Holzer, *Frankfurter Rundschau* (in German), November 6, 1980, pg. 3, centers attention on "good old America," and concludes that "the majority of the people of the most powerful Western nation have gotten exactly what they have been longing for."

From Paris *Le Monde* (in French), November 6, 1980, pg. 1, in an Editorial, "Rejection Phenomenon," there is the opening statement: "The crushing repudiation of President Carter by the U.S. voters reflects above all personal failure of a man who had scarcely more than his sincerity and good will to offer." It is on his general attitude, on that famous "leadership," that Mr. Carter has been "judged and rejected." He [President Reagan] has been able to rally the mass of middle class people who want "things to change" at home and abroad and who, although enlisted under the banner of moral order which the president-elect loftily claims to follow, are "pushing for change."

Laurence Radway, "The Curse of Free Elections," *Foreign Policy*, Fall 1980, pp. 61-73, discusses Presidential candidates who have conformed to the public mood (Harry Truman, John Kennedy, Stuart Symington, Lyndon Johnson, Barry Goldwater, Richard Nixon, Gerald Ford, Jimmy Carter, Ronald Reagan, and George Bush) and those who have been reluctant to do so (Thomas Dewey, Dwight Eisenhower, Adlai Stevenson, Hubert Humphrey, Eugene McCarthy, George McGovern, and Edward Kennedy) and concludes that most of the winners are in the group that catered to the electorate's definition of national self-interest.

From the *Madrid Domestic Service* (in Spanish), at 2300 GMT, November 5, 1980, the Secretary General of the Spanish Socialist Workers Party, Felipe Gonzalez, is quoted as having said, "Reagan's election from a point of view of domestic politics is a clear manifestation of a conservative tendency in American society, and I think that it is best to recognize this fact and not try to explain it with deceitful words."

From the *Frankfurter Allgemeine* (in German), November 6, 1980, pg. 1, Commentary, signed G-N, "Europe May Hope," describes the return of the

Republicans to the White House as a "plus" in the fields of economic and finance policy, saying, "Europeans have always gotten along better with Republican than with Democratic Presidents. The foreign policy of the Republicans is usually less ambitious and less missionary. Despite modest aims, it [the Republican foreign policy] has usually been more successful with regard to security and peace."

My conclusion from this extensive survey of foreign news is that the American people now believe that this nation, as a nation, can formulate new policies for national security and that those policies should include increased defense spending.

Though mood is difficult to put into words, General Robert E. Huyer, United States Air Force, Commander-in-Chief, Military Airlift Command, attempted the impossible. In "Patriotism Lies In Nation's Soul [*The Officer*, July 1980, pg. 12]," Huyer makes a plea for Americans to vote ... the voting record " ... is a national disgrace. The majority can no longer be silent." General Huyer is convinced the nation needs to hear the voice of the silent majority.

When President Carter released what was perceived by many to be classified information about defense-related issues, and he did it in the name of national security, those close to the Carter White House remained loyal, but the Democratic Party fragmented. [An Editorial from Paris, *Le Monde* (in French), November 6, 1980, pg. 1, "Rejection Phenomenon."] " ... Throughout his presidency, Mr. Carter used the national backing given to him in 1976 without succeeding in keeping the loyalty of the regional and social groups which were the foundation of his success at that time." The details are there and then the conclusion: "The President's rather cold nature and his frequent vacillations worked against the emergence of the sympathetic feeling which properly exercised power always creates. This emotional and political bankruptcy brought about the collapse of the Democratic coalition which, since Roosevelt, to a greater or lesser degree, united the labor world, the minorities—especially the large Catholic minority—and the South."

Secretary of Defense Harold Brown went on national television [ABC-TV "Issues and Answers (transcribed text)," Sunday, August 17, 1980] to defend President Carter's nuclear policy. The B-1 bomber was also discussed. A question by Mr. McWethy reminded Secretary Brown that he had " ... appeared at the Democratic National Convention," that he was " ... stepping up [his] speaking schedule." And Brown replied, "I am speaking out to defend the Administration's defense and foreign policies of which I'm a contributing architect ... "

PART TWO

Nuclear War Strategy

If you are going to fight a limited nuclear war,
then you really should find a willing target

MAD—Mutual Assured Destruction—depends upon having ICBMs—Inter-Continental Ballistic Missiles—aimed and ready to fire [Brodie, Bernard (1946). *The Absolute Weapon: Atomic Power and World Order*. New York: Harcourt, Brace, a classic work for the notion of deterrence from which MAD strategy is supposed to have evolved]. Detailed reference is given at the beginning of PART ONE.

The endorsement of the use of armed force as a means of extending communist influence comes from the *Communist Manifesto* (1848), composed by Karl Marx (1818-1883) with the aid of Friedrich Engels (1820-1895), while in Brussels [refer to commentary by Ebenstein, William (1962). *Great Political Thinkers*, Section 23: Totalitarian Communism, pg. 675, New York: Holt, Rinehart and Winston]. "What makes totalitarian communism an issue of peace or war is not its opposition to capitalism, but its determination to impose its philosophy by force of arms (pp. 673-690)."

The use of Europe as a battlefield is now openly discussed in Europe in connection with the modernization of NATO ["Schlachtfeld Europa: Die neue Heeresdoktrin der USA," von Konrad Ege, pp. 1438-1448, *Blätter für deutsche und internationale Politik*, December 1982, Pahl-Rugenstein Verlag, Köln].

The use of nuclear weapons on the "battlefield," in retaliation to conventional weapons, has almost lost its meaning because of the increased sophistication of "conventional" systems. Nevertheless, I still stand firm: I am opposed to the use of weapons of destruction as an acceptable means of deciding national superiority.

PART TWO

Chapter A

Anti-City Strategy

"Authority to Order the Use of Nuclear Weapons (United States, United Kingdom, France, Soviet Union, People's Republic of China)," Subcommittee on International Security and Scientific Affairs of the Committee on International Relations by the Congressional Research Service, Library of Congress, December 1, 1975, 94th Congress, 1st Session, Committee Print,

U.S. Government Printing Office, Washington, DC, is referenced frequently in this part of the book.

" . . . the use of 'small tactical nuclear weapons, . . . and authority to use them should be given to local commanders' (pg. 2, above)." U.S. strategic policy " . . . excludes a first strike, but does not rule out the first use of nuclear weapons (pg. 1, above)."

A broad overview of "Evolving Deterrent Policy" is given by Richard B. Foster, September 29, 1981, written Congressional Testimony, refer to Subsection A022.

Doubt of anti-city targeting is expressed by R. Jeffrey Smith, "Pentagon Moves Toward First Strike Capability," *Science*, Vol. 216, pp. 596-598, May 2, 1982, which includes a discussion of preemptive First Strike option. On pg. 598, in the same journal, "Another in a Series of Counterforce Weapons . . . Pentagon target—only 7% against cities . . . targeting of military facilities is not retaliatory."

The use of nuclear weapons in Europe was discussed by President Eisenhower. See "Special Message to the Congress Transmitting Agreement With Italy for Cooperative Uses of Atomic Energy of Mutual Defense," Dwight D. Eisenhower, January 17, 1961, [*Congressional Record*, March 7, 1961, vol. 107, pg. 1095] for text of agreement. " . . . if an attack on NATO should occur, Italian forces could, under the direction of the Supreme Allied Commander for Europe, effectively use nuclear weapons in their defense." [*Public Papers of the Presidents of the United States*, Dwight D. Eisenhower: 1960-1961, pg. 1035, U.S. Government Printing Office, Washington, DC.]

A019 The logic of geography

The well-established Russian tradition for the use of force comes directly from the *Communist Manifesto* (1848), written by Karl Marx (1818-1883) with the aid of Friedrich Engels (1820-1895). The teachings were made political reality in Russia by Vladimir Ilyich Ulyanov (1870-1924) who called himself Lenin, a name derived from the River Lena, which flowed through the region of Siberia where he was exiled January 1897 [Ebenstein, William (1962). *Great Political Thinkers*. New York: Holt, Rinehart and Winston, pg. 683].

The advantage of the aerospace industries of the United States following World War II is documented in detail [*Manufacturing Engineering*, Vol. 88, No. 1, January 1982, the "SME Golden Anniversary Issue 1932-1982, A Review of Manufacturing and the Society which Guides Its Progress," published by the Society of Manufacturing Engineers].

One of the more detailed analyses of Russian arms development is given by John M. Collins (1980). *U.S.-Soviet Military Balance*, to be ordered from Aviation Week and Space Technology Book Club, McGraw-Hill, Inc., P.O.Box 457, Hightstown, New Jersey 08520. Author comments about John Collins are given in Subsection A001: The threatening aspect of peace, Notes and References.

A020 Silo positioning in the Soviet Union

Underground silo construction is a necessary part of long-range missile installation. Many short-, medium-, or so-called intermediate-range missiles can be fired from launch platforms that are transportable. The Office of Technology Assessment of the United States Congress completed a study of basing modes for intercontinental ballistic missiles ["MX Missile Basing: Summary," OTA-ISC-139, June 1981, refer to Subsection A032 for additional comments about the MX basing mode].

A review of aerial surveillance is provided by *RUSI* (Journal of the Royal United Services Institute for Defense Studies), June 1978, pg. 64, "National Technical Means of Verification," by Colonel E. Asa Bates, Jr., United States Air Force (retired from the Directorate of Plans Organization of the Joint Chiefs of Staff).

Arguments in favor of improved and extended military use of space are given by Daniel Graham (retired U.S. Army, Lieutenant General, 1976), member of the American Security Council, Co-Chairman of the Coalition for Peace Through Strength, Director of Project High Frontier [*State of the Nation*, Vol. 2, No. 8, pg. 1, August 1982]. General Graham is reported to have named Congressman Newt Gingrich (Republican-Georgia) as an enthusiastic supporter of the "High Frontier" initiative, with the 47 Members of the House Space Caucus not far behind.

In the United States Senate, Malcom Wallop (Republican-Wyoming) is an active supporter of research and development of space-based lasers [*Congressional Record*, July 1, 1980, pg. S9074, Amendment No. 1784].

Locations of Soviet Union intercontinental ballistic missile fields and deployment areas for mobile intermediate-range SS-20s are depicted on a map of the U.S.S.R. Soviet fields generally run along the Trans Siberian Railway and northward around Moscow [*Aviation Week and Space Technology*, June 16, 1980, pg. 75]. "Special Report: Modernization Strategic Forces," essentially fills the entire 280 pages of this issue, but the survey of Soviet Union strategic nuclear weapons is given in the above mentioned Special Report, pp. 67-76.

A021 The arithmetic of counting bombs

The SALT II Treaty was written to limit the number of launch vehicles, not the number of bombs [refer to Subsection C028: National Technical Means].

"Bomb counting" has become difficult, if not impossible ["Authority for the Use of Nuclear Weapons," pg. 20, Section: "The Soviet Union," says, "The Ministry may stockpile weapons . . . until the weapons are turned over to the military (as is the case with the Energy Research and Development Agency, now the Department of Energy, in the United States)]. Elizabeth Pond, "The Real Euromissile Tally [*Christian Science Monitor*, November 27, 1981, pg. 12]," writes both fact and commentary to assist the reader.

A022 Survival becomes a way of life

The Russian tradition of fighting against people, the American, against nature, attributed to Alexis de Tocqueville (1805-1859), is taken from Richard B. Foster, Senior Director, Strategic Studies Center, SRI International, "Forecastability of National Security Telecommunications Requirements," a statement for the House Subcommittee on Investigations and Oversight of the House Committee on Science and Technology, released September 29, 1981, taken from SRI/BTL study entitled "National Strategic Command-Control-Communications to 1975," the study performed 1959-1962 for the then Chief Signal Officer, represented by Harold Silverstein, who regrets he cannot be here today serving on this panel, "A Retrospective Look at Some of the Basic Issues Connected with National Command, Control, and Communications." The hearings were conducted by Congressman Albert Gore, Jr. (Democrat-Tenn), Chairman of the Subcommittee; Don Fuqua (Democrat-Florida), Chairman of the full Committee; Larry Winn, Jr. (Republican-Kansas), Ranking Minority Member.

A023 Escalation and nuclear holocaust

Escalation to "the use of all weapons" is quoted from *Authority for the Use of Nuclear Weapons*, pg. 21. "Soviet strategy calls for a capability not only to deter its potential enemies from attacking it but to wage a nuclear war and win it (see pg. 18)."

The ability of the United States to immediately assess [nuclear] damage and retaliate in a studied [limited] war-fighting fashion is discussed by Richard B. Foster, on pp. 3-4, in the SRI International Report, referenced in Subsection A022. "[The United States] has invested heavily in weapon systems and military manpower, but far too little attention has been paid to providing survival and enduring C3 (read it C-cube with the meaning: Communications service Command in exercising Control over forces) systems to support and control these weapons and forces." Foster also discusses Soviet leadership—the CPSU Central Committee (the Communist Party of the Soviet Union)—the serious reader is encouraged to thoroughly digest Foster's SRI International Report.

The American military appears in no mood to be controlled by political folderol as it was in Vietnam ["Rolling Thunder and the Law of War," by W. Hays Parks, *Air University Review*, Jan-Feb 1982, pp. 2-23]. "On 2 March 1965—the beginning of the 43-month bombing of North Vietnam . . . Rolling Thunder was one of the most constrained military campaigns in history. The restrictions imposed by this nation's **civilian** leaders were **not** based on the law of war but on the obvious **ignorance** of law . . . to the detriment of those sent forth to battle . . . The McNamara-Johnson program for execution of Rolling Thunder can be considered to have **ignored all principles of war.**"

Barbara Tuchman discusses the Vietnam War in *Guns of August* [reviewed in *Parameters*, March 1980, pp. 2-9, (journal published by the Army War College, Carlyle, Penn.)]. For Commentary and Reply, see *Parameters*, June 1980, pg. 88; and then *Yankee*, August 1980, has "Interview: Barbara Tuchman."

For a discussion of First Strike, Second Strike, and Launch on Warning, refer to Stanley Sienkiewicz, Research Notes: "Observations on the Impact of Uncertainty in Strategic Analysis," *World Politics*, Vol. XXXII, October 1979, pp. 90-110, and included references.

PART TWO

Chapter B

Soviet Adventurism Flourishes

The Soviet endorsement of the use of armed force as a means of imposing the philosophy of Marxism theses . . . the execution of theses into deeds . . . is taken from a reprint Joseph Stalin, *Foundations of Leninism* (1924). International Publishers (1939) as provided by Ebenstein, William (1962). *Great Political Thinkers*. New York: Holt, Rinehart and Winston, pp. 726-740. Refer also to PART TWO, Notes and References, *Communist Manifesto*.

B024 Expanding the sphere of influence

The launch-radius for short- and long-range missiles, as it centers on the Soviet Union, is shown by Kevin N. Lewis, "Intermediate-Range Nuclear Weapons," *Scientific American*, Vol. 23, No. 6, pp. 63-73, December 1980. Lewis also published "The Prompt and Delayed Effects of Nuclear War," *Scientific American*, July 1979.

Military objectives that remain the same in peacetime and wartime come from the Clausewitzian view that war is a continuation of peacetime policy [Paul H. Nitze, "Strategy in the Decade of the 1980s," *Foreign Affairs*, Fall 1980, pp. 82-101].

A recent article by Aleksandr Solzhenitsyn, *Foreign Affairs*, Spring 1980, discusses "Misconceptions about Russia Are A Threat to America," pg. 797. "The smooth and effortless course of the West's long retreat could not go on forever, and it is now coming to an end; the brink may not have been reached, but it is already the merest step away. Since the outlying borders were never defended, the nearer ones will have to be held. Today the Western world faces a greater danger than that which threatened it in 1939."

For a step-by-step advance of Russian military adventurism, see *U.S. News and World Report*, May 11, 1981, pp. 30-31, "Where Soviets Flexed Their Military Muscle: 28 Examples of Russian Coercion," taken from a published study by Stephen S. Kaplan, Washington's Brookings Institution, "Diplomacy of Power: Soviet Armed Forces as a Political Instrument," also updated.

B025 The Soviet Union is land locked

The geography of the Soviet Union is the message of Vice Admiral Sir Ian McGeoch (retired), Editorial, *Naval Forces*, Vol. 1, No. 3, pg. 3, 1980; he refers to the quotation from Alexis de Tocqueville (Subsection A022) and adds the caution that the oceans " . . . are becoming even more important as the scene of confrontation—of naval diplomacy." The closing sentences touch upon the exciting idea that American alliance could " . . . gradually assume the character of a free association of mainly maritime states."

The remark by Mark Evans, a radio personality in Washington, DC, appointed U.S. Ambassador to Norway during the Reagan Administration, was informal, "He who controls the coast of Norway, controls the world." The remark was made very much in the spirit of the female response to the male, "He who controls the door knob, controls the world." Nevertheless, the remark is consistent with recent published articles [McGwire, Michael, "The Rationale for the Development of Soviet Seapower," *Naval Review 1980. United States Naval Institute Proceedings*, Vol. 106/5/927, May 1980, pp. 155-183; and Dunn, Keith A., "Power Projection or Influence: Soviet Capabilities for the 1980s," *Naval War College Review*, September-October 1980, pp. 31-47].

B026 Minority rule

The use of modern electronic technology by the citizens (or the military) within any society will transform the lives of the individuals [John Naisbitt (1982), *Megatrends*. Warner Books, Inc., A Warner Communications Comp., 73 Rockefeller Plaza, New York 10019]. This transformation is a threat to any minority rule because it democratizes information and such social, political, and economical change motivated by the assimilation of technology tends to be unpredictable.

The general concept of minority rule is contained in the *Communist Manifesto*, refer to the beginning of PART TWO, Notes and References.

B027 The separation of faith and reason

A candid look at the disruptive teachings of the Church is provided by Arthur E. Morgan, *One True Faith: As a Cause of War* (1948), Henry

Regnery Co., Hinsdale, Illinois, *Human Affairs Pamphlet*, Vol. 36, pg. 5, "One of the chief age-old methods to this end [causing conflict] is to create the belief that our particular faith, unlike others, was given to us from heaven, and, therefore, is beyond criticism or inquiry." Morgan is also critical of the military, " . . . a dominant cult with ingrown and medieval philosophy."

Morgan continues, "Competitive indoctrination is one of the greatest crimes of mankind (pg. 5)." One statement from Morgan, well worth contemplation: "It might be said with equal plausibility that Christianity never settled anything (pg. 21)."

Criticism of the church for teaching violence and religious conflict is not new. Jean Bodin (1530-1596) wrote of the "War of Religion" that started in France in 1562, " . . . [France] needed citizens who preferred the prosaic stability of France in the present, to the poetic bliss of heaven in the future." Bodin eventually arrives at a "theistic position of rational belief in God, above any particular Church or organized religion," first printed in 1841, but written in 1588, *Colloquium Heptaplomeres*, given in commentary by William Ebenstein (1962), *Great Political Thinkers*, New York: Holt, Rinehart and Winston, pg. 348.

Also refer to *The Encyclopaedia Britannica*, Vol. IV, 1911, pg. 110, Cambridge, England: at the University Press, New York, 120 West 32nd Street. *Colloquium heptaplomeres de abditis rerum sublimium archanis*, written in 1588, published first by Guhrauer in 1857, a philosophy of naturalism in the form of a conversation between seven learned men—a Jew, a Mohammedan, a Lutheran, a Zwinglian, a Roman Catholic, an Epicurean, and a Theist. The conclusion to which they are represented as coming is that all seven will live together in charity and toleration, and cease from further disputation as to religion.

It is curious that Leibnitz, who originally regarded the *Colloquium* as the work of a professed enemy of Christianity, subsequently described it as a most valuable production. [It should be recalled that much of this writing from Bodin provides an update and extension for the teachings of Aristotle.]

Andrei Sakharov, "An Appeal," *Parade*, Sunday, August 16, 1981, Newspaper Magazine Section, "Thoughts on Progress, Peaceful Coexistence, and Intellectual Freedom."

PART TWO

Chapter C

The NATO Alternative

For deployment of nuclear weapons in Europe refer back to PART TWO, Chapter A, Notes and References: "Authority To Order the Use of Nuclear

Weapons." Also refer to Subsection B024, Notes and References, "Intermediate-Range Nuclear Weapons," by Kevin N. Lewis.

C028 National Technical Means

One term in urgent need of detaled, if not exhaustive, debate is National Technical Means of Verification. The time has come for the American people to be far more concerned about realistic verification methods than arms control negotiations [*SALT II: Illusion and Reality*, Robert C. Johansen, World Order Models Project, Working Paper Number Nine (1979), Institute for World Order, Inc., 777 United Nations Plaza, New York, New York 10017].The reader is also referred to *Alternatives: A Journal of World Policy*.

The conclusions of Johansen are consistent with my own, "[arms negotiations] have ... legitimized existing nuclear arsenals ... they exclude multilateral monitoring ... they ... allow the superpowers to hold the world's peoples as nuclear hostages."

Johansen goes on to explain why SALT is more a charade than an arms reversal program. The SALT II focuses attention on launch vehicles, not bombs, "The SALT II limits on the number of strategic launchers will still allow the placement of new missiles (e.g., the MX) in existing silos and many more warheads on those [launch] vehicles. In addition to the strategic arsenal to which the President referred [President Carter], the United States has 22,000 tactical weapons, many of which are several times the power of the Hiroshima bomb. SALT II puts no limit on tactical weapons (see pg. 3)."

The serious reader should consult, "Principal Findings by the Senate Select Committee on Intelligence on the Capabilities of the United States to Monitor the SALT II Treaty," a working document provided December 14, 1979, through the office of Senator Richard G. Lugar (Republican-Indiana), Member of the Senate Select Committee on Intelligence.

Two common references are: *RUSI* (Journal of the Royal United Services Institute for Defense Studies), June 1978, pg. 64, "National Technical Means of Verification," by Colonel E. Asa Bates, Jr., USAF (retired) and *Proceedings of the U.S. Naval Institute*, June 2, 1980, pp. 42-51, "Photographic Satellite Reconnaissance," by Commander Cecil B. Jones, Jr., U.S. Navy (retired).

A response to the U.S. use of "apparently highly vulnerable" satellites is provided by Deborah Shapley, "Soviet Killer Satellites: U.S. Ponders a Response," *Science Magazine*, September 3, 1976, which, in turn, references Ted Greenwood, *Scientific American*, 228, 14, February 1973.

The optimistic assessment that verification technology has "improved to meet all expectations" represents the view of those interested to **use** satellite systems for global monitoring for peaceful purposes, not those who would like to continue their own emphasis on research and development ["Resolution on Proposal for Establishment of International Satellite Monitoring Agency," passed by the Plenary Session of the United Nations General Assembly, December 9, 1982, where the vote should be noted: 126

"yes," 9 "no" (including U.S.S.R.), and 11 "abstain" (including U.S.), reported by Howard G. Kurtz and Brenda Curtis, December 14, 1982, War Control Planners, Inc., P.O.Box 19127, Washington, DC 20036, Tele: (202) 785-0708].

The U.N. Document, E.83.IX.3: "The Implications of Establishing an International Satellite Monitoring Agency," may be ordered from United Nations Publications, Room A-3315, New York, New York 10017. The price is $12.50. Please specify whether you want to receive French or English version.

C029 Technology transfer

The need to transfer technology for coordinated operations becomes evident by reading "Special Report: Modernizing Strategic Forces," *Aviation Week and Space Technology*, June 16, 1980, which runs through most of the issue, but refer to pp. 77-91 for emphasis on electronic capabilities.

The concept of redundancy in weapons systems was born following World War II, prior to the arrival of the information age and revolutionary changes in communications systems ["Philosophers at the Pentagon," William J. Broad, *Science*, Vol. 210, October 24, 1980, pp. 409-412]. C3 (Communications, Command and Control), a new systems approach based on least action principle—based on function rather than structure—is introduced. It sounds exciting, but the reader should beware: any dependable system would have to be a three-component system—structure, function, and interaction, or a four-component system—structure, function, and interaction as a function of time.

There is also an 87-page study from the Naval Postgraduate School, Monterey, California, dated: July 1980, by K.E. Woehler, "Ilya Prigagine: Second Law of Thermodynamics—The Application of the Maximum Entropy Principle to Models of Military Command and Control," that has great potential.

C030 Theater Nuclear Forces

The United States negotiated a military modernization agreement with its NATO allies December 12, 1979 [*Aviation Week and Space Technology*, Modernizing Strategic Forces, June 16, 1980, pp. 271-275, 277-281]. The initial operational timetable for deployment is December 1983. This modernization includes deployment of 572 Ground Launch Cruise Missiles and Pershing II ballistic missiles. All 108 Pershing II ballistic missiles, intended for use against "time-urgent" targets are to be deployed in West Germany. The 464 cruise missiles, with a reported range of 2,500 kilometers (1,552 miles), are to be deployed: 160 in West Germany, 112 in Great Britain, 96 in Italy, 48 in Holland, and 48 in Belgium.

The wisdom of this NATO-modernization, especially the 1983 deployment of the U.S. forward-based systems in Europe, is questioned [*National Review*,

December 12, 1980, pg. 1504, "The End of Socialist Anti-Communism," by William R. Kintner].

The sophistication of the Pershing II terminal guidance system is discussed in the above mentioned Special Report: Modernizing Strategic Forces [*Aviation Week and Space Technology*, June 16, 1980, pg. 290].

Uncertainty about the deployment of U.S. land-based nuclear missiles in Europe continues [*Daily Sentinel*, Grand Junction, Colorado, Tuesday, January 18, 1983, front page, "Zero Option"], indicating that both the U.S. and West Germany are still insisting " . . . all rockets are supposed to be removed from the European part of the Soviet Union and they are supposed to be scrapped."

The Russian complaint is " . . . about the number of [U.S. or U.S. endorsed] weapons, also in this part of the world, not in any way regulated by any agreements or treaties . . . " [Bonn, West Germany (AP), was the source of the above mentioned January 18, 1983, "Zero Option" report.]

"The very intent of the Pershing II missile is to demonstrate to the Soviet planners that should they initiate a European war, the NATO response would be a nuclear assault on Soviet territory at a level **below** that of an all-out attach involving the American arsenal of Minutemen ICBMs [Mark Hopkins, "Our New Euromissiles and Theirs," *The New Leader*, October 6, 1980, pp. 6-8]."

The Washington Quarterly, Fall 1980, contained a collection of papers prepared for a conference held at the Palais d'Egmont in Brussels, September 1-3, 1979. The conference was devoted to the future of the North Atlantic Alliance.

An interesting "additional contribution" is printed in *The Washington Quarterly*, Winter 1980, pp. 100-125, "Theater Nuclear Forces in Europe: Is NATO Running Out of Options," by Uwe Nerlich, " . . . without better understanding of how the alliance got into its present condition, Western governments will continue to choose between quick fixes and deliberate diffusion of issues, which, taken together, have produced more than twenty years of blind incrementalism."

C031 The reality of de-coupling

The NATO (North Atlantic Treaty Organization) was formed following World War II (1949), as a "major Western military alliance, with prime responsibility for opposing Communist forces in Europe." [*The Hammond Almanac* (1980). Hammond Almanac, Inc., Maplewood, New Jersey 07040, pg. 719.]

A review, "European theater nuclear forces," appeared in the *Bulletin of the Atomic Scientists*, October 1980, pp. 32-37, by Coit Dennis Blacker and Farooq Hussain. A total of 108 Pershing II surface-to-surface missiles [the Pershing II, with sufficient range to reach into the Soviet Union, was to replace the Pershing I already deployed] and 464 ground-launched cruise missiles [with range up to 2,500 kilometers] were to be deployed, a

"Eurostrategic" level that could (perhaps) limit the fighting of a nuclear war to the European continent.

The withdrawal of American troops is also being considered. The authors appear to want to **avoid** military de-coupling, where I would tend to favor it. The coupling of nations that I advocate is electronic coupling, not weapons coupling.

The suggestion by Steven L. Canby ["Territorial Defense in Central Europe," *Armed Forces and Society* (An Interdisciplinary Journal), Vol. 7, No. 1, Fall 1980, pp. 51-67] that the Germans mobilize their own civilians appears to have merit. At least the Germans would know their own terrain and their own language. They would also know the mood of their own people when it came time to make the decision to fight a war.

The immense complexity of the European issue—the fact that the Europeans cannot "decouple" themselves politically, or economically, from the Americans, and then demand that military coupling be maintained as usual—and at least a hint of the wisdom of the "dissolution of the Atlantic Alliance" can be gleaned from Pierre Lellouche ["Europe and Her Defense," *Foreign Affairs*, Spring 1981, pp. 813-834, an essay taken from a wider study, "The New Dimensions of European Security"]. The closing near-suggestion by Lellouche, that European nations might want to chart their own course for the future, provides a welcome breath of fresh air.

The quotation is from President Truman: "To protect this area against war," declared Truman at the signing ceremony for the creation of the North Atlantic Alliance, "will be a long step toward permanent peace in the whole world." [Henrikson, Alan K., "The Creation of the North Atlantic Alliance, 1948-1952," *Naval War College Review*, May-June 1980, pp. 4-39, on the 30-year anniversary of NATO.]

Doubt about the future role of NATO military theater doctrine is also expressed in the two-part series: Mercer, Donald L. (Major-US Army), "How Viable an Option? The Warsaw Pact Short-Warning Nuclear Attack," *Military Review*, Vol. LX, No. 10, October 1980, pp. 23-31 and Vol. LX, No. 11, November 1980, pp. 28-36. Mercer places emphasis on the fact that war is an integral part of Soviet politics, while the United States continues to view war as a breakdown of the political process.

All nations should be treated equally under the force of the rule of law, that is the position that I advocate. The time has come to review the justification for American participation in NATO . . . did the founders of the North Atlantic Alliance "necessarily mean the permanent stationing of large numbers of American troops abroad in a highly integrated, U.S.-dominated, command structure [Henrikson, Alan K., referenced above]?"

The United States now has a global responsibility, a responsibility to use military-operated global-monitoring systems, if they are going to treat all nations equal under the rule of law. In view of modern electronic capabilities and existing treaty agreements, the United States should learn to treat all nations with equal favor. The only problem is that the American people are going to have to be willing to make the sacrifice of the transition.

The operation and maintenance of global information networks would be "manpower intensive." Every citizen in the United States would be required to work full time as a "national soldier," just to keep the information flowing. When assessed within the broad context of national needs, not the tunnel vision of destruction as the only means of defense, the real-time operation of global information systems could make the military service organizations cost effective (refer to PART FIVE, Chapter C: The National Weather Service). A combined military-civilian national service organization would be dedicated to the operation of detection and early warning systems, for both natural and man-made disaster. And the information generated by the monitoring systems, would become a national resource.

The complexity of "interoperating" and "standardizing" electronic equipment, once it has been fielded, is usually underestimated, even by the experts. But, in any case, doing it now sounds far more political than technical [*Signal*, April 1979, NATO—30th Anniversary Issue, pp. 15-19, "The evolution of NICS (Nato Integrated Communications System)," by Sir John Anderson and pp. 43-45, "Improving NATO Through Armaments Collaboration," by Walter B. LaBerge]. *Signal* is a journal of the Armed Forces Communications and Electronics Association, the AFCEA.

PART TWO

Perspective

Deterrence is MAD

The nesting instinct of Mother Russia remains rooted in centuries of tradition. "The Great Patriotic War [the Second World War, 1941-1945] imposed burdens and costs on the population that far outweigh any possible benefits . . . the more cohesive a society, the more likely it is that civilians will accept sacrifices in living standards . . . " [*World Development*, Vol. 9, No. 8, August 1981, Special Issue: The Two World Wars and Economic Development, pp. 793-803, "The Impact of War on Russian and Soviet Development," by Peter Gatrell.]

The two reluctant partners of law have usually been codified in language by two different words, one to distinguish the abstract aspect of law, another, the concrete sense of the word: Latin (lex, jus), French (loi, droit), German (gesetz, recht). In the English language, in a most pragmatic fashion, law is law [Clarence Morris (1959), Editor. *The Great Legal Philosophers*, University of Pennsylvania Press, Philadelphia, pg. 274 footnote: Jeremy Bentham].

Simone Weil was dedicated to the 5th century B.C. teachings of Pythagoras. She used logos and nomos (pneuma): logos was the Soul of the World; pneuma, the divine fire or lightning, eternally living, two-edged as a sword (pg. 13), so even the **absolute** dualism of pneuma is clearly stated.

In the writings of Simone Weil, dynamic dualism was translated reciprocal duties. " . . . she was called to serve the French provisional Government in England [1942]. She prepared for them a long study of the reciprocal duties of the individual and the State, later to become famous in English as *The Need for Roots*."

Her fondness for pre-Christian teachings did not stop there. "The passages in the Bible (Genesis, Psalms, St Paul) concerning Melchisedec prove that from the dawn of Israel there existed outside Israel a service of and knowledge of God situated on the selfsame level as Christianity and infinitely superior to anything Israel itself has ever possessed (pg. 108). Our civilization owes nothing to Israel and very little to Christianity; it owes nearly everything to pre-Christian antiquity—Germans, Druids, Rome, Greece, Aegeo-Cretans, Phoenicians, Egyptians, Babylonians (pg. 109)." [Simone Weil (1974), *Gateway to God*, Fontana Books, copyright William Collins Sons & Co Ltd Glasgow, edited by David Raper with collaboration of Malcolm Muggeridge and Vernon Sproxton (original in French—her dedicated translator and interpreter was Richard Rees).]

The root word logos has wandered to logic, legible, intelligence; while nomos appears as a suffix in astronomy, aeronomy, deuteronomy. " . . . but no systematic collection of Greek law has come down to us." Nevertheless, the dualism of law appears to have made its necessary transition from the ancient dualism of "fear and faith," to the modern dualism of "faith and reason," during the 5th century B.C. For a commentary on these sketchy written records of Greek law, see "Greek Law," *The Encyclopaedia Britannica*, Eleventh Edition (1910), Vol. XII, pg. 501, Cambridge, England: at the University Press, New York, 120 West 32nd Street.

Plato's *Republic* [(translated by F.M. Cornford, Oxford University Press, 1945), reprinted by William Ebenstein (1962), *Great Political Thinkers*, Holt, Rinehart and Winston, New York, pg. 13] does confront social reality with "what ought to be" and Plato's student Aristotle (384-322 B.C.) wrote *Politics* . . . in the history of political philosophy no one has surpassed Aristotle in encyclopedic interest and accomplishment [refer to Ebenstein, William (1962), pp. 64-74].

Modern day emphasis on Roman law comes from Justinian code, *Corpus Juris Civilis*. Yet still, if one reads carefully, there is also the dualism of internal and external history in Roman law ["Roman Law," *The Encyclopaedia Britannica*, Eleventh Edition (1910), Vol. XXIII, pg. 526, see above].

" . . . the ancient Hebrews, Aristotle, and Cicero, alike, ascribed the source of law elsewhere than in statute . . . they were in agreement that these rights had no human origin, that they were immutable and eternal." [Weinberger, Andrew D. (1962), *Freedom and Protection: The Bill of Rights*, Greenwood Press Pub., Westport, Conn., pg. 9.]

A good general reference for 5th century B.C. Greek dualism is Arthur Koestler (1959), *Sleepwalkers*. A History of Man's Changing Vision of the Universe, "Pythagoras of Samos," pg. 26, New York: The Macmillan Comp.

Jean Bodin (1530-1596) picked up and followed the teachings of Aristotle (except Bodin recognized that slavery was unjust), so his entire concept of the national state is an update of Aristotle's organic view of diversity [Ebenstein, William (1962), *Great Political Thinkers*. New York: Holt, Rinehart and Winston. Reprint of "Six Books on the State," pp. 349-356].

"In his *Theses on the Fundamental Tasks of the Second Congress of the Communist International* (dated July 4, 1920), Lenin elaborates his belief in the right of the minority to lead and rule the majority . . . Even after the dictatorship of the proletariat is established . . . the dictatorship of the proletariat is necessary . . . until the majority of the workers have rid themselves of the capitalistic ideology." Lenin's justification of dictatorship rests ultimately . . . on his profound conviction that the majority of the people is incapable of understanding and acting "correctly." Refer to commentary by Ebenstein, William (1962). *Great Political Thinkers*. Holt, Rinehart and Winston, New York., pp. 686-687, which continues, "The General Will of the proletariat is therefore, for Lenin, not what the majority of the proletariat actually think, but what they would think if they were familiar with the correct Marxian analysis of social and economic development."

The free use of modern electronic technology in the Soviet Union could encourage social and economic change that would violate rule by the "well-informed minority." This is the very serious difficulty with the existing concept of minority rule in the Soviet Union.

I stand firm on my belief that all authority originates in the will of the majority . . . as does Alexis de Tocqueville, *Democracy in America* [Reprinted by Ebenstein, William (1962), referenced above, pg. 541]. "I think that democratic communities have a natural taste for freedom: left to themselves, they will seek it, cherish it, and view any privation of it with regret. But for equality, their passion is ardent, insatiable, incessant, invincible: they call for equality in freedom; if they cannot obtain that, they still call for equality in slavery. They will endure poverty, servitude, barbarism—**but they will not endure aristocracy**."

"The evils which freedom sometimes brings with it are immediate, they are apparent to all, and all are more or less affected by them. The evils which extreme equality may produce are slowly disclosed; they creep gradually into the social frame; they are only seen at intervals, and at the moment at which they become most violent, habit already causes them to be no longer felt."

The dualism of individual freedom and equality eventually became a central theme of Alexis de Tocqueville. "The advantages which freedom brings are only shown by length of time; and it is always easy to mistake the cause in which they originate. The advantages of equality are instantaneous, and they may constantly be traced from their source (pg. 540)."

Prime Minister Clement R. Attlee explained (September 12, 1945), his conception of democracy: "Democracy is not just majority rule, but majority rule with due respect to the rights of minorities. It means that while the will of the majority must prevail, there shall be full opportunity for all points of view to find expression [Ebenstein, William (1962), referenced above, pp. 755-756]."

The United States had the military superiority in the 1950s to conquer the world by force, but did not use it [Collins, John M. (1980), *U.S.-Soviet Military Balance: Concepts and Capabilities, 1960-1980*, New York: McGraw-Hill, Inc., but should be ordered through Aviation Week and Space Technology Book Club, McGraw-Hill, Inc., P.O. Box 457, Hightstown, New Jersey 08520].

A clear statement of perceived American military superiority comes from Alan K. Henrikson who reviews the formation of the North Atlantic Alliance, 1948-1952, on the occasion of its 30-year anniversary [Alan K. Henrikson, "The Creation of the North Atlantic Alliance 1948-1952," *Naval War College Review*, May-June 1980, pp. 4-39], where he reports statements made at the time. Henrikson concludes, "The image of American military dominance at the end of World War II . . . was still so powerful, however, that alternative patterns of leadership could scarcely be conceived." The "top post" (of NATO) would go to an American.

The great age of imperialism comes to an end . . . The Soviet and Chinese Communist empires are seen as the only major imperial systems . . . Western imperialism was obviously declining in strength, and at a time when "Communist expansionism" was seeking to step into the vacuum created thereby (pg. 609, Snyder, referenced below). . . the Communist leaders went to extremes in their denunciation of the West. "Soviet Premier Nikita S. Khrushchev, on September 23, 1960, as head of the Soviet Russian delegation to the opening of the 15th session of the United Nations General Assembly," made his formal presentation, Canadian Prime Minister Diefenbaker, on September 26, 1960, in the debate of the "Issue of Western Imperialism versus Soviet Colonialism." [Louis L. Snyder, Editor (1962), *The Imperialism Reader: Documents and Readings on Modern Expansionism*, D. Van Nostrand Comp., Inc., 120 Alexander Street, Princeton, New Jersey, pg. 595, 609.]

The openness of the democratic process clearly limits the capacity of American officials to bluff foreign governments. Therefore, truth is the only alternative [Representative Jim Courter (Republican-New Jersey), a Member of the House Armed Services Committee, "Truth is a powerful weapon," *Washington Star*, "Point of View", pg. 9, August 9, 1980, an evening newspaper terminated Friday, August 7, 1981, in Washington, DC].

Anyone who doubts "truth" being the only alternative for the American people should listen to Pearl Baily sing all four verses of the "Battle Hymn of the Republic." The voice of Pearl Baily will erase all doubt. [Words were written by Julia Ward Howe at the famous Willard Hotel in 1861 after her visit of Army camps near Washington, DC (the Hotel, located within 5-minutes walking distance of the White House, is scheduled to be restored). The words were published by James Russell Lowell, Editor, *Atlantic Monthly,* February 1862. The words are sung to the music of "John Brown's Body," a melody that originated at camp meetings where the name, "My Brother, Will You Meet Us," was used. The music is considered by available library references to be anonymous, though many claims have been made to the contrary.]

PART THREE

Delivery of Nuclear Warheads

If this is evolution, then methinks I prefer creation

The "Development of Guided Missiles for Warfare: Origin" says, "The evolution of the guided missile as a military weapon began with rockets, which were first used by the Chinese against the Tartars in the Battle of Pien King in 1232." The discussion continues, "The British employed military rockets . . . during the War of 1812." [*Guided Missileman* (1958), Bureau of Naval Personnel, Navy Training Courses, United States Government Printing Office, Washington, DC, pg. 14.]

The destructive effect of a missile can be increased by either improving the accuracy or by carrying a larger destructive load [*Guided Missileman*, referenced above, pg. 14].

The nation's strategic nuclear policy, especially the policy of deterrence of nuclear war by assured destruction has existed since World War II. Deterrence is briefly surveyed by Lawrence J. Korb (1979). *The Fall and Rise of the Pentagon*, Greenwood Press, Westport, Conn., pp. 98-102. "By 1967, when they had developed a triad force of 1,054 ICBMs (Inter-Continental Ballistic Missiles), 656 SLBMs (Submarine Launched Ballistic Missiles), and about 500 long-range bombers, American planners felt they had generated a sufficient quantity and variety of delivery systems to maintain an 'assured destruction' capability against the Soviet Union . . . " In fact, " . . . the United States possessed more than assured destruction. By the mid-1960s it [the United States] had overkill capability. Its strategic forces had the capacity to destroy the Soviet Union at least five times over."

Atmospheric influence on the flight of a guided missile is discussed in scientific (technical) journals. A more readable explanation is given in *Guided Missileman* (1958), referenced above, pg. 35, Chapter 3: "Factors Affecting Missile Flight."

PART THREE

Chapter A

Land-based Missiles

The justification for altering the United States nuclear policy of "assured destruction by massive retaliation" was that the policy was "too clumsy" . . . the United States needed more choices than "simply the option of an all-out attack on the enemy's population or industry . . . " [Lawrence J. Korb

(1979), *The Fall and Rise of the Pentagon*, Greenwood Press, Westport, Conn., pg. 100, where Korb refers to the opinions of James Schlesinger, who became Secretary of Defense, April 1973 . . . "the youngest Secretary of Defense (Schlesinger was forty-four years old) and the first with no prior military experience . . . "]

"This nation ought to develop a capacity to launch a limited or surgical nuclear attack against such military targets as missile silos or airfields." This strategy is now known as the "counterforce" strategy or "flexible response," the strategy officially endorsed by President Carter when he signed PD-59 (Presidential Directive-59). Refer to PART ONE, Chapter C: At the White House: A domestic policy for war, and included references.

"In Schlesinger's view, the McNamara concept was now outdated [Lawrence J. Korb (1979), as given above, pg. 101] . . . it was no longer sufficient to have the capability to destroy between one-fifth and one-fourth of the Soviet population and half its industrial capacity . . . In light of . . . Soviet efforts to disperse and protect vital industries, a new measure of assured destruction was needed . . . Henceforth, the United States strategic nuclear forces had to be configured to prevent the Soviet Union from ever recovering militarily, politically, and economically."

Korb goes on to explain that the "McNamara concept could be implemented by delivering only 400 one-megaton equivalents for a retaliatory strike . . . the Schlesinger strategy meant that approximately 8,500 warheads would be required for adequate target coverage."

"Nonetheless, Schlesinger's arguments prevailed . . . and DOD [the Department Of Defense] received funds for increasing the accuracy and yield of its land- and sea-based missiles, developing terminal guidance, and embarking on a cruise missile program [Lawrence J. Korb (1979), as given above, pg. 101]." The date is 1973, and public discussion of the implications of national defense funding policies is sadly lacking, in my opinion, a fault of the legislative, not the executive, branch of the federal government.

A032 MX—Missile eXperimental

The basing options for the MX are reviewed in a pamphlet published by the Office of Technology Assessment, Congress of the United States, Washington, DC 20510 ["MX Missile Basing: Summary," OTA-ISC-139, June 1981]. The full report, "MX Missile Basing," can be purchased from the Superintendent of Documents, U.S. Government Printing Office, Washington, DC 20402.

The Carter Administration decided to go forward with the engineering development of the MPS (Multiple Protective Shelter) for the MX [OTA-ISC-139, June 1981, as referenced above, pg. 3], a basing mode that would involve hiding the missiles among a large number of shelters.

Another alternative for updating the land-based ICBM force was the MAP (Multiple Aim Point), a plan that would require digging up to twenty different holes or silos for each missile. This alternative would use the existing Minuteman missiles [OTA-ISC-139, June 1981, referenced above, pg. 28].

The Utah-Nevada basing of the MX-missile system attracted national attention in late 1980 [*Manchester Guardian*, November 30, 1980, pg. 8, "America's nuclear nut-in-a-cup or how MX runs rings around SALT," by David Leigh; *Air University Review*, Vol. XXXI, No. 5, July-August 1980, pp. 3-10, "The Case for the MX," by Lawrence J. Korb; *Air University Review*, Vol. XXXI, No. 5, July-August 1980, pp. 11-25, "The MX-Basing Mode Muddle," by Donald M. Snow; *Iron County Record*, July 23, 1981, pg. A-3, "Expert says MX won't work," by Lynette Sawyer; *Iron County Record*, July 2, 1981, pg. A-1, "Anti-MX citizens lobby in D.C.," by Diana Quinn; *Iron County Record*, July 2, 1981, pg. A-1, "Group cautiously confident about MX," by Diana Quinn].

The housing of the MX in Minuteman missile silos (or Titan silos "hardened against the strongest thing the Soviets now have") was actively discussed by President Reagan [*Phoenix Gazette*, October 2, 1981, pg. A-1, "State Most Likely Site of 1st MX: Choice not final," by G.G.LaBelle].

A Titan II missile exploded in its silo and for a short time the hazards of the liquid-fuel Titan (the oldest and biggest ICBM in U.S. inventory) attracted national attention [*Time*, September 29, 1980, pg. 33, "Arkansas's Missile Scare," by Dennis A. Williams]. The Titan's achilles heel (there are 53 of them) is its liquid propellant . . . once it escapes into the air and combines with the oxidizer . . . it explodes [*Norfolk Virginian-Pilot*, September 24, 1980, "Titan Strikes Again."]. The 1,000 Minutemen, solid-fueled rockets carrying multiple warheads, are "considered more effective militarily."

A033 ICBMs are "dumb" bombs

The distinction between "dumb" and "smart" bombs corresponds roughly to the technical distinction: a dumb bomb follows a ballistic-type trajectory; a smart bomb cruises along a low-altitude flight path much like an airplane.

"At the heart of modern theories of nuclear strategy lies the premise of accuracy . . . a missile fired 6,000 miles can land within 600 feet of a target no more than 150 feet in diameter." The Titan II (first introduced in 1962 and carrying a nine-megaton warhead) is now "officially deemed to have a CEP (Circular Error Probable) of 4,200 feet." The Titan III (carries three-335 kiloton warheads) is "officially estimated to have a CEP of 600 feet."

An intercontinental ballistic missile is, however, far more like an artillery shell than might be supposed . . . from the "moment of final burn-out . . . it is on its own." The authors go on to discuss atmospheric effects on the trajectory [*New York Review of Books*, November 20, 1980, pp. 40-43, "The Myth of Missile Accuracy," by Andrew Cockburn and Alexander Cockburn], that could cause a warhead to drift 1,065 feet to 1,320 feet off target . . . and those errors come only from "varying and unpredictable atmospheric densities and other winds."

The Kwajalein Missile Range is discussed in journals published for the defense community, for example, "Kwajalein Range Plays Unique Role," by Benjamin M. Elson, *Aviation Week and Space Technology*, June 16, 1980, pg. 223 and "Krems Facility Supports Advanced Technology," by Benjamin M. Elson, *Aviation Week and Space Technology*, July 14, 1980, pp. 52-54.

A034 The "disposable" rocket engine

For a description of the booster engine and undependable targeting accuracy upon re-entry into the earth's atmosphere refer back to Subsection A033: ICBMs are "dumb" bombs, the article by Andrew Cockburn and Alexander Cockburn (1980).

The cost of the Saturn-V rocket booster engine is reported to be twice that of a C-5A airplane [*Enterprise* (1979), by Jerry Grey, William Morrow and Comp. Inc., New York, pg. 19].

A035 The payload

TNT estimated equivalence is the usual way of reporting the "size" of a nuclear warhead. The atomic (fission) bomb dropped on Hiroshima was 20 kilotons; the "small" (fusion) warheads carried by Minuteman III missiles (there are three of them on each missile) are 335 kilotons each ["The Myth of Missile Accuracy," referenced in Subsection A033: ICBMs are "dumb" bombs].

A036 The reality of pork barrels

At least some of the people in Nevada and Utah were not eager to accept the construction money for the MX shelters [refer back to Subsection A032: MX-Missile eXperimental]. Such questions as, "who will pay for schools and utilities," were not uncommon [*Chicago Tribune*. October 26, 1980, pg. 15, "Small-town woman editor takes on the MX system," by William Currie].

The Mormon Church, headquartered in Salt Lake City, Utah, formally announced its opposition to deployment of the MX missile system in Utah and Nevada [*New York Times*. May 6, 1981, pg. 1, "Mormon Church Opposes Placing MX Missiles in Utah and Nevada," it was a statement issued by the Church President, Spencer W. Kimball and two Counsellors. The complete name of the Mormon Church is The Church of Jesus Christ Of Latter-Day Saints.].

A037 Priorities for land use

A lot of people don't understand that 50% of the west is owned by the federal government ["A Plea for Understanding," by Marvin Stone, *U.S. News and World Report*. March 2, 1981, pp. 79-80].

The Department of Interior has been systematically shutting off state and local input into land-use decisions [*Rocky Mountain News*, February 6, 1982, pg. 102, "Lamm attacks Reagan's land policies," by Bob Diddlebock].

PART THREE

Chapter B

Sea Launch

The United States is an island. With the expectation that we will soon be able to "pass a law against nuclear weapons [Admiral Rickover, as referenced in PART THREE, Perspective]," the United States should concern itself with concentrating its "armed forces" with the Navy and Marine Corps [Lawrence J. Korb (1979), *The Fall and Rise of the Pentagon*, Greenwood Press, Westport, Conn., pg. 173]. Korb explains the advantages of giving highest priority to the Navy when structuring "conventional" forces.

B038 Keeping weapons at sea

Land-based missiles merely act as a target ["Move MX Missiles Out to Sea," by John E. Draim, *National Review*, December 12, 1980, pg. 1500, for comments on Project Hydra].

Project Hydra, as it was headed by Lt. Cmdr. John E. Draim in the 1960s, advocates putting the MX at sea [*Reader's Digest*, September 1980, pp. 101-105, "Should Our Missile Force Go To Sea?" by Melvin R. Laird, Secretary of Defense from 1969-1973, who is now the *Reader's Digest* Senior Counsellor].

Editorial comments by John E. Draim, Captain, U.S. Navy (Retired), advise the American taxpayers of the advantages of putting weapons at sea ["A Floating U.S. Force of Missiles," by John E. Draim, *Washington Star*, September 25, 1980].

The quotation, " . . . to stop putting cannons in the village square," was apparently quoted first by George C. Wilson, *Washington Post*.

The new navigation system is the constellation of satellites, NAVSTAR, described in Subsection B040: Navigation to the rescue.

International management of navigation on the open seas depends upon a negotiated agreement among nations for the 12-mile width (in some cases the 200-mile width) for territorial sea, the limit of national control [*Regimes for the Ocean, Outer Space, and Weather* (1977), by Seyom Brown, Nina W. Cornell, Larry L. Fabian, and Edith Brown Weiss, Brookings Institution, 1775 Massachusetts Ave., N.W., Washington, DC 20036, pp. 35-49, 113-120].

The 12-mile limit would "... bring under national control ... more than 100 straits that were previously considered international water ways." It would subject missile-carrying submarines to the regulations of "innocent passage," passage through these straits on the surface of the water.

B039 Like Ivory soap, it floats

The "float-launch" principle depends upon launching missiles from a floating position in water. The buoyancy of the water actually adds "lift" and provides faster acceleration on takeoff than is possible (for the same power) with a land-based launcher [Refer back to Subsection B038: Keeping weapons at sea, John E. Draim, *National Review*, and Melvin R. Laird, *Reader's Digest*].

Robert C. Truax, the officer in charge of jet propulsion for the Ship's Installation Division of the Navy's BuAer (Bureau of Aeronautics) in 1942, was an early advocate of the "big dumb booster," an early version of sea launch. Truax called his project "Sea Dragon [*Enterprise*, by Jerry Grey (1979), William Morrow and Comp., Inc., New York, pg. 27, 59]."

Submarine Launch of a Ballistic Missile (SLBM) is, of course, an entirely different launch option from the float launch. The Navy is reported to have 10 Polaris submarines, each carrying 16 ballistic-type missiles (a total of 160 missiles) and 31 Poseidon submarines, each carrying 16 ballistic missiles (a total of 496 missiles).

The Navy's new submarines are each expected to carry 24 Trident I missiles onboard (and each missile is to carry 8 warheads). Since every Navy missile carries multiple warheads (MIRV—Multiple Independently targetable Re-entry Vehicles—or MARV—MAneuverable Re-entry Vehicle), the number of warheads will always exceed the number of missiles. [*Defense Daily*, October 29, 1980, pg. 297, "Administration to temporarily cut U.S. SLBMs by 160 launchers."]

The old Poseidon missiles are reported to have a range of 2,500 miles; the new Trident I missile, a longer range of 4,000-6,000 miles [*Los Angeles Times*, September 11, 1980, pg. 1, "Costly but Untried: U.S. Weapons Systems—Are They Dependable," by Robert C. Toth and Norman Kempster, fifth in a series].

The plan to build 27 of these giant Trident submarines is, however, running into contract difficulties [*U.S. News and World Report*, March 30, 1981, pp. 21-22, "Inside Story of the Trident Debacle," by Orr Kelly].

Nevertheless, the United States has already announced plans for constructing a Trident submarine base on the east coast. "The Navy has chosen Kings Bay, Georgia, as the site for a $1.4 billion Trident submarine base. King's Bay, to be completed by 1990, will complement the Trident base at Bangor, Washington, which is scheduled to become operational next year [*Aerospace Daily*, October 28, 1980, pg. 320, Navy Chooses Georgia Site As East Coast Trident Base]."

The United States Department of Navy is required by events as well as by political directive to maintain a 'two-ocean navy' with inadequate resources. It is well to remember the statement of a much respected author in 1874: "Wipe out North America and you will have anarchy—the complete decay of modern commerce and civilization [Karl Marx, *The Poverty of Philosophy*, reprinted in *Sea Power*, Vol. 23, No. 9, September 1980, The Foreword to Jane's]."

The *Finale* [*Sea Power*, referenced above] makes a strong plea for intelligent and timely use of electronics. "The Micro-Processor Revolution promises to be an even more climactic period than the Industrial Revolution and those navies which fail to appreciate its impact in sufficient time will be even less capable of fulfilling the requirements of their politicians than in the last few years." It is equally necessary to note the emphasis the author places on "total collaboration between uniformed and civilian staff."

Another public advocate of sea power, and certainly an outspoken opponent of land-based MX systems, is John B. Oakes, former senior editor of the *New York Times* ["MX: Tick, Tick, Tick," by John B. Oakes, *New York Times*, October 21, 1980, pg. 19].

The United States Navy offers the only immediate way for the American people to move all nuclear weapons off the land . . . as step one toward phasing them out completely. That is to say, because people live on the land, elimination of land-based systems must happen today, not tomorrow, and not next week, today.

The U.S.S.R. has 2,200 silos housing ballistic missiles . . . it would take 2 megatons per silo to ensure destruction . . . a so-called crater effect which, unlike any other nuclear strike, calls for an explosion at ground level . . . the radioactivity . . . the radioactivity of a 1 megaton explosion makes 6 million tons of ground radioactive . . . the Russian people would be largely exterminated. ["Carter's Response," *Le Figaro* (in French), August 12, 1980, pg. 1, 3]."

Of course, nuclear warheads whether launched from land or sea, are still going to pollute or incinerate the upper atmosphere when they explode. Each Trident I missile carries 8 warheads, and there are 24 missiles on each submarine—a total of 192 targets some 5,000 miles away. Yet each warhead exploding over each of the 192 targets is . . . 5 times more powerful than the atomic bomb that devastated Hiroshima [*U.S. News and World Report*, March 30, 1981, referenced above].

A nuclear submarine is "nuclear" because of the nuclear power plant it carries on board, not because of nuclear warheads the missiles may or may not carry. And getting rid of nuclear-powered submarines is equally important. The disposal of radioactive waste through "burial at sea," as it was sanctioned between 1946 and 1970, off the Farallon Islands (near San Francisco), is not yet approved by the EPA . . . as the reactors rust and decay, the radioactivity could get into the marine food chain ["Deep-six sub-scuttling scheme," *San Jose Mercury*, October 27, 1980].

The United States already has "well over a hundred nuclear-powered naval vessels . . . another sizable number [are] in the navies of the Soviet Union, France, and the United Kingdom ["Navy Considers Scuttling Old

Nuclear Subs," by Luther J. Carter, *Science*, September 26, 1980, pg. 1495]."
Perhaps it is time to mandate the navies of the world to use some new improved diesel engine for power . . . one of those that "almost" burns water.

B040 Navigation to the rescue

NAVSTAR (NAVigation System using Time And Ranging)-GPS (Global
Positioning System), when it becomes fully operational in 1987, will further enhance our C3I capabilities (read it C-cube-I; it means Communication, Command, Control, and Intelligence) and is advertised as being compatible with associated NATO systems ["C3I Satellite Systems," by Paul
A. Chadwell, *National Defense*, June 1980, pp. 50-53, 190-192].

Though the original justification for the NAVSTAR system was the improved technology—the advancement in the state-of-the-art in producing
space-borne clocks capable of sustained real-time accuracy—by the time it
becomes operational, the internal components will be antiquated unless
something is done to update them.

The U.S. Air Force is designated service responsibility for NAVSTAR implementation and the "budget" for manpower and resources is so grossly
inadequate that the performance of the system will remain orders of
magnitude below its potential. The operational system has already become
dedicated to bureaucratic bumbling within the Department of Defense
rather than to user utility by the service organizations.

"It is the navigator's dream come true ["Quick Fix: Navigation Satellites
Are Proving Useful To Many Users Besides the U.S. Military," by Arlen
J. Large, *Wall Street Journal*, July 9, 1981, pg. 50]."

Navigation systems now in operational use are described more fully in
Dutton's Navigation and Piloting, 13th Edition, 1978, Elbert S. Maloney,
Naval Institute Press, Annapolis, Maryland (satellite navigation, pg. 749;
Omega, pg. 733).

My plea to place nuclear weapons with the United States Navy is also
an endorsement of the "committee system." The committee system
developed out of the federal form of government as part of a "series of checks
and balances" to prevent any one group within the government from becoming too powerful . . . this device of inviting argument [discussion] between
conflicting interests . . . which we call the "foulup factor" in our equation
of performance . . . was obviously the result of a deliberate decision to give
up the doubtful efficiency of a dictatorship in return for a method of protection of individual freedom, rights, privileges, and immunities. This committee system runs contrary to "total unification."

Unification theory subscribes to the idea that not only money but also
manpower can be "managed," a theory that I now forcefully reject. In my
opinion, you manage money, you motivate people. The money may be effectively managed according to the total unification theory; the activities
of people should be motivated and coordinated through committee system
representation.

Unification theory is discussed by James E. Hewes, Jr. (1975), *From Root to McNamara: Army Organization and Administration, 1900-1963*, Center of Military History, United States Army, Washington, DC, for sale by Superintendent of Documents, U.S. Government Printing Office, Stock Number 0800-00202, see pp. 301-303 for above quotations.

Hewes describes this **centralization-decentralization** issue as a continuing struggle between the "rationalists and the traditionalists." Rationalists claim that traditionalists give equal attention to decisions over "the issuance of toilet paper and belt buckles . . . as the deployment of missiles [James E. Hewes, Jr. (1975), referenced above, pp. 371-374]."

All things considered, having a belt buckle to hold up your pants and toilet paper to finish the job at hand, one cannot help but appreciate the traditionalists. Nevertheless, the rationalists appear to want to manage both money and manpower—both procurement and people—as though a purchase order or a memorandum is all that is needed. The rationalists appear unable to appreciate the deliberate attempts of the traditionalists to "fragment power and responsibility" among competing bureaus [Hewes (1975), referenced above, pp. 367-368].

The career people carried the continuity, while politically appointed secretaries came and went with "little knowledge of these details." Hewes is describing the sporadic behavior of the political appointee, but there are many who would argue in favor of that breath of fresh air from the outside world. Nevertheless, bringing NAVSTAR onboard will not be easy. The issue of centralization-decentralization sits at the heart of the philosophy of making the system operational.

The "smallest, busiest" armed service of the United States is still the Coast Guard, and the U.S. Congress is still going to have to make a few immediate, but firm, decisions about increased funding ["The Coast Guard Today—Grace Under Pressure," by Merle Macbain, a retired Navy Commander, *Sea Power*, August 1980, pp. 21-28]. As NAVSTAR goes operational the Coast Guard will need an entire new generation of electronic equipment. Search And Rescue is a national service in need of increased resources, both money and manpower, to correspond to its ever expanding role in our daily lives. And Search And Rescue should remain a primary responsibility of the U.S. Coast Guard even though it is the smallest and the busiest armed service. And, yes, that is correct—I still think the Coast Guard should be an armed service, not merely a uniformed service, until more electronic support is provided.

PART THREE

Chapter C

Airplanes or Cruise Missiles

A cruise missile is a "pilotless aircraft using . . . jet-propulsion technology . . . and can be remotely controlled and guided to [its] target [*Enterprise* (1979) by Jerry Grey, New York: William Morrow and Comp. Inc., pg. 37]." The controversy of the pilotless versus the piloted aircraft started in the United States following World War II. It continues yet today.

C041 An "invisible" airplane

The use of "stealth" technology, especially as the information was released to the public during the closing days of the Carter Administration, was reported and surveyed in PART ONE, Chapter E: A Quick Fix.

The large, powerful fleet of B-29 aircraft was produced by the United States by the end of World War II, a national decision that permitted the delivery of the new nuclear [atomic] bombs of great weight [*Enterprise* (1979), Jerry Grey, pg. 37, refer to Chpt. C: Airplanes or Cruise Missiles, Notes And References].

A dispatch on Secretary of Defense Harold Brown's press conference in Washington, DC, "The U.S. Air Force Is Flying 'Invisibly,' " was published in West Germany [*Die Welt*, August 25, 1980, pg. 5] to assure our European NATO allies that . . . this does not involve the development of a completely new airplane but the testing of a complicated [sophisticated] installation of electronic countermeasures . . . the flight test of an 'invisible' plane . . . is based on the secret development of an electronic 'magic hood.' The technical explanation that follows makes it clear that the magic hood is monitoring the frequency of the incoming [probing] radar pulse. The on-board radar then returns a 'false echo' so the enemy weapon flies toward an electronically created [false] image.

Since any coding of the transmitted enemy radar pulse would immediately allow the enemy radar to detect and reject a returned false echo, one can only wonder about the operational success of the magic hood installation. Nevertheless the 30-year old U.S. Air Force B-52 long-range bombers of the Strategic Air Command are to be electronically shielded so they can fly over the Soviet Union carrying their 20 units of air-launch cruise missiles that would also eventually be electronically shielded from enemy radar detection so they could fly over the Soviet Union . . . and hit their target.

For an American story about the B-52 bomber upgrade, refer to "U.S. B-52 Bomber Fleet Being Upgraded," by Robert R. Ropelewski [*Aviation Week and Space Technology*, June 16, 1980, pg. 192]. The ALCM (Air Launch Cruise Missile) is a different missile from the GLCM (Ground Launch Cruise Missile) because airplanes are moving, the ground is not. Also refer to

"ALCM to Enter Inventory Next Year," by Jeffrey M. Lenorovitz [*Aviation Week and Space Technology*, June 16, 1980, pg. 176], to learn that the ALCM for the B-52G has a [theoretical] 1,350-mile range, the range of a so-called medium-range missile.

At about the same time, the *Financial Times* (published in Frankfurt and London), August 15, 1980, announced a major international missile agreement, "NATO partners sign major missile pact," for the United Kingdom and West Germany to develop ASRAAM (Advanced Short Range Air-To-Air Missiles) while the United States would develop AMRAAM (Advanced Medium Range Air-To-Air Missiles).

C042 The "disposable" airplane

A "disposable" airplane . . . a cruise missile . . . is an "unmanned vehicle, designed as a weapon, which travels above the Earth's surface along a course . . . that can be altered by a mechanism within the vehicle itself . . . this vehicle destroys itself in carrying out its mission [*Guided Missileman* (1958), referenced in PART THREE, Notes and References]."

Notes and References for cruise missile mania continue in Subsection C043: Offense becomes the defense.

C043 Offense becomes the defense

The United States Congress has been told in secret briefings that the U.S. Army needs "pre-clearance" for using tactical nuclear weapons ["U.S. Army Wants Pre-Clearance To Use N-Weapons in Europe," by Walter Pincus, *Denver Post*, July 21, 1982, pg. A-3 (reprinted from *Washington Post*, no date given)]. The briefings centered around "a look at the doctrine of the future" taken from "Air Land Battle 2000." An Army spokesman said, " . . . it would like release of nuclear weapons to come earlier in the battle."

A law should be passed against the use of all nuclear weapons [Admiral Hyman Rickover, *60 Minutes*, to be references in PART THREE, Perspective]. If one follows this suggestion from Admiral Rickover, then the use of tactical nuclear weapons would be terminated even before it starts.

Let the great minds of American military men be devoted to a creative purpose. The world needs real-time information flow. The American people need real-time information flow. The American military should be collecting and using remote sensing information. The American people should be interpreting that same information and acting in a responsible fashion.

The national purpose is now and must remain protection of the environment for the common economic good of all mankind. Real-time information is still the best offensive weapon.

"In response to the Soviet nuclear build-up . . . the deployment of mobile SS-20 ballistic missiles, the NATO ministers agreed that 572 U.S. missiles should be deployed in Europe ["UK discloses sites and date for Cruise Missiles," by Elinor Goodman, *Financial Times*, June 18, 1980, pg. 1]." The

U.S. Air Force base at Greenham Common, Berkshire, is to be used as the main UK operating base . . . six flights will be housed there. Another four flights will be based at the disused airfield of RAF Molesworth in Cambridgeshire. These missiles (a total of 160 ground-launched cruise missiles) are reported to have a range of 1,500 miles, a range comparable to that reported for the U.S.S.R. rail-mounted mobile missile, the T-4A. The Soviet T-2 and T-4 intermediate-range missiles are reported to have 1,000- to 1,500-mile range [*A Guide to National Defense: The organization and operations of the U.S. Military Establishment* (1964), by Patrick W. Powers, New York: Frederick A. Praeger, pp. 88-90: Soviet Nuclear-Delivery Forces].

The horror of cruise missile mania is briefly stated by Jack Anderson ["3 Nations to Begin Cruise Missile Project," by Jack Anderson, *Washington Post*, December 8, 1980, pg. B-15]. " . . . small, pilotless jets that hug the ground to evade enemy radar [detection] . . . deliver nuclear warheads 1,500 miles away." The three nations that are mentioned are Israel, South Africa, and Taiwan. "Taiwan would be able to destroy Peking . . . Israel would be able to deliver warheads from its own backyard to any of its Arab enemies in the Middle East, and even deep inside the Soviet Union." The important point made by Mr. Anderson is that " . . . four cruise missiles can be installed on a single truck and hidden, ready to go, in an ordinary garage . . . precisely what the United States plans to do with its cruise missiles earmarked for deployment in Britain."

PART THREE

Chapter D

Satellite Launch

The use of military-operated Earth-orbiting satellites for global monitoring of the natural environment, the effective use of modern electronic technology for the common economic good of all nations, that is the destiny of the United States. The American military, the American industry, and the American people through their strong central government can either fulfill that destiny or the nation can commit internal suicide.

In my opinion, the United States has to take the lead and the American people have to pay the bill. The potential benefits of global monitoring appear in any case to be significantly greater than the costs of deploying and operating the systems [*Regimes for the Ocean, Outer Space, and Weather*, pg. 134, referenced in Subsection B038: Keeping weapons at sea].

Global monitoring of the natural environment should require **prior consent from no one**. No one nation owns the air, land, or sea, in so far as the use or the abuse of it has impact on the total environment. Global environmental management is a must for the survival of the human race on planet earth, and nowhere is the management of the environment more important than with the regulation of proposed military-related destruction. Passing a law against the use of nuclear weapons is necessary for the protection of the Earth's atmosphere ["The Atmosphere After a Nuclear War," Paul J. Crutzen and John W. Birks, *Ambio*, June/July 1982 (the Journal is published in Sweden)].

There is one nation and one work force, and the future of the nation depends upon wise use of human resource. " . . . beyond any single explanation, each of which has an element of truth, the secret [of American success] lies in the confidence the society has in its citizens . . . the ability of its citizens to decide for themselves and in the capacity of their intelligence [*The American Challenge*, by J.-J. Servan-Schreiber, New York: Atheneum (1968), translated from French (1967) by Ronald Steel, pg. 253]."

D044 Your technology, my technology

The chronology of the space age given by Jerry Grey [*Enterprise* (1979), William Morrow and Comp. Inc., 105 Madison Ave., New York, New York 10016, pp. 267-275] is certainly one of the more convenient and entertaining. The October 4, 1957, launch of the Soviet Sputnik I is, however, so well known that most Americans can recite it from memory.

It is the January 31, 1958, launch of Explorer I by the United States that attracted far less attention. The July 29, 1958, creation of the American civilian space agency NASA appears to have attracted no public attention at all.

The history of the birth of NASA is reviewed by Jerry Grey [*Enterprise*, referenced above, pp. 42-53]. This exciting U.S. history identified Senator Lyndon Johnson (Democrat-Texas) as the driving force for the formation of the civilian space agency.

A comparatively morbid outlook for the same time period is presented by the United Nations ["The Arms Race: Satellites, Missiles, Nuclear," by A. G. Mezerik, Editor, *International Review Service*, Vol. III, No. 38, November 1957; and "Outer Space," by A. G. Mezerik, Editor, Vol. VI, No. 56, 1960, *International Review service*, United Nations Bureau: Room 352, 15 Washington Place, New York, 3, New York, U.S.A.]. The chronology of events given by Mezerik [Vol. VI, No. 56, pp. 25-38] for 1939-1959 is comprehensive. The date given for the first successful U.S.S.R. test of an ICBM is August 26, 1957, prior to the October launch of Sputnik I.

The lack of coordination between the civilian- and military-oriented space programs is exaggerated by the news media because few people perceive the "militarization of space" as a positive national effort. The headline: "U.S. Plans Big Spending Increase For Military Operations in Space," could easily have triggered a negative emotional response from many Americans, while the subtitle: "Program Includes Better Satellites, Gathering of Intelligence and a Cargo Role for the Shuttle," could have gone without notice [*New York Times*, Sunday, October 17, 1982, front page]. The information in the text of the article is fragmented to the point of being almost meaningless, at least for the average non-technical reader.

Whether Richard Halloran has a poor grasp of the "national space effort" or the final article is the handy work of an editor, one can never know. The headline could better have implied that President Reagan had made a very wise decision with regard to defense spending. " . . . after a quarter-century of mostly peaceful exploration of space, the United States has [finally] begun a vast expansion of its [national] military operations [of Earth-orbiting satellites for the benefit of all mankind, including an increased effort toward environmental monitoring]." The "there" at the end of the sentence is misplaced. The increase in defense spending is clearly intended for military-operated Earth-orbiting satellites, as is remarked elsewhere in the article, **not** for space exploration.

D045   Hail COLUMBIA, a Space Shuttle at last

The excitement of the shuttle landing swept across the country, Tuesday, April 14, 1981, "Shuttle Glides to Triumph: Columbia Weathers Fiery Pass: Welcome Home! Beautiful! Beautiful!" by John J. Fialka, *Washington Star*, front page. NASA officials pronounced its a perfect mission 1:21 p.m. Eastern Standard Time . . . Columbia pilots John Young and Robert Crippen made aerospace history today.

The Wednesday Special, April 15, 1981, *Washington Star*, front page, continued the story. "Touchdown," said communicator Joe Allen . . . and Young became a hero. The quote to remember from Young . . . after waiting in the cockpit of the shuttle for more than one hour, "We're still in here and if we're gonna get this thing operational, we're gonna have to work on this a little more . . . do you realize we could have done a whole initial orbit by now?" That remark accurately reflects the frustration of all who would like to have national operational capabilities realized . . . right now . . . and even right now would not be soon enough. It is time to start doing. Let the doers do, let everyone else sit in a conference room and talk, or go play tennis. Let them do anything, except interfere with those who are able to get the job done.

The contrast on the front page of the April 15, 1981, *Washington Star* is severe. At the top of the page was the shuttle story, at the bottom was a picture of the flag-draped casket of Omar Bradley being carried to the burial site at Arlington Cemetery. Bradley, the nation's last 5-star general, had died the week before in New York at the age of 88. The new arrives, and the old departs—it is so typical military that one has to take pause to pay tribute to those who dedicate their lives to service.

The history of the development of the space shuttle from the perspective of a NASA engineer is provided by Jerry Grey [*Enterprise* (1979), referenced in Subsection A034: The "disposable" rocket engine]. Practical inadequacies of the small cargo bay and the iterim upper stage are described on pp. 94-96. The typical orbit for the space shuttle would be 175-250 miles or perhaps 150-300 miles (see pg. 59, pp. 160-163).

Such engineering matters have also made news in the *Christian Science Monitor*, "Air Force elbows industry for more room in space shuttle's cargo hold," by Clayton Jones, September 12, 1980, pg. 4.

The White House Rose Garden was the scene of the ceremonies and luncheon for 160 guests; the picture in the newspaper was of Astronaut John W. Young receiving the Congressional Space Medal of Honor from President Reagan [*Washington Star*, May 20, 1981], and Jeremiah O'Leary quotes President Reagan, " . . . nothing binds our abilities except our expectations." I agree with President Reagan, bring on the expectations.

The combined cost now comes to $500 billion a year for arms ["The $500 billion arms bill," by Richard L. Strout, *Christian Science Monitor*, September 12, 1980, pg. 23]. Spending that $500 billion (the $500 billion appears to be the world expenditure on arms) for the use of electronics and the development of global information systems would be quite an "expectation," but it is certainly realistic, given the anti-war mood of so many people in the world today.

The United States now has a $500 billion federal budget [*Enterprise* (1979), referenced above, pg. 247]; we need only to view all federally funded activities as "the use of electronics for common economic good within the constraints imposed by natural law."

D046 The militarization of space

The use of increased defense spending to hasten the use of electronics is the best news yet from the Reagan Administration [*New York Times*, Sunday, October 17, 1982, front page, "U.S. Plans Big Spending Increase For Military Operations in Space: Program Includes Better Satellites, Gathering of Intelligence and A Cargo Role for the Shuttle," by Richard Halloran].

Electronics can certainly decrease if not eliminate our national need to produce weapons of destruction " . . . information, navigation, weather, communications, all of those things that contribute to a better allocation of forces." This effect is the so-called "force multiplier" effect that is opening the door to the use of information as the primary "weapon" for the "war of ideas," the eternal war of the future.

A dated but informative article about laser technology is printed in *National Geographic*, December 1966, pp. 858-881, "The Laser's Bright Magic," by Thomas Meloy. A more technical article is printed in *Scientific American*, December 1981, pg. 51, "Laser Weapons," by Kosta Tsipis. In both cases, the reader learns that the use of laser light, for anything other than research purposes, is only in its infancy.

The appeal from Senator Malcom Wallop (Republican-Wyoming) to fund laser research is one I endorse. Though the Senator uses "weapons arguments" in his "Dear Colleague" letter released June 25, 1980, 9:09 a.m., Washington, DC, he is dedicated to using increased defense spending to . . . redefine DARPA's [Defense Advanced Research Projects Agency] program in laser research. Perhaps by now Senator Wallop has realized that one does not dare to use lasers, or anything else, to destroy nuclear weapons in the upper atmosphere. The Senator has a reputation for doing his homework. Once he is told of the hazards of incinerating the upper atmosphere with nuclear explosions, he will respond. Malcom Wallop is not one to stand on formality.

Senator Wallop also authored an article that stresses the importance of changing defense spending priorities because " . . . technology is rendering the balance of terror obsolete." The good Senator is trying to encourage public debate, to " . . . lay to rest the MAD phantom (the delusion of Mutual Assured Destruction)." Wallop is interested to protect American lives and American homes ["Opportunities and Imperatives of Ballistic Missile Defense," by Malcom Wallop, *Strategic Review*, Fall 1979, pp. 13-21].

A technical survey of the status of Soviet and U.S. directed-energy technology, by senior military editor Clarence A. Robinson, Jr., and senior avionics editor Philip J. Klass, is provided by *Aviation Week and Space Technology*, July 28, 1980, pg. 32. The military need to rely upon a civilian work force is no where more glaringly evident than with this laser research and development.

PART THREE

Chapter E

Hiroshima

"Sixteen hours ago . . . " the statement is made by the President of the United States. He is announcing the dropping of the atomic bomb on Hiroshima [*Public Papers of the Presidents of the United States*, Harry S. Truman, 1945 (April 12 to December 31, 1945), pg. 197, United States Government Printing Office, Washington, DC, printed 1961]. "It was to spare the Japanese people from utter destruction . . . (pg. 199) that the ultimatum of July 26 was issued at Potsdam. Their [the Japanese] leaders promptly rejected that ultimatum. If they do not now accept our terms they may expect a rain of ruin from the air, the like of which has never been seen on this earth."

This statement on the atomic bomb 1945, by Harry S. Truman, is conveniently available in *The Illustrated Heritage Dictionary and Information Book*, pp. 1750-1751, Boston: Houghton Mifflin Comp. (1977), a dictionary commonly sold for use in the home or secondary schools.

E047 People are easy to kill

The Japanese government reply had said of the Potsdam warning, "To us its meaning does not seem of great worth, just something to be ignored [refer to Presidential Papers, Harry S. Truman, given above].

The description of the Hiroshima bomb "Little Boy," its explosive power of 20,000 tons of TNT, and the destruction of the "crater-like" area on the Ota River delta is given by Kirk, John and Robert Young, Jr. (1941), *Great Weapons of World War II*, New York: Bonanza Books, pp. 344-347.

E048 Accuracy was the problem

For the military or political merit of the bombing of Hiroshima refer to Libby, Leona Marshall (1979), *The Uranium People*, Crane Russak, Charles Scribner's Sons, New York, pg. 243 and included references.

All remarks from Major Claude Robert Eatherly, Commander of the lead plane STRAIGHT FLUSH are taken from Eatherly's letters published by Gunther Anders (1961), *Off Limits für das Gewissen*, Rowholt Verlag GmbH, Reinbek bei Hamburg, First American edition *Burning Conscience* (1962) by Gunther Anders, New York: Monthly Review Press.

For an assessment of the use of ground forces versus the [indiscriminate] use of bombing read *They Fought Alone* (1963) by John Keats, Philadelphia: J. B. Lippincott Comp., pg. 416. "It was Fertig's passionate belief that guerrilla operations are always victorious."

E049 A commanding responsibility

The story of the trial of Tomoyuki Yamashita, the General of the Japanese military, who "plunged to his death at the end of a rope on American gallows" for failure to retain control over the actions of his men is related by George F. Guy, "The Defense of General Yamashita," *Yearbook. 1981. Supreme Court Historical Society*, 1511 K Street, N.W., Washington, DC 20005. George Guy believed " . . . that the U.S. Supreme Court erred in handling the Yamashita case . . . "

"The soldier that defends a nation today can ultimately be no more responsible or no more moral than the nation itself in international relations ["Morality and the Military Profession," by Malham M. Wakin, *Parameters*, June 1980, pg. 95]."

Military responsibility is further discussed by William W. Bishop Jr., *International Law. Cases and Material*, 1962, Little, Brown and Comp., pg. 778, "Nürnberg Trial of War Criminals," reference to The Caroline Case, *Moore's Digest of International Law*, Vol. II, pg. 412.

"The Ethics of War," by Barrie Paskins and Michael Dockrill, *Parameters*, March 1980, pg. 102, emphasizes the responsibility of the American people in a decision to use military action as a means of implementing their foreign policy.

E050 The weapons strike back

All remarks about Eatherly and the guilt of using untried technology are taken from Eatherly's letters, referenced in Subsection E048: Accuracy was the problem.

The meaning of the word "weapon" needs to be clarified. The weapons that strike back are "lethal weapons," they are machines of destruction. In contrast, there are many vitally important "pieces of equipment," such as radar, sonar, jeeps, trucks, typewriters, radios, C-47s, and bulldozers, that may be far more important to the outcome of a war [Kirk, John and Robert Young Jr. (1941), *Great Weapons of World War II*, Bonanza Books, New York]. The authors define lethal weapons in the introductory remarks. According to these authors, information could well be a "weapon" in the "war of ideas" that we are now fighting. Information could well be used for constructive, rather than destructive, purposes.

No American male is immune to the horrors of having been responsible for the destruction of human life, partly because of the intensity of emotional involvement at the time of the action ["Haunted Survivors of the USS Bullhead," by Joseph P. Mastrangelo, *Washington Post*, Style Section F-1, August 16, 1981].

As for the "collective guilt of a nation," I do **not** believe that such a thing exists. One cannot transfer guilt, or credit, or responsibility, to the nation, to the government, or to any other man-made institution. The people are guilty. Every citizen of the United States is "guilty." Guilt is an individual thing. Just like integrity, just like faith; guilt belongs to you. And responsibility belongs to you.

My thoughts always return to the words of Adlai Stevenson who said something like " . . . you have to be fighting for the love of something, not the fear of something." Americans have always been fighting for the love of an ideal that combines faith and reason, but, with modern weapons, the Americans are in the process of rethinking their concept of "fighting." An interesting book by Senator McIntyre references remarks from Adlai Stevenson [*The Fear Brokers* (1979), Thomas J. McIntyre, Philadelphia: Pilgrim Press, pg. 339].

The basic problem with U.S. nuclear strategy is that both use and possession of nuclear weapons have to be outlawed. Nuclear explosion would alter the chemistry of the upper atmosphere, and there is no known way for man to control that chemistry once it has been artificially altered. In that sense, it really does not matter who is guilty. When there is no atmosphere to sustain life as we know it, there will also not be anyone around to assign guilt.

PART THREE

Perspective

System Failure knows no Limit

The book by C.P. Snow, *Science and Government* (1961), Harvard University Press, Cambridge, Mass., is recommended reading for scientists and non-scientists alike. Those "cardinal choices," those that "determine in the crudest sense whether we live or die," should be made by the people, that is the joy of this do-it-yourself government we call democracy.

The "security of the secret" is a myth and we have lived with the myth long enough. Since World War II, we have nothing but secrets in the arena of nuclear strategy and we are not one darn bit more secure because of it. We now have to let go of the past, " . . . the arrival of novelty implies a loss of the past [*Process and Reality* (1960), by Alfred North Whitehead, Harper Torchbooks, Harper and Row, Pub. (original copyright, 1927, The Macmillan Comp.), pg. 516]."

The difficulty with rigid thought patterns in the military-industrial complex, the difficulty of preparing today's military to fight yesterday's war, is discussed by Donald L. Mercer (Major-U.S. Army), "How Viable an Option: The Warsaw Pact Short-Warning Nuclear Attack," *Military Review*, Vol. LX, No. 10, October 1980, pp. 23-31 (Part I); Vol. LX, No. 11, November 1980, pp. 28-36 (Part II). But, in all fairness to the military and the industry, one must remember that no one else in this country is on the "technology frontier," no one else has to get rid of those "rigid" thought patterns in such a rapid fashion. Being on the frontier of modern technology is not easy . . . especially when you have to depend upon decisions made my the United States Congress to obtain your funding.

To get some idea of the rate at which ideas have to be up-dated, the rate at which ideas become obsolete in U.S. industry, take a look at the Special Golden Anniversary Issue of *Manufacturing Engineering*, January 1982, as referenced for the Preface. The President of SME has a message for everyone.

Jerry Grey retells the story of Philomena Grodzka [*Enterprise* (1979), referenced in Subsection D044: Your technology, my technology, see pp.151-154]. Grodzka criticizes NASA's method of selecting experiments and investigators for space processing. Grodzka was especially critical of the institutionalization of space by vested interests—a priesthood of technology: keepers of the sacred flame of knowledge—a priesthood that excludes new-comers to the "club" (and I might add, also excludes "old-comers" if they happen to be females who steadfastly refuse to conform to the male standards for deciding) in order to preserve their own established (perhaps even decaying) supremacy, whether corporate or individual. "So what happens," she said, "is that you get a lot of tired old ideas. But if they didn't work before, why should they work now (pg. 153)?" Yes, a rigid thought pattern is often associated with a particular male. To reject the thought pattern would be equivalent to rejecting the male. And, oh dear me, that is a no, no, just ask any of my male colleagues.

The inability of the scientific community to respond to a new idea (that idea does not need to be "new," it can be ancient, but different from the status quo) has been well documented and traced through history by Arthur Koestler [*Sleepwalkers* (1959), A History of Man's Changing Vision of the Universe, New York: The Macmillan Comp.]. Starting with Pythagoras of Samos (425 B.C.), the "founder of science as the word is understood today (see pg. 26)," the determination of the male scientist to reject new ideas is well documented. And the writing style of Koestler makes for enjoyable reading.

The best way to get rid of nuclear weapons is to pass a law against them. Admiral Hyman George Rickover (retired U.S. Navy) said, " . . . just outlaw all nuclear weapons, so start off with [an international meeting]. Then we outlaw nuclear reactors too. That's what I would do. And I think this is a very propitious time . . . [military expenses are] completely unproductive and using up so much of the people's taxes. I think this is a fine thing that the President could do." [The typescript is from CBS-TV *60 Minutes*, WDVM, 7 p.m., Washington, DC, March 28, 1982, provided through the Office of the Assistant Secretary of Defense for Public Affairs. Also refer to PART FIVE, Subsection B096: Military-industrial divorce, for comments from Rickover.

PART FOUR

Detection and Early Warning

If the gift of foresight is our most effective weapon,
then information flow is the live ammunition

"Major advances in civilization are processes that all but wreck the societies in which they occur." The quotation is attributed to Alfred North Whitehead by Marshall McLuhan [*The Medium is the Massage* (1967), New York: Bantam Books, Inc.] in the Introduction.

The rate at which the American way of life is being altered by the use of modern computers is "rapid," but the change in the quality of life is assessed differently, depending upon the perspective of the author: Christopher Riche Evans [*Micro-Millenium* (1979), New York: Viking Press]; John Wicklein [*Electronic Nightmare* (1981), New York: Viking Press]; and John Naisbitt [*Megatrends* (1982), New York: Warner Books]. The degree of uncertainty is captured by Naisbitt, "As a society we have been moving from the old to the new. And we are still in motion. Caught between eras, we experience turbulence. Yet amid the sometimes painful and uncertain present, the restructuring of America proceeds unrelentingly."

The global use of operational remote sensing systems for the combined civilian-military mission of environmental protection awaits a political decision in the United States; it awaits a national policy that would mandate the creation of the systems within the government service organizations. Jerry Grey talks about the need for this national policy decision [*Enterprise* (1979), New York: William Morrow and Comp. Inc., pg. 146]; the matter is discussed in detail in PART FIVE, Chapter C: The National Weather Service.

The problem with a Congressional mandate for remote sensing services, no matter the timing of its arrival, is that the work force needed for data handling and data interpretation has been so dramatically underestimated that most members of the U.S. Congress would not be able to comprehend the scope of the shortage. To have a national expectation to have such information systems operating continuously would only compound the problem.

One preliminary but staggering assessment of the manpower shortage was provided by the International Institute for Aerial Survey and Earth Sciences (ITC), 350 Boulevard 1945, P.O.Box 6, 7500 AA Enschede, The Netherlands [ITC Journal, 1981-2, pp. 171-183, "Education and training in remote sensing applications," F. C. d'Audretsch, S. A. Hempenius, C. Voute, and T. Woldai]. The purpose of the paper was " . . . to provide Member States [the paper was prepared for the United Nations Committee on the Peaceful Uses of Outer Space, January 1981] with the necessary information to enable them to assess their requirements and identify their national and international policies on education and training in the applications of satellite remote sensing data."

The ITC is the International Training Center originally located in Delft, The Netherlands, closely affiliated with related departments of the Technical University (refer to PART FOUR, Chapter B, Notes and References, for additional author comments).

"The new frontiers of human creativity in every area lie in information systems and their utility . . . the signs and instruments of power are no longer armed legions or raw materials or capital [as traditionally defined] . . . The wealth we seek . . . lies in the human spirit . . . the ability of man to think and to create [*The American Challenge* (1967), by J.-J. Servan-Schreiber, translated from French into English by Ronald Steel (1968), New York: Atheneum, pp. 276-277]."

PART FOUR

Chapter A

A Spy in the Sky

The "resolution" is what determines the detail a remote sensing device can record. A device with "good resolution" can distinguish ("see") small objects; a device with poorer resolution can see only bigger objects. "They used to talk about reading license plates from orbit. Now we're able to see the bolts that hold the license plate on [*Enterprise* by Jerry Grey, pg. 147, referenced above]."

The question, of course, is who needs the resolution, and why? Or, more importantly, why should the resolution be a secret? Local TV news crews fly around taking aerial photographs of what ever strikes their fancy. Private aircraft fly around seeing what ever they can see. The surface of the Earth is not a secret, for most of us ordinary citizens.

In 1969, Americans were already publicly advocating the use of "spy" satellites to help monitor any agreement the superpowers might reach for arms control [*U.S. News & World Report*, November 24, 1969]. During the 1960s, electronic reports and photographs were both being received and recorded only to be air-dropped back to earth in canisters.

The possibility of instant intelligence by electronic relay from communication satellites was only a gleam (or a beam) in the eye of the scientist. The 1962 Canadian-launched Alouette ionospheric-monitoring radar-type satellite did, however, transmit analogue data back to ground stations as it was collected. The data were recorded on magnetic tape as they were received. It was the tape-to-film conversion, that was done on the ground, that was done with great delay. The evaluation and interpretation of the information taken from the film was done with even greater delay.

A051 The world turns

The "ideal" orbit offered by launch from the latitude of Cape Canaveral is an inclined orbit of 28.5° [*Enterprise* (1979), by Jerry Grey, pg.96 and pp. 160-163, as referenced at the beginning of PART FOUR]. To go from that low inclined orbit, a height of 150 to 300 miles, up to a geosynchronous orbit of 22,300 miles above the equator, requires an extra "tug."

The polar orbit, the so-called "sun-synchronous" pole-to-pole pass preferred for many Department of Defense operational needs, is best achieved by launch from Vandenberg Air Force Base in California [*Enterprise*, by Jerry Grey, pp. 128-129].

The more than urgent need for a "national orbital strategy" has already been made public by Lieutenant General Richard C. Henry, United States Air Force, Commanding General of the Air Force Space Division, who calls for and defines national orbital strategy, especially the need to develop a management system for launch priorities and orbital positioning ["Old Problems, New Solutions Surfacing in Space Programs," by Richard Hartman, *Defense Electronics*, December 1980, pp. 55-58].

A052 Information relay with delay

The idea of transmitting one billion bits of information per second, the idea of transmitting "the entire contents of all 30 volumes of the *Encyclopedia Britannica* in one second," was reported by the *Armed Forces Journal International*, February 1980, pg. 59. [Their printed text should be corrected to read "as fast as one gigabit (one billion bits) of information every second." One million bits of information per second would be only one megabit.]

The same article also explains " . . . such a satellite could relay over 250,000 phone calls simultaneously, compared with the roughly 24,000 telephone conversations which today's communication satellites can handle."

Two tutorial papers are available to explain the basics of communication satellites ["Global Satellite Communications," by Burton I. Edelson, *Scientific American*, February 1977, pp. 58-73; and "The Satellite TV Primer — thousands watch satellite TV every day . . . here's how they do it and what they see," by Robert B. Cooper, Jr., *Amateur Radio*, November 1979, pp. 13-26]. The emphasis is on information transfer, **not** the collection of data by remote sensing.

A053 Interrogation and relay with delay

The advantage of local monitoring, using an "immersed sensor," is that it is continuous. Also a sensor located on the ground can be repaired; if need be, replaced. Interrogation of ground- or water-based sensors is easy enough to do when an orbiting satellite passes overhead.

A054 The "look-and-see" satellite

The "passive" observer satellite capabilities were referenced in PART TWO, Subsection C028: National Technical Means.

The primary difference between the routine monitoring use of National Technical Means and the spy satellites of Detection and Early Warning is the haste with which the information must be processed and interpreted.

Eric Burgess (1961), *Long-Range Ballistic Missiles*, New York: The Macmillan Comp., gives a general discussion of relevant times as they relate to the launch of nuclear warheads. An ICBM (Inter-Continental Ballistic Missile) would travel 5,500 nautical miles in approximately 30 minutes;

its approximate burn-out velocity would be 22,000 feet per second; the warhead would re-enter the lower atmosphere at a 25° angle; it would approach a target at 250 miles per minute. For a range of 5,000 miles, the highest point in the trajectory (the apogee) would be 700 miles, a little more than 1,000 kilometers.

Response times at lift-off are typically measured in seconds, however, not minutes. The sequence from lift-off, through the booster engine ignition and burn-out (182-200 seconds), through the 2nd, 3rd, and 4th stages (237, 246, 268 seconds), up to the 700-mile apogee, would be nearly 600 seconds or 10 minutes [Eric Burgess (1961), given above, pp.196-200].

One of the primary means of detecting a heat source is an IR (Infra Red) scanning device. The MIDAS (the MIssile Defense Alarm System) satellite carries one such infra red detection payload but several satellites would have to be placed in 24-hour stationary orbits to provide complete global coverage [Eric Burgess (1961), referenced above, pp. 204-206].

A055 The "listen-and-hear" satellite

The "ferret" reconnaissance space craft was utilized by the United States during the 1960s ["Space Patrol—How The U.S. Watches The Russians," *U.S. News & World Report*, November 24, 1969]. Passive-observer satellite capabilities are also discussed in PART TWO, Subsection C028: National Technical Means.

A056 The "active" observer

Decisions to use active or passive observers appear not to be based on rational thought. The decision making process is based instead on an obscure principle of "budget constraint," where a variety of options are all under-funded so the emphasis is never focused on making any one system operational on a realistic time schedule. The duration of the funding is adequate for "prototype" testing, evaluation, or development, but **never** for utilization of the equipment or the information for operational needs. Projects are funded to hire "senior scientists" to develop hardware, but the scientists themselves have little or no sense of data handling, data display, or data interpretation, even for their own needs. The scientific goal is research, the commitment to national service is lacking.

A057 Effective lifetime of the payload

The *New York Times* has finally started mentioning the extended lifetime of U.S. satellites ["U.S. Plans Big Spending Increase For Military Operations in Space: Program Includes Better Satellites, Gathering of Intelligence, and A Cargo Role for the Shuttle," by Richard Halloran, October 17, 1982, front page, continued on page 60. (It is a series of three articles; the second was printed October 18; the third, October 19.)]. The extended lifetime of a payload translates into fewer launches, and certainly the need for the U.S. to launch fewer spy satellites than the Soviet Union.

PART FOUR

Chapter B

Real-Time Monitoring

The sophistication of the equipment, coupled with the expense of purchasing and operating remote sensing systems for continuous global monitoring and real-time information exchange, has created a challenge for the United States, especially for Goddard Space Flight Center in the Maryland outskirts of Washington, D.C. ["A Global Information Complex," by Howard and Harriet Kurtz, *IEEE Aerospace and Electronic Systems Society Newsletter*, May 1983, pp. 1-2].

Real-time receiving, processing, and editing of raw remote sensing data are perhaps the most serious problems now facing this country. Either that information will remain in the public domain to be sorted, processed, interpreted, and transferred to all users or it will be made available only to a select few. Those few would then have the luxury of using that information for their own vested interests.

The impossibility of handling remote sensing data by hand is discussed by Paul F. Krumpe, 1976, *The World Remote Sensing Bibliographic Index*, Tensor Industries, Inc., Fairfax, Virginia. Stephen Barber says that the problem with the National Security Agency is that "it tapes so much eavesdropping data from all over—from the sky, from giant scanner sites around the world, from radio and radar intercepts—that there are literally tons of material constantly awaiting transcription ["Noise Interferes," by Stephen Barber, *Far Eastern Economic Review*, February 25, 1977, pg. 28]."

Miles Copeland discusses the reliability of satellite information; he decides in favor of satellite data rather than espionage information. Copeland concludes, " . . . espionage information is always, by its very nature, questionable ["The Functions of Strategic Intelligence," by Miles Copeland, *Defense and Foreign Affairs Digest*, February 1977]."

One of the more informative journals for the user of remote sensing systems is the *IEEE Aerospace and Electronic Systems Society Newsletter*, Melvin N. Abramovich, Editor, 10708 Shelly Court, Garrett Park, Maryland 20896 USA, Tele: (202) 722-2200. This Society announced in its May 1983 issue, pg. 12, that the IEEE Society on Social Implications of Technology (SSIT) had issued a statement opposing Government restrictions on information [flow] not directly involved with military operations. The position says that SSIT "opposes government efforts to impose restrictions on the free flow of scientific and technical information other than with respect to specific classified details directly concerning weaponry, military plans, and the like."

The elitest attitude could be encouraged by concentrating the development of more and more automation in the hands of a few; system performance would then become more and more independent of human participation, human judgement, and human incentive. That elitest approach is, however, a "dead-end approach" for the human race ["Remote Sensing," by C. Voute, *ITC Journal*, 1982-1, pp. 37-44].

In that article Prof. Dr. Voute outlines three operational modes for handling remote sensing data; he concludes that the third is really the only acceptable option: decentralize and diversify. All related job opportunities should depend upon national scientific and technological self-reliance. Though this decentralization and diversification cannot take place overnight, it could now make steady progress.

The mailing address for ITC (the International Training Center) is given at the beginning of PART FOUR: Notes and References. A small booklet, available by writing to the ITC, lists regional training centers in developing countries, and lists courses taught in the English language (some classes are also taught in French).

The International Institute for Aerial Survey and Earth Sciences (ITC) was founded in 1951 as a contribution from the Netherlands to international development co-operation, on the initiative of Prof. Dr. Ir. W. Schermerhorn, first Prime Minister of the Netherlands after World War II, and in response to a United Nations recommendation.

It would seem that the time has come for the United States to found such a training institute. An International Training Center in the United States would, however, have to emphasize the continuous interpretation and use of remote sensing data from atmospheric monitoring. The training and education would have to include the use of real-time (digital) data display for instant assimilation. And much would have to be done to support weather-dependent or weather-sensitive operations.

Training and education for the use of remote sensing data could be certified through existing colleges and universities in the United States but the bulk of the preliminary teaching would logically go to vocational training schools. Those schools are already authorized to pursue and certify less than four-year degree-granting programs.

Secondary schools could also start teaching classes in global circulation and pattern recognition. Students could trace the fate of toxic materials entering the atmosphere in their own home town—carbon monoxide generated as automobile exhaust, jet fuel dumped by aircraft before landing, fumes of chemical spray carried aloft.

B058 Sorting signal from noise

Sorting signal from noise from a moving source, from an airplane or a satellite payload requires similar computer capability. The AWACS (Airborne Warning And Control System) is a Boeing E-3A, a modified Boeing 707-32B airframe topped with a 30-foot rotating radome employing advanced radar, computer, and communication technology. The idea is that the signal is transmitted and the echo received by a radar in motion ["Arms Control, Regional Stability, and the Taiwan Relations Act," by A. James Gregor and Maria Hsia Chang, *Journal of Strategic Studies*, May 1980, pp. 3-25].

The possibility of civilian use of AWACS attracted attention during the Air Traffic Control strike ["U.S. Eyed AWACS for Air Control," by Shifrin Carole, *Washington Post*, August 13, 1981, pg. A-16]. That was the first time many civilians had thought about the use of a flying radar, and the intrigue of sorting signal from noise with the computer in motion. The use of AWACS is mentioned in Subsection C065: Airborne Warning And Control System.

B059 The hazard of the digit

"Advantages of digital transmission over current analog methods include improved signal quality, compatibility with planned digital terrestrial links, and more efficient use of available band width and power, enabling the system to handle a greater volume of [information transfer] traffic." ["Digital transmission equipment for satellite systems," author unknown, *Telecommunication Journal*, Vol. 44, II, 1977, pg. 54.]

The hazard of digitizing or quantitizing information is a user-oriented, not a technology-oriented, concern. The hazard is that the digitizing process has been pre-determined by some engineer. In that case, all the user-operator can do in his primitive state where he is now constrained to function is to switch the equipment on or off. And, unfortunately, that simplistic mode of data collection, of using pre-determined digitizing options, is a mode designed only for idiots, intended to remain standard in future systems ["Remote Sensing," by C. Voute, an article written in English, available from The Netherlands, referenced in PART FOUR; Chapter B].

The selection of user options for digital density would require software that is not yet being developed. It would require a departure from fully automated systems. Such user-oriented software is the only software that could eventually assure full utility of an operational system. Such user-oriented software is the only software that can transform a trained operator into a participating user. Full utility of a system implies that software has been developed to accommodate the needs of the user, to achieve maximum machine efficiency, to allow user judgement for the selection of digitizing density at the time of data collection. That means, the decision for recording detail is transferred from the design engineer to the person who has to interpret the data.

The digitizing process, especially the use of the binary number system, the flip-flop circuit where the numbers are either "zero" or "one," is discussed by Joseph Weizenbaum, 1976, *Computer Power and Human Reason*, San Francisco: W. H. Freeman and Comp., Chapter 3: How Computers Work, pp. 73-110.

A single character in a binary number is a bit. BIT is an abbreviation for B-inary dig-IT. A byte is a word; there are 16- and 8-bit bytes ["The Chip: Electronic Mini-marvel that is Changing Your Life," by Allen A. Boraiko, *National Geographic*, October 1982, pp. 420-458; and "Silicon Valley: High Tech, High Risk, and High Life," by Moira Johnston, *National Geographic*, October 1982, pp. 459-477]. Both articles are written for readers with a non-technical background. A healthy portion of the editorial credit should go to the Senior Science Editor for *National Geographic*, Mr. Kenneth Weaver.

B060   The sensor is smart

The miniaturization of electronics has enabled engineers and scientists to include electronic data processing capabilities in the design of remote sensors for satellite payloads. The two articles in the October 1982 issue of *National Geographic* are recommended background reading, see Subsection B059.

Reconnaissance satellites have achieved increasing importance for early warning and arms control monitoring as land-based reconnaissance systems have become more and more vulnerable to political dispute [Seyom Brown, Nina W. Cornell, Larry L. Fabian, and Edith Brown Weiss, 1977, *Regimes for the Ocean, Outer Space, and Weather*, The Brookings Institution, 1775 Massachusetts Ave., N.W., Washington, DC 10036, pg. 133], covert operations more and more vulnerable to political abuse. These authors also point out the need for a combined military-civilian work force in the United States.

A standard reference for the use of military Earth-orbiting reconnaissance satellite systems is the book by Philip J. Klass, 1971, *Secret Sentries in Space*, New York: Random House. Also refer to "Spies in the Sky," by Philip J. Klass, *New York Times Magazine*, September 3, 1972, pg. 35.

B061   A file cabinet in the sky

As more and more electronic equipment is placed in the satellite payload, the limiting factor for the user will eventually become our inability to tell time, our inability to communicate a reference time signal from one place to another. In 1955, the instabilities in the clock (oscillators) were go great as to mask the instabilities of the HF (High Frequency) radio dissemination. But clocks have been improved. Today, the stability of the clock far exceeds the capabilities of the dissemination links ["The science of time and its inverse," by Roger L. Freeman, *Telecommunications Journal*, Vol. 44, II, 1977, pg. 66]. The author starts with a history of time—the Julian calendar (46 B.C., Before Christ, not Before Computer), the Gregorian reform (1582), and the definition of the second with the Cesium-133-atom—and provides a wealth of information about NBS (National Bureau of Standards) time-frequency standards and formats.

B062   Information at a glance

Now that personal computers are becoming more popular ["The boom is on in New Personal Computers," by William J. Hawkins, *Popular Science*, November 1982, pg. 93], many American children are learning the value of computer graphics—the ease of assimilating information presented as a picture ["Coming: A New Generation of Super-realistic Computer Images," by Charles A. Miller, *Popular Science*, November 1982, pg. 67].

PART FOUR

Chapter C

Identification: Friend or Foe

General background information for the use of active radar observing is provided by Eric Burgess, 1961, *Long-Range Ballistic Missiles*, New York: The Macmillan Comp. and Eric Burgess, 1957, *Guided Weapons*, New York: The Macmillan Comp.

C063   The active observer

C064   The active electronic fence

C065   Airborne Warning And Control System

C066   A flying transponder

C067 The case of the false echo

C068 The air space merger

PART FOUR

Chapter D

Detecting the Explosion

"The Atmosphere After a Nuclear Attack," by Paul J. Crutzen and John W. Birks, *Ambio*, June/July 1982 (a journal published in Sweden), provides an introduction to the idea of nuclear explosions causing artificially initiated atmospheric change. The atmospheric model used to describe background behavior could be improved. There is uncertainty in the geographic distribution of the number and size of nuclear explosions and also in the altitude of the explosions. A variety of operational and atmospheric parameters could be adjusted for future considerations. But the risk of incinerating the upper atmosphere, the risk of imposing irreversible change in atmospheric chemistry, atmospheric dynamics, atmospheric transmission properties, would still remain severe.

The use of a network of ground-based seismic sensors or of a constellation of satellite-borne flash detectors can be understood by studying background material presented by Ola Dahlman and Hans Israelson, National Defense Research Institute in Sweden. Their book *Monitoring Underground Nuclear Explosions*, published in 1977 by Elsevier Scientific Publishing Comp., 335 Jan van Golenstraat, P.O.Box 211, Amsterdam, The Netherlands, is the best available. The Partial Test Ban Treaty of 1963 is discussed; also the Comprehensive Test Ban Treaty.

Background material for test ban treaty negotiations can be obtained by writing directly to Frank Blackaby, Director, Stockholm International Peace Research Institute (SIPRI), Bergshamra, S-171 73 Solna, Sweden, Tele: 08-55 97 00.

D069   Underground nuclear testing

Seismological recording-reporting techniques are discussed by Ola Dahlman and Hans Israelson, 1977, *Monitoring Underground Nuclear Explosions,* referenced for Chapter D, pp. 52-107. The leakage of radioactivity from at least five underground tests in U.S.S.R. and from at least two in the U.S. had been detected outside territories of the countries (pg. 14).

"The Carter Administration has caved in to the nuclear-weapons [national] laboratories, which want to continue to test bombs and are opposed to a meaningful agreement that will stop the spread of nuclear weapons ["The Atomic-Weapons Lobby Is Gaining," Norman Solomon, *The Nation,* October 11, 1980, pp. 335-338]."

D070   Atmospheric nuclear testing

Ola Dahlman and Hans Israelson discuss satellite reconnaissance (pg. 329); they also review specifically negotiated treaty requirements for satellite verification through remote sensing and global information systems (pp. 337-356), referenced for Chapter D. The first part of the book goes into some detail of non-productive negotiations to ban nuclear testing.

Atmospheric contamination from dust, dirt, and debris carried aloft by the updraft of a nuclear explosion is examined by Paul J. Crutzen and John W. Birks, "The Atmosphere After a Nuclear Attack," *Ambio,* June/July 1982.

The first hydrogen bomb was built by the United States. That bomb was exploded, as a test, November 1, 1952 (the testing of this thermonuclear device was reported February 2, 1954), on the Island Elugelab, one of the Marshall Islands in the Pacific Ocean. This test, known as Operation Ivy (I is the ninth letter of the alphabet and this was the ninth big test of an atomic- or hydrogen-bomb) sent up a ball of fire more than three miles wide. Elugelab Island vanished. The only trace of it was a hole in the bottom of the ocean, 175 feet deep ["Outer Space," by A. G. Mezerik, *International Review Service,* Vol. VI, No. 56, 1960, pp. 25-38].

D071   The false hope of ABM

United States Senator Malcom Wallop (Republican-Wyoming) has been actively involved in review and public debate of ballistic missile defense systems ["Opportunities and Imperatives of Ballistic Missile Defense," by Malcom Wallop, *Strategic Review,* Fall 1979, pp. 13-21]. Also see Notes and References, PART TWO, Subsection D046.

Launch parameters and lift-off behavior for intercontinental ballistic missiles are discussed by Eric Burgess, 1961, *Long-Range Ballistic Missiles,* New York: The Macmillan Comp., pp. 196-197. Also see Notes and References, PART THREE, Subsection A054.

PART FOUR

Chapter E

Network Decentralization

The purpose of decentralization of communication and information transfer networks is the freedom of choice it provides to the users. And freedom of choice is the central freedom for the survival of capitalism as we would like to think it can survive. "The natural tendency of capitalism is toward a continuous improvement in the average standard of living . . . a progressive enrichment of many." The remarks are taken from *The Anti-Capitalistic Mentality*, by Ludwig von Mises, 1956, D. Van Nostrand Comp., Inc., Princeton, New Jersey. Mises continues, "What gives to the individual as much freedom as is compatible with life in that particular society, is the operation of market economy. In the market economy, a person is free to choose." Excerpts from the book are provided in *U.S. News & World Report*, October 19, 1956, "What's Behind the War on Business," by Ludwig von Mises, pp. 156-175.

E072   A down to earth message

The ARPANET (Advanced Research Projects Agency NETwork) is an operational, computerized, packet switching digital network, sponsored by the Department of Defense, that provides a capability for geographically separated computers to communicate with each other. The ARPANET is a resource-sharing, host-to-host network-linking capability designed for a wide variety of computers at research centers.

ARPANET mail should be addressed to: Elizabeth Feinler, Manager, ARPANET Network Information Center, Room J 2021, SRI International, Menlo Park, California 94025, Tele: (415) 859-3695/Telex: 334463. Computer network development is discussed by Lawrence G. Roberts and Barry D. Wessler, "Computer network development to achieve resource sharing," American Federation of Information Processing Societies Conference Proceedings, Vol. 36, 1970, pg. 540, American Federation of Information Processing Societies Press, 210 Summit Avenue, Montvale, New Jersey 07645.

The ARPANET Directory: NIC48000, November 1980, was prepared for: Defense Communications Agency, Washington, DC 20305; it was produced and published by: Network Information Center, SRI International, Menlo Park, California 94025, provides a wealth of user information.

E073   A package of information

Packet switching is becoming an attractive alternative to circuit switching for the transmission of digital data sets [Roy D. Rosner, 1982, *Packet Switching: Tomorrow's Communication Today*, Lifetime Learning Publications, A division of Wadsworth, Inc., Belmont, California].

E074   Democratization of information flow

Computer access to information flow is discussed in the ARPANET Directory referenced in Subsection E072.

PART FOUR

Chapter F

Communication Satellites

Working references for communication satellites were given at the beginning of PART FOUR, Chapter A, Subsection A052, Burton I. Edelson, 1977, and Robert B. Cooper, 1979.

Michael E. Kinsley, 1976, *Outer Space and Inner Sanctums: Government, Business, and Satellite Communication*, John Wiley and Sons Ltd., Baffins Lane, Chichester, Sussex, England, traces and documents the history of communication satellites in the United States beginning with the Communications Satellite Act of 1962, with concern for economic history and regulatory practices.

F077   Boost and return

Refer to Burton I. Edelson, 1977, and Robert B. Cooper, 1979.

F078   The receiver on the ground

Refer to Burton I. Edelson, 1977, and Robert B. Cooper, 1979.

F079   The transmitter is the target

Refer to Burton I. Edelson, 1977, and Robert B. Cooper, 1979.

PART FOUR

Chapter G

Use it or lose it

"It is a dreary mission that America has established for herself . . . the defender of an intolerable status quo . . . the spokesman for the smug and rich in their efforts to ward off the encroachments of the desperate and the miserable." [Ronald Steel, 1964, *The End of Alliance*, New York: Viking Press, pg. 136.]

G080 Automation is the enemy

Refer to Joseph Weizenbaum, 1976, *Computer Power and Human Reason*, W. H. Freeman Comp.; Weizenbaum stresses the importance of human intelligence over artificial (computer) intelligence. The book is required reading for those interested in changing priorities in defense spending to favor human judgement instead of automation.

G081 Industrial push

G082 The fault is me

G083 User pull

G084 Back to computer basics

G085 Technology is culture

G086 People with a purpose

PART FOUR

Perspective

Information is Firepower

Immanuel Kant (1724-1804) wrote about war, " . . . in the natural state of war, the stronger prevail." Kant used "war" to mean a natural state, a manifestation of eternal dynamic dualism. Kant explains, "War does not imply or does it require hostility." [Refer to *The Great Legal Philosophers*, by Clarence Morris, Editor (1959), University of Pennsylvania Press, Philadelphia, pg. 259.]

The destruction of human life and the destruction of property became a goal rather than an unfortunate consequence of the fighting. "The U.S. Navy and the U.S. Air Force competed with each other to see who could drop more tonnage on North Vietnam . . . Some Army and Marine units engaged in body count sweepstakes in South Vietnam [Lawrence J. Korb (1979), *The Fall and Rise of the Pentagon*, Greenwood Press, Westport, Conn., pg. 9]."

The references to faith and reason according to the teachings of Saint Thomas Aquinas (1226-1274) are reprinted by Ebenstein, William [*Great Political Thinkers* (1962), New York: Holt, Rinehart and Winston, pg. 213].

The stagnation of the "balance of power" and the sameness of "equality" imposed by the conformity of the rule of law have introduced rigid (static) thought patterns that now permeate the American way of life. The purpose of this book is to encourage departure from that conformity, to introduce dynamic dualism into the decision making process.

William James (1842-1910) popularized dynamic dualism in the decision making process but he gave it only the name, pragmatism [*Pragmatism* (1914), Longmans, Green, and Comp., Lecture I, as given in the Preface, Notes and References]. James recognized not only the importance of continuity and creativity as essential partners, but also the overwhelming urgency for preserving both as participants in the decision making process. Thus, pragmatism, as William James used it, included the "fourth dimension," it included the time-dependent interaction of continuity and creativity.

William James, a student of John Stuart Mill (1806-1873), was greatly impressed with the writings of an "aristocratic Frenchman," Alexis de Tocqueville (1805-1859). Both Mill and Tocqueville wrote extensively on the dualism of liberty and subjugation. As I understand the intent of their writings and their concept of human behavior, liberty and subjugation were dynamic dualing partners. Subjugation would carry the continuity; liberty would provide the creative, refreshing pulse of energy. William Ebenstein is a convenient reference [*Great Political Thinkers* (1962), New York: Holt, Rinehart and Winston, pp. 522-588].

The doctrine of massive retaliation—massive destruction of human life and property through the use of nuclear weapons—had been the "intellectual underpinnings" of our national security during the Eisenhower years of the 1950s. In the early 1970s, to compensate for any shortage of military manpower, Secretary of Defense James Schlesinger made public statements to the effect that this nation would initiate nuclear warfare to repel attack with conventional weapons [Lawrence J. Korb (1979), *The Fall and Rise of the Pentagon*, Greenwood Press, Westport, Conn., pg. 41, which includes reference to James Schlesinger, *Annual Report of the Secretary of Defense, FY1975*, March 4, 1974, pp. 3-6].

This all-new American institution, the modern-day utility of democratic-capitalism to sustain an armed peace for the industrial elite, was brought to the attention of the American people by President Eisenhower. "We have been compelled to create a permanent armament industry of vast proportions . . . This conjunction of an immense military establishment and a large arms industry is new in the American experience . . . We recognize the imperative need for this development. Yet we must not fail to comprehend its grave implications. The potential for the disastrous rise of misplaced power exists and will persist." ["Farewell Radio and Television Address to the American People," by Dwight Eisenhower, January 17, 1961, 8:30 p.m., *Public Papers of the Presidents of the United States*, 1960-1961, Dwight D. Eisenhower, pg. 1038.]

The NEW era is an era of Natural Eternal War of global (electronic) monitoring. The American military mission of real-time Detection and Early Warning is completely compatible with the broader long-term humanitarian mission of Global Environmental Monitoring.

It is interesting to note that Isaac Asimov (1975), *Science Past - Science Future*, Ace Books, A division of Charter Communications, Inc., Grosset and Dunlap Comp., New York, arranged his collection of reprints as a TEAM effort. The divisions in that book are: Technology, Environment (Physical Science), And Man (Life Science). It seems that the TEAM concept provides a convenient, if not necessary, representation of our current dynamic interactive thinking.

"We live in a global village . . . a simultaneous happening . . . Real, total war has become the information war . . . the latest technologies have rendered [destructive] war meaningless. The hydrogen bomb is history's exclamation point. It ends an age-long sentence of manifest violence. The cold war is the real war . . . [it] surrounds us . . . [it] involves everybody—all the time—everywhere [Marshall McLuhan (1967), *The Medium is the Massage*, New York: Bantam Books, Inc.]."

One last plea for the continuation of the eternal war of deciding without resort to violence is made by Marshall McLuhan (1971), *From Cliche to Archetype*, New York: Pocket Books, pg. 133. McLuhan quotes from *The Joys of Yiddish* by Leo Rosten, "Knowledge, among Jews, came to compensate for worldly rewards. Insight, I think, became a substitute for weapons: one way to block the bully's wrath is to know him better than he knows himself."

Senator Barry Goldwater (Republican-Arizona), a "great friend" of the Air Force Academy and Chairman of the Academy Board of Visitors, was in Colorado Springs, Colorado, to deliver the 25th Air Force Academy commencement address. Goldwater told the cadets . . . they should not be worried by any sense of national bewilderment . . . they should also witness an upsurge in patriotism and a "return to God." The Senator was optimistic about the future; he told the class of 1983 that " . . . he expects the cadets to live to see a day when war will be done away with because of the United States' great technological abilities." [*Gazette Telegraph*, Colorado Springs, Colorado, June 2, 1983, pg. 1, "Goldwater sees more Latin conflict: Senator addresses cadets," by Sue McMillin.]

PART FIVE

Information Politics

If freedom of the press is the best insurance,
then it is time to pay the premium

The "press leak" operates through informal channels. The "leak" mechanism attracted national attention when it was suspected that the Carter Administration had used it to release sensitive information about defense spending priorities, refer to PART ONE, Chapter E: A Quick Fix.

The release of the Pentagon Papers by Daniel Ellsberg, the "History of U.S. Decision-Making Process on Vietnam Policy, 1945-1967," is reviewed in the Special Issue of *Manufacturing Engineering*, January 1982, pg. 212, as referenced in the Preface, Notes and References.

PART FIVE

Chapter A

SALT Treaties

The Prohibition Amendment, the Eighteenth Amendment to the U.S. Constitution, went into effect January 16, 1920. The Twenty-first Amendment was adopted December 5, 1933: Section 1. The Eighteenth Article of Amendment to the Constitution of the United States is hereby repealed [Sol Bloom (1937), *The Story of the Constitution*, pp. 93-94, The United States Constitution Sesquicentennial Commission, House Office Bldg., Washington, DC].

The life of Charles Evans Hughes (1862-1948) is documented in the two-volume masterpiece by Merlo Pusey (1951), *Charles Evans Hughes*, New

York: The Macmillan Comp. and was recently reviewed in the *Year-book.1981.Supreme Court Historical Society*, pp. 95-112, "Hughes Exhibit Catalogue: Charles Evans Hughes: The Eleventh Chief Justice." Much of my information about Hughes was obtained from that exhibit at the Supreme Court Building, "Charles Evans Hughes Display."

My first visit was on a rainy afternoon, May 19, 1981, at 1:25 p.m. With the gracious assistance of Security Officer Surles, I was able to locate every display of interest to me, and to borrow a pencil. Especially the display, "Secretary of State/World Statesman (1921-1929)," was helpful. Being able to see original documents, letters, and news clippings was not only informative, it was also stimulating: "Hughes stunned the world at the opening session of the Washington Arms Conference when he presented his proposal for disarmament, November 12, 1921, as he grappled with the recurring controversy over naval arms limitation."

"Treaties and other international agreements provide a major part of the international rights and obligations of the United States . . . many of them lie in unwritten customary law [Louis Henkin (1972), *Foreign Affairs and the Constitution*, The Norton Library, W. W. Norton and Comp. Inc., New York, pg. 187]," but, as Henkin explains in the Preface, " . . . the law of foreign affairs [for the United States] fell somewhere between the constitutional lawyer and the international lawyer, perhaps nearer to the latter, but his credentials in constitutional law were not universally accepted." Thus the question of "how the U.S. Constitution governs the conduct of foreign relation" does not receive the sustained attention or the extended exposition it deserves.

Standard references to international law are to be recommended [Grenville Clark and Louis B. Sohn (1958), *World Peace Through World Law*, Harvard University Press, Cambridge, Mass.; William W. Bishop, Jr. (1962), *International Law: Cases and Materials*, Little Brown, and Comp.], but the book by Henkin is certainly the best I used. It is written from the combined perspective of the U.S. Constitution and foreign affairs.

The illusion of prohibition type legislation for arms control is discussed by Robert C. Johansen (1979), *SALT II: Illusion and Reality*, Working paper No. Nine, Institute for World Order, Inc., 777 United Nations Plaza, New York, New York 10017. " . . . it is hard to believe that arms opponents would be in any worse position if there had been no SALT at all."

Johansen goes on to explain that the SALT process has helped "legitimize" MIRVs (Multiple Independently targetable Re-entry Vehicles), cruise missiles, the MX (Missile eXperimental), and a shift to a nuclear war-fighting capability. I agree with Johansen, " . . . SALT is more a charade than an arms reversal program."

It is necessary to focus attention on the tendency of the SALT process to "exclude multilateral monitoring (pg. 1, 8)." Multilateral monitoring or "trans-national monitoring agencies" would provide equal opportunity for all nations to access remote sensing information. That is to say, one reason to reject SALT-efforts is because they are "imperialistic;" the SALT-process says the "Big Two" have the right to hold the world population hostage while they threaten "instant genocide." The SALT-process is bilateral and, therefore, unacceptable.

A short version of this working paper by Robert C. Johansen was printed in the May 1979 issue of *Harper's* magazine.

A087 Equality for all nations

George Washington's Farewell Address to the People of the United States, a reprint from a facsimile of the manuscript which Washington gave to Claypoole's *American Daily Advertiser*, September 19, 1796, Philadelphia, is available in the book by Sol Bloom (1937), *The Story of the Constitution*, pp. 135-145, referenced in Chapter A, above.

A088 No force for enforcement

According to the Charter of the United Nations no one nation can use its own military force to enforce an international agreement. The complete Charter of the United Nations is conveniently printed in *The Random House Dictionary of the English Language*, The Unabridged Edition (1967), Jess Stein, Editor-in-Chief, New York: Random House, pp. 1941-1946.

A089 International regulatory activities

"There can be no greater error than to expect, or calculate upon real favours from Nation to Nation. 'Tis an illusion which experience must cure, which a just pride ought to discard." [Washington's Farewell Address as reprinted by Sol Bloom (1937), *The Story of the Constitution*, pg. 144, referenced in Chapter A above.

The elimination of the possibility of a "surprise" attack would also eliminate, or at least decrease, the possibility of accidental nuclear war. PART FOUR of this book is devoted to the feasibility of the use of detection and early warning systems for the purpose of eliminating the element of surprise. PART FIVE, Chapter C: National Weather Service, focuses attention on the service aspect of national service organizations.

A090 Verification to the rescue

National Technical Means of verification was discussed and referenced in PART TWO, Subsection C028: National Technical Means. Herbert Scoville, Jr. discusses "Verification of Nuclear Arms Limitations," *Bulletin of Atomic Scientists*, October 1970, pg. 8.

Fundamental to the issue of verification is the question of method. For the United States the question of method dates back to July 21, 1955, when the "Open Skies" proposal was made by President Eisenhower [Statement on Disarmament Presented at the Geneva Conference]. The September 19, 1955, Eisenhower response to a letter received from Nikolai Bulganin, Chairman, Council of Ministers, U.S.S.R., clearly indicates Soviet refusal of the proposal. Instead of the "Open Skies" policy advocated by the United States, the Soviets wanted to be given the right to actively police activities of the American people within the United States, " . . . to station inspection teams at key points . . . " Refer to *Public Papers of the Presidents*, Dwight D. Eisenhower, 1955, pg. 713, 715.

The "Open Skies" policy was again offered to Soviet reconnaissance aircraft, on a reciprocal basis, in 1960. The Soviets again refused. The 1960 offer was basically the same offer that had been made, and refused, five years earlier ["Radio and Television Report to the American People on the Events in Paris," May 25, 1960, Dwight D. Eisenhower, *Public Papers of the Presidents*, 1960-1961, pg. 443, as referenced above].

I endorse the proposal by Eisenhower, "A major American goal is a world of open societies." The Soviet preference for having inspection teams patrol the areas of (military or national) interest would run contrary to American ideals. There are other public advocates of an "Open Sky" policy [Edward Teller, "Re-open the Skies: Seventeen years ago President Eisenhower proposed the Open Skies policy," *New York Times*, April 25, 1971, an Op-Ed piece; and Ray S. Cline (1976), *Secrets, Spies and Scholars: Blueprint of the Essential CIA*, Acropolis Books, Ltd., Washington, DC]. In that book, Cline also addresses the broader question of the availability of information flow to the American people.

A comprehensive survey of the question of information availability was prepared by the Congressional Research Service of the Library of Congress, "Intelligence Community: Reform and Reorganization," by Mark M. Lowenthal, CRS Issue Brief 76039, dated: May 7, 1976, updated periodically.

A091   Creating a wartime economy

The direct correlation between political power and government spending . . . staunch Federalists welcomed it, Republicans feared it, but both were painfully aware of its existence [Hill, Peter P. (1971), *William Vans Murray: Federalist Diplomat: The Shaping of Peace with France: 1797-1801*, Syracuse University Press, Syracuse, New York, pg. 228].

The closed decision making process within the defense community is now attracting national attention thanks to the efforts of many, including the Council on Economic Priorities, 84 Fifth Avenue, New York, New York 10011; Tele: (212) 691-8550. Especially the Council on Economic Priorities *Newsletter*, June 1981, CEP Publication N81-4, is devoted to a summary of the study "The Iron Triangle: The Politics of Defense Contracting," by Gordon Adams and Geoff Quinn. The study identifies the three centers— the Congressional, the Executive (the Department of Defense), and private industry—as "a community of shared interests and assumptions which defends itself against outsiders." The authors make recommendations for "increasing public participation in military policy-making and weapons procurement decisions."

One can still argue in favor of electing mature people, say those born prior to 1932, to the United States Congress—those with practical experience outside the legal profession.

The funding that is being suggested to create a "wartime economy" is the funding currently available through the defense budget. The spending priorities could be shifted to favor the use of electronics for continuous global monitoring, with the idea that continuous information flow would reduce the need for excessive overkill in weapons systems.

PART FIVE

Chapter B

The Invisible Government

The political "mood" of the country was assessed from the foreign press, from the press as the nation was viewed from outside at the time of the 1980 presidential election [see PART ONE, Perspective, Notes and References].

The adjustment of federal spending should be viewed within a context of national purpose, not merely as an exercise in accounting. Refer to PART ONE, Subsection A004: "Demand-side" economics. The American people would "demand" that their tax dollars in the defense budget be spent for electronics . . . that their tax dollars be used to provide a driving force for economic expansion.

A "shotgun wedding" within the world of electronics would breakdown traditional barriers as it did with increased war production prior to World War II [*Manufacturing Engineering*, Special Golden Anniversary Issue, January 1982, "Industry at war," pp. 79-114]. " . . . General Motors was drawn into the airplane business by way of the production of motors . . . the Allison engine (pg. 82)." The Ford Motor Company (using assembly line techniques) would "lay the genesis of the Willow Run Bomber Plant, an outstandingly successful contributor to the war effort (pg. 83)." *Manufacturing Engineering* is a publication of the Society of Manufacturing Engineers, One SME Drive, P.O.Box 930, Dearborn, Michigan 48128.

The importance of synchronizing defense spending and economic growth cannot be emphasized enough. As this nation emerged from economic depression in 1934, the "Big Three," the existing dominating automotive industries: General Motors, Ford, and Chrysler, strengthened their stranglehold on the industry . . . despite the upbeat note in industry, the small manufacturers were finding the going increasingly difficult [*Manufacturing Engineering*, January 1982, pg. 50, Special Issue referenced above].

This very serious matter of protecting "some 50,000 subcontractors and suppliers (mostly small- and medium-sized businesses)" has been recently addressed by legislation: H.R.5540, The Defense Industrial Base Revitalization Act, introduced by Representatives James J. Blanchard (Democrat-Michigan) and Stewart B. McKinney (Republican-Connecticut), House Subcommittee on Economic Stabilization of the House Committee on Banking, Finance, and Urban Affairs. The interested reader could learn of the current status of that legislation by contacting the Subcommittee Chairman.

B092   Fire the bookkeeper

Congressional oversight responsibility extends not only to the Budget Committee ["'No Small Change," by Mark Shields, discussing U.S. Senate Budget Committee Chairman Pete V. Domenici (Pietro Vichi - Italian immigrant parents), *Washington Post*, March 20, 1981, pg. A-23] but also to taxation policies and monetary control through the Federal Reserve [John Maynard Keynes (1958), *A Treatise on Money*, Vol. I: The Pure Theory of Money; Vol. II: The Applied Theory of Money, London: Macmillan and Co., Ltd.]. The framers of the Federal Reserve Act apparently had " . . . implicit faith in what has come to be called the commercial loan theory (Vol. I, pg. 89)."

Practical aspects of the Federal Reserve System are discussed by Ritter and Silber [Lawrence S. Ritter and William L. Silber (1970), *Money*, New York: Basic Books]. Especially monetary policy versus fiscal policy (pg. 163) is clarified. The authors state, "The best stabilization policy is no stabilization policy at all (pg. 195)." The history of the Federal Reserve is reviewed on pg. 11. I am certainly sympathetic with the conclusion of Ritter and Silber: the money supply should be set on "automatic pilot" and left alone (pg. 195).

Public criticism of the monetary policies of the Federal Reserve continues, "The centralized money market in the United States is in New York and the New York Federal Reserve Bank has dominated the other eleven districts to the point where the latter are usually not even consulted when decisions are made by the Open Market Committee." [Cleon Skousen, "The Federal Reserve: Broken Promises," the second in a series of articles about the Federal Reserve System, detailing the history and the purpose of the system, *State of the Nation*, Vol. 2, No.7, July 1982, pg. 4.]

The Paperwork Reduction Act [H.R.6410] specifically addresses "information management [An Editorial by John F. Judge, *Government Executive*, October 1980]." Those aspects of the new Bill generated by Representative Jack Brooks (Democrat-Texas) would create an "Office of Federal Information Policy headed by an Administrator and subordinate to the Director of the Office of Management and Budget . . . it [the new Bill] also provides for the delegation of all authority and responsibility to administer the law to the Administrator." Editor Judge is expressing serious displeasure with the Paperwork Reduction Act when he goes on to suggest, "Why not just create the cabinet Department of Automated Information and have done with it."

An informative pamphlet, prepared by the Information Industry Association, 316 Pennsylvania Ave., S.E., Suite 400, Washington, DC 20003, Tele: (202) 544-1969, Robert S. Willard, Moderator, Information Policy Discussion Group, December 12, 1980, provides "An Assessment of 1980 and a View Toward 1981: The Information Perspective." The Honorable Al Gore, Jr. (Democrat-Tenn.), Member, U.S. House of Representatives; Richard M. Neustadt, White House Domestic Policy Staff; and Richard E. Wiley, Kirkland and Ellis (Dick Wiley was Chairman of the FCC—Federal Communication Commission—in 1976 at the beginning of the present four year cycle, the year in which National Information Policy, or the "Blue Book," was put together) were panelists. " . . . H.R.6410, the Paperwork and Information Policy bill was signed . . . yesterday (December 11, 1980), as a matter of fact (pg. 3)."

The good news/bad news information policy joke by Mr. Willard (pg. 8) is worth reprinting: " . . . a staffer walked into a Congressman['s office] and said we've got this tremendous new area that no one is paying attention to. There is so much to be done in the area of information that you can make all sorts of new policy; you can really make a significant contribution: that's the good news. The bad news is that nobody in the world is interested in it, and you probably won't get re-elected if you concentrate on it." (Laughter)

Mr. Neustadt [Information Policy Discussion Group, above, pg. 16] referred to H.R.6410, " . . . that bill is a little train with two box cars on it. One is paperwork reduction. The other was Congressman Brooks' Office of Information and Regulatory Affairs, which is going to be a permanent part of OMB, substantially staffed, with responsibility for coordinating federal information activities . . . That unit in OMB is now going to be a major player in the Executive Branch's communication policy development."

For the official record refer to *Congressional Record*, House: December 1, 1980, pp. H11374-H11380: Paperwork Reduction Act of 1980. The quotations in the text are taken from this section of the *Congressional Record*.

B093 "Constitutional Dictatorship"

The reference to "Constitutional Dictatorship" is taken from A Brief History of Emergency Power: A Working Paper, prepared by the Special Committee on National Emergencies and Delegated Emergency Powers, United States Senate, 93d Congress, 2d Session, July 1974, U.S. Government Printing Office, Washington, see Foreword, pg. v, a study by the late Clinton Rossiter. The Working Paper—all 140 pages—was reproduced October 10, 1974, by the Library of Congress, Congressional Research Service.

" . . . hundreds of emergency statutes confer enough authority on the President to rule the country without reference to normal constitutional

312   *Notes and References*

process [National Emergencies and Delegated Emergency Powers, Senate Report No. 94-922, 94th Congress, 2d Session, Final Report, Special Committee on National Emergencies and Delegated Emergency Powers, May 28, 1976, U.S. Government Printing Office, Washington, DC, pg. 18]."

While " . . . occasions may arise when the Executive [the President] must exert a broad discretion in meeting special exigencies or emergencies for which the legislative power has provided no relief and/or existing law will not grant necessary remedy . . . that decision to terminate a constitutional dictatorship, like the decision to institute one, should never be in the hands of the man who constitutes the dictator [Working Paper referenced above, pp. 1, 121-123]."

Federal Emergency Management Executive Order 12148, July 20, 1979 . . . and "in order to transfer emergency functions to the Federal Emergency Management Agency, it is hereby ordered . . . " [Weekly Compilation of Presidential documents, v. 15, no. 29, July 23, 1979: 1277-1284, "Administration of Jimmy Carter, 1979," reproduced by the Library of Congress, Congressional Research Service, July 30, 1980.]

Also refer to "Background and Status of Executive Order 11490: The Assignment of Emergency Preparedness Functions," by Harold C. Relyea, Government Division, Congressional Research Service, The Library of Congress, Washington, DC 20540, July 29, 1976, for a survey of Executive Orders, including E.O.11490, and for the assignment of emergency preparedness functions to executive agencies and departments [*Federal Register*, Vol. 34, No. 209, Thursday, October 30, 1969, Part II, pp. 17567-17599]. The assignment continues with E.O.11921, from President Ford [*Federal Register*, Vol. 41, No. 116, pp. 24294-24336].

"Despite the lack of any specific authority to take unilateral emergency actions, some legal authorities argue that the constitutional clause granting executive power to the President implicitly authorizes him to take such actions . . . others argue that such powers stem from the 'take care' clause [Presidential Emergency Powers over Domestic Affairs: Executive Order No. 11490 and PRM (Presidential Review Memorandum) No. 32, by Raymond Natter, Issue Brief Number IB80087, Congressional Research Service, The Library of Congress, Originated: September 25, 1980; Updated: February 20, 1981, pp. 1, 3, 5]."

"War Powers of the Presidents: A Selective Bibliography," is available from The Army Library, Pentagon 1-A-518 (1st floor, A-ring, Room 518), compiled August 1978. The document includes a list of Public Laws-War Powers.

"Selected Pro and Con Materials on War Powers Legislation," a compilation of articles taken from various editions of the *Congressional Record*, reproduced by the Library of Congress, Congressional Research Service, February 24, 1971, JX 4552, is recommended to the serious reader of constitutional law.

B094 America First

The "isolationists" were everywhere [*Manufacturing Engineering*, January 1982, Special Issue, pg. 70, as referenced in Preface section]. The "chronology of events" is taken from that same Special Issue, "Industry in the depression 1932-1939," pp. 37-78.

Arsenal of Democracy, a book by Burnham Finney (1941), Whittlesey House, New York, a division of McGraw-Hill Book Comp. Inc., is referenced in Preface section.

B095 A real-time response

The President of the United States has emergency authority for domestic action . . . Under 10 USC 333, the President can use the militia or armed forces to suppress "conspiracy," if it is likely that "any part" of the people in a state will be deprived of some constitutional rights, and the state itself refuses to act . . . Under 18 USC 1383, the President has authority to declare any part or all of the United States military zones. People in such zones can be jailed for a year for violating any "executive order of the President." It is not clear that these arrests would be reviewed in Court . . . 5 USC 701 excludes actions taken under declaration of martial law . . . for a government that is supposed to be "of the people, by the people, for the people," it sounds more like a dictatorship.

Under emergency circumstances, communication is the first priority ["The Changing Environment for National Emergency Preparedness and Its Communications Support," by Francis P. Hoeber, testimony before Committee on Science and Technology, Subcommittee on Investigations and Oversight, U.S. House of Representatives, Chairman Albert Gore, Jr., September 29, 1981].

The testimony of Dr. Thomas G. Belden, "Indications, Warning, and Crisis Operations," presented the strongest testimony advocating renewed emphasis on human resource [presented September 30, 1981]. The written testimony submitted by Belden had already been published ["Indications, Warning, and Crisis Operations," by Thomas G. Belden, Intelligence Community Staff, Washington, DC].

A time of national emergency, the same as a time of war, is a time when the people substitute national priorities for those of private individuals [James N. Rosenau, Editor (1961), *International Politics and Foreign Policy*, New York: The Free Press, Chpt. 33: Motivation for War, by Klaus Knorr, pg. 295].

The need to combine national service responsibilities, especially the use of civilian expertise by the military, is noted by George C. Wilson ["Military Seeking to Add 72,000 Civilians to Payroll," *Washington Post*, August 14, 1981, pg. A-13].

B096   Military-industrial divorce

The importance of human resource rather than hardware is discussed by Thomas G. Belden, as referenced in Subsection B095: A real-time response.

The Story of the Constitution, by Sol Bloom (1937), The United States Constitutional Sesquicentennial Commission, House Office Bldg., Washington, DC, pp. 52-53, has been a convenient reference for Amendments passed prior to 1935.

The re-organization of the federal government is discussed in a report by the Murphy Commission, "Organization of the Government for the Conduct of Foreign Policy," June 27, 1975, 278 pps., U.S. Government Printing Office, Washington, DC.

Refer to PART SIX, Chapter E: Purification of the Pentagon, Notes and References, for a discussion of the use of the Congressional Veto for reorganization of the Executive.

Coordination of the industrial use within the Federal Emergency Management Agency (FEMA) would be in good hands with General Louis Giuffrida, Director. At least the high-technology requirements of the United States Air Force for communications/information transfer in time of national emergency would be well represented. "High-technology" must, for the purpose of federal emergency management, include not only hardware but also software development.

According to the written statement by Dr. Richard S. Beal, Special Assistant to the President, White House, September 22, 1981 [submitted to the House Committee on Science and Technology, Subcommittee on Investigations and Oversight, for hearings on Information Technology and Emergency Management], FEMA is responsible for "effective application" of science and technology to the field of "emergency management," a statement that makes almost no sense to me. Application implies utility, and utility implies people. It has been my experience that you do not "manage" people. You manage money, but you motivate people.

Industrial emphasis on one-of-a-kind military-sponsored prototype development, while neglecting the broad civilian market of practical use, is criticized by Robert de Grasse, Jr., Director of the Council on Economic Priorities ["Costs of Defense Spending Not Told in Dollars Alone," by Robert de Grasse, Jr. and David Gold, *Boulder Daily Camera*, Boulder, Colorado, December 31, 1981 taken from the *New York Times*, no date given]. Refer back to PART FIVE, Subsection A091, for the mailing address for Council on Economic Priorities. The general theme of reorganization of the Department of Defense would support a dramatic shift toward human resource— the service aspect of the military service organizations—away from the procurement of hardware.

One of the more colorful critics of the Department of Defense has to be Admiral Hyman George Rickover (retired U.S. Navy): "I don't know why we have a Defense Department. I really don't know. I don't know what it does. No one knows [*60 Minutes*, WDVM, CBS-TV, Washington, DC, March 28, 1982]." Morley: " . . . We asked him [Rickover] to come to *60 Minutes*.

He wouldn't." He said, "Why don't you use my final testimony before the Joint Economic Committee of Congress?" We did. [The typescript of the *60 Minutes* program is available from the Department of Defense, Assistant Secretary for Public Affairs, 000027.]

PART FIVE

Chapter C

National Weather Service

The question of real-time access to digital data sets is a topic covered by "Information For The 1980s," Final Report of the White House Conference on Library and Information Services, 1979, Superintendent of Documents, U.S. Government Printing Office, Washington, DC 20402. The National Commission on Libraries and Information Science, 1717 K-Street, N.W., Suite 600, Washington, DC 20036, is a source for a wealth of background material.

The final recommendation of the Conference requests the U.S. Congress to provide a statutory base: "A National Library and Information Services Act is needed . . . The Act should establish a new statement of [national] purpose for Federal action in this area . . . "

In my opinion, human initiative is far more important than statutory base. The federal agencies and departments would do well to encourage innovation rather than condemn it. Innovation may well be "disruptive," it is also necessary. For effective use of information resources, new "information initiatives" will have to cut across existing "traditional" administrative barriers, or they will not be new initiatives and they certainly will not be innovative.

The low profile of the Department of Commerce has been criticized by Senator William V. Roth, Jr. (Republican-Delaware) who referred to the Department of Commerce as a "bureaucratic graveyard [National Press Club, Tuesday noon, February 22, 1983]." Roth suggested the creation of a Cabinet-level Department of Trade. The talk was informative but the topic of "information as a trade commodity" was passed over lightly.

The controversial issue of public domain versus private sector is covered in detail in the Final Report of the White House Conference on Library and Information Services, referenced above. Part Two, Resolution C-12: Telecommunication Networks, reads more like a wish list than a realistic resolution, but the intent of the report goes in the right direction.

C097 "Born classified"

The lack of consistency between European NATO countries, Canada, and the United States for the classification of research results is understandable. For one thing, the United States government does not control internal affairs in foreign countries. For another, research results become known and their practical applications appreciated at different times and in different ways in different countries. Thus, the importance of a particular research result will be perceived one way in the United States, some other way in another country. To be more specific, the sensitive nature of a particular application of a research result may not be universally endorsed.

C098 The basic waste of basic research

The International Geophysical Year (IGY), a major global scientific undertaking, marked the launch of the United States' first artificial satellite, the eighteen-pound Explorer I, January 31, 1958, almost 3 months after the Soviet launch of Sputnik I, October 4, 1957 [Jerry Grey (1979), *Enterprise*, New York: William Morrow and Comp., Inc., pp. 21-22, 40-45].

Enterprise is "the story of real people who made dreams come true," but the emphasis of the book in on hardware. The scientific value of the space program, especially atmospheric or environmental monitoring, receives only modest attention from Grey.

The neglect of the development of improved routine operations came about naturally in the scientific community. Career "rewards" in the scientific community were institutionalized to favor scientist who "published" their results. The results did not have to be "good" science and they did not have to be anything that could be used to improve services. The results only had to be "new." Thus, any new instrument flown on a satellite payload brought new measurements, and "new results."

Undue emphasis on "publish or perish" presupposes that "senior executives" who award funding contracts know best. The entire process, in either case, focuses undue emphasis on the male need to decide who is "above or below" the other [Anne Wilson Schaef (1980), *Women's Reality*, Minneapolis, Minn., Winston Publishers], rather than the national need to get something done . . . to achieve maximum utility of creative human resource.

The view that all opinions should be freely published, that the ideas themselves should contend for followers, that "truth" and "untruth" are eventually sorted out, that the scientific community would be most healthy when "diverse opinions have a chance to clash," is expressed by ITT (International Telephone and Telegraph) in their 25th Anniversary advertisement [*National Review*, December 31, 1980]. I enthusiastically endorse that view.

With freedom of the press, the question is: who should pay the bill? At the moment, tax dollars are being used by government laboratories to pay "page charges" to professional organizations to publish scholarly works. By private sector standards, that would be advertisement—the scientist (or scientific laboratory) originating the writing is expected to pay to have the material put into print. But then this becomes a fuzzy area for advertising. When you start examining money sources, you quickly come full circle. The Golden Rule still applies: Gold Rules.

The entire question of the neglect of service organizations is only a narrow aspect of the broader national dilemma—the neglect of creative human resource. Human resource has been under-utilized; the development of "elitest" one-of-a-kind hardware has taken precedence. Only now is the national emphasis starting to shift to utility—only now is it being recognized that the user of hardware is the one who creates economic prosperity, not the producer. Refer to PART FOUR, Chapter G: Use it or lose it.

C099 Research for service

The type of research that should be funded by the government is a controversial matter. There is only one thing certain: human resource should dominate research. The service aspect of service organizations, including military service organizations, should become more important than the development of hardware. And national emphasis will have to shift from management to leadership, where human resource is concerned. Management is needed for money or things; leadership is needed for people.

Past national emphasis on the management of money has distorted our national perception of human endeavor. The United States is often perceived from foreign countries as teetering on the brink of intellectual bankruptcy; as having lost sight of the difference between people and money or things.

Joseph Weizenbaum has spoken out strongly "against the imperialism of instrumental reason." Weizenbaum continues, "Scientists ... have detached science and knowledge from contact with the real world." [Joseph Weizenbaum (1976), *Computer Power and Human Reason*, W.H. Freeman and Comp., San Francisco, pg. 258, 265.] One pointed remark by Dr. Weizenbaum seems especially relevant, "We can count, but we are rapidly forgetting how to say what is worth counting and why (pg. 16)."

The legislative history of the NOAA mission, especially as it relates to the service responsibilities of the National Weather Service, is like the legislative history of most other service-oriented government agencies, it just grew.

Political issues that surround the collection of "weather data" are more complex than many people realize. Taking an aerial picture of a cloud on a cloudy day is one thing; taking an aerial picture over the same place on a clear day reveals the surface of the earth below. This broad question of aerial reconnaissance is addressed in Presidential Directive/National Security Council-54, known as PD-54, signed November 16, 1979, by Zbigniew Brzezinski, "Civil Operational Remote Sensing." That Directive " ... amplifies [policy] established in PD/NSC-37: National Space Policy and PD/NSC-42: Civil and Further National Space Policy."

The first paragraph of PD-54 is deleted. Other than that, the Directive is unclassified. The combined responsibilities of the Departments of Defense and Commerce, which includes National Oceanic and Atmospheric Administration / National Weather Service, are clearly stated for "dual polar orbiting meteorological programs." The Directive states that " . . . any new polar orbiting satellites . . . will be jointly developed and procured by Defense, Commerce, and NASA to maximize technology and to minimize cost."

PD-54 also establishes a Program Board within the Department of Commerce for "continuing federal coordination and regulation . . . " The following federal organizations are mentioned: Defense, Interior, Agriculture, Transportation, Energy, State, NASA, CIA, AID, EPA, and EOP, although it would seem that the NSF (the National Science Foundation) should eventually be included.

Dr. John B. Slaughter, past Director of the National Science Foundation, an appointee for the Carter Administration, was an advocate of integrating applied and basic research. Congressional efforts to place more emphasis on applied, or relevant, research are identified with Representative George E. Brown (Democrat-California). Congressman Brown, with the able support of his personal staff, introduced a bill that would create a new agency, a National Technology Foundation ["A science-technology rift," by Robert Cooke, *Boston Globe*, December 11, 1980].

C100   Getting the harvest to the market

A "transfer chain" to move scientific knowledge out of the scientific disciplines and into the marketplace—into the hands of the user—is only now being developed. A decrease in government spending may well be a blessing in disguise. Adversity could encourage people to use what they know, rather than spend more tax dollars to explore something new and different.

Joseph Weizenbaum talks at length about modern man's actions affecting the whole planet, how modern man can determine the future for the entire human race . . . how we are "the trustees for future generations [Joseph Weizenbaum (1976), *Computer Power and Human Reason*, W. H. Freeman and Comp., San Francisco, pg. 262]."

C101   The surface of the globe is no secret

On a cloudy day, you see clouds. On a clear day, you see everything else ["Is Espionage Necessary for Our Security," by Herbert Scoville, Jr., *Foreign Affairs*, April 1976].

C102   Pattern in motion

"Pattern in motion" is an extremely powerful concept that can insure instant information assimilation. Within the scientific community, Stanislaw Ulam, a well known American mathematician (born in Poland), has pioneered the use of pattern in motion. Ulam realizes the necessary use of pattern in motion for information display ["Metamagical Themas: Strange Attractors: mathematical patterns delicately poised between order and chaos," by Douglas R. Hofstadter, *Scientific American*, November 1981, pg. 22].

C103 The vanity press of the nation

Digital access to the *Congressional Record* and the *Federal Register* is limited because of a lack of software development. Private or public libraries, for example, the library here at Mesa College, Grand Junction, Colorado, or the Public Library downtown, do not yet have space or facilities for user terminals. Also libraries at secondary schools have been slow to provide user terminals for accessing digital data sets. Whether students need meteorological information, legislative history, or government generated data sets, access is limited.

C104 The military-civilian work force

The urgent need to combine the military-civilian work force now surrounds us. The Special Advertising Section in *Aviation Week and Space Technology*, December 1, 1980, pp. 47-110, written by Information Age, Inc., located in Westport, Conn., a company that specializes in advertising data processing and related technologies, gives an up-to-date indication of human resource needed to effectively use electronic equipment now entering this society. Their emphasis on the "needs of the user" is a necessary and healthy sign (pg. 66, for example).

The necessity to combine the military-civilian work force is evident in the writing of Joseph Weizenbaum (1976), "Human society is therefore inevitably faced with the task of wisely distributing the scarce resource that is its scientific talent." [Referenced above in Subsection C100: Getting the harvest to the market, see pg. 265.]

Specifically word processor software selection is discussed by Phillip Good [*Small Business Computers*, May/June 1983, pp. 42-48, "Choosing Computers," by Phillip Good].

The Eagle computer, a user-friendly machine with a CP/M operating system, has been described by Kenneth Skier [*Popular Computing*, December 1982, pp. 82-86, "Popular Reviews: Hardware: Old Wine in New Bottles?" by Kenneth Skier]. The Eagle systems use "Spellbinder" software for text editing [Phillip Good, *Small Business Computers*, referenced above].

Presidential Directive-54 mandates the coordination of the Departments of Defense and Commerce [refer back to Subsection C099: Research for service], but the Directive provides no funding to either.

The concept of "total force," the 1968 post-Vietnam doctrine for military manpower, involves . . . integration of the National Guard and reserves into active duty components . . . in those areas where the reserves have capabilities . . . they [the reserve forces] were totally integrated into all of the Pentagon's war plans. The DoD no longer had separate active duty and reserve components but a total force [Lawrence J. Korb (1979), *The Fall and Rise of the Pentagon*, Greenwood Press, Westport, Conn., pp. 38-40]. This "total force" concept described by Korb appears to be in agreement with my concept of a combined military-civilian work force. It also appears compatible with the citizen-soldier responsibilities endorsed by our founding fathers. [PART SIX, Subsection A105: This job belongs to you.]

PART FIVE

Perspective

Learn to love a snoop

The mobilization of the industry in the United States prior to World War II, especially the creation of a new industrial base for munitions manufacturing, is outlined in the Golden Anniversary issue of *Manufacturing Engineering*, January 1982, as referenced for the Preface.

The manpower estimates for industrial support are taken from *Arsenal of Democracy*, by Burnham Finney (1941), Whittlesey House, New York, a division of McGraw-Hill Book Comp., Inc., pg. 5.

Natural Eternal War, the use of dynamic dualism in the decision making process, was referenced for the Preface.

The importance of the freedom of information exchange is an ongoing theme for Jack Anderson ["Why I Tell Secrets," by Jack Anderson, *Washington Post*, Sunday Parade Magazine Section, November 30, 1980, pp. 20-25]. In that particular article, Mr. Anderson goes right to the heart of a very serious problem within the federal government: " . . . when a reporter charges the government with deceit or dishonesty . . . our elected [or appointed] leaders, instead of rushing to correct the abuse, are concerned more with chastening the reporter and exposing the identity of the varlets who squealed."

Mr. Anderson goes on to justify his own investigative type of reporting: "One of the seemingly irreversible currents I have observed during 32 years of covering Washington politics is the hankering of our leaders to transform themselves from servants into sovereigns, to replace Abraham Lincoln's government 'of the people, by the people, and for the people' with a government of privilege, majesty, and omnipotence."

It would be to the advantage of the American people if investigative reporting could soon become the "fourth branch of government." Only reporters, authors, and the President of the United States (and some wonder about the President), have immediate access to all Departments, Agencies, and Commissions for the sake of conducting ongoing investigations of "glaring contradictions in official policy." Because our country was formed by "a scattering of peoples with no common denominator of religion, geography, or ethnic origin, American patriotism is grounded in common adherence to a distinct set of ideals. Expounded by Jefferson and popularized further by Lincoln, they concern the rights of the people—to know, to dissent, to be treated equally, to rule themselves, to run their government processes, to be the judges of government and not its subjects. It is this distinctly American ideal that lends nobility to the endeavor of the investigative reporter and raises it above its grubby appearances," wrote Mr. Anderson near the end of his Parade article.

There is nothing "grubby" about the investigative reporting of Mr. Anderson. And his pointed condemnation of "hands off patriotism" is both timely and necessary. Such alien patriotism " . . . preached by government officials will lead only to the eventual collapse of an uncriticized, corrupt shell."

It is interesting to note that the tone of a United States government publication agrees with a claim by Mr. Anderson, " . . . federal agencies have not balked at violating the U.S. law . . . in their zeal . . . to discover my sources." ["A Brief History of Emergency Powers in the United States," a working paper prepared by Special Committee on National Emergencies and Delegated Emergency Powers, United States Senate, July 1974, 93d Congress, 2d Session, Committee Print, U.S. Government Printing Office, Washington.] That working paper, a chronological history of the American government in times of emergency, written by Dr. Harold Relyea, cautions firmly against authority conferred upon rulers of this country " . . . without reference to normal constitutional process."

PART SIX

The Birth of the Nation

If the meek shall inherit the Earth,
then what will happen to all us hawks

Slowly the American people are realizing that not only political but also economic freedom is needed if they are going to pursue their own national goals, and their own patriotic ideals. Advocates of national independence are publishing articles in *The Freeman*, sponsored by the Foundation for Economic Education, Inc., 30 South Broadway, Irvington-on-Hudson, New York 10533. The bottom line is freedom of choice, " . . . support of free market economics has more to do with belief in the moral value of free choice, than with any purely economic concern with efficiency [a review by John Chamberlain, *The Freeman*, Vol. 32, No. 10, pg. 632, October 1982, *Back To Basics*, by Burton Yale Pines (1982), New York: William Morrow]."

The Council on Economic Priorities, 84 Fifth Avenue, New York, New York 10011, Tele: (212) 691-8550, is able to provide a wealth of information on the politics and economics of defense contracting.

Michael Roemer comments about the controversial aspects of economic independence in his article, "Dependence and Industrialization Strategies." Roemer makes the claim ". . . that Western economics has not yet accepted national independence as a fundamental goal of development [*World Development*, Vol. 9, No. 5, May 1981, pp. 429-434, a multi-disciplinary international journal devoted to the study and promotion of world development, that tends to present a broad overview of economic options]."

PART SIX

Chapter A

The American Military Tradition

The citizen-soldier of Colonial times created a military tradition that ran contrary to centuries of brutality that had gone before. "The idea of citizen-soldier . . . a duty and an obligation . . . a political symbol and military reality . . . has been an operative factor in civic education, contributing to civilian supremacy and viable patriotism ["Patriotism and the U.S. All-Volunteer Military," by Morris Janowitz, *Air University Review*, Jan-Feb 1982, pg. 31].

A comprehensive discussion of justification for "war" is given by Jean Bodin (1530-1596), as reprinted and translated in "Six Books on the State [William Ebenstein (1962), *Great Political Thinkers*, New York: Holt, Rinehart, and Winston, pg. 356]." The importance of the commitment of the citizen to his own [national] military [service] becomes self-evident in these writings.

A105 This job belongs to you

"By the rude bridge that arched the flood, Their flag to April's breeze unfurled . . . " taken from The Concord Hymn by Ralph Waldo Emerson.

The Big Bang Theory for the beginning of the universe is generally well known [see Carl Sagan (1975), *The Cosmic Connection*, Dell Pub. Co., Inc., New York, pg. 249].

A106 Aristocracy in democracy

The history of the citizen-soldier, including hours of discussion and reference searching, was provided by the head librarian, Colonel Cross, at the National Guard Association of the United States, 1 Massachusetts Avenue, N.W., Washington, DC, Tele: (202) 789-0031. The National Guard Association building is a pleasant 12-minute walk from the Russell Senate Office Building. And it is open daily. If you can manage an invitation for early morning coffee, you can get off the Red Line at Union Station, and walk the distance in 5 minutes.

Remarks about the career (professional) military may sound derogatory. They are intended to show the hazards of "inbreeding" in any elitist (professional) organization.

The history of the National Guard, and arguments in favor of the citizen-soldier concept of national service, are available from the National Guard Association cited above. Also see "The New National Guard," *The Century Magazine*, Vol. XLIII, February 1982, pg. 483; "Civilian in Peace, Soldier in War," DA PAM 130-2, January 1967, a bibliographic survey of the Army and Air National Guard.

A special feature story by Peter Marshall, former Chaplain for the United States Senate, is printed inside the back cover, *Military Review*, July 1980. In the same July 1980 issue of *Military Review*, see "Managing Soldiers: A Personal Philosophy of Management," by Lt. Colonel Joel E. L. Roberts. Also see "Our Reserve Forces Today," by Colonel W. D. McGlasson, *Retired Officer*, September 1980, pg. 15.

A107 The individual and the common good

The conflict that now exists between the Soviet Union and the United States is often perceived as a philosophical conflict between subjugation and liberty, as though one were right and the other wrong, as though one were good and the other evil, as though the existence of one should or could exclude the existence of the other. On the contrary, the acceptance of both liberty and subjugation is easily understood within the context of pragmatism as popularized by William James (1914), *Pragmatism*, A New Name for Some Old Ways of Thinking, Longmans, Green, and Co., pp. 130-137.

A108 Passion and patriotism

Opposition to the professional army came from those with an intense dislike for the British Red Coats. The speeches of Patrick Henry provide strong arguments against a standing army [William M. Goldsmith (1974), *The Growth of Presidential Power*, Vol. 1: The Formative Years, Part V: The President as Commander in Chief, pg. 367].

Albert Einstein appears to have thought of war, much like those of his generation thought of sex, he made no distinction as to motive or purpose.

The purpose of this book is to try to rescue the "good" of war, to do away with the need for destruction and violence, to create a dynamic decision making process responsive to human needs.

In spite of claim of Rheinhold Niebuhr (1932), *Moral Man and Immoral Society*, New York: Charles Scribner's Sons, the American people are "moral man and moral society," or they are no democracy. The American people have to do their own deciding. This is a government of the people, by the people, for the people, and the people are responsible. As Joseph Weizenbaum wrote, " . . . the range of one's responsibilities must be commensurate with the range of efforts [Joseph Weizenbaum (1976), *Computer Power and Human Reason*, W. H. Freeman and Comp., San Francisco]." With that in mind, it is necessary for many Americans to extend their attention to the survival of the entire human race.

An article by Clarence Manion (1896-1979), "Legalized Immorality," is published in the July 1982 issue of *The Freeman*, pg. 426. Manion long served as Dean of the College of Law, Notre Dame University. His book, *The Key To Peace*, dated 1950, is available from the Foundation of Economic Education, 30 South Broadway, Irvington-on-Hudson, New York 10533. And you can't beat the price, $2.00. Manion takes the position, "Government should do for the people [only] what people are unable to do for themselves." As I look around me, and as I talk to concerned people, I would say, there is just not much the people in this country cannot do for themselves, as individuals. It is the coordination of information exchange and environmental monitoring, in the form of national policy, that could use a little help.

PART SIX

Chapter B

The Unity of the Nation

The unity of the nation advocated in this book comes from the living organic concept of the nation. Generally speaking, the unity of a nation can be based upon two different concepts: one is the living organic concept, the other is a mechanistic one. Aristotle (384-322 B.C.) laid the foundation for the organic; the mechanistic concept is older, having been propounded by the Sophists a century before [William Ebenstein (1962), *Great Political Thinkers*, New York: Holt, Rinehart, and Winston, pg. 680].

Plato (427-347 B.C.), the teacher of Aristotle, appears to have been the first to reject the view that the state is an instrument to be manipulated, to be used for purposes and ends higher than itself.

Political theory that would have the nation a natural community, an organism with all the attributes of a living system, continued its early stages of development in Greece, but it appears to have been largely ignored in Roman Law. Jean Bodin (1530-1596) became the last strong advocate of the organic or natural living concept of the nation state.

Advocates of the mechanistic view, Thomas Hobbes (1588-1679), John Locke (1632-1704), and John Dewey (1859-1952), revived it in modern times—and government organization has become a piece of machinery devised by man [William Ebenstein (1962), *Great Political Thinkers*, referenced above, pp. 344-413].

I agree with Ebenstein (pg. 680, as referenced above), " . . . classical democracy and classical Marxism . . . both wrongly assume that any system of society can be devised that can achieve perfect harmony of interests." It would seem to me that the time has come for man to cease with his mechanistic efforts to "devise" systems within which to confine human behavior, to focus attention instead on the interpretation of existing natural or "divine" law. For a classical narrative that develops this concept of living unity, read Jean Bodin, "Colloquium Heptaplomeres," referenced in PART TWO, Subsection B027.

B109 The Spirit of the Constitution

By accepting the laws of nature and the practices of states, as had gone before, writers and scholars known as Grotians (taken from the name of Hugo Grotius (1583-1645), the father of international law), brought into being the fundamental concepts of natural law that guide human behavior. Refer to the writings of Emmerich de Vattel (1758), *The Laws of Nations*, as reported by Clarence Morris (1959), *The Great Legal Philosophers*, as referenced below.

The most famous of the Grotians were the German mathematician and philosopher Christian Wolff (1679-1754) and the Swiss diplomat Emmerich de Vattel (1711-1767), who popularized Wolff's ideas in his *Le Droit des Gens*, translated as *The Laws of Nations*. An interested reader is encouraged to consult Clarence Morris (1959), Editor of *The Great Legal Philosophers*, University of Pennsylvania Press, Philadelphia, pp. 80-133 and introductory material.

Those Articles of Confederation served in an unsatisfactory fashion as the basic law of the new nation until the Constitution of the United States was written and then ratified in 1789 [Sol Bloom (1937), *The Story of the Constitution*, The United States Constitutional Sesquicentennial Commission, House Office Bldg., Washington, DC, pg. 30].

The failure of the Articles of Confederation can be read in greater detail in the standard reference: Louis H. Pollack (1966), *The Constitution and the Supreme Court: A Documented History*, The World Pub. Comp., 2231 West 110th Street, Cleveland, Ohio, Part I: Declaring Independence and Adopting the Constitution, Chapter B: The Articles of Confederation, pp. 24-51.

B110 A strong central government

In his extensive work, *The Spirit of the Laws*, Charles Louis de Secondat, Baron de Montesquieu (1689-1755), concluded that political freedom could be maintained only by separating the Executive, Legislative, and Judicial powers of government. Many of the ideas expressed by Montesquieu appear, however, to have originated from the writings of John Locke (1632-1704), as discussed by Clarence Morris (1959), pp. 134-158, and pg. 159, reference given in Subsection B109.

The powers and duties compel each of the three branches of government to "check and balance" the other two. For that reason, the written Constitution of the United States remains paramount to any particular Legislative, Executive, or Judicial authority [Sol Bloom (1937), pg. 53, referenced in Subsection B109].

The text of the United States Constitution with readable numbered text is available as a pocket-sized book, Robert A. Maurer and George J. James (1925), *The Constitution of the United States*, D. C. Heath and Comp., Boston. A convenient home reference for the text of the U.S. Constitution is *The Random House Dictionary of the English Language*, the unabridged edition, Jess Stein, Editor in Chief (1967), New York: Random House, pp. 1937-1940.

B111 The Gettysburg Address

The dedication ceremonies for the military cemetery at Gettysburg, Pennsylvania, were held November 19, 1863, to commemorate the Battle of Gettysburg, fought July 1, 2, 3, 1863, considered to be the turning point of the American Civil War [*Encyclopaedia Britannica*, Vol. XI, Eleventh Edition (1910), Cambridge, England: at the University Press, 120 West 32nd Street, New York, see Gettysburg, pg. 911].

B112 The more perfect Union

"A house divided against itself cannot stand," the speech was given by Abraham Lincoln at the Republican State Convention, Springfield, Illinois, June 17, 1858. That opening phrase is a paraphrase of the Biblical verse, Mark 3:25.

"My paramount object in this struggle is to save the Union . . . " [Abraham Lincoln, Letter to Horace Greeley, August 22, 1862, *The Illustrated Heritage Dictionary*, Boston: Houghton Mifflin Comp., 1977, pg. 1678]. A better reference, but more difficult to locate, is *The Lincoln Reader*, Edited by Paul M. Angle, New Brunswick, Rutgers University Press (1947), a book that includes reprinted materials from many collections.

The Union is much older than the Constitution. It was formed, in fact, by the Articles of Association in 1774 . . . And, finally, in 1787, one of the declared objects for ordaining and establishing the Constitution was "to form a more perfect Union." [Abraham Lincoln: First Inaugural Address, 1861.]

" . . . extreme unification of the state is clearly not good . . . If self-sufficiency is to be desired, the lesser degree of unity is more desirable than
the greater." [William Ebenstein (1962), referenced at the beginning of
PART SIX, Chapter B, see pg. 80.] This thesis, as presented by Aristotle,
claims that the "best" political community is the one that survives. Aristotle is arguing against, " . . . the greater the unity of the state, the better."
   The "contradiction" in all the writings seems to be with the meaning
of the word "unity." Unity is not desirable when unity implies imposed
uniformity or sameness, where economic unity is a living unity, one that
is desirable, one that could well preserve the diversity of individuality of
the people. Elizabeth Cheny (1944) has written about this living unity from
the perspective of the Baha'i Faith [*Prophecy Fulfilled*, Baha'i Publishing
Trust, Wilmette, Illinois].

PART SIX

Chapter C

The Power of the President

   The nation has been a nation of doers. It is a commonly held conviction
that the United States is a nation of "doers," more than a nation of
"thinkers." The text is also an endorsement of pragmatism: "James asked
for a new prophet, one who could demonstrate that all our different motives,
rightly interpreted, pull in one way." [Paul K. Conkin (1968), *Puritans and
Pragmatists*, New York: Dodd, Mead, and Co., see William James pp.
266-344.]
   Truth is an "instrument," truth in an idea means its power to "work."
Truth is used "to marry old opinion to new fact, so as to show a minimum
jolt, a maximum continuity [William James (1955), *Pragmatism*, Meridian
Books, The World Publishing Co., New York (original copyright 1814), pp.
58, 61, 67-69]." James continues, "If the hypothesis of God works satisfac-
torily . . . then it is true (pg. 296)." As truth (or theory) is introduced, there
are three classic stages through which it passes, "a new theory is attacked
as absurd; then it is admitted to be true, but obvious and insignificant;
finally, it is seen to be so important that its adversaries claim that they
themselves discovered it (pg. 198)."
   The constitutional question of the Power of the President, because it em-
bodies the authority to order the use of nuclear weapons, is the most urgent
matter facing the American people today. A serious reader is referred to
Louis Henkin (1975), *Foreign Affairs and the Constitution*, Norton Library,
W. W. Norton and Comp., New York, Chapter II: The President, and Chapter
IV: Separation of Powers, for Commander-in-Chief, pg. 50, and pg. 278 fn.
where President Truman is quoted as having said, " . . . the President's

powers would have made Caesar or Genghis Khan or Napoleon bite his nails with envy.''

The fine art of attaching undreamed-of-importance to well-known truths is a simple reference to an intuitive process. "Truth is intuitive . . . '' [Virginia Woolf (1927), *To The Lighthouse*, A Harvest Book, Harcourt, Brace, and World, Inc.]

C113   That fragile line of presidential succession

The United States Constitution, Article II, Section 1, Clause 6, contains the statement, "In Case of the Removal of the President from Office . . .'' [Sol Bloom (1937), *The Story of the Constitution*, pg. 72, referenced in PART SIX, Subsection B109.]

The highest ranking "Officer'' following the President and Vice President is the Secretary of State [Sol Bloom (1937), *The Story of the Constitution*, pg. 177, referenced in PART SIX, Subsection B109]. "Question: In the event of the death, resignation, removal, or disability of both President and Vice President, who would become President? Answer: In accordance with the Presidential Succession Act of 1886, the succession would devolve upon the Secretary of State . . . ''

The use of the word "Officer'' in the U.S. Constitution, when given a strict interpretation, applies only to those in the Executive; it purposefully excludes the Legislative. Thus, when following a strict interpretation of the U.S. Constitution, there is no way presidential succession can pass out of the Executive, into the Legislative to include the Speaker of the House or the President pro tempore of the Senate [Louis Henkin (1975), *Foreign Affairs and the Constitution*, New York: Norton Library, W. W. Norton & Comp. Inc.].

A comprehensive report, Presidential Succession: A Short History, Report No. 78-244 GOV, Congressional Research Service, January 25, 1979, written by Ronald C. Moe, Specialist in American National Government, Government Division, gives a detailed review of the use of the word "Officer'' starting on pg. 22. A discussion of the U.S. Senate opposition to having the Secretary of State next in line of succession, following the President and the Vice President, starts on pg. 6. The Presidential Succession Act of 1792 starts on pg. 5. One of the standard references used by Moe is Ruth C. Silva (1951), *Presidential Succession*, Ann Arbor, Michigan: University of Michigan Press.

Alexander Meigs Haig, Jr. is quoted by the news media as having said, "As of now I am in control here in the White House, pending return of the Vice President . . . Constitutionally you have the President, the Vice President, and the Secretary of State [*Washington Post* and *Washington Star*, Tuesday, March 31, 1981].'' That statement by Haig clearly signified to the entire world that the United States was **not** in a state of national emergency, that the Secretary of State held a higher rank as "Officer'' in the Executive than the Secretary of Defense.

C114 Freedom from fear

The individual freedoms of American citizens are protected by the first ten Amendments to the United States Constitution, the Bill of Rights. The fight for the passage of a bill of rights conducted by Patrick Henry at the Virginia Convention is reviewed in Chapter XXV: Amendments to the Constitution [Sol Bloom (1937), *The Story of the Constitution*, pp. 44-53, as referenced in PART SIX, Subsection B109].

Compatible with this constitutional concern for individuality is the quotation, " . . . the consequence of such a philosophy of pragmatism is the well-known democratic respect for the sacredness of individuality," quoted on the cover of the book by William James, *Pragmatism*, reprinted in 1955 by Meridian Books, The World Pub. Co., New York. Those writings of William James focus on the central concern for free will, free choice, and intelligent "actions" of individuals.

For another perspective of "freedom," read Victor E. Frankl's, *Man's Search for Meaning*, New York: Washington Square Press.

Franklin D. Roosevelt's First Inaugural Address was intended to lift the sagging spirits of the nation. " . . . the only thing we have to fear is fear itself . . . " Roosevelt's Four Freedoms Speech was delivered 1941, to give the nation a set of idealistic goals that would act as inspiration for the people during the World War II, the War Roosevelt was about to enter.

C115 Freedom from want

C116 Freedom of speech

C117 Freedom of worship

Early settlers taught and respected the rigid ideology of their own particular church [Arthur E. Morgan (1948), Henry Regnery Comp., Hinsdale, Illinois, Human Affairs Pamphlet, Vol. 36, pg. 5].

The first attempt to legislate religious freedom in this country, the "Act for the liberties of people," was approved by the Maryland General Assembly in 1639 [Robert Allen Rutland (1955), *The Birth of the Bill of Rights 1776-1791*, Institute of Early American History and Culture, University of North Carolina Press, Chapel Hill].

The role of the Constitutional Convention of Virginia and the June 26, 1788, ratification is unique, especially the challenge of Patrick Henry [Sol Bloom (1937), *The Story of the Constitution*, pg. 45, referenced in Subsection B109]. "Virginia in 1786, after a seven-year bitter struggle led by Jefferson and Madison, passed the Bill for Establishing Religious Freedom granting complete religious liberty. The Virginia Bill is the first known law of its kind anywhere . . . " [Andrew D. Weinberger (1962), *Freedom and Protection: The Bill of Rights*, Greenwood Press Publishers, Westport, Connecticut, pg. 21.]

The Church had become a formal source for extraneous rules, a concern common to many [Truman G. Madsen (1966), *Eternal Man*, Deseret Book Co., Salt Lake City, Utah]. A broader concern for the worship of material goods, rather than spiritual matters, is expressed by Stanwood Cobb (1970), *The Rise of Religious Liberty in America*. Cobb goes on, however, to address the timely issue of nationalism [Stanwood Cobb (1970), *The Destiny of America*, Baha'i Publishing Trust, Wilmette, Illinois]. "Nationalism is a necessary step in the evolution of greater unities upon the planet (pg. 11)," and Cobb's view of nationalism is positive. "May this American democracy be the first nation to establish the foundation of international agreement (pg. 10) . . . On one hand America is materialistic; but on the other hand, America is deeply religious, more vitally so, perhaps, than any other country (pg. 16)."

The concepts of religious purpose are based upon dynamic dualism, a fundamental law of nature as man perceives nature today.

C118 The power of the President

The fact that the Office of the President of the United States carries with it two distinctly different responsibilities attracted national attention during the 1956 campaign to re-elect Dwight D. Eisenhower to a second term in the White House ["Which Commander-in-Chief," by David Lawrence, *U.S. News & World Report*, October 12, 1956, pg. 152]. Lawrence was concerned that the United States have a military man, not a novice, to run foreign affairs, that the "political" decisions that needed to be made were of a military nature.

The comparison of the trends in military build-up for the Eisenhower and Kennedy Administrations is outlined by Stephen E. Ambrose, "The Military Impact on Foreign Policy [Stephen E. Ambrose and James A. Barber, Jr. (1972), *The Military and American Society*, New York: The Free Press, pp. 121-136]."

The role of the military in the society, the consequences for those who have and have not served, and the influence of military training methods on basic education, are discussed by Morris Janowitz, "Characteristics of the Military Environment [*The Military and American Society*, pp. 166-173, referenced above]."

PART SIX

Chapter D

War Powers of Congress

The power to declare war . . . is legislative. And legislative acts belong to the Congress. The best defense of Constitutional war powers as a legislative power was made by James Madison, in the Pacificus (Alexander Hamilton)-Helvidius (James Madison) Letters [Louis Henkin (1975), *Foreign Affairs and the Constitution*, The Norton Library, W. W. Norton & Co., Inc., Notes Section, pg. 297]. James Madison represented the great middle ground of national identity, apart from the pro-British leanings of Hamilton and the pro-French biases of Jefferson [Irving Brant (1950), *James Madison, Father of the Constitution 1787-1800*, The Bobbs-Merrill Comp., Inc., Indianapolis, Indiana, pg. 39].

"The Constitution makes no provision for suspending the distribution of power in the United States Government in time of emergency." [National Emergencies and Delegated Emergency Powers, Senate Report No. 94-922, 94th Congress, 2d Session, Final Report of the Special Committee on National Emergencies and Delegated Emergency Powers, U.S. Government Printing Office, Washington, DC (1976), pg. 18 and references given on page 21. A Staff Report on Emergency Preparedness in the United States is attached.]

A scholarly work on the separation of powers—so much separation "as the nature of a free government will admit; or as is consistent with that chain of connection that binds the whole fabric of the constitution in one dissoluble bond of unity and amity . . ." [Louis L. Jaffe and Nathaniel L. Nathanson (1968), *Administrative Law: Cases and Materials*, Boston: Little, Brown and Comp., Chapter 1: The Constitutional Position of the Administrative Agency (The introduction deals with the general theory of the separation of powers, "Is there a divine right of powers to be separate?"), Section A: Constitutionality and Practice of Delegation, pg. 35 and then pg. 38 ff.]

D119 The national emergency

Special Legislative powers—war powers—were conferred on the President and other Officers, Boards, and Commissions as a result of the National Emergency Proclamation of December 16, 1950 [National Emergency and Delegated Emergency Powers, Senate Report No. 94-922, pg. 3, as referenced above].

In 1973, after becoming alarmed about the power of the President to control the use of American military abroad, the United States Senate established a Select Committee on National Emergencies and Delegated

Emergency Powers to examine the desirability and possible consequences of terminating those powers [refer to Senate Report No. 94-922, Preface and Introduction, pg. 1, as referenced above].

More recently Senator J. James Exon reminded the American people of the purpose of the War Powers Resolution (Public Law 93-148). When money was being authorized for a Rapid Deployment Force, Exon reminded the people that the Congress was funding "an increased capability to extend the reach of our [American] military power in an expedited manner." [Department of Defense Authorization Act, 1981, Senate Report No. 96-895, 96th Congress, 2d Session, Conference Report to accompany H.R.6974, see pg. 49.]

The War Powers Resolution passed the U.S. Senate, 75-20, October 10, 1973; the House vote passed, 244-170, on October 12; the House adopted the conference report [House Joint Resolution 542] 238-123, October 12. The Congress dealt President Nixon a "stunning setback" November 7, 1973, when it voted to override his veto of legislation limiting the president's powers to commit U.S. forces abroad without Congressional approval. The House overrode the veto by a "cliff-hanging vote," 284-135, only four votes over the two-thirds majority necessary under the Constitution to override. Four hours later, the Senate completed the process with a 75-18 vote to override the veto, a comfortable 13-vote margin over the two-thirds majority. Reaction from the White House . . . was "swift and sharp." In his October 24 veto message to Congress, Nixon had branded the war powers resolution as both dangerous and unconstitutional [*Congressional Quarterly Almanac*, 1973, pg. 905].

A comprehensive bibliography: Congress, The President, and the War Powers: A Bibliography, 75-209F, was prepared by the Congressional Research Service of the Library of the Congress: Vita Bite, Lois McHugh, Leneice Nen Wu, Analysts in International Relations, Foreign Affairs Division, September 22, 1975.

At the time the Special Senate Committee began its work, January 6, 1973, four emergency proclamations remained in force: the national emergencies declared by Harry S. Truman on December 16, 1950 (the Truman Korean War Emergency), Franklin Roosevelt on March 9, 1933 (to cope with the current banking crisis), Richard Nixon on March 23, 1970 (to deal with the Post Office strike), and Richard Nixon on August 15, 1971 (to implement currency restrictions and to enforce controls on foreign trade), see Senate Report No. 94-922, pp. 2-3, referenced above.

"The continuation of these states of emergency was significant, since any declaration of emergency triggers numerous laws which, taken together, give the President extraordinary power." Many examples are given: Statute 10 USC 712 permits the President, during a "war or a declared national emergency" to "detail members of the Army, Navy, Air Force, and Marine Corps to assist in military matters" in any foreign country [taken from Senate Report No. 94-922, pp. 3-4, referenced above].

President Ford "acted under his constitutional war powers to protect the lives and property of Americans ["The Mayaguez Incident and the Constitution," by Raoul Berger, *New York Times*, May 23, 1975 (No. 143-75-34)]."

It seems the founding fathers and the Congress had other ideas and Berger explains the "inherent power" of the President to be a euphemism for " . . . exercise of a power that was not conferred." Raoul Berger is the Charles Warren senior fellow in American legal history at Harvard Law School and author of "Executive Privilege: A Constitutional Myth," which sounds rather impressive to me.

Anthony Lewis, "A Chorus of Yahoos," *New York Times*, May 26, 1975 (No. 146-75-60), issues a complaint against the Congress, " . . . when it acts on foreign affairs it seeks power without responsibility."

President Carter took action pursuant to the International Emergency Economic Powers Act, which grants the President of the United States authority "to deal with any unusual and extraordinary threat to the national security, foreign policy, or economy of the United States" to block Iranian Government Property [50 U.S.C.A. sec. 1701 et seq., also the National Emergencies Act, 50 U.S. C. sec. 1601 et seq., and 3 U.S. C. sec 301], reported in the Weekly Compilation of Presidential Documents, vol. 15, no. 46, November 19, 1979: pp. 2117-2118: Executive Order 12170, November 14, 1979. The use of American military for the Iranian rescue attempt was justified by emergency proclamation.

D120   War in the absence of war

The Senate Select Committee on National Emergencies and Delegated Emergency Powers reported in 1973 that Congress had transferred awesome magnitudes of power to the Executive without having reexamined the cumulative effects of that delegation [Senate Report No. 94-922, pg. 1, referenced at the beginning of PART SIX, Chapter D].

When asked in a press conference what should or might constitute a national emergency, Vice President Bush replied, [it is] a matter of judgement on the part of the President [transcript of White House press conference].

One of "the underlying factors generating interest in the authority of the President and other Federal officers to order the use of nuclear weapons" is the concern which several Members of Congress have expressed relating to the U.S. strategic policy which excludes First Strike, but does not rule out the first use of nuclear weapons. "Excluded from its scope is a discussion of the broader question of whether the President may initiate a war (i.e., order a first strike) except in the event an attack or invasion is imminent ["Authority to Order the Use of Nuclear Weapons (United States, United Kingdom, France, Soviet Union, People's Republic of China)," Subcommittee on International Security and Scientific Affairs of the Committee on International Relations, by the Congressional Research Service of the Library of Congress, 94th Congress, 1st Session, December 1, 1975, U.S. Government Printing Office, Washington, DC (Subcommittee Chairman Clement J. Zablocki, Democrat-Wisconsin), Summary on pg. 1]. Andrew C. Mayer, Specialist in National Defense, Foreign Affairs Division, Congressional Research Service, Library of Congress, October 16, 1975, was largely responsible for the background research that produced the report.

The more controversial question of the President's authority to commit forces to combat without the consent of Congress, is discussed in "The War Power," Congressional Research Service, "Constitution of the United States of America—Analysis and Interpretations," Senate Document No. 92-82, U.S. Government Printing Office, Washington, DC, pg. 323.

D121   Commander-in-Chief by invitation only

"Don't call use, we'll call you." I and Patrick Henry (1787) seem to share the same view. The powers of the President as Commander-in-Chief, particularly in time of war, overshadow all other executive responsibilities, and throughout the history of the presidency these powers have been the principle source of strength and growth in the office [William M. Goldsmith (1974), *The Growth of Presidential Power*, Vol. 1: The Formative Years, Part V: The President as Commander-in-Chief, pg. 367]. "At the Virginia convention, Patrick Henry pounced upon the section [of the Constitution] dealing with presidential power, pouring forth great scorn on the President's jurisdiction over the armed forces . . . Your President may easily become king . . . "

Within the written Constitution, the sole granting of War Powers to the President of the United States is contained in the "Commander-in-Chief" designation [Sol Bloom (1937), *The Story of the Constitution*, Art. 2, Sect. 2, Cl. 1, pg. 73, referenced in Subsection B109].

Arguments given by Alexander Hamilton, at the time the Constitution was to be ratified, downgraded the "Commander-in-Chief" to be "first general" [Louis Henkin (1975), *Foreign Affairs and the Constitution*, pg. 50, 278, referenced at the beginning of PART SIX, Chapter D].

A comprehensive discussion of Constitutional Sources of Presidential Power comes from Louis Henkin (1975), starting on pg. 39 . . . consideration of the President's powers in foreign affairs, a consideration that extends immediately to the Commander-in-Chief designation, pg. 50, begins with the language of the Constitution . . . Presidents found in that [foreign policy] clause substantive, policy making authority. Presidents claimed authority to make rules for the government and regulation of the land and naval forces, although that power was explicitly given to Congress (Art. I, Sec. 8, Cl. 14); they have used troops for political purposes and have even taken action **not** involving use of the armed forces for military reasons (pg. 51). Thus the announcement of national emergency by presidential proclamation as a means of relating "war and declared national emergency" appears to have started with President Roosevelt. President Truman (December 1980) and then President Johnson (January 1968) ordered the use of American military (combat) troops abroad.

The "take care" clause for the President is taken from ART. II, Sec. 3, Cl. 1 of the Constitution, " . . . he shall take Care that the Laws be faithfully executed," see Sol Bloom (1937), *The Story of the Constitution*, pp. 69-73, referenced in Subsection B109. The Congressional War Powers are stated in Art. I, Sec. 8 of the Constitution, " . . . The Congress shall have

Power To declare War . . . To raise and support Armies . . . To provide and maintain a Navy; To make Rules for the Government and Regulation of the land and naval Forces; To provide for calling forth the Militia to execute the Laws of the Union, suppress Insurrections and repel Invasions."

D122 Madison responds to Pacificus

The Helvidius-Pacificus Letters of Madison and Hamilton should not be confused with the *Federalist Papers*. The Hamilton-Madison Dispute over the President's authority: Secretary of Treasury Alexander Hamilton, The First Letter of "Pacificus," June 29, 1793, is reprinted on pg. 398. Reply by Representative James Madison: The First Letter of "Helvidius," August-September 1793, on pg. 405. Introductory remarks start on pg. 396. [William M. Goldsmith (1974), *The Growth of Presidential Power*, Vol. 1: The Formative Years, New York: Chelsea House Publishers.]

D123 The power of public opinion

A strong advocate of direct democracy is Alvin Toffler (1980), *The Third Wave*, New York: Morrow.

The Declaration of Independence, "In Congress, July 4, 1776: the unanimous Declaration of the thirteen united States of America," a reprint from the copperplate facsimile made in 1923 and the list of 56 signers that includes John Hancock as President of the Congress, is given on pp. 132-134 [Sol Bloom (1937), *Story of the Constitution*, pp.132-134, referenced in Subsection B109].

George Wythe, Richard Henry Lee, and Th. Jefferson signed for Virginia. It is interesting to note, "On Jefferson's grave is the epitaph he himself composed, indicating that he thought the writing of the Declaration of Independence to be, along with two other public acts, achievements more memorable than his eight years as President." [Louis H. Pollak (1966), *The Constitution and the Supreme Court. A Documented History*, The World Pub. Comp., 2231 West 110th Street, Cleveland, Ohio, Vol. 1, pg. 22.]

The force of public opinion can be expressed through the "Congressional Veto of Executive Actions," an Issue Brief from the Congressional Research Service, No. IB76006, written by Thomas J. Nicola, American Law Division, Clark F. Norton, Government Division, John T. Melsheimer, American Law Division, printed February 3, 1976; updated June 17, 1981, Major Issues System. Statutory provisions by which Congress authorizes a Federal program to be administered by the Executive but retains the legal authority to disapprove all or part of the program before final implementation have become increasingly frequent in recent years. These statutory provisions which subject a variety of proposed executive actions to congressional review are commonly known as "congressional veto" devices. Although the constitutionality of the congressional veto has yet to be finally resolved by the Supreme Court, it has been the object of considerable discussion since the beginning of its use in the 1930s (The Legislative Appropriation Act of 1932: 47 Stat. 413).

The reader is at this point reminded that "New Deal" was the name Franklin D. Roosevelt gave his political programs. The chief measure designed to promote industrial recovery, the National Industrial Recovery Act, established the National Recovery Administration. In 1935, the Supreme Court declared the National Recovery Administration unconstitutional.

PART SIX

Chapter E

Purification of the Pentagon

The reorganization of the Department of Defense into a Department of Military Affairs, a reorganization that would move the responsibility for the coordination of the industrial base into a new Department of Industrial Resources, or perhaps into the existing Federal Emergency Management Agency, could be done using the Congressional veto of Executive actions, as referenced in Subsection D123.

This Congressional veto originated for the purpose of controlling Executive reorganization legislation, to grant President Hoover the authority to reorganize Executive departments. This Congressional oversight responsibility took on renewed importance with the review of Procedures for Congressional Review of Agency Rules, Agency Accountability Act of 1981, and the Regulatory Reform Act of 1981—all part of an effort by the Reagan Administration to get rid of unnecessary government regulation. It remains to be seen just how effective the White House can become in getting "government off the backs of the people." The mood of the country now seems to favor (Republican) big business rather than (Democrat) big government, but decreasing government control will not be easy.

The Congressional veto device was employed in the War Powers Act (P.L. 93-148). That act was designed to restrict the authority of the President to order the use of American armed forces in combat operations in foreign nations, see pg. 2, Congressional Research Service Issue Brief No. IB76006, cited in Subsection D123.

The need to re-examine the organization of the civilian-staffed, industry-oriented, Department of Defense, and the national purpose it was created to serve, will pass from the level of necessity to an elevated level of imperative the day the American people finally decide to endorse the thinking expressed by the late General of the Army Douglas MacArthur: for the American people and the American military there is no such thing as security, there is only opportunity. And the present opportunity at the Pentagon has become inviting and exciting.

The time is right for the American people to decide how they would like to institutionalize dynamic dualism in the deciding making process. This dualism: centralized control and committee participation, has always been at the Pentagon; it remains only for the American people, and the United States Congress, to recognize its value. The dynamic dualism of deciding by interaction of centralized and committee methods is discussed at length by James E. Hewes,Jr. (1975), *From Root to McNamara: Army organization and administration, 1900-1963*, published through the Center of Military History, United States Army, U.S. Government Printing Office, Washington, DC 20402, Stock Number 0800-00202. Hewes refers to this dualism as traditionalists versus rationalists. The rationalists would favor a centralized pyramid-style command structure; the traditionalists, a more de-centralized, self-sufficient working unit, pp. 366-374.

Dynamic dualism would have the rationalists and traditionalists coordinate their efforts; the interaction of the two would pursue the same ideal. The interaction of the two would be constructive reinforcement, rather than destructive annihilation. The interaction would be cooperative in its purpose, because the two would share the same goals; but competitive in nature, because their methods of achieving those goals would differ. The methods of the rationalist would compliment the methods of the traditionalist—the continuity of the rationalists would dominate at one time; the creativity of the traditionalists at another. It is that energy-momentum exchange between the two that would sustain an unrelenting forward motion in pursuit of our national ideals.

E124 Defense can't fight a war

The Korean and Vietnam conflicts are prime examples of the civilian-administered Department of Defense trying to fight a war through presidential proclamation and administrative purchase order.

The Special Senate Committee on National Emergencies and Delegated Emergency Powers generated a wealth of comprehensive background material with its review of the authority of the President to order the use of American military on foreign soil. The final report from the Committee made an emphatic plea to the American people, and to the Congress of the United States: " . . . the National Emergencies Act, HR 3884 [should] be passed as soon as possible, to terminate special powers possessed by the President . . . to establish procedural guidelines for the handling of future emergencies with provisions for regular Congressional review." That Final Report, Senate Report No. 94-922, was referenced at the beginning of Chapter D; it is worth reading in its entirety.

The justification for the formation of the Special Senate Committee on National Emergencies and Delegated Emergency Powers is clearly stated: "Interest in the question of emergency powers stems from the United States' experience in the Viet Nam War and the incursion into Cambodia. The President's ability to commit Americans to warfare [to order the use of lethal weapons of combat] without any Congressional declaration of a state of war disturbed many Senators (see pp. 1-2)."

The decision to fight in Vietnam was proclaimed by the President, it was endorsed by the complacency of the Congress [Louis Henkin (1975), *Foreign Affairs and the Constitution*, pp. 52-54, 101, complete reference given in PART SIX: Chapter C]. "American participation in hostilities in Korea and in Viet Nam began on the President's sole authority." After a lengthy review of the process, Henkin concludes, "He [the President of the United States] needed the approval of Congress, and the question—a different question, with different constitutional overtones—was whether he had it." The implication to the reader is, Yes: through Congressional appropriation and Congressional cooperation, the President had the consent he needed.

A time of war was intended by our forefathers to be a time when the citizens of the nation assign a higher priority to the common good than to their own individual needs and desires. Ernie Pyle (1943, 1944), *Brave Men*, Scripps-Howard Newspaper Alliance, reprinted by Henry Holt and Co., New York, Chapter 22: Brass Hats, pg. 306, writes about the attitude and behavior of Lieutenant General Omar Nelson Bradley. Pyle proclaims, and rightly so (pg. 465), "We won because we were audacious. We have won this war because our men are brave."

This book has progressively redefined the meaning of war and peace. A time of peace could now become a time when the citizens of the nation assign a higher priority to the common good than to their own individual needs and desires. In other words, the common good could now become the common economic good, in the form of perpetual economic prosperity. And the pursuit of that prosperity could be a national peacetime pursuit. The natural dueling partner for common economic good would be, of course, the special interests of individuals. In other words, war and peace would coexist; they would interact as dynamic partners.

Political abuse of the U.S. military in Vietnam is discussed in PART TWO, Subsection A023: Escalation and nuclear holocaust.

E125 Defense can't win the peace either

The life of James Forrestal reflects his involvement with the political precursors of the Department of Defense. Source material is available from Miss Cross, Chief of the reference librarians at the Army Pentagon Library.

Recommended reading for those seriously interested in Purification of the Pentagon is anything and everything written by Lawrence J. Korb. For example, "The Executive and the Joint Chiefs," *Society*, July/August 1980, pp. 56-60; and *The Fall and Rise of the Pentagon*, referenced at the beginning of PART THREE.

Korb makes the claim that "the presidency has entered into a post-imperial phase" while the "force planning environment" of the Department of Defense has become both complex and unstable. The underlying issue is still dualism: the continuity of the professional military men and the creative energy of the citizens.Continuity and creativity: the answer is the same: both should be institutionalized. It is the dynamic interaction between continuity and creativity that sustains forward motion in pursuit of national ideals.

Prophetic words were written for the American people by Ernie Pyle at the end of his book, *Brave Men*, A Last Word (pg. 466): "All we can do is fumble and try once more . . . try out of memory of our anguish . . . and be as tolerant with each other as we can (reference for *Brave Men* given in Subsection E124)."

That final Chapter of *Brave Men* was written in the latter part of August 1944. Ernest Taylor "Ernie" Pyle (1900-1945), born near Dana, Indiana, was a war correspondent whose syndicated columns told millions of Americans how their boys lived and died during World War II. Writing with humor and sensitivity, Pyle became one of the best loved reporters. He traveled with American troops on nearly every front in Africa and Europe before he went to the Pacific. A Japanese machine-gunner killed Pyle on Ie Shima (island) during the battle for Okinawa.

At the Pentagon, on the second-floor E-ring, in the news division sponsored by the Assistant Secretary of Defense for Public Affairs, is a memorial to Ernie Pyle: "—30—"

A general overview of this time in national history (1937-1945) is given in the Special Issue, *Manufacturing Engineering*, see Notes and References, Preface.

Grand strategy has become a more or less incidental by-product of the administrative process of the defense budget [James E. Hewes, Jr. (1975), pg. 300, as referenced at the beginning of Chapter E].

Political abuse—Congressional involvement in the weapons procurement process—has become "overbearing." Undesirable side effects of Congressional actions are discussed in detail by Lawrence Korb (1979) in his concluding Chapter 6: Unsolved Problems (pg. 175), *The Fall and Rise of the Pentagon*, Greenwood Press, Westport, Conn.

E126 The last great balance of power

" . . . the Congress of Vienna, the machinery of coercion devised by Metternich [Prince Klemens Wenzel Nepomuk Lothat von Metternich, 1773-1859, an Austrian statesman], restored the old royal lines and endeavored to create among the nations of Europe a harmony and a stability which would make a recurrence of revolutionary violence impossible . . . international machinery known as the Congress system was devised to defend the political arrangements of 1815 and to crush any attempt to upset them [*Civilization Past and Present*, 1962, T. Walter Wallbank, Alastair M. Taylor, and Nels M. Bailkey, Chicago: Scott, Foresman, and Comp., pp. 501-507, Chapter 21: To the Barricades! Reaction and Revolution: 1815-1830]."

Jeremy Bentham (1748-1832), founder of Utilitarianism, was a man willing to translate political science into government and administration, to translate natural science into technology and industry, to pragmatically and relentlessly interpret and implement the dualism of pain and pleasure. Bentham's life spanned "a long period of transition in British history: while experiencing 18th century autocracy at its worse, he could perceive the firm outlines of 19th century democracy." One could view Bentham's later life as an effort to implement the transition: from the bullet to the ballot [William Ebenstein, 1962, *Great Political Thinkers*, New York: Holt, Rinehart, and Winston, pp. 496-521].

The utilitarian methods of Bentham also carried over to religion. Bentham found . . . religion was useless at best, and positively harmful in its more sinister manifestations [William Ebenstein, pg. 504, given above].

The formation of the United Nations Organization following World War II dates back to the wartime meetings of the Big Three: the United States, the Soviet Union, and Great Britain. An informal Great Power Conference was held at Dumbarton Oaks, Washington, DC, August 21, 1944-September 28, 1944. The Dumbarton Oaks Proposals, the communique of October 9, 1944, the published proposals for the Establishment of a General International Organization (an Assembly in which all members would be represented) and a Council with a Great Power nucleus to carry the *main* responsibilities for peace and security, recorded far reaching agreement.

That meeting at Dumbarton Oaks was held prior to the drafting conference, April 25, 1945, at the Opera House, San Francisco, under the sponsorship of the Big Five Nations: China, England, France, the Soviet Union, and the United States. The United States Senate passed the proposed Charter 89 to 2, July 28, 1945; the Big Five and a majority of member nations had signed the agreement by October 24, 1945. [H. G. Nicholas, 1971, *The United Nations as a political institution*, London: Oxford University Press, pp. 1-6, for background information.]

E127   An armed peace for the industrial elite

The National Security Act of 1947 justified the formation of the National Military Establishment, the forerunner of the Department of Defense [James E. Hewes, Jr., 1975, referenced in Subsection E125]. A convenient review of the formation of the Department of Defense is provided by Lawrence J. Korb, "The Executive and the Joint Chiefs," *Society*, July/August 1980, pp. 56-60.

The origins of NSC-68 (National Security Council-68) are discussed by Sam Postbrief, *Naval War College Review*, March-April 1980, pp. 34-57 and May-June 1975, pg. 51.

Biographies of Secretaries for the Department of Defense are available from the reference librarians at the Pentagon Army Library.

A severe but humorous criticism of McNamara's Army and his clean, functional lines of Defense reorganization says, "It's a good thing we were created by God and not Bob McNamara. He would have designed us differently. In separate components: a bucket of blood, a bundle of bones, a package of tissues, and a swirl of hair." [Robert Leider, "When Computers Control Maintenance: Brains Lose Out," *Rocky Mountain News*, Denver, Colorado, June 15, 1980.]

The industrial abuse of the military appears to have originated with the Congress. It is based on an ancient American tradition: money motivates, and it also gets votes. Intellectual curiosity and individual initiative are diseases against which all should be vaccinated at a very early age. This pork barrel philosophy places high political priority on sending federal dollars to the home state. It appears to be the same political priority system that favors federal subsidy for tobacco, milk, grain.

E128 The uniqueness of service

The first four Executive Departments—State (Foreign Affairs), Treasury, War, and the Post Office—existed under the Articles of Confederation, refer to Sol Bloom, 1937, Subsection B109.

The first nine secretaries of defense came primarily from the business community [Lawrence J. Korb, 1979, *The Fall and Rise of the Pentagon*, refer to Subsection E125]. Korb cites *Men at the Pentagon*, by C. W. Borklund, New York: Praeger, 1966, for biographical information for the first eight secretaries.

The history of the development of the War Department is reviewed briefly by Edward Bernard Glick, 1955, *Peaceful Conflict*, Stackpole Books, Harrisburg, Pennsylvania. Glick places special emphasis on the administration of the Civilian Conservation Corps. A more detailed and more recent history, starting with the National Security Act of 1947, is given by James E. Hewes, Jr., 1975, referenced in Subsection E125. Hewes also provides Appendix A: Principal Laws and Regulations Governing the Organization of the War Department and the Department of the Army, 1903-1963 (pg. 376).

"National Security Act, July 26, 1947 (published in War Department Bulletin No. 11, July 31, 1947) provides for the unification of the armed services, including a separate Air Force, in a loose federation, and the National Military Establishment, under a Secretary of Defense with little authority." The National Security Act Amendments, August 10, 1949, (published in the Department of Army Bulletin No. 22, August 22, 1949) gave the Secretary of Defense more authority over the services . . . and directed adoption of program or functional budgets that effectively "eliminated the traditional individual budgets . . . "

Department of Defense Reorganization Act, August 25, 1958, . . . replaced the service secretaries as executive agents of the President . . . and authorized the Secretary of Defense to reorganize non-military functions of the services as he saw fit in the absence of Congressional objection.

The monumental flaw in the Act is the introduction of the idea that the military performs non-military functions. The logic escapes me. The logic has also ruined the service aspect of the military service organizations. That Amendment also created an Office of Director of Defense Research and Engineering at the assistant secretary level. Secretary of Defense Robert S. McNamara was a rationalist . . . who sought to apply pure reason and scientific method to military organization [James E. Hewes, Jr., pg. 366].

Centralizing authority, growing dependence on computer technology, increasing use of automatic data processing, all were consequences of the rational methods of management, rather than the traditional, of trying to treat the military like a machine rather than a living system [James E. Hewes, Jr., pg. 374]. The rational method of management caters to centralization of authority, the traditional system to rule by committee. At the time of McNamara, the Navy appears to have been the strongest advocate of the traditional methods of the Committee System as favored by the Joint Chiefs of Staff [James E. Hewes, Jr., pg. 303, reference given in Subsection E125].

It should be kept in mind that the National Security Act of July 26, 1947, War Department Bulletin referenced above, also created the Central Intelligence Agency and the National Security Council. The formation of those two organizations put an official stamp of approval on secrecy within the defense community and started the decision making process down the road to elitism.

After 1969 . . . the threat to overwhelm and exclude the military from the national security decision-making process came primarily from Henry Kissinger. As Executive Assistant for National Security Affairs, the former Harvard professor sought to dominate the entire national security decision-making apparatus . . . Lawrence J. Korb, 1979, *The Fall and Rise of the Pentagon*, pg. 92, referenced in Subsection E125.

The reorganization idea presented in this Chapter would have the U.S. Army responsible for domestic military affairs, except for patrol of coastal areas where the U.S. Coast Guard would remain actively involved. The highest priority for armed force and armed readiness would go to the U.S. Navy and Marine Corps. That would leave the U.S. Air Force on the High Frontier. The U.S. Air Force would have to develop and use Earth-orbiting satellites for global monitoring systems and global information networks. This suggested reorganization appears compatible with the second viewpoint presented by Lawrence J. Korb, 1979, *The Fall and Rise of the Pentagon*, pg. 173, referenced in Subsection E125.

PART SIX

Chapter F

The Politics of Foreign Policy

The concept of a TEAM effort (Technology, Environment, And Man) is introduced as a necessary method for implementing Global Environmental Monitoring, the GEM of the future. No one can know for sure how to implement this TEAM effort, but considering its long-term implications, one can only guess that it will require a fourth branch of government, an investigative or research branch to become more active. In that respect, it is necessary to repeat the thinking of Jeremy Bentham (1748-1832): " . . . investigation is increasingly becoming a fourth branch of government, without which the traditional three (the legislative, executive, and judicial) cannot properly function. Government has ceased to be a day-to-day affair of simple dimensions, confining itself to the maintenance of law and order, and now requires long term planning, particularly in relation to national defense and social welfare [William Ebenstein (1962), *Great Political Thinkers*, New York: Holt, Rinehart, and Winston, pg. 505]." To national defense and social welfare mentioned by Bentham, I am adding natural constraint imposed by the natural environment.

In the United States today, this responsibility for the fourth branch of government has been picked up by the press. Investigative reporting is the answer. And Jack Anderson is the master [*Washington Post*, daily column].

F129 Patriotic industries

Industries in the United States will become patriotic industries when the people become patriotic citizens. The tendency has been for the United States, as a matter of national policy, to foster national trade dependence. Patriotic industries would encourage national self-sufficiency and national economic independence.

When talking about "petro-dollars," Jean-Jacques Servan-Schreiber [*The World Challenge* (1981), New York: Simon and Schuster, A division of Gulf and Western Corp.] writes, "The American Government no longer controlled the expansion of its own currency (pg. 25)." A more popular book, written for the American reader, is *Miracle on Main Street*, by F. Tupper Saussy (1980), Spencer Judd Publications, Sewanee, Tenn. 37375.

The Federal Reserve System (1913) has grown by spurts and jerks. "There would almost certainly have been no Federal Reserve System if its advocates had heralded it as an instrument for continuous monetary management. This function of the Federal Reserve developed only several years later when the international gold standard had broken down . . . " [Lester Chandler (1959), *The Economics of Money and Banking*, New York: Harper and Row, Pub., pg. 161 forward]. For historical remarks about the economic development of the United States, see pg. 17.

Whether the Federal Reserve is "useless or lethal" may be difficult to decide, but the book by Lawrence S. Ritter and William L. Silber (1970) makes interesting reading [*Money*, New York: Basic Books, pg. 198].

Just as people make democracy work, they also make economy work. " . . . the most important relic [of government participation in collective planning] is the idea that government is responsible for the functioning of the economy." [Clarence B. Carson, "The Relics of Intervention: Part 4: New Deal Collective Planning," *The Freeman*, Vol. 32, No. 7, pg. 414, July 1982, one of a series.]

Washington's Farewell Address is reprinted in *The Story of the Constitution* by Sol Bloom (1937), refer back to Subsection B109 for the reference.

F130   From scientist to Senator

The most important dualism for the American people today is "science and religion," science is the only truly American way of expressing and teaching truth. The utility of faith and reason, or science and religion, in the interaction of man with his natural environment is explained by Arthur Koestler (1959), in his review of the 5th century B.C. and the teachings of Pythagoras of Samos [*Sleepwalkers*, New York: Macmillan Co.], see A history of man's changing vision of the universe, pg. 26.

In the pragmatic movement in the United States, William James is quoted as having said that his "predestined mission" was "to find a philosophic truth that would justify religion without alienating science." Refer especially to Lecture I: The Present Dilemma in Philosophy, pg. 28 [Charles Morris (1970), *The Pragmatic Movement in American Philosophy*, New York: George Braziller]. William James uses science and religion as the example for what I am calling dualism in the decision making process. James' pragmatic method is the mediating way of thinking, it is primarily a method of settling metaphysical disputes that otherwise might be interminable [William James (1955), *Pragmatism*, New York: Meridian Books, The World Publishing Co., (original copyright 1907), pg. 43].

Religion and natural science are fighting a joint battle in an incessant, never relaxing crusade against skepticism and against dogmatism, against disbelief and against superstition and the rallying cry in this crusade has always been and always will be "on to God." Max Planck is being quoted in an article about Sir John Eccles, temporarily at Georgetown University Campus, "Photons, Philosophy, and the Eccles of the Mind: The Complete Scientists' Encounters With the Soul," by Sandy Rovner, *Washington Post*, March 15, 1981, pg. F-1.

Gerald Holton says that having a "scientifically illiterate majority of people" has put decision making in the hands of a "knowledgeable scientific-technological elite," and Holton identifies this exclusive decision making process as "our present danger." ["A Widening Gulf Between Science and the Rest of Us," by Martin Kaplan, *Washington Star*, Monday, May 11, 1981, pg. C-1.] The occasion was the delivery of the 10the annual Thomas Jefferson Lecture, where Holton quotes Thomas Jefferson, "You're not a free citizen if you can't participate intelligently . . . " and cautions . . . if you want to rebel [demonstrate], then you should do it in informed ways.

Dwight D. Eisenhower, in his Farewell Address in 1961, cautioned the American people of precisely the same danger, that " . . . public policy itself could become the captive of a scientific technological elite." [Dwight D. Eisenhower, 1960-1961, *Public Papers of the Presidents of the United States*, pg. 1038, U.S. Government Printing Office.] That caution from Eisenhower has been largely ignored. The immediate alternative is to attach some urgency to the election of capable scientists to public office.

There are many senior scientists and/or engineers now developing an increased awareness of public policy. Certainly Jerry Grey, Carl Sagan, and Joseph Weizenbaum are prime examples and their writings are referenced in this book. Of course, John Glenn is already a member of the United States Senate [*The Right Stuff*, by Tom Wolfe (1980), New York: Farrar, Straus, and Giroux, Inc., pg. 257, 263, 287], but one man is a rather slow start, considering the magnitude of neglect of the problem. Freeman Dyson, mentioned in the text, wrote "Death of a Project," *Science*, Vol. 149, pg. 141-144, in 1978.

The participation of scientists in politics is not without precedence. "The active part which [Sir Issac] Newton had taken in defending the legal privileges of the university against the encroachments of the crown had probably at least equal weight with his scientific reputation when his friends chose him as a candidate for a seat in parliament . . . " [*Encyclopaedia Britannica*, 1911, Vol. XIX, pg. 589, Cambridge, England: at the University Press, New York, 120 West 32nd Street]

The advantages of science in politics and the uses of conflict [dynamic dualism] to generate progress, are discussed by Walter Bagenot (1826-1877), economist and journalist, graduate of the University of London [*Physics and Politics*, London: D. Appleton and Comp., 1848], refer especially to Chapter II: The Use of Conflict, pg. 41.

F131   From advocate to lobbyist

Through the ages religious leaders have acknowledged the "prophetic advantages" of scientists. The present century is no exception. See "Paris Talks," addresses given by Abdu'l-Baha' in Paris in 1911, published in 1979 by the Baha'i Publishing Trust, 27 Rutland Gate, London SW7 1PD; Theosophical Society, Paris, pg. 127, Fourth Principle: The Acceptance of the Relation Between Religion and Science (pg. 130, pp. 141-145). " . . . religion that does not walk hand in hand with science is itself in the darkness of superstition and ignorance . . . it is impossible for religion to be contrary to science. Even though some intellects are too weak or too immature to understand truth, the true principles of all religions are in conformity with the teachings of science."

F132 To teach is to transfer

A transfer of sophisticated electronic hardware into a non-technical society creates junk. This fact has been demonstrated time and time again, right here in the United States, as many disciplines of social or biological sciences, banks, public utilities, and even government agencies try to learn to use computers. The transition to the computerized systems has been fraught with disappointment. The user simply refuses to use the equipment. Either the user does not know anything about the equipment, or the equipment, including the software, was not designed with the needs of the user in mind, or both.

F133 Information is the trade commodity

The automobile was an industrial success but an economic failure. The United States House Committee on Patents condemned the efficiency of industrial progress [*Manufacturing Engineering*, January 1982, pg. 38, pp. 40-41, see the reference given in PART ONE, Subsection A002: Technology push]. The manufacture of the automobile, using the efficiency of the assembly line, had created unemployment. It would be the use, not the production, of the automobile that would later alter lifestyle and economic conditions in the United States.

The uniqueness of munitions as a trade commodity is discussed by Anthony Sampson, 1978, *The Arms Bazaar*, New York: Bantam Books in association with Viking Press. "The arms business has always insisted that it is like any other business, with no special moral responsibility . . . but the ordinary citizen is right in thinking that the arms trade, like narcotics and slavery, is different from other trades (pg. 386)."

PART SIX

Chapter G

The Presence and the Purpose

Action-reaction physics is usually attributed to Sir Issac Newton (December 25, 1642-March 20, 1727) because Newton formalized modern (equilibrium) physics. Newton also paid great attention to theological studies . . . it is well known that Newton had begun to study the subject of prophecies before the year 1690, before he was 48 years old [*Encyclopaedia Britannica*, Vol. XIX, pg. 591, 1911, Cambridge, England, referenced in Subsection F130]. Nevertheless the excessive emphasis on the balance of the equilibrium state is the fault of those who later taught and institutionalized equilibrium physics. It has nothing to do with the likes or dislikes of Newton himself [Bronowski, J., 1973 *The Ascent of Man*, Boston: Little, Brown and Co., pp. 221-227].

John Locke, in 1690, wrote the *Second Treatise of Civil Government*. Locke said, " . . . the prince and the legislature are subordinate to basic natural law." [Andrew D. Weinberger (1962), *Freedom and Protection: The Bill of Rights*, Greenwood Press Pub., Westport, Conn., pg. 10.] The American people would do well to take that statement by John Locke seriously.

F134   Fight or flight is not enough

The American war correspondent Ernie Pyle contrasted the joyous mood of the pilots with the grimness of the men in the trenches [Ernie Pyle (1943, 1944), *Brave Men*, Original copyright Scripps-Howard Newspaper Alliance, pg. 293, also refer to PART SIX, Subsections E124 and E125].

John Keats describes "the butchering of Americans" by the Japanese [*They Fought Alone*, J. B. Lippincott Comp., Philadelphia and New York, pg. 409], it is the story of Wendell Fertig in the Philippines, and his passionate belief that guerrilla operations are always victorious.

G135   The Letter of the Law

The enactment of the prohibition amendment, the Eighteenth Amendment to the United States Constitution, was passed swiftly; it was offered to the States by the Congress on December 18, 1917; it was in effect January 16, 1920. Congress voted the repeal of the Eighteenth Amendment on February 20, 1933, with certificate of the adoption of the Twenty-first Amendment, December 5, 1933 [Sol Bloom (1937), referenced in Subsection B109].

G136   The Spirit of the Law

The principles of the law of nature and of nations, in the hands of Hugo Grotius (1583-1645), turn into a general examination of the "just causes of action," written as an examination of the just causes of war. And the "dichotomy" of the law of nature and nations is maintained throughout. Whatever the terminology, the international law of Grotius was a unified whole [developed around the natural law of dynamic dualism], fundamentally different from the conceptions of the scholastics. Without doubt, the outstanding feature of the international law of Grotius is tolerance.

The concept of "just war" permeates the writings of Grotius who " . . . urged moderation for reasons of humanity, religion, and far-sighted policy." The writings of Grotius should be required reading for anyone seriously interested in the non-violent decision making process, who shares "the desire and hope for reunion of the Christian Churches." The great work of Grotius is essentially a treatise on the "law of war." Even though Grotius used a phrase from Cicero, *De jure belli ac pacis*, on the Law of War and Peace, for his title, Grotius treats the law of peace as "most incidental." [Arthur Nussbaum (1954), *A Concise History of the Law of Nations*, New York: Macmillan comp., pp. 102-114, also refer to Subsection B109]

According to Henry James Summer Main (1897), *Ancient Law*, London: John Murray, Albemarle Street, Sixteenth Edition, pg. 96 (first edition was published in 1861), "The greatest function of the Law of Nature was discharged in giving birth to modern International Law of War." It is that Law of War, the law of how to make a decision during a time of rapid (if not violent) change, that we must continue to develop.

G137 Do it—a nation in action

The American military is this nation in action [" . . . a breed of its own," pg. 293, *Brave Men*, by Ernie Pyle, referenced in Subsection F134].

The Farewell Address, "Duty-Honor-Country," by General Douglas MacArthur (January 26, 1880-April 5, 1964) is reproduced in *The Army Officer's Guide*, Preface, the 41st Edition, by Lieutenant Colonel Lawrence P. Crocker, U.S. Army (retired), Stackpole Books, Cameron and Keiker Streets, Harrisburg, Pennsylvania 17105. The complete speech was recorded and is available commercially.

G138 The mystique of presence

There is no known measure for the value of the mystique of presence [Peter P. Hill (1971), *William Vans Murray: Federalist Diplomat: The Shaping of Peace with France, 1797-1801*, Syracuse University Press, pg. 228]. The value of the mystique of presence, as it related to World War II in the Philippines and the guerrilla activities of Wendell Fertig, is discussed by John Keats (1963), *They Fought Alone*, referenced in Subsection F134.

The importance of economic independence and the right to free trade has become a popular theme in the journal of *World Development*, published by Pergamon Press, Ltd., see, for example, Vol. 9, No. 5, pg. 429-434, May 1981, "Dependence and Industrialization Strategies," by Michael Roemer, and included references.

The idea that the American people pay in excess of other nations for an international effort is not without precedence. H. G. Nicholas (1971), *The United Nations as a Political Institution*, Chapter 1: Origins, London: Oxford University Press, explains that the United States now pays more to the United Nations than other nations with the same political status.

G139 Stand your ground

The telic response of the whole follows from the organic concept for the living nation [refer to Notes and References, Preface, especially the writings of Aristotle]. The idea of having the United States Navy become the sole custodian for nuclear weapons during this time of transition was presented in PART THREE: Chapter B: Sea Launch Options.

G140 There is a nation standing behind you

The think-do dualism, like faith and reason or science and religion, has become so much a part of the American way of life that it is attracting attention in the political arena. "U.S. Faith in Reason Is World's Last Best Hope," by N. P. Kannan, *Washington Post*, March 10, 1981, pg. A-13. Kannan quotes President Reagan as having referred to the United States as "the last, best hope of man on earth." The quotation "last, best hope on earth," is attributed to Abraham Lincoln [*The Air Force Officer's Guide*, Twenty-third Edition (1976), by Major General A. J. Kinney, United States Air Force (retired), Stackpole Books, Harrisburg, Penn., pg. 4]. Kannan goes on to explain, "This society is not perfect . . . but the American culture is relatively young and perhaps more able to absorb new ideas." And, I might add, especially young enough to absorb the use of modern electronic technology. It is interesting to note that Kannan refers to Alexis de Tocqueville for his optimistic thoughts about democracy in America.

Dualism in the decision making process was popularized in the United States by William James [Refer to *Pragmatism*, in Subsection F130].

The organic concept of the living nation receives strong support in the writings relating to the teachings of Aristotle [refer to Notes and References, Preface].

The importance of growth of information industries in the private sector is discussed in PART FIVE: Information Politics. The timely arrival of a breath of fresh air, refers to the information industries. The "sensory system" that alerts the nation to danger is described in PART FOUR: Detection and Early Warning.

The monetary flow, the blood supply that circulates at near-constant volume, is a more timely, and more controversial, analogy. "Set the money supply on automatic pilot and then leave it alone [Lawrence S. Ritter and William L. Silber (1970), *Money*, New York: Basic Books, pg. 195]."

PART SIX

Perspective

Tell it like it is

Astronaut John Glenn circled the globe in free flight [*The Right Stuff*, by Tom Wolfe (1979), New York: Farrar, Straus, and Giroux, Inc., pg. 257].

That the prestigious American Eagle should be "in flight," rather than sitting perched with his olive branch and bundle of arrows (the traditional Eagle on the President's seal) is only a suggestion of the dynamic future of this country.

"Retreat, hell! We just got here." [*The Marine Officer's Guide*, Fourth Edition, Colonel Robert D. Heinl, Jr., United States Marine Corps (retired), Naval Institute Press, Annapolis, Maryland (1977), pg. 1.] The quotation is attributed to a company commander of the U.S. Marines, 1918. The primary mission of the Marine Corps—readiness—has become the primary mission of this book and, hence, of this nation. The Marine Corps traces its origin back to November 10, 1775, when the Continental Congress . . . formed two battalions of Marines.

Bibliography

Alphanumeric characters following each entry refer to Notes and References.
One letter with three numbers refers to notes for a numbered subsection.
One number alone refers to notes for the introduction to a numbered Part.
One number with one letter refers to notes for a Chapter within a Part.
One number with PER refers to notes for the Perspective (the final section) of a Part.
PREF refers to notes for the Preface.

Abdu'l-Baha', *Paris Talks from 1911*, Baha'i Pub. Trust, London, 1979. F131

Adams, Gordon and Geoff Quinn, *Council on Economic Priorities Newsletter*, "The Iron Triangle," June 1981. A091

Alfven, Hannes, *Bulletin of Atomic Scientists*, Re: split between bomb and anti-bomb scientists, January 1981, pp. 4-5.   1D

Ambrose, Stephen E. and James A. Barber, *The Military and American Society*, New York: Free Press, 1972. C118

Anders, Gunther, *Off Limits für das Gewissen*, Rowholt Verlag GmbH, Reinbek bei Hamburg, 1961. E048

_____, *Burning Conscience*, New York: Monthly Review Press, 1962. E048

Anderson, Jack, *Washington Post*, "3 Nations to Begin Cruise Missile Project," December 8, 1980, pg. B-15. C043

_____, *Washington Post, Parade Magazine Section*, "Why I Tell Secrets," November 30, 1980, pp. 20-25. 5PER

_____, *Washington Post*, "Stealth: The Story Behind a Secret," October 13, 1980, pg. C-27. E017

_____, *Washington Post*, Re: investigative reporting, the fourth branch of government, daily column.   6F

Anderson, Sir John, *Signal*, "The Evolution of NICS," April 1979, pp. 15-19. C031

Angle, Paul M., *The Lincoln Reader*, New Brunswick: Rutgers University Press, 1947. B112

Aquinas, Saint Thomas (1226-1274), Re: dualism of faith and reason, see William Ebenstein, 1962. 4PER

Aristotle (384-322 B.C.), *Politics*, see William Ebenstein, 1962. 2PER

Asimov, Isaac, *Science Past-Science Future*, Grosset and Dunlap, 1975. 4PER

Attlee, Clement, "Democracy is not just majority rule," September 12, 1945, see William Ebenstein, 1962. 2PER

Audretsch, F. C., et al., *ITC Journal*, "Education and training . . . " 1981-2, pp. 171-183.   4

Bagenot, Walter, *Physics and Politics*, London: D. Appleton and Co., 1848. F130

Barber, James A., *The Military and American Society*, see Stephen E. Ambrose, 1972. C118

Barber, Stephen, *Far Eastern Economic Review*, "Noise Interferes," February 25, 1977, pg. 28.   4B

Barclay, William, *Flesh and Spirit*, Baker Book House, Grand Rapids, Michigan, 1976. PREF

Bates, E. Asa. Jr., *RUSI*, "National Technical Means of Verification," June 1978, pg. 64. A020

Beal, Richard S., Testimony: Information Technology and Emergency Management, United States House Committee on Science and Technology, September 22, 1981. B096

Belden, Thomas G., Testimony: Information Technology and Emergency Management, United States House Committee on Science and Technology, September 30, 1981. B095

Bentham, Jeremy (1748-1832), Re: fourth branch of government, see William Ebenstein, 1962, pg. 505.   6F

Berger, Raoul, *New York Times*, "The Mayaguez Incident and the Constitution," May 23, 1975. D119

Birks, John W., *Ambio*, see Paul J. Crutzen, June/July 1982.   3D

Bishop, William W., Jr., *International Law. Cases and Material*, Boston: Little, Brown, and Co., 1962. E049

Bite, Vita, et. al., *Congress, The President and the War Powers*, Congressional Research Service 75-209F, September 22, 1975. D119

Blackaby, Frank, Director, Stockholm International Peace Research Institute, Re: monitoring nuclear testing, Sweden. 4D

Blacker, Coit Dennis and Farooq Hussain, *Bulletin of Atomic Scientists*, "European theater nuclear forces," October 1980, pp. 32-37. C031

Blanchard, James J., HR5540, "The Defense Industrial Base Revitalization Act," 1983. 5B

Bloom, Sol, *The Story of the Constitution*, U.S. Constitution Sesquicentennial Commission, House Office Building, Washington, DC, 1937. E018

Bodin, Jean (1530-1596), Re: Six Books on the State, see William Ebenstein, 1962. 6A

_____, Re: Colloquium Heptaplomeres (written in 1588, published in 1841), see William Ebenstein, 1962, pg. 348. B027

_____, *War of Religion*, written 1562, published 1588, see William Ebenstein, 1962. B027

Boraiko, Allen A., *National Geographic*, "The Chip: Electronic Mini-marvel that is Changing Your Life," October 1982, pp. 420-458. B059

Brandt Commission, *Parameters*, "North-South: A Program for Survival," review, June 1980, pg. 93. A006

Brant, Irving, *James Madison, Father of the Constitution*, The Bobbs-Merrill Comp., Indianapolis, Indiana, 1950, pg. 39. 6D

Broad, William J., *Science*, "Philosophers at the Pentagon," October 24, 1980, pp. 409-412. C029

Brodie, Bernard, UCLA Working Paper, "The Development of Nuclear Strategy," February 1978. 1

_____, *Strategy in the Missile Age*, Princeton University Press, Princeton, New Jersey, 1959. 1

_____, *The Reporter*, "Unlimited Weapons and Limited War," November 8, 1954, pp. 16-21. 1

_____, *The Absolute Weapon*, New York: Harcourt, Brace, 1946. 2

Bronowski, J., *The Ascent of Man*, Boston: Little, Brown, and Co., 1973. 6G

Brooks, Jack, *Government Executive*, see John F. Judge, October 1980. B092

Brown, George E., *Boston Globe*, see Robert Cooke, December 11, 1980. C099

Brown, Harold (interviewed), *ABC-TV, Issues and Answers*, August 17, 1980. C011

Brown, Seyom, et al., *Regimes for the Ocean, Outer Space, and Weather*, Brookings Institution, Washington, DC, 1977. B038

Brzezinski, Zbigniew, Presidential Direction 54: Civil Operational Remote Sensing, November 16, 1979. C099

Buckley, William F., Jr., *Washington Star*, "Launch Under Attack," November 5, 1980, pg. 21.   1C

Bulganin, Nikolai, Re: open skies policy, see Dwight D. Eisenhower, September 19, 1955. A090

Burgess, Eric, *Long-Range Ballistic Missiles*, New York: Macmillan Comp., 1961. A054

_____, *Guided Weapons*, New York: Macmillan Comp., 1957.   4C

Burt, Richard, *New York Times*, "Carter Denies Directing Disclosure of Stealth Program," September 21, 1980, pg. 33. E016

_____, *New York Times*, "Muskie Rebuffs Soviets on Nuclear Strategy Criticism," September 17, 1980, pg. 3. D014

Caesar, Julius (100?-44 B.C.), Re: absolute power of a ruler, see Louis Henkin, 1972, pg. 278 fn.   6C

Canby, Steven L., *Armed Forces and Society*, "Territorial Defense in Central Europe," Fall 1980, pp. 51-67. C031

Carole, Shifrin, *Washington Post*, "U.S. Eyed AWACS for Air Control," August 13, 1981, pg. A-16. B058

Carson, Clarence B., *The Freeman*, "The Relics of Intervention," July 1982, pg. 414. F129

Carter, Luther J., *Science*, "Navy Considers Scuttling Old Nuclear Subs," September 26, 1980, pg. 1495. B039

Chadwell, Paul A., *National Defense*, "C3I Satellite Systems," June 1980, pp. 50-53, 190-192. B040

Chamberlain, John, *The Freeman*, Re: Burton Yale Pines, October 1982, pg. 632.   6

_____, *The Freeman*, "Supply Side Economics," June 1981, pg. 381. A004

Chandler, Lester, *The Economics of Money and Banking*, New York: Harper and Row, 1959. F129

Chappell, Bill, Re: background study for defense appropriations, see John M. Collins, 1980.   1A

Cheny, Elizabeth, *Prophecy Fulfilled*, Baha'i Publishing Trust, Wilmette, Illinois, 1944. B112

Clark, Grenville and Louis B. Sohn, *World Peace Through World Law*, Harvard University Press, Cambridge, Mass., 1958.   5A

Claypoole, *American Daily Advertiser*, Philadelphia, Re: Washington's Farewell Address, September 19, 1796. A087

Cline, Ray. S., *Secrets, Spies and Scholars*, Acropolis Books, Ltd., Washington, DC, 1976. A090

Cobb, Stanwood, *The Destiny of America*, Baha'i Publishing Trust, Wilmette, Illinois, 1970. C117

_____, *The Rise of Religious Liberty in America*, see *The Destiny of America*, 1970. C117

Cockburn, Andrew and Alexander Cockburn, *New York Review of Books*, "The Myth of Missile Accuracy," November 20, 1980, pp. 40-43. A033

Cockburn, Alexander, *New York Review of Books*, see Andrew Cockburn, November 20, 1980, pp. 40-43. A033

Collins, John M., *U.S.-Soviet Military Balance*, McGraw-Hill, Hightstown, New Jersey, 1980.   1A

_____, *U.S.-Soviet Military Balance*, Congressional Research Service, Library of Congress, published as a series, 1978-1979.   1A

_____, *New York Times*, Re: *U.S.-Soviet Military Balance*, September 28, 1980, pg. 16.   1A

Conkin, Paul K., *Puritans and Pragmatism*, Meridian Books, The World Pub. Co., 1955, pp. 266-344.   6C

Cooke, Robert, *Boston Globe*, "A science-technology rift," December 11, 1980. C099

Cooper, Robert B.,Jr., *Amateur Radio*, "The Satellite TV Primer ... " November 1979, pp. 13-26. A052

Copeland, Miles, *Defense and Foreign Affairs Digest*, "The Functions of Strategic Intelligence," February 1977.   4B

Corddry, Charles W., *Baltimore Sun*, "Defense Chief Explains Shift in War Strategy," August 21, 1980, pg. 8.   1C

Cornford, F. M. (translator), *The Republic of Plato*, see William Ebenstein, 1962. 2PER

Courter, Jim, *Washington Star*, "Truth is a Powerful Weapon," August 9, 1980, pg. 9. 2PER

Crocker, Lawrence P., *The Army Officer's Guide*, Stackpole Books, Harrisburg, Penn., 41st Edition. G137

Cross, Colonel, Reference Librarian, National Guard Association, Washington, DC, 1980-1981. A105

Cross, Mrs., Reference Librarian, Army Library, Pentagon, 1980-1981. G086

Crutzen, Paul J. and John W. Birks, *Ambio*, "The Atmosphere After a Nuclear Attack," June/July 1982.   3D

Currie, William, *Chicago Tribune*, "Small-town woman editor takes on MX system," October 26, 1980, pg. 15. A036

Dahlman, Ola and Hans Israelson, *Monitoring Underground Nuclear Testing*, Elsevier Scientific Pub. Comp., 1977.   4D

Dallas, Daniel B., Editor, *Manufacturing Engineering*, SME Golden Anniversary Issue, January 1982. PREF

David, Rene and John E. C. Brierley, *Major Legal Systems in the World Today*, Free Press, Collier-Macmillan Ltd., London, 1968 (original in French, 1964).

Dewey, John (1859-1952), Re: instrumentalist view of nation-state, see William Ebenstein, 1962. PREF

Diddlebock, Bob, *Rocky Mountain News*, Denver, "Lamm Attacks Reagan's Land Policies," February 6, 1982, pg. 102. A037

Diefenbaker, *The Imperialism Reader*, see Louis L. Snyder, September 26, 1960, pg. 595, 609. 2PER

Dinneen, Gerald (interviewed), *Government Executive*, "Information Engineering," June 1980, pg. 16. A002

Dockrill, Michael, *Parameters*, see Barrie Paskins, March 1980, pg. 102. E049

Draim, John E., *National Review*, "Move MX Missiles Out to Sea," December 12, 1980, pg. 1500. B038

_____, *Washington Star*, "A Floating U.S. Force of Missiles," September 25, 1980. B038

Dunn, Kieth A., *Naval War College Review*, "Power Projection or Influence," Sept-Oct 1980, pp. 31-47. B025

Dyson, Freeman, *Science*, "Death of a Project," Vol. 149, 1978, pp. 141-144. F130

Ebenstein, William, *Great Political Thinkers*, New York: Holt, Rinehart and Winston, 1962. PREF

Eccles, Sir John, *Washington Post*, see Sandy Rovner, March 15, 1981, pg. F-1. F130

Edelson, Burton I., *Scientific American*, "Global Satellite Communications," February 1977, pp. 58-73. A052

Ege, Konrad, *Blatter fur deutsche und international Politik*, "Schlachtfeld Europe," December 1982, pp. 1438-1448.   2

Eisenhower, Dwight D., *Congressional Record*, Re: use of nuclear weapons by Italy, March 7, 1961, 1095.   2A

_____, *Public Papers of the Presidents*, Re: open skies policy, July 21, 1955, May 25, 1960. A090

_____, *Public Papers of the Presidents*, Re: open skies policy, January 17, 1961. 4PER

_____, *Public Papers of the Presidents*, Re: letter to Nikolai Bulganin, September 19, 1955. A090

Ellsberg, Daniel, *Manufacturing Engineering*, Re: Pentagon Papers, January 1982, pg. 212.   5

Elson, Benjamin M., *Aviation Week & Space Technology*, "Krems Facility Supports Advanced Technology," July 14, 1980, pp. 52-54. A033

_____, *Aviation Week & Space Technology*, "Kwajalein Range Plays Unique Role," June 16, 1980, pg. 223. A033

Emerson, Ralph Waldo (1803-1882), Re: And fired the shot heard round the world: Concord Hymn. A105

Engels, Friedrick (1820-1895), *Communist Manifesto*, see Karl Marx, 1848. 2

Epstein, William, *Scientific American*, "A Ban on the Production of Fissionable Material for Weapons," July 1980, pp.43-51.   1C

Evans, Christopher Riche, *Micro-Millenium*, New York: Viking, 1979.   4

Feinler, Elizabeth, ARPANET Information Center, SRI International, See ARPANET Directory. E072

Fertig, Wendell, *They Fought Alone*, see John Keats, 1963. G137

Fialka, John J., *Washington Star*, "Shuttle Glides to Triumph," April 14, 1981, pg. 1. D045

_____, *Washington Star*, "Stealth News Called Political by House Panel," February 5, 1981, pg. 3. E016

————, *Washington Star*, "Brown Outlines New U.S. Policy on Nuclear Strategy," August 21, 1980, pg. 3.   1C

Finney, Burnham, *Arsenal of Democracy*, New York: Whittlesey House, 1941. PREF

Fox, Daniel J., *International Security*, see Jacek Kugler, Spring 1980, pp. 105-138.   1

Foster, Richard B., *SRI International Report*, "Forecastability of National Security Telecommunications Requirements," September 29, 1981. A022

Frankl, Victor E., *Man's Search for Meaning*, New York: Washington Square Press. C114

Freeman, Robert L., *Telecommunications Journal*, "The science of time and its inverse," Vol. 44, II, 1977, pg. 66. B061

Gardner, Martin, *Scientific American*, "Mathematical Games," December 1981, pg. 18. A004

Gatrell, Peter, *World Development*, "The Impact of War on Russian and Soviet Development," August 1981, pp. 793-803. 2PER

Genghis Khan (1162-1227), Re: absolute power of rulers, see Louis Henkin, 1972, pg. 278 fn.   6C

Gerasimov, Gennadi, *Washington Star*, "A Soviet view of the nuclear directive," August 27, 1980, pg. 9. D015

Glasser, William and William Powers, *Stations of the Mind*, New York: Harper and Row, 1981.   1A

Glenn, John, *The Right Stuff*, see Tom Wolfe, 1980, pg. 257, 263, 287. F130

Glick, Edward Bernard, *Peaceful Conflict*, Stackpole Books, Harrisburg, Penn., 1955. E128

Goldsmith, William M., *The Growth of Presidential Power*, Vol. 1 and 2, New York: Chelsea House Pub., 1974. C013

Goldwater, Barry, *Gazette Telegraph*, Colorado Springs, Colorado, see Sue McMillin, June 2, 1983. 4PER

Gonzalez, Felipe, Madrid Domestic News Service, Spain, Re: political mood in United States, November 5, 1980, 2300 GMT. 1PER

Good, Phillip, *Small Business Computer*, "Choosing Computers," May/June 1983, pp. 42-48. C104

Goodman, Elinor, *Financial Times*, "UK discloses sites . . . " June 18, 1980, pg. 1. C043

Gore, Albert, Jr., Information Industry Association Breakfast, see Robert S. Willard, December 12, 1980. B092

Graham, Daniel, *State of the Nation*, "High Frontier," August 1982, pg. 1. A020

Grasse, Robert de, Jr. and David Gold, *Daily Camera*, Boulder, Colorado, "Costs of Defense Spending Not Told In Dollars Alone," December 31, 1981. B096

Greenwood, Ted, *Scientific American*, Re: use of Earth-orbiting satellites for global monitoring, February 1973. C028

Gregor, A. James and Maria Hsia Chang, *Journal of Strategic Studies*, "Arms Control, Regional Stability . . . " May 1980, pp. 3-25.   4B

Grey, Jerry, *Enterprise*, New York: William Morrow and Co., Inc., 1979. A034

Grodzka, Philomena, Re: rejecting rigid thought patterns, see Jerry Grey, 1979, pg. 151-154. 3PER

Grotius, Hugo (1583-1645), *Law of War and Peace*, see Clarence Morris, 1959. B109

_____, Re: international law of war, see Arthur Nussbaum, 1954. G136

Guy, George F., *Yearbook: Supreme Court Historical Society*, "The Defense of General Yamashita," 1981. E049

Gwertzman, Bernard, *New York Times*, "Muskie Wasn't Told . . . " August 10, 1980, pg. 1. D015

Haig, Alexander Meigs, Jr., *Washington Post*, Re: "I am in control at the White House . . . " March 31, 1981. C113

_____, *Washington Star*, Re: "I am in control at the White House . . . " March 31, 1981. C113

Halloran, Richard, *New York Times*, "U.S. Plans Big Spending Increase . . . " October 17, 1982, pg. 1. D044

_____, *New York Times*, "Defense Secretary Fires Some Political Missiles," September 7, 1980, pg. E-2. E016

Hartman, Richard, *Defense Electronics*, "Old Problems, New Solutions . . . " December 1980, pp. 55-58. A051

Hawkins, William J., *Popular Science*, "The boom is on in New Personal Computers," November 1982, pg. 93. B062

Heinl, Robert D., *The Marine Officer's Guide*, Naval Institute Press, Annapolis, Maryland, 1977. 6PER

Henkin, Louis, *Foreign Affairs and the Constitution*, New York: W. W. Norton and Comp., 1972.   5A

Henrikson, Alan K., *Naval War College Review*, "Creation of the North Atlantic Alliance, 1948-1952," May-June 1980, pp. 4-39. C031

Henry, Patrick (1736-1799), Re: the President of the United States could become a king, see Sol Bloom, 1937, Chapter XXV. C114

———, *The Growth of Presidential Power*, see William M. Goldsmith, 1974, pg. 367. A108

Henry, Richard C., *Defense Electronics*, Re: national orbital strategy, December 1980, pp. 55-58. A051

Hewes, James E., Jr., *From Root to McNamara*, U.S. Government Printing Office, Washington, DC, 1975. B040

Hill, Peter P., *William Vans Murray: Federalist Diplomat*, Syracuse University Press, Syracuse, New York, 1971, pg. 228. A091

Hobbes, Thomas (1588-1679), Re: instrumentalist view of nation-state, see William Ebenstein, 1962. PREF

Hoeber, Francis P., *SRI International Report*, "The Changing Environment for National Emergency Preparedness . . . " September 29, 1981. C010

Hofstadter, Douglas R., *Scientific American*, "Metamagical Themas: Strange Attractors," November 1981, pg. 22. C102

Holton, Gerald, *Washington Star*, see Martin Kaplan, May 11, 1981, pg. C-1. F130

Holzer, Werner, *Frankfurter Rundschau*, Germany, "Hope for Yesterday," November 6, 1980, pg. 3. 1PER

Hopkins, Mark, *The New Leader*, "Our Euromissiles and Theirs," October 6, 1980, pp. 6-8. C030

Howe, Julia Ward, *Atlantic Monthly*, "Battle Hymn of the Republic," February 1862. 2PER

Hussain, Farooq, *Bulletin of Atomic Scientists*, see Coit Dennis Blacker, October 1980, pp. 32-37. C031

Huyer, Robert E., *The Officer*, "Patriotism Lies In Nation's Soul," July 1980, pg. 12. 1PER

Israelson, Hans, Re: monitoring underground nuclear explosions, see Ola Dahlman, 1977.   4B

Jaffe, Louis L. and Nathaniel L. Nathanson, *Administrative Law*, Boston: Little, Brown, and Comp., 1968, pg. 38.   6D

James, William, *Pragmatism*, New York: Meridian Books, World Pub. Co., 1914. PREF

_____, *Pragmatism*, Longmans, Green and Comp., 1907. 4PER

Janowitz, Morris, *Air University Review*, "Patriotism and the U.S. All-Volunteer Military," Jan-Feb 1982, pg. 31.　6A

_____, Re: role of the military in society, see Stephen E. Ambrose and James A. Barber, Jr., 1972, pp. 166-173. C118

Jefferson, Thomas (1743-1826), *Washington Star*, see Martin Kaplan, May 11, 1981, pg. C-1. F130

_____, Re: Declaration of Independence, see Sol Bloom, 1937.　6

Johansen, Robert C., *SALT II: Illusion and Reality*, Institute for World Order, New York, 1979. C028

Johnston, Moira, *National Geographic*, "Silicon Valley: High Tech . . . " October 1982, pp. 459-477. B059

Jones, Clayton, *Christian Science Monitor*, "Air Force elbows industry . . ." September 12, 1980, pg. 4. D045

Jones, Clayton, *Christian Science Monitor*, "Air Force elbows industry . . . " September 12, 1980, pg. 4. D045

Judge, John F., *Government Executive*, Editorial, Re: Paperwork Reduction Act, October 1980. B092

Kannan, N. P., *Washington Post*, "U.S. Faith in Reason . . . " March 10, 1981, pg. A-13. G140

Kant, Immanuel (1724-1804), Re: war does not require hostility, see Clarence Morris, 1959, pg. 259. PREF

Kaplan, Martin, *Washington Star*, "A Widening Gulf Between Science and the Rest of Us," May 11, 1981, pg. C-1. F130

Kaplan, Stephen, *U.S. News & World Report*, "Where Soviets Flexed Their Military Muscle," May 11, 1981, pp. 30-31. B024

Keats, John, *They Fought Alone*, Philadelphia: J. B. Lippincott Comp., 1963. E048

Kelly, Brian J., *Chicago Sun-Times*, "Carter's New A-Policy: Deterrent or Trigger," August 17, 1980, pg. 10.　1C

Kelly, Orr, *U.S. News & World Report*, "Inside Story of the Trident Debacle," March 30, 1981, pp. 21-22. B039

Kemp, Jack F., Re: background study for defense appropriations, see John M. Collins, 1980.　1A

Kempster, Norman, *Los Angeles Times*, see Robert C. Toth, September 11, 1980, pg. 1. B039

Keynes, John Maynard, *A Treatise on Money*, London: Macmillan and Comp., 1958. B092

Khrushchev, Nikita S., *The Imperialism Reader*, see Louis L. Snyder, September 23, 1960, pg. 595, 609. 2PER

Kimball, Spencer W., *New York Times*, "Mormon Church Opposes Placing MX Missiles in Utah and Nevada," May 6, 1981, pg. 1. A036

Kinney, A. J., *The Air Force Officer's Guide*, Stackpole Books, Harrisburg, Penn., 1976. G140

Kinsley, Michael, *Outer Space and Inner Sanctums*, New York: John Wiley and Sons, 1976.   4F

Kintner, William R., *National Review*, "The End of Socialist Anti-Communism," December 18, 1980, pg. 1504. C030

Kirk, John and Robert Young Jr., *Great Weapons of World War II*, New York: Bonanza Books, 1941. E047

Klass, Philip J., *Aviation Week & Space Technology*, Re: directed-energy technology, July 28, 1980, pg. 32. D046

———, *New York Times Magazine*, "Spies in the Sky," September 3, 1972, pg. 35. B060

———, *Secret Sentries in Space*, New York: Random House, 1971. B060

Knorr, Klaus, Re: motivation for war, see James N. Rosenau, 1961. B095

Koestler, Arthur, *Sleepwalkers*, New York: Macmillan and Comp., 1959. 2PER

Korb, Lawrence J., *Air University Review*, "The Case for the MX," July-August 1980, pp. 3-10. A032

———, *The Fall and Rise of the Pentagon*, Greenwood Press, Westport, Conn., 1979.   3

Krumpe, Paul F., *The World Remote Sensing Bibliographic Index*, Tensor Industries, 1976.   4B

Kugler, Jacek and A.F.K. Organski, *International Security*, "Deterrence and the Arms Race," Spring 1980, pp. 105-138.   1

Kurtz, Howard and Harriet Kurtz, *Checkpoint*, "Global Information Cooperative," September 1979.   1

———, *IEEE Aerospace and Electronic Systems Society Newsletter*, "A Global Information Complex," May 1983, pp. 1-2.   4B

LaBelle, G. G., *Phoenix Gazette*, "State Most Likely Site of 1st MX," October 2, 1981, pg. A-1. A032

LaBerge, Walter B., *Signal*, "Improving NATO Through Armaments Collaboration," April 1979, pp. 43-45. C031

Laird, Melvin R., *Reader's Digest*, "Should Our Missile Forces Go To Sea?" September 1980, pp. 101-105. B038

Lamoureaux, Naomi R., *The Freeman*, Re: From Antitrust to Supply-Side Economics, June 1981, pg. 381. A004

Large, Arlen J., *Wall Street Journal*, "Quick Fix: Navigation Satellites . . . " July 9, 1981, pg. 50. B040

Lawrence, David, *U.S. News & World Report*, "Which Commander-in-Chief?" October 12, 1956, pg. 152. C118

Leider, Robert, *Rocky Mountain News*, Denver, Colorado, "When Computers Control Maintenance . . . " June 15, 1980. E127

Leigh, David, *Manchester Guardian*, "America's nuclear nut-in-a-cup," November 30, 1980, pg. 8. A032

Lellouche, Pierre, *Foreign Affairs*, "Europe and Her Defense," Spring 1981, pp. 813-834. C031

Lenin (Vladimir Ilyich Ulyanov, sometimes called Nikolai, 1870-1924), *Theses on the Fundamental Tasks of the Second Congress of the Communist International*, July 4, 1920, see William Ebenstein, 1962. 2PER

Lenorovitz, Jeffrey M., *Aviation Week & Space Technology*, "ALCM to Enter Inventory Next Year," June 16, 1980, pg. 176. C041

Lerner, Max, Re: The Supreme Court and American Capitalism, see Robert G. McCloskey, 1957. A006

Lewin, Leonard C., *Report from Iron Mountain*, New York: Dial Press, Inc., 1967. PREF

Lewis, Anthony, *New York Times*, "A Chorus of Yahoos," May 26, 1975. D119

Lewis, Flora, *Washington Star*, "The Super Bureaucracy: Time to Check the NSC," September 12, 1980, pg. 11. D015

Lewis, Kevin N., *Scientific American*, "Intermediate-Range Nuclear Weapons," December 1980, pp. 63-73. B024

_____, *Scientific American*, "The Prompt and Delayed Effects of Nuclear War," July 1979. B024

Libby, Leona Marshall, *The Uranium People*, New York: Crane Russak, Charles Scribner's Sons, 1979, pg. 243. E048

Lincoln, Abraham (1809-1865), Re: A nation divided against itself cannot stand, *Bible*, Mark 3:25 (paraphrase), June 17, 1858. B112

———, Re: "last best hope on earth," see A. J. Kinney, 1976, pg. 4. G140

———, Gettysburg Address (Lincoln wrote five different versions, the fifth version represents as exactly as can be known the speech he delivered, November 19, 1863; he signed only the copy he made in 1864), *The World Book Encyclopedia*, Chicago: World Book-Childcraft International, Inc., 1980, pg. 164. B111

Locke, John (1632-1704), Re: instrumentalist view of the nation-state, see William Ebenstein, 1962. PREF

Lord, John, *Beacon Lights of History*, New York: James Clarke and Co., 1883. A002

Lowell, James Russell (Editor), *Atlantic Monthly*, see Julia Ward Howe, February 1862. 2PER

Lowenthal, Mark M., Congressional Research Service, CRS-Issue Brief 76039, "Intelligence Community: Reform and Reorganization," May 7, 1976. A090

Lugar, Richard G., Member, Senate Select Committee on Intelligence, "Principal Findings . . . to Monitor the SALT II Treaty," Working Paper, December 14, 1979. C028

MacArthur, Douglas (January 26, 1880-April 5, 1964), Re: Farewell Address: Duty-Honor-Country, May 1962, see Lawrence P. Crocker. G137

Macbain, Merle, *Sea Power*, "The Coast Guard Today . . . " August 1980, pp. 21-28. B040

Madsen, Truman G., *Eternal Man*, Deseret Book Co., Salt Lake City, Utah, 1966. C117

Main, Henry James Summer, *Ancient Law*, London: John Murray, 1897 (first edition 1861). G136

Maloney, Elbert S., *Dutton's Navigation and Piloting*, Naval Institute Press, Annapolis, Maryland, 1978. B040

Manion, Clarence (1896-1979), *The Key to Peace*, Notre Dame University, available from *The Freeman*. A108

———, *The Freeman*, "Legalized Immorality," July 1982, pg. 426. A108

Marshall, Leona, *The Uranium People*, see Leona Marshall Libby, 1979. E048

Marshall, Peter, *Military Review*, feature story inside cover, July 1980. A106

Marx, Karl (1818-1883), *Communist Manifesto*, 1848, see William Ebenstein, 1962.   2

_____, Re: The Poverty of Philosophy, *Sea Power*, September 1980, B039

Mastrangelo, Joseph P., *Washington Post*, "Haunted Survivors of the USS Bullhead," August 16, 1981, pg. F-1. E050

Maurer, Robert A. and George J. James, *The Constitution of the United States*, Boston: D. C. Heath and Comp., 1925. B110

Mayer, Andrew C., Re: authority to order the use of nuclear weapons, Committee Print, 94th Congress, 1st Session, December 1, 1975.   2A, D120

McCloskey, Robert G., *Essays in Constitutional Law*, New York: Alfred A. Knopf, 1957. A006

McGeoch, Sir Ian, *Naval Forces*, Editorial, Vol. 1, No. 3, 1980, pg. 3. B025

McGlasson, W. D., *Retired Officer*, "Our Reserve Forces Today," September 1980, pg. 15. A106

McGwire, Michael, *United States Naval Institute Proceedings*, "The Rationale for the Development of Soviet Seapower," May 1980, pp. 155-183. B025

McIntyre, Thomas J., *The Fear Brokers*, Philadelphia: Pilgrim Press, 1979. E050

McKinney, Stewart B., HR5540, "The Defense Industrial Base Revitalization Act," 1983.   5B

McLuhan, Marshall, *From Cliche to Archetype*, New York: Pocket Books, 1971. 4PER

_____, *The Medium is the Massage*, New York: Bantam Books, 1967.   4

McMillin, Sue, *Gazette Telegraph*, Colorado Springs, Colorado, "Goldwater sees more Latin conflict ... " June 2, 1983, pg. 1. 4PER

Meloy, Thomas, *National Geographic*, "The Laser's Bright Magic," December 1966, pp. 858-881. D046

Mercer, Donald L., *Military Review*, "How Viable an Option? The Warsaw Pact ... " October 1980, pp. 23-31; November 1980, pp. 28-36. C031

Mezerik, A. G., *International Review Service*, "The Arms Race," Vol. III, No. 38, November 1957. D044

_____, *International Review Service*, "Outer Space," Vol. VI, No. 56, 1960. D044

Mill, John Stuart (1806-1873), Re: dualism in pragmatism as implemented by William James, see William Ebenstein, 1962, pp. 522-588. 4PER

Miller, Charles A., *Popular Science*, "Coming: A New Generation of Super-realistic Computer Images," November 1982, pg. 67. B062

Moe, Ronald C., Congressional Research Service Report No. 78-244 GOV, "Presidential Succession," January 25, 1979. C113

Montesquieu, Charles Louis de Secondat (1689-1755), *The Spirit of the Laws*, see Clarence Morris, 1959, pp. 134-158. B110

Morgan, Arthur E., *One True Faith: As a Cause of War*, Henry Regnery Co., Hinsdale, Illinois, 1948. B027

Morris, Charles, *The Pragmatic Movement in American Philosophy*, New York: George Braziller, 1970. F129

Morris, Clarence, *Great Legal Philosophers*, Philadelphia: University of Pennsylvania Press, 1959. 2PER

Murphy Commission, "Organization of the Government . . . " U.S. Government Printing Office, Washington, DC, June 27, 1975. B096

Naisbitt, John, *Megatrends*, New York: Warner Books, 1982.   4

Napoleon, Bonaparte (1769-1821), Re: absolute power of rulers, see Louis Henkin, 1972, pg. 278 fn.   6C

Natter, Raymond, Congressional Research Service Issue Brief No. IB80087, "Presidential Emergency Powers . . . " February 20, 1981. B093

Nerlich, Uwe, *Washington Quarterly*, "Theater Nuclear Forces: Is NATO Running Out of Options?" Winter 1980, pp. 100-125. C030

Neustadt, Richard M., Information Industry Association Breakfast, see Robert S. Willard, December 12, 1980. B092

Newton, Sir Isaac (December 25, 1642-March 20, 1727), Re: the man and his ideas, see J. Bronowski, 1973, pp. 221-227.   6G

―――, *Encyclopaedia Britannica*, Cambridge, England: at the University Press, New York, Vol. XIX, 1911, pg. 591, 589.   6G

Nicholas, H. G., *The United Nations as a Political Institution*, London: Oxford University Press, 1971. G139

Nicola, Thomas J., "Congressional Veto of Executive Actions," Congressional Research Service, CRS-Issue Brief IB 76006, June 17, 1981, update. D123

Niebuhr, Rheinhold, *Moral Man and Immoral Society*, New York: Charles Scribner's Sons, 1932. A108

Nitze, Paul H., *Foreign Affairs*, "Strategy in the Decade of the 1980s," Fall 1980, pp. 82-101. B024

Noel, John V., *Division Officer's Guide*, Naval Institute Press, Annapolis, Maryland, 1972.   1C

Nussbaum, Arthur, *A Concise History of the Law of Nations*, New York: Macmillan Comp., 1954. G136

Oakes, John B., *New York Times*, "MX: Tick, Tick, Tick," October 21, 1980, pg. 19. B039

O'Leary, Jeremiah, *Washington Star*, Re: expectations of the nation, May 20, 1981. D045

Organski, A. F. K., *International Security*, see Jacek Kugler, Spring 1980, pp. 105-138.   1

Parks, W. Hays, *Air University Review*, "Rolling Thunder and the Law of War," Jan-Feb 1982, pp.2-23. A023

Paskins, Barrie and Michael Dockrill, *Parameters*, "The Ethics of War," March 1980, pg. 102. E049

Pincus, Walter, *Denver Post*, "U.S. Army Wants Pre-Clearance . . . " July 21, 1982. pg. A-3. C043

Pines, Burton Yale, *Back To Basics*, New York: William Morrow, 1982.   6

Planck, Max Karl Ernst Ludwig (1858-1947), *Washington Post*, see Sandy Rovner, March 15, 1981, pg. F-1. F130

Plato (427-347 B.C.), *Republic*, see William Ebenstein, 1962. 2PER

Pollack, Louis H., *The Constitution and the Supreme Court*, New York: The World Pub. Comp., 1966. B109

Pond, Elizabeth, *Christian Science Monitor*, "The Real Euromissile Tally," November 27, 1981, pg. 12. A021

_____, *Christian Science Monitor*, "Deterring Nuclear War," August 26, 1980, pg. 12. D015

Postbrief, Sam, *Naval War College Review*, "Departure from Incrementalism . . . " March-April 1980, pp. 34-57.   1D

Powers, Patrick W., *A Guide to National Defense*, New York: Frederick A. Praeger, 1964. C043

Powers, William, *Stations of the Mind*, see William Glasser, 1981.   1A

Prigagine, Ilya, Re: Second Law of Thermodynamics, see K. E. Woehler, July 1980. C029

_____, Re: Second Law of Thermodynamics, see Jeremy Rifkin, 1980. C029

Pusey, Merlo, *Charles Evans Hughes*, New York: Macmillan Comp., 1951. 5A

Pyle, Ernie (1900-1945), *Brave Men*, New York: Henry Holt and Co., 1943, 1944. E124

Pythagoras of Samos (425 B.C.) Re: founder of modern science, see Arthur Koestler, 1959, pg. 26. 3PER

Quinn, Diana, *Iron County Record*, Utah, "Group cautiously confident about MX," July 2, 1981, pg. A-1. A032

_____, *Iron County Record*, Utah, "Anti-MX citizens lobby in D.C.," July 2, 1981, pg. A-1. A032

Quinn, Geoff, *Council on Economic Priorities Newsletter*, see Gordon Adams, June 1981. A091

Radway, Laurence, *Foreign Policy*, "The Curse of Free Elections," Fall 1980, pp. 61-73. 1PER

Raper, David (editor), *Gateway to God*, Re: Simon Weil, 1974. 2PER

Reagan, Ronald, Re: last best hope on earth, *Washington Post*, see N. P. Kannan, March 10, 1981, pg. A-13. G140

Rees, Richard (translator), *Gateway to God*, Re: Simon Weil, 1974. 2PER

Relyea, Harold C., Congressional Research Service Report, "Background and Status E.O.11490," July 29, 1976. B093

_____, Committee Print, "A Brief History of Emergency Powers . . . " July 1974. 5PER

Rickover, Hyman George, *CBS-TV 60 Minutes*, Washington, DC, WDVM, 7 p.m., March 28, 1982. 3PER

Rifkin, Jeremy, *Entropy*, New York: Viking, 1980. C029

Ritter, Lawrence S. and William L. Silber, *Money*, New York: Basic Books, 1970. B092

Roberts, Joel E. L., *Military Review*, "Managing Soldiers," July 1980. A106

Roberts, Lawrence G. and Barry D. Wessler, *American Federation of Information Processing Society Conference Proceedings*, "Computer network development . . . " Vol. 36, 1970, pg. 540. E072

Robinson, Clarence A., Jr., *Aviation Week & Space Technology*, Re: directed-energy technology, July 28, 1980, pg. 32. D046

Roemer, Michael, *World Development*, "Dependence and Industrialization Strategies," May 1981, pp. 429-434.   6

Roosevelt, Franklin D., Four Freedoms speech, January 6, 1941, see *Illustrated Heritage Dictionary*. C114

Ropelewski, Robert R., *Aviation Week & Space Technology*, "U.S. B-52 Bomber Fleet . . . " June 16, 1980, pg. 192. C041

Rosenau, James N., *International Politics and Foreign Policy*, New York: Free Press, 1961. B095

Rosner, Roy D., *Packet Switching*, Lifetime Learning Pub., 1982. E073

Rosten, Leo, *The Joys of Yiddish*, see Marshall McLuhan, 1971. 4PER

Roth, William V., National Press Club Luncheon, Re: Department of Trade proposal, February 22, 1983.   5C

Rovner, Sandy, *Washington Post*, "Photons, Philosophy, and the Eccles of the Mind," March 15, 1981, pg. F-1. F130

Rutland, Robert Allen, *The Birth of the Bill of Rights 1776-1791*, University of North Carolina Press, Chapel Hill, 1955. C117

Sagan, Carl, *The Cosmic Connection*, New York: Dell Pub. Co. Inc., 1975. A105

Sakharov, Andrei, *Washington Post, Parade Magazine Section*, "An Appeal," August 16, 1981. B027

Sampson, Anthony, *The Arms Bazaar*, New York: Bantam Books, 1978. F133

Saussy, F. Tupper, *Miracle on Main Street*, Spencer Judd Pub., Sewanee, Tenn., 1980. F129

Sawyer, Lynette, *Iron County Record*, Utah, "Expert says MX won't work," July 23, 1981, pg. A-3. A032

Schaef, Anne Wilson, *Women's Reality*, Winston Pub., 1980. C098

Scheer, Walter, *With Enough Shovels: Reagan, Bush and Nuclear War*, New York: Random House, 1982. B007

_____, *Los Angeles Times*, "Bush Assails Carter Defense Strategy," January 24, 1980.   1

Schemmer, Benjamin F., *Air Force Journal*, "U.S. Has Been Flying Virtually Invisible Aircraft for over Two Years," September 1980.   1E

Schlesinger, James, Annual Report of the Secretary of Defense FY75, see Lawrence J. Korb, 1979. 4PER

Scoville, Herbert, Jr., *Foreign Affairs*, "Is Espionage Necessary for Our Security," April 1976. C101

_____, *Bulletin of Atomic Scientists*, "Verification of Nuclear Arms," October 1970, pg. 8. A090

Servan-Schreiber, J.-J., *The American Challenge*, New York: Atheneum, 1968.   3D

Shapley, Deborah, *Science Magazine*, "Soviet Killer Satellites," September 3, 1976. C028

Shields, Mark, *Washington Post*, "No Small Change," March 20, 1981, pg. A-23. B092

Sienkiewicz, Stanley, *World Politics*, "Observations on the Impact of Uncertainty . . ." October 1979, pp. 90-110. A023

Silber, William L., *Money*, see Lawrence S. Ritter, 1970. F129

Silva, Ruth, *Presidential Succession*, University of Michigan Press, Ann Arbor, 1951. C113

Simes, Dimitri K., *International Security*, "Deterrence and Coercion in Soviet Policy," Winter 1980-1981, pp. 80-103. C012

Skier, Kenneth, *Popular Computing*, "Popular Review: Hardware . . . " December 1982, pp. 82-86. C104

Skousen, Cleon, *State of the Nation*, "The Federal Reserve: Broken Promises," July 1982, pg. 4. B092

Sloss, Leon, *Los Angeles Times*, "No: Its Evolutionary . . . " August 31, 1980, pg. 3. D015

Smith, R. Jeffrey, *Science*, "Pentagon Moves Toward First Strike Capability," May 2, 1982, pp. 596-598.   2A

Snow, C. P., *Science and Government*, Harvard University Press, Cambridge, Mass., 1961. 3PER

Snow, Donald M., *Air University Review*, "The MX-Basing Mode Muddle," July-August 1980, pp. 11-25. A032

Snyder, Louis L., *The Imperialism Reader*, D. Van Nostrand Comp., 1962. 2PER

Sohn, Louis B., *World Peace Through World Law*, see Grenville Clark, 1958. 5A

Solomon, Norman, *The Nation*, "The Atomic-Weapons Lobby is Gaining," October 11, 1980, pp. 335-338. D069

Solzhenitsyn, Aleksandr, *Foreign Affairs,* "Misconceptions about Russia Are a Threat to America," Spring 1980, pg. 797. B024

Stalin, Joseph, *Foundations of Leninism,* see William Ebenstein, 1962, pp. 726-740.   2B

Steel, Ronald, *The End of Alliance,* New York: Viking, 1964.   4G

————, translator of, *The American Challenge,* see J.-J. Servan-Schreiber, 1968, pp. 276-277. 4PER

Stein, Jess (Editor), *Random House Dictionary of the English Language,* New York: Random House, 1967. A088

Stone, I. F., *Washington Star,* "Casualties in a Limited Nuclear War," August 23, 1980, pg. 11. D015

Stone, Marvin, *U.S. News & World Report,* "A Plea for Understanding," March 2, 1981, pp. 79-80. A037

Strout, Richard L., *Christian Science Monitor,* "The $500 billion arms bill," September 12, 1980, pg. 23. D045

Surles, Security Officer, Charles Evans Hughes Display, Supreme Court Building, May 19, 1981, 1:25 p.m., pouring rain and had to borrow a pencil.   5A

Szulc, Tad, *The New Republic,* "The New Brinksmanship," November 8, 1980, pp. 18-21.   1C

Tatu, Michel, *Le Figaro,* Paris, France, "Toward a Counterforce Doctrine," August 8, 1980, pg. 24. B009

Teller, Edward, *New York Times,* "Re-open the Skies . . . " April 25, 1971. A090

Thaler, Richard, *Journal of Economic Behavior and Organization,* "Toward a Positive Theory of Consumer Choice," March 1980, pp. 39-60. A004

Tocqueville, Alexis de (1805-1859), *Democracy in America,* written 1835-1840, see William Ebenstein, 1962. 2PER

————, Re: Democracy in America, see Richard B. Foster, Testimony, September 29, 1981. A022

————, *Washington Post,* see N. P. Kannan, March 10, 1981, pg. A-13. G140

Toffler, Alvin, *The Third Wave,* New York: William Morrow, 1980. D123

Toth, Robert C. and Norman Kempster, *Los Angeles Times,* "Costly but Untried," September 11, 1980, pg. 1. B039

Truax, Robert C., "Sea Dragon," see Jerry Grey, 1979, pg. 27, 59. B039

Truman, Harry S., Re: absolute power of rulers, see Louis Henkin, 1972, pg. 278 fn.   6C

_____, *Public Papers of the Presidents of the United States*, U.S. Government Printing Office, Washington, DC, 1945, pg. 197.   3E

Tsipis, Kosta, *Scientific American*, "Laser Weapons," December 1981, pg. 51. D046

Tuchman, Barbara, *Parameters*, Re: commentary on *Guns of August*, June 1980, pg. 88. A023

_____, *Yankee*, Re: interview and commentary, August 1980. A023

_____, *Guns of August*, review, *Parameters*, March 1980, pp. 2-9. A023

Tuerck, David G., *The Freeman*, Re: Rational Expectations and Supply Side Economics, June 1981, pg. 381. A004

Ture, Norman B., *The Freeman*, Re: Supply Side Analysis and Public Policy, June 1981, pg. 381. A004

Ulam, Stanislaw, Re: the importance of pattern, see Douglas R. Hofstadter, November 1981, pg. 22. C102

Ulyanov, Vladimir Ilyich, see Lenin, July 4, 1920. 2PER

Vattel, Emmerich de (1711-1767), *The Law of Nations*, see Clarence Morris, 1959. B109

Vaughn, Robert L., *Manufacturing Engineering*, "President's Message," January 1982, pg. 4. A002

Von Mises, Ludwig, *The Anti-Capitalistic Mentality*, D. Van Nostrand Comp., 1956.   4E

_____, *U.S. News & World Report*, "What's Behind the War on Business," October 19, 1956, pp. 156-175.   4E

Von Raven, Wolfram, *Die Welt*, Germany, "Not New, but Effective," August 19, 1980, pg. 6. C012

Voute, C., *ITC Journal*, "Remote Sensing," 1982-1, pp. 37-44.   4B

Wagner, Richard E., *The Freeman*, Re: The Enterprise System, June 1981, pg. 381. A004

Wakin, Malham M., *Parameters*, "Morality and the Military Profession," June 1980, pg. 95. E049

Wallbank, T. Walker, et al., *Civilization Past and Present*, Chicago: Scott, Foresman and Comp., 1962. A005

Wallop, Malcom, *Congressional Record*, Re: spaced-based lasers, July 1, 1980, pg. S9074. A020

_____, Re: Dear Colleague letter, United States Senate, released, June 25, 1980, 9:09 a.m. D046

_____, *Strategic Review*, "Opportunities and Imperatives . . . " Fall 1979, pp. 13-21. D046

Warnke, Paul C., *Los Angeles Times*, "Yes: The Revision of U.S. Strategy Implies a Belief in Limited War," August 31, 1980, pg. 3. D015

Washington, George (1732-1799), Re: Farewell Address to the people, printed September 19, 1796, see Sol Bloom, 1937. A089

Weil, Simone, *Gateway to God*, Glasgow: Fontana Books, 1974. 2PER

_____, *The Need for Roots*, Re: study of reciprocal duties of individual and the State, 1942. 2PER

Weinberger, Andrew D., *Freedom and Protection: The Bill of Rights*, Greenwood Press, Westport, Conn., 1962. PREF

Weizenbaum, Joseph, *Computer Power and Human Reason*, San Francisco: W. H. Freeman and Comp., 1976. C099

Whitehead, Alfred North, *Process and Reality*, Harper Torch Books, Harper and Row, 1960; also New York: Macmillan Comp., 1927. 3PER

Wicklein, John, *Electronic Nightmare*, New York: Viking, 1981.   4

Wiley, Richard E., Information Industry Association Breakfast, see Robert S. Willard, December 12, 1980. B092

Willard, Robert S., Information Industry Association Breakfast, "An Assessment of 1980 . . . " December 12, 1980. B092

Williams, Dennis A., *Time*, "Arkansas's Missile Scare," September 29, 1980, pg. 33. A032

Wilson, George C., *Washington Post*, "Military Seeking to Add 72,000 Civilians . . . " August 14, 1981, pg. A-13. B095

_____, *Washington Post*, "Change in Nuclear Target Policy Not a Radical One, Brown Says," August 21, 1981, pg. 1.   1C

Woehler, K. E., Naval Postgraduate School Study, "Ilya Prigagine: Second Law of Thermodynamics," July 1980. C029

Wolfe, Tom, *The Right Stuff*, New York: Farrar, Straus, and Giroux, Inc., 1980. F130

Wolff, Christian (1679-1754), *The Law of Nations*, see Clarence Morris, 1959. B109

Woolf, Virginia, *To The Lighthouse*, New York: Harcourt, Brace, and World, Inc., 1927.   6C

Young, Robert, Jr., *Great Weapons of World War II*, see John Kirk, 1941. E047

List of reports or topics

Analyses of Effects of Limited Nuclear war, Committee Print: 94th Congress, 1st Session, September 18, 1975. D014

ARPANET Directory, SRI International Network Information Center, November 1980. E072

Authority To Order The Use Of Nuclear Weapons, Committee Print, 94th Congress, 1st Session, December 1975. C012

Colloquium Heptaplomeres, *Encyclopaedia Britannica*, Eleventh Edition, 1911, Vol. IV, pg. 110. B027

Comprehensive Test Ban Treaty, see Ola Dahlman and Hans Israelson, 1977, Appendix.   4D

Computer Advertising Special Section, *Aviation Week & Space Technology*, December 1, 1980, pp. 47-110. C104

Eighteenth Amendment, United States Constitution, see Sol Bloom, 1937. E018

Executive Order 12148, see Harold C. Relyea, July 20, 1979. B093

Executive Order 11490, see Harold C. Relyea, July 29, 1976. B093

Executive Order 11921, see Harold C. Relyea, July 29, 1976. B093

Greek Law, *Encyclopaedia Britannica*, Eleventh Edition, 1911, Vol. XII, pg. 501. 2PER

Guided Missileman, Bureau of Navy Personnel, 1958.   3

Hughes Exhibit Catalogue: Charles Evans Hughes, Supreme Court Historical Society Yearbook, 1981, pp. 95-112.   5A

Illustrated Heritage Dictionary and Information Book, Boston: Houghton Mifflin Comp., 1977, pg. 1750-1751.   3E

Modernization of Strategic forces, Special Report, *Aviation Week & Space Technology*, June 16, 1980. A020

MX Missile Basing, OTA-ISC-139, June 1981. A020

North-South: A Program for Survival, Brandt Commission, *Parameters*, June 1980, pg. 93. A006

Partial Test Ban Treaty of 1963, see Ola Dahlman and Hans Israelson, 1977, Appendix.   4D

Presidential Directive/National Security Council-37, "National Space Policy," see Zbigniew Brzezinski. C099

Presidential Directive/National Security Council-42, "Civil and Further National Space Policy," see Zbigniew Brzezinski. C099

Presidential Directive/National Security council-54, "Civil Operational Remote Sensing," see Zbigniew Brzezinski, see Francis P. Hoeber. C099

Re: Administration to temporarily cut U.S. SLBMs . . . *Defense Daily*, October 29, 1980, pg. 297. B039

Re: A New Life for a High-Flying Bird, *Time*, December 22, 1980, pg. 64. E016

Re: Carter's Response, *Le Figaro*, August 12, 1980, pg. 1. B039

Re: Deep-six sub-scuttling scheme, *San Jose Mercury*, October 27, 1980. B039

Re: Digital transmission equipment for satellite systems, *Telecommunication Journal*, Vol. 44, II, 1977, pg. 54. B059

Re: Europe May Hope, *Frankfurter Allgemeine*, Germany, November 6, 1980, pg. 1. 1PER

Re: Gigabits of information transfer, *Armed Forces Journal International*, February 1980, pg. 59. A052

Re: Information Engineering, *Government Executive*, June 1980, pg. 16. A002

Re: Information for the 1980s, White House Conference on Library and Information Services, 1979. A004

Re: NATO partners sign major missile pact, *Financial Times*, London, August 15, 1980. C041

Re: Navy Chooses Georgia Site . . . *Aerospace Daily*, October 28, 1980, pg. 320. B039

Re: New nuclear strategy, *Aftenposten*, Oslo, Norway, August, 18, 1980, pg. 2. B009

Re: New nuclear strategy, *Frankfurter Allgemeine*, Germany, August 12, 1980. pg. 8. B009

Re: New nuclear strategy, *Helsingin Sanomat*, Helsinki, Finland, August 16, 1980, pg. 2. B009

Re: North Atlantic Alliance, *The Washington Quarterly*, Fall 1980. C030

Re: North Atlantic Treaty Organization, *Hammond Almanac*, New Jersey: Hammond Almanac, Inc., 1980, pg. 719. C031

Re: Paperwork Reduction Act, *Congressional Record*, December 1980, pp. H11374-H11380. B092

Re: Partners in preparedness, *National Defense*, June 1980. A002

Re: PD-59 Affair, *Washington Post*, August 22, 1980. D015

Re: PD-59: Why? *Los Angeles Times*, August 15, 1980. D015

Re: Queen Beatrix urges N-arms reduction, *Boulder Daily Camera*, Colorado, April 22, 1982. PREF

Re: Rejection phenomenon, *Le Monde*, France, November 6, 1980, pg. 1. 1PER

Re: Selected pro and con materials on war powers legislation, Congressional Research Service, JX 4552, February 24, 1971. B093

Re: Space patrol — How the U.S. watches the Russians, *U.S. News & World Report*, November 24, 1969. A055

Re: Stealth disclosure, *Defense Daily*, September 23, 1980, pp. 111-115.   1E

Re: Titan strikes again, *Pilot*, Norfolk, Virginia, September 24, 1980. A032

Re: U.S. Air Force Is Flying Invisibly, *Die Welt*, Germany, August 25, 1980, pg. 5. C041

Re: What is Muskie's role, *Denver Post*, Colorado, August 21, 1980. D015

Re: Zero option, *Daily Sentinel*, Grand Junction, Colorado, January 18, 1983, pg. 1. C030

Re: Zumwalt, E. R., letter and stealth, *Journal of Commerce*, September 11, 1980, pg. 4. E017

Roman Law, *Encyclopaedia Britannica*, Eleventh Edition, 1911, Vol. XXIII, Pg. 526. 2PER

Senate Document No. 92-82, War Powers. A005

Senate Report No. 94-922, National Emergencies and Delegated Emergency Powers, 94th Congress, 2d Session, May 28, 1976. A005, 6D

Twenty-first Amendment, United States Constitution, see Sol Bloom, 1937. E018

United Nations Document: E.83.IX.3, Implications of Establishing an International Satellite Monitoring Agency, Spring 1983. C028

War Powers Act (Public Law 93-148), Congressional Research Service Issue Brief No. IB76006, see Thomas Nicola.   6E

Index

ABM, Anti-Ballistic Missiles, 32, 116, 146
academic disciplines,
  political turf of, 159
accidental nuclear holocaust. *See* nuclear
  holocaust, accidental
acquired skill. *See* natural dueling partners,
  born talent and acquired skill
action-reaction partners, 4
  See also natural dueling partners
action-reaction response, 3, 222-223
  See also human action, motivated by fear
advanced industrial society, 86
adventurism. *See* Soviet adventurism
AEC, Atomic Energy Commission. *See*
  United States, Department of Energy
Aegean Sea, 42
Afghanistan,
  invasion of, 13, 53
Airborne Warning And Control System, 72,
  109-110
airplanes,
  invisible to radar, 69
  pilots fly, 68
    See also human judgement
  without pilots, 68, 70-71
    See also missile, cruise
air space, 106-107, 111
  controlled, 112
  merger, 111
  safety, 106-107, 111-112
air traffic control, 112
Aleutian chain, 109
Alexander, Czar of Russia, 210

alliances,
  dissolving, 9, 209-211
  See also coupling
America First, 153-154
American Eagle, 10, 177-178, 231-233
  glide-perch dualism of, 177-178
  nest egg of, 230-233
  selectivity of the perch of, 177-178
  soaring and selecting of, 177-178
  See also natural dueling partners
American ideals, 30, 130, 132, 136, 148,
  176-178, 223
  See also national ideals
American industry, 72, 138
  See also industrial base
American independence, 30, 176, 213
American military, 38, 47, 56, 64, 75, 129,
  138, 168-172, 176-177, 181, 206-209
  ambience of the, 221
  cadence for the living, 176
  destroying the nation, 171, 207
  epitaph for, 88
  heartbeat of the nation, 176, 228-229
    See also, living nation, organic
      concept of
  industrial abuse of, 38
  inventing the future, 176, 231-232
  manipulated by a political minority,
    38, 207-209, 211, 227
    See also Vietnam War
  peacetime mission for, 212-213, 231-232
  presence, 45, 221-222,
    ambience of, 221

creativity of, 223
electronic, 223, 226-227
mystique of, 226-227
superiority, 5, 8, 13-14, 21, 30, 206, 209
campaign promise of, 21
created by technology push, 5
the nation in action, 225-229
tradition, 177-179, 206-207
American nation, *vi*, 72-73, 176, 226-229
See also living nation, organic concept of
American nest egg, 230-233
double yolk of, 232-233
American people, the, 27, 29, 37-38, 57, 62,
72, 77, 79, 83, 86, 88, 90, 128, 131-132,
136, 138, 140-141, 156, 168, 172,
179-181, 205, 215, 228-230, 232-233
central authority of the United States
government, 199
guilt of, 83
protection of, 74
responsibility of, 179
thinking and acting like a people, 228-229
voice of, 215
American population,
protection of, 64, 116
survivability of, 12
American Revolution, 176, 184, 207
fight for political independence, 176
the First, 176
American tax dollars, 87, 118, 153-154, 168
for detection and early warning, 154
for electronic industries, 148, 154
for electronics, 154
for information industries, 47, 168
invested in,
information dissemination, 7
information gathering, 7
information processing, 7
See also defense spending
American taxpayers, 19, 87, 104, 127
pay the premium, 139-141
pay the price, 227
American Telephone & Telegraph, 119
American tradition, 30, 36-37, 88
American voters, 29, 86, 171
attracting the attention of, 10, 16
See also public opinion, power of
Anders, Gunther, 83
Aquinas, Saint Thomas, 137
Arctic watch-dog, 109
aristocracy,
in democracy, 178
of virtue and talent, 178
armed peace of the industrial elite, 9, 170,
211-212
destructiveness of the, 170
arms build-up, 142
Arms Control and Disarmament Agency,
146
arms control negotiations, 21-23, 142, 146

arms limitation talks, 22
See also Strategic Arms Limitation Talks
Arsenal of Democracy, 154, 169
Articles of Confederation, 184
ASS, yours or mine. *See* air space, safety
assimilation of technology, 52-53
impact on the human soul, 53
atmosphere,
destruction by nuclear explosion, 87, 113,
115-117
disturbed by exploding bombs, 56, 58-59,
71, 87
incineration of, 114, 116
needed to sustain life, 117
re-entry into, 59, 67
re-entry vehicle, 75
there is only one, 106, 117
trajectory through, 58, 108-109
atmospheric chemistry, 113, 115
artificially changed, 113, 115-117
atmospheric conditions,
along trajectory path, 58-59, 108-109
influence on people, 52
atmospheric contamination, 115-117
atmospheric physics, 159-160
atmospheric science, 159-160
atomic bomb, 79, 86
See also bomb, fission; nuclear reaction,
fission
atomic clock, 65
Atomic Energy Commission. *See* United
States, Department of Energy
AT&T. *See* American Telephone &
Telegraph
attack, nuclear, 2, 23
See also surprise attack
Austad, Mark Evans, 42
Austria, 210
authority. *See* natural dueling partners,
authority and responsibility
authority to order the use of nuclear
weapons. *See* nuclear weapons,
authority to order the use of
automated electronic hardware, 128
automated weapons, 5, 129, 212
military dependence on, 212
automation,
eliminating the need for people, 129, 212
enemy of individuality, 129
replacing people, 5, 68-71, 129
responsibility for the failure of, 82
scientists who favor, 5, 129
civilians who favor, 68, 70
AWACS. *See* Airborne Warning And
Control System

balance,
artificially contrived, 172, 209-211
of military power, 4, 88, 172, 176, 211, 221
threat of disturbing the, 172

of supply and demand, 6, 221
of terror, 4, 32, 88, 210-211
of trade, 221
stagnation of, 172, 176, 209-210, 221
See also natural dueling partners
Ballistic Missile Defense, 117
Ballistic Missile Early Warning System, 108
See also missile, ballistic
Baltic Sea, 41
barter system, 216
See also Perpetual Economic Prosperity
basic research, 159, 161
basic waste of, 159-160
with a purpose, 161
Berlin, 14, 80
Big Bird camera satellite, 97
Big Three, 210
See also Europe, Great Power system of
bilateral agreements,
avoidance of, 144
Bill of Rights, 145
Blackbird. *See* SR-71
black-box mentality, 5, 129
Black Sea, 42
BMD. *See* Ballistic Missile Defense
BMEWS. *See* Ballistic Missile Early
Warning System
Bodin, Jean, 51
Boeing 707, 109-110
bomber airplanes,
B-52, 59, 69, 72
B-29 Superfortress, 69, 81
strategic, 69
bombing of Hiroshima, 79-83
accuracy of the bomb, 80, 82
bombs,
accuracy of gravity, 80, 82
almost, 36
American-made, 36
atomic, 79, 86, 115
dumb. *See* missile, ballistic,
intercontinental
fission, 60, 79, 86
fusion, 60, 86
gravity, 72, 80, 82
hydrogen, 60, 64, 86, 115
smart. *See* missile, cruise
the arithmetic of counting, 36
thermonuclear. *See* bombs, hydrogen
born classified, 158
born talent.*See* natural dueling partners,
born talent and acquired skill
Boston, Massachusetts, 179
Boulder Laboratories, Boulder, Colorado,
161
See also National Bureau of Standards;
National Oceanic and Atmospheric
Administration
Brave Men. See Pyle, Ernie
British Red Coats, 179

Brown, Harold, Secretary of the Department
of Defense, under President Carter,
17-18, 20-21, 26, 29
budget, 149
Bureau of the Budget, 150
See also United States, Office of
Management and Budget
Bush, George, Vice President of the United
States, under President Reagan, 2,
11-16, 201
Bush, James L., 14

camera. *See* remote sensing, passive
Canada, 108
capitalism,
what we once called, v
See also democratic-capitalism; Perpetual
Economic Prosperity
cardinal choices, 86
Carter Administration, 21, 23, 57, 150, 166
Carter defense strategy, 12, 16-17
Carter Directive,
new nuclear strategy, 17
See also Presidential Directive/National
Security Council-59
Carter, election defeat of, 16-17, 29-30
Carter, Jimmy (James Earl), 39th president
of the United States, 1977 to 1981,
15-17, 21, 26, 29, 200, 216
Carter response, 15, 26
Carter White House, 16, 18, 21, 24, 26, 29
casualty estimate, 22
Central Intelligence Agency, 12
character of people,
climate bias in, 52
Cheyenne Mountain, Colorado Springs,
Colorado, 108
China. *See* People's Republic of China
Christian reform, 194
Christian teachings, 194
Christianity, 195
Church, 194-196
disruptive teachings of, 43
See also natural dueling partners, Church
and State
CIA. *See* Central Intelligence Agency
citizen-soldier, 177-179, 181
See also natural dueling partners,
citizen-soldier
Civil War, vi, 186-187, 215
Confederacy, 187
Confederate Armies, 186
Union Forces, 186
Clark, *ABC-TV Issues and Answers*, 17-18
classified information. *See* information,
classified
Clausewitzian view, 41
Clear, Alaska, 108
climate, influence on people, 52
Colonial times, 177-179

Columbia space shuttle, 75-76, 111
combat readiness,
    guise of, 171
common economic good. *See* Perpetual
    Economic Prosperity
common good, 148, 154, 179
    See also natural dueling partners, common
        good and special interests,—individual
        rights and common good
communication networks,
    centralized, 104, 118
    decentralized, 104, 118-119
    democratized, 118-119
    fixed wire, 119, 126
    microwave relay, 119, 126
    nationalized, 119
    underground cables, 119
communication satellites. *See* satellites,
    communication
Communist Party, 41-43, 51, 53
    Central Committee of, 41
Comprehensive Test Ban Treaty, 114
    verification of, 114
    See also global monitoring systems
computer
    basics, 133
    products, 129, 134
    programmers,
        born talent of, 133
    software, 103
        development, 132-133
        dependence on intuition, 132
        production, 90
    systems, 132
        human resource in, 132
        manpower intensive, 133
    users, 128
Confederacy, 187
Confederate Armies, 186
conflict of interest, 208-209
    See also industrial base, coordination of;
        Pentagon, moving the industry out of
Congress. *See* United States Congress
Congress of Vienna, 210
    See also Europe, Great Power system of
Congressional Record, 166
Consolidated Space Operations Center, 111
Constitution. *See* United States Constitution
Constitutional Convention, 181
constitutional dictatorship, 151-152
constitutional law, 9, 51, 200
    as living mirror, 198
    war powers, 199-201
constitutional mandate,
    To repel Invasions, 8, 10, 63, 143, 148,
        172, 200
Continental Army, 179
Continental Congress, 181
continuous information flow, 9, 90, 137, 146,
    170-172

a replacement for artificially stimulated
    fear, 9
    See also global information systems
continuous monitoring,
    of launch operations, 9, 146-147
    of silo construction, 9
continuous global monitoring. *See* global
    monitoring systems
Coughlin, Charles E., Father, 153
coupling,
    through National Technical Means, 46-50
    through Theater Nuclear Forces, 48-49
creation. *See* natural dueling partners,
    evolution and creation
creative action, 128, 134
creative human energy,
    focused, 173
    release of, 136
    See also war, creative aspects of
cruise missiles. *See* missile, cruise
CSOC. *See* Consolidated Space Operations
    Center
cultural heritage, 133
culture,
    being created, 133
    technology is, 133
Czechoslovakia,
    invasion of, 13

data base,
    electronic, 147
    graphic display of, 105
    sorting of, 104
    See also remote sensing; satellite
        monitoring systems
data sets, 160, 166-167
    electronic access to, 167
    one time users of, 160
data transfer,
    real time, 100-101
    See also continuous information flow
decision making process, 136, 149, 210
    dynamic adjustment in, 210-211, 221
    dynamics of, 137, 210
    non-destructive, 137
    non-violent, 137
Declaration of Independence, 205
declaration of war, 199-201, 204-205
    is legislative, 199, 203-204
de-coupling,
    Europe from the United States, 49
defense contracts, 7, 129
Defense Department. *See* United States
    Department of Defense
defense spending, 2, 60-61, 131, 136, 146,
    158
    as campaign issue, 13, 29
    as driving force, 149, 169
    competitive aspect of, 158, 169
    for Congressional districts, 60

increase in, 7, 23, 29, 60-61, 136, 146,
    149-150, 153-154, 168, 171-172
political power of, 147, 169
priorities, 7, 131-132, 150, 156
    shift in, 6, 7, 132, 154, 156, 223
    See also economic growth; industrial base,
        all-new; technology push
delivery systems. *See* missile delivery
    systems
demand pull, as guiding principle, 5, 131
    of the user, 5, 131
    See also economics, demand-side, all-new;
        natural dueling partners, technology
        push and demand pull
democracy, 176, 180, 182
    do-it-yourself government, 131, 231-233
    self-government, 168, 182-183
    spirit of, 177
Democrat, 11, 29, 140
democratic-capitalism, *v, vi*, 170, 176, 188
    as a way of life, *vi*, 9, 198, 211, 232-233
    cohesiveness of, 188
    dualism of, 232-233
    economic dichotomy, 52
    modern miracle of, 170
    nest egg of, 230-233
Democratic Party, 29
    fragmented, 29
democratic process,
    openness of, 53
Denmark, 41
destruction,
    from surprise attack, 2
    threat of, 2, 8, 22
detection and early warning, 8, 49, 87, 89,
    108, 131, 135, 137, 158, 167-168
    for protection of natural environment, 168
    for protection of people, 168
    for protection of property, 168
    of man-made disaster, 158, 167
    of natural disaster, 158, 167
deterrence, 48-49, 51
    failure of, 8, 12-13
    national policy of, 8, 22
    See also Mutual Assured Destruction
deuterium-tritium mixture, 115
    See also bombs, hydrogen
DEW line, *See* Distant Early Warning line
digital
    revolution, 118
    switching. *See* packet switching
dinosaurs,
    of defense establishment, 49
disposable
    airplane, 70-71
        See also missile, cruise
    launch vehicle, 59
        See also rocket engine
Distant Early Warning line, 108
dualism,

dynamic, 2-3, 37
static. *See* balance
wave-particle, 137, 173
dueling partners. *See* natural dueling
    partners
Dulles, John Foster, Secretary of the
    Department of State, under President
    Eisenhower, 14
"Duty-Honor-Country." *See* MacArthur,
    Douglas
dynamic dualism,
    decision making process, 137, 210-211,
        221-222
    See also natural dueling partners
    partners in, 137
    pragmatic interpretation of, 222
Dyson, Freeman, 217

Eatherly, Major Claude Robert, 81, 83
economic
    dichotomy. *See* democratic-capitalism
    expansion, 7
    growth, 150
        feeding it, 148
        See also defense spending
    independence. *See* national economic
        independence
    opportunity, 172, 176
    policy, 17, 172, 176
    prosperity, 6, 128, 169, 172, 183, 206-207,
        215-216, 220
        assuring national unity, 183, 206
        driving force for national unity, 215
        from computer use, 220
        See also Perpetual Economic Prosperity
    recovery, 149, 157
    security. *See* Perpetual Economic
        Prosperity
    stagnation, 156, 172, 220
    transition, 7, 157, 168, 220
economics,
    demand-side, 6
    all-new, 6
    supply-side, 6
economy,
    wartime, 147
Edwards Air Force Base, 76
    See also United States Air Force
Eisenhower, Dwight David, 34th president
    of the United States, 1953 to 1961, 74,
    197, 209
electronic
    coupling. *See* National Technical Means
    fence, 108
    jamming, 69
    scanning, 69, 107
    warfare. *See* warfare, electronic
electronics, 154
    user-friendly, 72

elitest attitude, 9, 170, 179-180
  of an aristocracy, 178
  of scientists, 129, 159
  See also minority rule
Ellsberg, Daniel, 140
emergency, 8, 118-119, 179, 200-201
  See also national emergency; First Strike
emergency powers, 8, 151, 200-201
  are legislative, 152
  institutionalization of, 152
  of the President, 8, 151-152, 200-201
  See also war powers
Emerson, Ralph Waldo, 178
enemy,
  is me, 130
England, 38, 80, 86, 232
  independence from, 232
  King of, 179
Enola Gay, 81
environment,
  protection of, 62, 117
  See also atmosphere; Global
    Environmental Monitoring
equality,
  for all nations, 143, 146-147
equilibrium,
  dynamic. *See* natural dueling partners
  stagnation of. *See* balance, stagnation of
eternal war, 138, 170
  of deciding, 138, 170-172
  of ideas, *v*
  See also Natural Eternal War
Europe, 144, 153-154, 209-210, 222
  as a battleground, 32, 45, 48-50
  Great Power system of, 209-210, 221
evolution,
  of technology, 85, 87, 130-131
  of weapons systems, 17-18, 55, 85
  See also natural dueling partners,
    evolution and creation
Explorer satellite, 74, 159

FAA. *See* Federal Aviation Administration
faith,
  leap of, 44
  See also natural dueling partners, faith
    and reason
Farewell Address,
  MacArthur, Douglas, 225
  Washington, George, 143-144
favored friend, 9, 50, 106, 112
FCC. *See* Federal Communication
    Commission
fear,
  artificially stimulated, 9
  See also freedom from fear
fearful foe, 10, 50, 106-107, 112
Federal Aviation Administration, 67
Federal Communication Commission, 119
Federal Emergency Management Agency,
    152, 155, 213

Federal Register, 166
Federal Reserve System, 150, 215
Federalists, 147
FEMA. *See* Federal Emergency Management
    Agency
fight or flight, 222
  See also action-reaction response
firepower,
  information is. *See* information
  overkill,
    elimination of, 10
First Amendment,
  landmark decision of, 140
First Strike, 8, 9, 12, 18, 20, 201
  passive acceptance of, 15, 18, 19
  preemptive, 18, 19, 38, 201
  retaliation, 14, 18, 35, 38-39, 53
  See also nuclear weapons, authority to
    order the use of,
first use, 20, 32
fiscal policy. *See* United States, President of
fission bombs. *See* bombs, fission
Flyingdales Moor, Yorkshire, England, 108
Ford,
  Gerald Rudolph, 38th president of the
    United States, August 9, 1974 to 1977,
    200
  Henry, 128, 153, 220
  Model-T, 6, 220
  Motor Company, 211
    assembly line, 220
forefathers, 177, 208
foreign aggression, 9
foreign policy, 9, 15, 22-23, 32
  use of military action, 9, 22-23, 32, 206-207
  United States Senate, 2, 214-215
foreign politics,
  of the President, 214
Forrestal, James V.,
  Secretary of the Navy, under President
    Franklin D. Roosevelt, 208-209, 211
  Secretary of the National Military
    Establishment (Department of
    Defense), under President Truman,
    208-209
Fort McHenry, 56
founding fathers, 20, 172, 176, 184, 202-203,
    230, 232-233
France, 38
freedom "of,"
  choice, *v*, 168
  creative innovation, 193-194
  information exchange, *v*, 171
  religion, 194-195
  religious teaching, 195
  self-expression, *vi*, 196, 198
  speech, *vi*, 189, 193-194
  the press, 27, 139-141, 194
    pay the premium for, 139-141
  worship, 189
freedom "from,"

action-reaction response, 192-193
fear, 44, 83, 189, 192
want, 189, 192
freedom to work, 168
fusion bombs. *See* bombs, fusion,

GEM of the future. *See* Global
Environmental Monitoring
General Motors, 211
geography,
influence on nuclear strategy, 34
Germany, 4, 151
Gettysburg, 186
Address, 186
Battle of, 186
gift of foresight, 88-89
GLCM, Ground Launch Cruise Missile. *See*
missile, cruise, ground launch
Glenn, John H. Jr., first American in orbit,
111, 230
Global Environmental Monitoring, 127, 143,
171-172, 213, 223-225, 232
global information systems, 127
military-operated, 7, 48, 73, 77, 87, 128,
137, 145-146
real-time, 90, 145-146
global monitoring systems, 7-8, 48, 121, 127,
143, 146-147, 154, 166, 168, 219
military-operated, 46, 64, 91, 100-102, 128,
137, 143, 146, 223-226
global peacekeeping networks, 78, 127
military-operated, 78
global presence,
American naval, 41, 228
Goldwater, Barry, Republican Senator-
Arizona, 20
government,
branches of,
Executive, 185
Judicial, 185
Legislative, 185
democratic, 3
do-it-yourself, 131
of the several States, 185
self, 168
separation of powers in, 185
Government Printing Office, 166
GPS, Global Positioning System. *See*
NAVSTAR
Grand Monarchy, 210
See also Europe, Great Power system of,
Great Britain, 80
See also England
Great Powers. *See* Europe, Great Power
system of
Greece, 42
Grotius, Hugo, 51, 184, 224
Ground Launch Cruise Missile. *See* missile,
cruise, ground launch

Haig, Alexander Meigs, Jr., Secretary of the

Department of State, under President
Reagan, 190-191
Hamilton, Alexander, Secretary of the
Department of the Treasury, under
President Washington, 202-203
hawks, 230-231
in dove's clothing, 230-233
See also American Eagles; patriotic
Americans
Heaven and Earth, 106, 111, 177
Helvidius letters, 203
Hiroshima, Japan,
bombing of, 4, 79-83, 115
civilian casualty estimate, 80
Holy Alliance, 210
See Europe, Great Power system of
home
district, 86
state, 60
See also pork barrel
Hughes, Charles Evans, Secretary of the
Department of State, under President
Harding, 142
human
action,
motivated by fear, 189, 222-223
motivated by threat, 206-207
See also deterrence
behavior,
dualism of, 173, 228
false concept of, 209, 221-222
mechanical era of, 221, 224
NEW era of, 137-138
profound change in, 44, 170-173
See also natural dueling partners
drudge, 220
eliminate the need for, 220
incentive, 5, 128
insight, 72
intelligence, 68, 70, 129
interaction,
two components of, 137, 173
See also natural dueling partners
judgement, 5, 68-70, 129
life,
irradication of, 222
destruction of, 222-223
misery, 171, 189, 231
motivation, 134
participation, 5
potential, 154-155, 168
stored for emergency, 154-155
resource, 154-155, 167-168
coordination of, 167
creative use of, 68, 70
mobilization of, 154-155, 168
maximum utility of, 146
under-utilization of, 133, 145
See also national service organizations
spirit, 134
suffering, 171, 221, 231

prolonged by action-reaction response,
    221
tragedy, 222
hydrogen, 60
hydrogen bomb,
  Russian mastery of, 34
  See also bombs, hydrogen; warheads,
    thermonuclear

ICBM. *See* missile, ballistic,
    intercontinental
Icelandic saga, 88
Identification: Friend or Foe, 106, 110, 112
IFF. *See* Identification: Friend or Foe
IGY. *See* International Geophysical Year
Illinois, 73
incoming information,
  accepting signal, 101
  digitizing, 102
    hazard of, 102
  real-time sorting, 101
  rejecting noise from, 101
  See also remote sensing
In control at the White House. *See* Haig,
    Alexander Meigs, Jr.
India, 41
individual rights, 148, 154
  See also natural dueling partners,
    individual rights and common good
industrial base,
  all-new, 6, 128-129, 149-150, 155, 168,
    206-207
  computer products, 7, 129
  coordination of, 207
    at the Pentagon, 206-207
  elastic limit of, 147
  electronics, 154-155
  information technology, 149
  munitions, 7, 154-156, 168-172, 206
  of the nation, 6, 128, 147-150, 154-155,
    168-172, 206
  raw material for, 7, 129, 171
industrial mobilization, 4, 169-170
  See also World War II
industries,
  aerospace superiority, 34
  electronics, 148, 154-155
  information, 7, 128, 148, 154, 170-171
  munitions, 7, 23, 51, 130, 154-155, 169-172
  patriotic, 215
  service, 148
  software production, 90
information,
  access to, 151
  at a glance, 165
  classification of, 26-27, 146
  control of, 140, 146
  equal access to, 147
  exchange, 47, 147, 158, 220
    as economic equalizer, 43, 147, 220

  competitive aspect of, 158-159
  right to, 150-151
  U.S. restrictions on, 158-159
  flow, 47, 120-121, 137, 143, 146, 149-151,
    158, 166, 168, 220
    continuous, 86, 91, 137, 146-147
  democratization of, 121
  real-time, 90-91, 100-101, 146
  to strangle, 158
  industries. *See* industries, information
  in public domain, 158, 162, 164, 166-168
  is firepower, 24, 135, 226
  one-time users of, 160
  perishable commodity, 151
  policy, 150-151, 155
  politics, 139-140, 169
  resources, 150-151
  restricting access to, 146, 150-151
  saturation, 118
  systems, 7, 86-87
    See also global information systems
  transfer, 46-49, 120-121
    continuous, 86
    packet switching, 120-121
  users, 128
Information and Regulatory Affairs, Office
    of, 150
  See also United States, Office of
    Management and Budget
Inter-Continental Ballistic Missile. *See*
    missile, ballistic, intercontinental
international agreements, 146-147
  global monitoring for, 146-147
  rejection of, 147
  verification of, 146-147
international bankers, 153
international criminal law, 82,
  a new era of, 82-83
International Geophysical year, 159
international law, 184, 223
  against the manufacture, possession and
    use of nuclear weapons, 9, 117, 224
  all nations equal, 143-145
  conformity imposed by, 223
  for continuous monitoring, 9, 143, 224-225
  no force for enforcement, 144, 223-224
international regulatory activities, 143-147,
    223-224
international regulatory agreements,
    145-147, 223-224
  verification of 146-147
interventionists, 144, 153
invisible aircraft. *See* stealth technology
invisible citizens, 217
invisible government, 149
  See also United States, Office of
    Management and Budget
ionospheric physics, 161
  early research in, 161
Iowa, 74

Iowa Republican caucus, 11
isolationists, 144, 153

James, William, 37
Japan, 4
Japanese
  government,
    unconditional surrender of, 4
  military headquarters, 81
Jefferson, Thomas,
  Secretary of the Department of State,
    under President Washington, 203
  3d president of the United States, 1800 to
    1808, 178
Jesus Christ, 194
Johnson, Kelly, 24
Johnson, Lyndon Baines, 36th president of
  the United States, November 22, 1963 to
  1969, 74
Jungk, Robert, 83

Kamchatka Peninsula, 42, 109
Keats, John, 222
Kennedy, John Fitzgerald, 35th president of
  the United States, 1961 to November 22,
  1963, 197
Key, Francis Scott, 56
Korean War, 14, 207
Kwajalein Missile Range, 58

land,
  lord, 61-62
  owner, 61-62
  use, 57-58, 62
    priorities for, 61
  See also environment
land-based weapons. *See* missile, land-based;
  nuclear weapons, land-based
lasers in space, 77
  See also satellites, communication
launch on warning, 18-19, 201
  See also First Strike, preemptive
launch systems. *See* missile, launch systems
launch vehicle, re-usable, 76
  See also missile, launch vehicle; space
    shuttle
law,
  control by rule of, 27
  equality under rule of, 10
  letter of, 51, 145, 223-225
  spirit of, 51, 145, 223-225
laws,
  of nature, 4, 178, 184, 217
  See also natural law
lawyers, 217
  logic of, 217
leaking information,
  to the press, 24-25
  the politics of, 24-25

leap of faith, 44
Lee, Robert E., 186
Letter of the Constitution, 51, 223-224
  See also United States, Constitution of
Library of Congress. *See* United States
  Congress, Library of
limited nuclear war. *See* nuclear war
Lincoln, Abraham, 16th president of the
  United States, elected December 20,
  1860 to April 15, 1865, 73, 186-187
Lincoln Memorial, 187
Lindbergh, Charles A., 153
linkage, 13
  See also Soviet, sphere of influence
live ammunition, 72
live broadcast, 100
living nation, 176
  organic concept of, v, 227-233
  See also natural dueling partners
lobbyist,
  advocate to, 218
  homemaker as, 218
local residents, 61
loyal opposition, 11, 140
Lugar, Richard, G., Republican Senator-
  Indiana, 26

MacArthur, Douglas, General of the Army,
  225
MAD. *See* Mutual Assured Destruction
Madison, James,
  member, United States House of
    Representatives, 203
  4th president of the United States, 1808 to
    1816, 195, 204
Maginot Line, 87
majestic Ship of State, 230
major advances in civilization, 90
majority-minority dualism, 179
majority rule, 53-54, 179
Manila, Philippines, 82
Mariana Islands, 81
Marshall, George C.,
  Secretary of the Department of Defense,
    under President Truman, 211
  Secretary of the Department of State,
    under President Truman, 211
Marshall Islands, 58
Marx, Karl, 37
Maryland Toleration Act, 194
Massachusetts, 179
Mayaguez seizure, 200
McNamara, Robert S., Secretary of the
  Department of Defense, under
  Presidents Kennedy and Johnson, 19,
  140, 211
Mediterranean, 42
megaton equivalence. *See* TNT explosive
  equivalence

Middle East, 41
military
  command structure, 23, 42
  defeat, 4
  dictator, 151
    See also United States,
      Commander-in-Chief
  draft, 153
  force, 4
  industrial complex, 5, 9, 130
    Congressional control of, 9
    last great challenge, 9
  industrial divorce, 155-156
  industrial nest egg, 232-233
  intervention, 153
  mission,
    all-new, 172, 211, 213
    To repel Invasions, 8, 10, 63, 143, 148,
      172
  monarch, 196
    See also nuclear weapons, authority to
      order the use of
  needs, 5, 130
  service organizations, 9, 77, 85-86, 129,
    146, 155-156, 167-168, 170-172, 176,
    197-198, 212-213
    misdirected hostility toward, 198, 207
    national responsibility for, 9, 172, 213
    restoring identity to, 212,
    restoring uniqueness to 212-213
  strength,
    build-up of, 15
  target, 17, 81
  tradition. *See* American military tradition
  weather service, 158
minority rule, 42-43, 51, 53, 179
  See also natural dueling partners
Minuteman,
  missile, 35, 58
  silo, 87
  Spirit of '76, 179
missile
  accuracy. *See* missile, targeting accuracy
  anti-ballistic, 32, 116, 146
  attack, air-to-ground, 72
  ballistic, intercontinental, 12-13, 17, 19,
    32, 49, 56-59, 62, 64, 69, 71, 85-87, 116
  cruise, 68, 70-71
    ground-launch, 70-71
  delivery systems, 85-87, 137
  dinosaurs of, 87
Missile eXperimental, 13, 57, 87
  race track shelter, 57
missile,
  fleet ballistic, 64
  float launch, 65
  land-based dinosaurs, 87
  land-based systems, 34-35, 39, 41, 45,
    48-49, 57, 86-87
    threat of use, 86

launch systems, 34-35, 63
launch vehicle, 34, 36, 58-59
  reloading, 36
  sea launch, 63-65
  submarine launch, 64
  targeting accuracy, 17, 34, 56
    increased, 17, 19, 56
    lack of, 35-36
mobilization. *See* World War II, industrial
    mobilization for
Monetary Control Act, 216
money talks, 157
monitoring, satellite. *See* Global
    Environmental Monitoring
Montesquieu, Charles de Secondat, 185
mood of the country, 2, 16, 28, 30, 149, 154,
    183, 188-189, 233
  pro-defense, 3, 29, 149
  to sustain prosperity, 183, 188-189
Moral Man, 182
Mother Nature,
  laws of, 173
Mother Russia, 51, 53
MPS. *See* Multiple Protective Shelter
Multiple Protective Shelter, 56
munitions,
  production, 10
  economic dependence on, 10
  See also industrial base; industries
mushroom cloud, 115
Muskie, Edmund, Secretary of the
    Department of State, under President
    Carter, 21-23
Mutual Assured Destruction, 5, 22, 32, 34,
    40, 51
MX. *See* Missile eXperimental

Napoleon, 210
NASA. *See* National Aeronautics and Space
    Administration
nation, 175, 183-184, 186
  birth of, 175, 186, 230-233
  cohesiveness of, 183
  destiny of, 184, 230, 233
  economic fate of, 183
  unity of, 183
National Aeronautics and Space Act, 74
National Aeronautics and Space
    Administration, 74-75
National Bureau of Standards, 65, 161
national cemetery, 186
National Command Center, 131
National Defense Acts, 202
national
  defense policy, 155
  destiny, 73, 75, 144, 184
  economic
    cruelty, 156
    independence, 52, 176, 213, 216
    prosperity, 6, 30, 128, 155, 169

See also Perpetual Economic Prosperity
National Emergencies and Delegated
    Powers, Special Committee on, 151-152,
    200-201
national
  emergency, 8, 118-119, 152-153, 169
    declaration of, 8, 152
    powers, 8, 151-152, 200-201
    proclamation, 200
  goals, 5
National Guard, 167, 202
national
  ideals, 136, 215
  identity, 30, 136, 231
  independence, 29-30, 144-145, 210, 213
  information policy, 155
  needs, 6, 130-131, 161
    during wartime, 147-148
National Oceanic and Atmospheric
    Administration, 157, 161-162
national
  purpose, 6, 75, 149
    definition of, 149
    statement of, 186
    See also To repel Invasions
  readiness, 153
  remote sensing information, 168
  resources,
    divided between military-civilian, 73-74,
      167-168
    divided in space, 73-74
    government-generated, 168
  security, 16, 26, 30

National Security Act, 211
national
  service, 167-168, 197-198
    organizations, 134, 176-177, 197-198
    See also military service organizations
  space programs, 74-75
    competing, 74-75
    technological advantage, 128
National Technical Means, 46-47, 146
  of verification, 47-50, 146
national
  unity, 183, 206
    economic prosperity and, 183, 206
National Weather Service, 157, 165, 167
national
  work force, 167, 219
    military-civilian, 167
nation's bookkeeper, 150-151
NATO. *See* North Atlantic Treaty
    Organization
natural dueling partners, 5, 137, 176-177
  American people and American military,
    176, 230-233
  authority and responsibility, 131
  born talent and acquired skill, 132
  Church and State, 137

citizen-soldier, 177, 231
common good and special interests, 168,
    214
continuity and creativity, 176
democracy and capitalism, v, 170, 172,
    176, 232-233
Democrats and Republicans, 29
equality and freedom, 172
evolution and creation, 55, 172
faith and reason, 40, 43-44, 137, 172, 176
for forward motion, 172, 176
glide and perch, 177-178, 232
individual rights and common good, 154,
    172, 176, 179
letter and spirit
  of the Constitution, 51, 145, 223-225
  of the law, 51, 145, 223-225
liberty and subjugation, 172, 179-181
majority-minority rule, 179
male-female, 137
of the living future, 172, 176
science and religion, 137, 176, 196
soar and sit, 177-178, 232
sporadic-persistent, 172-173
stars and stripes, 232-233
State Department-Defense Department, 3,
    4, 7-8, 16, 21-23
supply and demand, 6
technological evolution and creative
    energy, 55, 172-173
technology push and demand pull, 5,
    130-131, 156, 215, 232
think-do, 138, 189, 228-229, 231-233
thought and deed, 231
tradition and radical change, 176
two-party system, 3, 29, 140-141
United States and the Soviet Union,
    179-181
war-peace, 3, 7-8, 21-23, 40-41, 176
wave-particle, 173
natural environment, 136, 143
  protection of, 136, 170-173
  See also Global Environmental Monitoring
Natural Eternal War, 137-138, 170-172

natural
  law, 4, 137-138, 172-173, 217, 224, 228-229
    prophetic advantage of, 217
  resources, 146
    minimum consumption of, 146

NAVSTAR, 65-67
Navy. *See* United States Navy
nest egg, 230-233
  double yolk of, 232-233
  See also democratic-capitalism
Nevada, 57
  test site, 114
NEW era. *See* Natural Eternal War
Newton, Sir Isaac, 221
Niebuhr, Rheinhold, 181

Nixon, Richard Milhous, 37th president of
    the United States, 1969 to August 9,
    1974, 16, 19, 200
NOAA. *See* National Oceanic and
    Atmospheric Administration
noise,
    rejection of unwanted, 101, 126
    See also incoming information
NORAD. *See* North American Air Defense
    Command
North Africa, 41
North American Air Defense Command, 108
North Atlantic Alliance, 50
North Atlantic Treaty Organization, 23, 45,
    48-50, 158
    modernization agreement, 45, 48, 50
North Sea, 41
Norway, 42, 127
Norwegian Sea, 42
nuclear
    attack, 9
        defense against, 116
        retaliation, 8, 12, 15, 18, 23
        See also First Strike
    destruction,
        threat of, 9, 206-207
        See also deterrence
    exchange. *See* nuclear war
    explosions, 113
        detection of 113-117
        heat from, 115-117
        updraft from, 115
    holocaust, 3, 39
        accidental, 10, 33, 85-86, 146
        threat of, 34, 206-207
        See also deterrence
    reaction,
        fission, 60, 86
        fusion, 60, 86
    strategy, 2, 4, 32-33
        anti-city, 33-34
        counter-force, 17-19, 56
        evolution of, 17-18
        geographic influence on, 40-42
        new, 16, 18-19
    targeting,
        against population centers, 34, 56
        new, 16, 18, 22-23, 56
    testing,
        atmospheric, 114-117
        underground, 113-114
    war, 2, 12, 60
        analysis of effects, 22
        fighting, 6, 13, 15-19, 58-59
        fighting and winning, 12-13, 18, 38,
            41-42
        strategy, 31, 51, 54
        threat of, 19
        winner in, 12
        winnable, 18

warheads.
    delivery of, 55, 60, 63-64
    explosion of, 113-117
    fission, 60
    fusion, 60
    kept at sea, 63
weapons,
    authority to order the use of, 8-9, 18, 20,
        38-39, 192, 196, 199-201, 205
    based at sea, 63-65
    battlefield. *See* nuclear weapons, short
        range
    demonstrations against, 156
    get rid of, 143
    land-based, 34-35, 39
    long-range, 13-14
    offensive, 71-72
    short-range, 13, 20
    tactical. *See* nuclear weapons, short
        range
    testing of, 113-115
    See also missile, ballistic; Theater
        Nuclear Forces

observing. *See* remote sensing
OMB. *See* United States, Office of
    Management and Budget
operational needs,
    of the military, 7
    See also demand pull

Pacificus letters, 203
packet switching, 120-121
Paine, Thomas, 207
pairs,
    static, 4
    See also balance, stagnation of
Paperwork Reduction Act
    opponents of, 150
    signed by Carter, 150
patriot,
    sunshine, 207
patriotic
    American, 181, 230-233
    See also American people
    enthusiasm, 181
pattern in motion, 165
    continuity of, 165
    pictures of information, 165
payload. *See* satellite, payload
peace,
    absence of war, 3
    See also armed peace
    achieved by threat. *See* deterrence
    definition of 4, 21
    foreign policy for, 21
    pursuit of, 21
    the very thin veil of, 4, 142
    threatening aspect of, 3
    through strength, 21

peacemakers,
  blessed are the, 169
Pearl Harbor, Hawaii, 153
  Japanese bombing of, 153
Pennsylvania, 186
Pentagon, 48, 88
  estimates of civilian casualties, 22
  moving the industry out of, 9, 155-156,
    206-207
Pentagon Papers, 140
Pentagon,
  press leak at, 24-26
  Pride of, 176, 231
    See also American military
  Purification of, 9, 155-156, 206-207
  wisest men in the land, 88
People's Republic of China, 38, 80
PEP of the nation. *See* Perpetual Economic
    Prosperity
Perpetual Economic Prosperity, 170-172
Persian Gulf areas, 41
Perspective, 28, 51, 85, 135, 168, 230
Peter the Great, 52
Peterson Field, Colorado Springs, Colorado,
    111
Petropavlovsk port, 42
photovoltaic cells, 76
  See also satellites; space, militarization of
Pine Tree radar line, 108
Planet Earth, 39, 61, 90, 92, 106, 117, 142,
    145, 224, 230
Plutonium, 60
Poland, 41
political
  credibility, 24
  dueling. *See* dualism, dynamic
  loyalty, 28, 141
    security blanket of, 28
  patronage, 10
  system,
    two-party, 3, 10, 141
    collapse of, 141
  thorns, 28-29
pork barrel, 60-61
Potomac River,
  foggy bottom, 28
Potsdam Declaration, 80
Potsdam, suburb of Berlin, 80
President,
  constitutional powers of, 190-192, 198,
    203-204
  power of, 151-152, 189
  vanishing power of, 26
    See also emergency powers; war powers;
      United States, President of
presidential
  campaign 1980, 2, 11, 15-16, 28-30
  campaign 1964, 20
Presidential Directive/National Security
    Council-59, 15-17, 23

presidential
  nomination 1980, 11
  succession, 190-192, 201
press,
  American, 15
  attention by, 18
  conferences,
    at the White House, 16
  known through, 19
press leak, 24-26
press,
  Soviet, 15
private sector, 158
  defense contracts in, 7
  profit in, 7
  proprietary information in, 158, 164
Prohibition, 142, 223
  failure of, 142, 223
prototype technology, 46
  See also technology push
Prussia, 210
public
  controversy, 3
  debate, 3, 131
  domain, 164
    information in, 158, 164
  endorsement, 17
  officials, 131
  opinion, 3, 29-30
    force of, 75, 183
    power of, 26-28, 205
    very loud voice of, 199
  watch-dog, 197
Puritans, 179
push-button
  delivery systems, 137
    See also missile, delivery systems
  warfare. *See* warfare, push-button
Pyle, Ernie, 208, 222

radar,
  detection, 69-70, 109-110
    avoiding, 106, 110
  echo return, 107, 109-111
  false echo return, 69-70, 110
  flying through the beam of, 25, 69, 106,
    110-112
  flying under the beam of, 25, 106, 112
  frequency resolution, 107
  line-of-sight, 109-110
  operation of, 106-107
  plane. *See* AWACS
  pulse, 107
  radiated power, 107
  resolution, 107
  scanning mode, 107, 110
  time resolution, 107
  tracking mode, 107
  transmitter-receiver, 107
  transponder, 110

Reagan Administration, 6, 155
Reaganomics, 149
    See also economics, supply-side
Reagan, Ronald, 40th president of the
    United States, 1981 to present, 6, 17,
    28, 64, 136, 149, 171, 190-191
    assassination attempt, 190-191
Reagan White House, 201
real-time monitoring, 100-101
    unwanted noise, 101
    wanted signal, 101
    See also continuous information flow
reason. *See* natural dueling partners, faith
    and reason
reconnaissance
    aircraft, 25, 72, 112
        See also SR-71
    satellites, 101
        See also Big Bird camera satellite
Redstone Arsenal, 65
religion, 195-196
    See also natural dueling partners, science
    and religion
remote control. *See* automation, replacing
    people
remote sensing, 25, 64, 90, 102-104, 106-107,
    137, 143, 158, 168
    active, 90, 106-107
    passive, 90-91, 107
    See also global monitoring systems
remote sensing data
    assimilation of, 104
    graphic display of, 104-105
    interpretation of, 104-105
    pattern in motion, 105
    sorting, 103-104
remote sensor, 102-103
    down-link transfer, 104
    educated, 104
    hardware, 103
    smart, 102-103
    software, 103
    up-link command, 103
Republican Administration, 74
Republican candidates, 11, 21, 73
    campaign, 17, 28
    nomination of, 2, 29, 140
research, 159-161
    neglect of utility, 160
    results, 163
    self-serving, 161
    with a purpose, 161
retaliation. *See* First Strike, retaliation
Revolutionary War, 176, 184, 207
rocket
    engine, 34, 59
        disposable, 59, 76
        liquid propellant, 64-65
        Saturn-V, 59
        solid propellant, 64-65

rockets,
    wartime use of, 56
Roman Catholic Church, 194-196
Roosevelt, Franklin Delano, 32d president of
    the United States, March 4, 1933 to
    April 12, 1945, 153-154, 192
Rose Garden, 29
row boat of democracy, 230
rule by law, 138, 143, 226
rule by natural law, 138
    equality for all nations, 143, 226
Russian people, 36-37, 52-53
    See also Soviet Union

SAC. *See* Strategic Air Command
Sagan, Carl, 217
SAGE, Semi-Automated Ground
    Environment, 108
Saipan Island, Marianas, 81
Sakharov, Andrei, 44
SALT. *See* Strategic Arms Limitation Talks
San Francisco, California, 210
satellite,
    drag, 99
        See also satellite orbit, decay
    ground-control, 99
    ground-station, 92-93, 123-125
    information relay, 93, 123-125
        with delay, 93
    monitoring systems, 100
        real-time, 100-101
        receiving raw data, 100
    orbit,
        decay, 99, 124
        equatorial, 92, 124
        fixed in space, 92-93
        geostationary, 92, 124, 164
        geosynchronous, 92, 124, 164
        inclined, 92
        polar, 92, 95, 164
    pass,
        overhead, 95, 103, 127
        pole-to-pole, 93
    payload, 60, 75-76, 102, 104, 123-124, 126
        effective lifetime of, 98-99, 124
    pictures, 163-164
        See also spy-in-the-sky; weather satellites
    systems,
        military-operated, 46, 48, 66-67, 73-75, 99
        operating costs, 99, 126-127
        See also global information systems
satellites,
    active observers, 98-99
    circling the globe, 10, 46-47, 92
    communication, 92, 94, 123-126, 158, 161
        central facility for, 124-125
    Earth-orbiting, 73-75, 77, 92-94, 160, 163,
        224
        down-link, 104, 124-125

up-link, 102-103, 124-125
ferret, 97
interrogation, 95
listen-and-hear, 97, 123
look-and-see, 96
passive observers, 96-99
radar-type, 98
relay with delay, 94-95
Silent Sally, passive, 98
Singing Sam, active, 98
technology inversion, 104, 126-127
Scheer, Walter, 2, 12-13
Schlesinger, James R., Secretary of the
    Department of Defense, under President
    Nixon, 16, 19
Schmidt, Helmut, 48
science and religion. *See* natural dueling
    partners, science and religion
scientific community, 159, 212, 214-215
communication failure within, 159
publish or perish, 160
technical assistance from, 163
scientists, 129, 158, 160-163, 216-217
dedicated public servants, 162
funded by tax dollars, 162
in the Congress, 216-217
in the federal government, 162, 216
Scoville, Herbert, 146
sea launch, 63-65
secrecy,
    government abuse of, 140
secret
    information, 26-27, 146
    project, 25
self-doubt, 227-228
    your only enemy, 228
self-government, 182
    American style, 184
    bedrock of the nation, 186
    roots of, 186
seismic data, 114
seismograph-type instrument, 113
    See also nuclear testing
sensory perception, 133
Separatists, 179
Shemya Island, Alaska, 109
signal,
    incoming,
        accepting wanted, 101, 126
        enhancing weak, 126
        protecting, 126
        rejecting noise, 101, 126
silo construction, 33, 35, 224
    near trans-Siberian railroad, 35
sixth sense, 133
Snow, C. P., 86, 88
social change,
    driven by technology, 43, 53
Social Security, 155
software. *See* computer software

Soviet
    adventurism, 13, 15, 32, 40-42, 53
    sphere of influence, 40-42
Soviet Union, 8, 13, 18, 34, 38-39, 41-42, 51,
    52-54, 57, 86, 117, 179-181, 232
    missiles aimed at, 13, 37
    nuclear exchange with, 5, 12-15
space,
    militarization of, 76-77
    nationalization of, 76
space programs, 73
    consolidation of, 76-77
    dividing the nation 73-74
space shuttle, 75-76
    Columbia, 75-76, 111
    truck, 76
SPADATS, Space Detection And Tracking
    System, 108
Spirit of the Constitution, 51
Sputnik I, 74
spy-in-the sky, 93, 100
    See also satellites, Earth-orbiting
SR-71, 25, 112
Star Spangled Banner, The, 56
stars and stripes. *See* natural dueling
    partners, stars and stripes
State Department. *See* United States,
    Department of State
stealth technology, 24-26, 69, 110-111
Stockman, David, Director of the Office of
    Management and Budget, 149
Straight Flush, 81
Strategic Air Command, 59, 71
    See also United States Air Force
Strategic Arms Limitation Talks, 36, 142,
    146
strategic
    means nuclear, 12
    triad, 10
    weapons. *See* nuclear weapons
stratosphere, 115
    See also atmosphere
Succession Act, 190-191
Sun, 156
Supreme Court. *See* United States, Supreme
    Court of
Supreme Law
    of the Land, 184, 187, 191, 218
    See also United States, Constitution
surprise attack, 8
    elimination of, 8, 46-47, 146-147
    passive acceptance of, 9
    See also First Strike
Sweden, 41
Sylvanus Thayer Award. *See* MacArthur,
    Douglas

TAC air. *See* Tactical Air Command
Tactical Air Command, 71-72
    See also United States Air Force

take care clause, 152
TEAM effort. *See* Technology, Environment,
    And Man
technological evolution, 85, 130-131
    dinosaurs of, 87
    freaks of, 87, 131-132
Technology, Environment, And Man, 136,
    176, 214
technology
    is culture, 53, 133
technology push, 4, 5, 22-23, 130-131, 156,
    215
    driving force for economic recovery, 5
    See also defense spending; natural dueling
        partners, technology push and demand
        pull
technology
    transfer of, 219
    use of untried, 83-84
teeter-totter of terror, 4, 211-212
    See also balance of power
Texas, 74
    Democrat, 74
Theater Nuclear Forces, 45, 48-50
thermonuclear devices. *See* bombs, hydrogen
They Fought Alone. See Keats, John
thinking and doing. *See* natural dueling
    partners, think-do
Thule, Greenland, 108
Tibbets, Colonel Paul W., Jr., 81
Tinian Island, 81
TNT explosive equivalence, 60, 79, 116
Tocqueville, Alexis de, 37
To repel Invasions, 8, 10, 63, 143, 148, 172,
    200
trade dependence, 216
    See also economic independence
trajectory path, 58, 108-109
    gravitational pull, 58
    of ballistic missile, 109
    See also atmospheric conditions
transmitter
    is the target, 126-127
transponder pulse, 106, 110-111
    coding of, 106, 110
treason, 201, 207
Trident submarine, 64
Truax, Robert C., 65
Truman, Harry S., 33d president of the
    United States, April 12, 1945 to 1953,
    50, 79-80, 140, 211
truth, 43, 190, 196
    common search for, 43, 196
    the most powerful weapon, 190
truths,
    well-known, 189-190
Turkey, 42
tyranny, 180, 203
    not easily conquered, 203
tyrant, rule by, 204

UN. *See* United Nations (United Nations
    Organization)
Uncle Sam, 29
    creative spirit of, 135
Union, 185, 187, 215
    created the States, 185
    of the several States, 185, 187
    preservation of, 187
    telic harmony of, 227
    the more perfect, 187-188, 227
Union of Soviet Socialist Republics. *See*
    Soviet Union
United Kingdom, 38
    See also England
United Nations, 114, 144-145
    Charter, 144-145, 210
    General Assembly resolution, 114
    Military Staff Committee, 145
    Security Council, 144
United States, the, 34, 37-39, 42, 49, 53, 64,
    69, 71-73, 86, 108, 118-119, 145, 179-181
    Air Force, 59, 65, 71-72, 87, 211, 226
        Edwards Air Force Base, 76
        Peterson Field, 111
        Tactical Air Command, 71-72
        Vandenberg Air Force Base, 58
        See also Strategic Air Command
    Army, 65, 211, 225
        See also Redstone Arsenal
    Coast Guard, 63
    Commander-in-Chief, 80, 83, 130, 153, 192,
        196-198, 202-203
        by invitation only, 202-203
        See also United States, President of
    Congress, 7, 19, 30, 51, 67, 75, 77, 87, 144,
        148, 150-151, 153-154, 167, 171, 180,
        190-191, 195, 202-205
        bringing new talent to, 10
        burden imposed by, 171
        Committee structure of, 11
        lagging behind controversy, 204-205
        Library of, 159
    Constitution, 7, 51, 140, 142, 167, 184-185,
        195, 202-203, 223-224
        a living mirror, 198
        Bill of Rights, 145, 195
        Eighteenth Amendment, 223
        First Amendment, 140, 167, 195
        landmark decision, 140
        Letter of, 184, 223-224
        Prohibition Amendment, 142, 223
        Spirit of, 184, 223-224
    Department of Agriculture,
        Forest Service, 161
    Department of Commerce, 157
        National Oceanic and Atmospheric
            Administration, 157, 161-162
        National Weather Service, 157, 165
    Department of Defense, 21-23, 111,
        155-156, 206-212

Assistant Secretaries of, 155
rivalry with Department of State, 3-4, 7-8,
  16, 21-22
Secretary of. *See* Brown, Marshall,
  McNamara, Schlesinger, Wilson
industrialization of, 211
Department of Energy, 64
Department of Health and Human
  Resources, 155
Department of Military Affairs, 156,
  206-207, 213
creation of, 156, 206-207, 213
Department of State, 21-23
rivalry with Department of Defense, 3-4,
  7-8, 16, 21-22
Secretary of, 190-191. *See* Dulles, Haig,
  Hughes, Muskie, Vance
Department of the Interior, 161
National Park Service, 161
Department of the Post Office, 212
Department of the Treasury, 212
Department of Transportation,
  Federal Aviation Administration, 67
Department of War, 212-213
Army Corps of Engineers, 212
Civilian Conservation Corps, 212
Executive branch,
  order of precedence, 190
government of, 180, 182
House of Representatives,
  Armed Services Committee, 155
  International Relations Committee, 38
  Speaker of, 190-191
is an island, 63
Military Academy, at West Point, 225
National Military Establishment, 208
Navy, 63-66, 87, 208, 211-212, 228
Bureau of Aeronautics, 65
Office of Management and Budget, 149-150
Patent Office, 220
President. *See* Carter, Eisenhower, Ford,
  Jefferson, Johnson, Kennedy, Lincoln,
  Madison, Nixon, Reagan, Roosevelt,
  Truman, Washington
President of, 24, 26-27, 45, 79, 130,
  151-153, 189-192, 196-201
Duties and Powers of, 190-191
fiscal policy of, 150-151
Senate, 73, 144, 148, 152, 210
Budget Committee, 22
elect scientists to, 216-217
Foreign Relations Committee, 22, 26
Intelligence, Select Committee on, 26
National Emergencies and Delegated
  Powers, Special Committee on, 150-151,
  200-201
President pro tempore, 190-191
Supreme Court of, 83, 140
threat of violence by, 206-207
Vice President of, 190-191

universe,
  big bang theory, 178
Uranium, 60, 79
user pull. *See* demand pull
U.S. *See* United States
U.S.-Soviet balance, 14
U.S.S.R. *See* Soviet Union
Utah, 57

Van Allen, James, 74
Vance, Cyrus R., Secretary of the
  Department of State, under President
  Carter, 22
Vandenberg Air Force Base
  See United States Air Force
Vattel, Emmerich de, 184
verification
  by remote sensing, 146-147
  of internation agreements, 146-147
  pays for itself, 147
Vietnam,
  American involvement in, 140
  loss of American lives, 140
  loss of military dignity, 140
  loss of national prestige, 140
  policy, 140
Vietnam War, 38, 140, 207-208
Virginia, 195
  State Convention of 1786, 195
Vladivostok, 35, 42
Von Braun, Wernher, 65

Wallop, Malcom, Republican Senator-
  Wyoming, 77
war,
  an absence of, 3
    achieved by threat, 3
  as human activity, 135, 169-171, 224
    See also Natural Eternal War
  blind condemnation of, 135
  creative aspect of, 136
  crimes, 83
    See also international criminal law
  declaration of, 19
  destructive aspect of, 135
  domestic policy for, 16
  false hopes of, 136
  hawks, 10, 175, 177
    materialistic, 177
    See also American Eagles
  in the absence of, 200
  limited. *See* nuclear war
  meaning of,
    transition in, 135, 222-225
    See also Natural Eternal War
  moral battleground for, 181
  of ideas. *See* Natural Eternal War
  potential, 5, 47, 148
  powers,
    contradiction of, 7, 151, 199

of the Congress, 7-8, 20, 199-201
of the President, 8, 151, 199-201
production, 149, 169, 206, 208-209
  See also World War II, industrial
    mobilization for
promising aspect of, 7-8
purpose of, 135-136, 171-173
void of purpose, 135
War Powers Resolution, 200
warfare,
  electronic, 87, 90, 110-111
  nuclear, 33, 38-39
  push-button, 33-34, 39, 48, 86, 88
war-fighting, 135, 170
  industrial support of, 169-170
warheads,
  thermonuclear, 60, 64, 115
  See also bombs
war-peace
  dualism. *See* natural dueling partners,
    war-peace; peace through strength
wartime
  economy, 147, 149, 170, 208-209
Washington Arms Conference, 142
Washington, DC, 121, 142, 187, 204
Washington, George,
  1st president of the United States, April
    30, 1789 to 1796, 143-144, 216
  Farewell Address, 143-144
wave-particle dualism. *See* natural dueling
    partners, wave-particle
wealth of information, *v*
weapon,
  gift of foresight as, 89
  information as, 137
  truth as, 190
weapons of destruction,
  conventional versus nuclear, 14-15
  in Europe. *See* Theater Nuclear Forces
weather, 52, 81, 87, 107, 129, 160-161,
    164-165
  satellites, 91, 163-164
We the People, 8
Whitehead, Alfred North, 90
White House, 11, 16, 149, 191, 197, 204
Wilson, Charles E., Secretary of the
    Department of Defense, under President
    Eisenhower, 211
Wolff, Christian, 184
World War I, 169, 208
World War II, 4, 8, 34, 46, 48, 69, 77, 130,
    142, 150, 153, 158, 169, 206, 208-211,
    222
  against Germany, 4
  against Japan, 4
  disastrous delay, 169
  industrial mobilization for, 4, 169, 211

X-ray flash, 113, 115
  See also nuclear explosions, detection of

Yamashita, Tomoyuki, General of the
    Japanese Army, 82-83

Zero Option, 48
Zumwalt, Elmo, Chief of Naval Operations,
    former, 26

About the Author

Unshakable faith in the no-nonsense qualities of the American people and in the military service organizations they have created is the striking feature in the writing style of Anna van Gogh. When you have a leak in the faucet, you call a plumber; when you are living with the threat of nuclear holocaust, you call the military. This nation, more than any other in the world, "cares enough to send the very best," and that very best can now be achieved by freeing the military service organizations from the technology push of the weapons industries, an industrial domination that has been endorsed, if not created, by the self-serving defense spending priorities of the United States Congress.

Anna van Gogh takes the position that the "armed peace of the industrial elite" has held the human race hostage long enough. PROMISE ME WAR brings the American military out of the closet of a closed decision making process and into the arena of common sense public debate. With an integrity of purposeful intent the American people are being asked to create an all-new industrial base for this nation; they are also being asked to provide popular endorsement for an international law against nuclear weapons, weapons that are, in any case, already obsolete.

The author's 22 years of professional contact with NATO defense establishments in Europe are evidenced by the highly personal quality of her writing. Intermittent affiliations with the Boulder Laboratories of the United States Department of Commerce, Boulder, Colorado, and the Max-Planck-Institute for Ionospheric Physics, Lindau, West Germany, become apparent in her approach to international agreement: treat all nations alike under the rule of law. There are no favored friends and there are no fearful foes.

Anna van Gogh's participation in military-related research programs progressed primarily through the Advisory Groups for Atmospheric Research and Development of NATO and the International Union for Radio Science, Arbeitsgemeinschaft for the Ionosphere, Bundesrepublik Deutschland, but many interpretations and applications of her research results were made possible only through the determined efforts of her colleagues at the Central Post Office, Darmstadt, West Germany.

In 1965, as a result of her identification of natural resonant phenomena excited by radar equipment operating onboard Earth-orbiting satellites, G. Goe (Anna van Gogh) became the only female atmospheric scientist to be awarded a Gold Medal by the United States government. Ironically, the author had already established residence in West Germany where she was intimately involved with the rearing of orphan children at the Ursuline Convent in Duderstadt. And it was in that female-dominated environment that she experienced a complete invasion of her inner self by the horrors of the destructiveness of war.

398

Anna van Gogh, through her dedicated use of pattern recognition, has developed a keen perception of harmony in the natural environment — the laws of nature dictate patterns of collective response for the whole, patterns of motion that are not in any way associated with the behavior of the individual parts. It is the author's uncanny sense for that collective behavior of the whole that has led her to view human behavior in the same collective manner.

The American people and the American military collectively form a living system — they are citizen cells in an organic nation-state in motion. And, rightly interpreted, the attitudes and the activities of those individuals do comprise a collective whole. They comprise a living nation that can now fulfill its own living destiny of global environmental monitoring or commit internal suicide.

About the Artist

Charles Ewing is basically a self-taught artist who now lives in southern Colorado. He acquired his initial disciplined training in wildlife illustration while working as a Peace Corps Volunteer in Chile. Those illustrations, mainly line drawings and oils, were published in a Field Guide to Chilean Mammals. Much of his creative incentive was acquired at an early age while watching his father, Frank C. Ewing, at work at the easel. It was not until Charles returned to the States in 1973, at the age of 27, that he began, as a full-time artist, directing much of his time and talent towards the perfection of his unique scratchboard technique.

About the Electronics

The text of the book was prepared on an Eagle IIe computer system, using the software package *Spellbinder* for text editing, a registered trademark of Lexisoft, Inc., with a CP/M operating base, a registered trademark of Digital Research, Inc. The ease of user control in the text editing mode is the primary convenience of the Eagle IIe system with *Spellbinder*.

The Eagle keyboard, with an overall width of 21 inches, is designed to support copy from which you are typing at its upper edge without interfering with the visual display on the monitor. The high-resolution, anti-glare, adjustable-intensity, 12-inch, green-phosphor monitor screen will display 80 characters per line, 24 lines, an adequate display for text editing. Eagle IIe/*Spellbinder* also has a command operating mode with dedicated function keys that reduces the learning time to near zero for the beginner.

Eagle IIe uses two 5 1/4 inch floppy, single-sided, double-density disks with 390 kilobytes of storage on each disk, or approximately 250 pages of typewritten text. The Eagle IIe computer word size is an 8-bit byte. The 64K (kilobyte) internal active memory was sufficient for entering, say, one chapter of the book before writing to "save" on the disk.

The computer, which includes the built-in display screen, is a single lightweight self-contained unit that you can easily carry around. The unit weighs 42 pounds but the weight is conveniently distributed so even I can lift it. All you do is move it, plug it in, and go to work.

Communication from the Eagle system at Graphics West to the CompuGraphic typesetter at Service Typographers was done using the Advanced Communication Interface, the standard 212A telephone modem with a standard transfer rate of 1200 baud. (A baud is a "bit" of computer jargon that refers to the so-many bits per second communication rate.) The typed material was read and corrected from computer print out *before* the material was communicated to the CompuGraphic.

Eagle systems are available locally from Bircham's Office Products, Inc., 204 Mountview Lane, Colorado Springs, Colorado 80907, Tele: (303) 599-8285, Mr. Edward G. Bircham, owner.